Global Dangers
Changing Dimensions of International Security

AN *International Security* READER

EDITED BY

Sean M. Lynn-Jones
and Steven E. Miller

THE MIT PRESS
CAMBRIDGE, MASSACHUSETTS
LONDON, ENGLAND

The contents of this book were first published in *International Security* (ISSN 0162-2889), a publication of The MIT Press under the sponsorship of the Center for Science and International Affairs at Harvard University. Except as otherwise noted, copyright in each article is owned jointly by the President and Fellows of Harvard College and of the Massachusetts Institute of Technology.

Richard H. Ullman, "Redefining Security," 8:1 (Summer 1983); Thomas F. Homer-Dixon, "On the Threshold: Environmental Changes as Causes of Acute Conflict," 16:2 (Fall 1991); Peter H. Gleick, "Water and Conflict: Fresh Water Resources and International Security," 18:1 (Summer 1993); Miriam R. Lowi, "Bridging the Divide: Transboundary Resource Disputes and the Case of West Bank Water," 18:1 (Summer 1993); Thomas F. Homer-Dixon, "Environmental Scarcities and Violent Conflict: Evidence from Cases," 19:1 (Summer 1994); Myron Weiner, "Security, Stability, and International Migration," 17:3 (Winter 1992/93); F. Stephen Larrabee, "Down and Out in Warsaw and Budapest: Eastern Europe and East-West Migration," 16:4 (Spring 1992); Stephen Van Evera, "Hypotheses on Nationalism and War," 18:4 (Spring 1994); Barry R. Posen, "Nationalism, the Mass Army, and Military Power," 18:2 (Fall 1993); V.P. Gagnon, Jr., "Ethnic Nationalism and International Conflict: The Case of Serbia," 19:3 (Winter 1994/95).

Selection and introduction, copyright © 1995 by the President and Fellows of Harvard College and of the Massachusetts Institute of Technology.

Library of Congress Cataloging-in-Publication Data
Global Dangers : changing dimensions of international security /
   edited by Sean M. Lynn-Jones and Steven E. Miller.
      p. cm. — (International security readers)
   Includes bibliographical references.
   ISBN 0-262-62097-9
   1. Security, International. 2. National security—International
cooperation. I. Lynn-Jones, Sean M. II. Miller, Steven E.
   III. Series.
JX1963.G62 1995
327.1'7'09049—dc20   94-24037
                                                           CIP

Contents

The Contributors

SEAN M. LYNN-JONES is Co-Editor of *International Security* and a Research Fellow at the Center for Science and International Affairs, Harvard University.

STEVEN E. MILLER is Editor-in-Chief of *International Security* and Director of the International Security Program at the Center for Science and International Affairs, Harvard University.

RICHARD H. ULLMAN is David K.E. Bruce Professor of International Affairs at the Woodrow Wilson School of Public and International Affairs at Princeton University.

THOMAS F. HOMER-DIXON is Director of the Peace and Conflict Studies Program at University College, University of Toronto.

PETER H. GLEICK is Director of the Global Environmental Program at the Pacific Institute for Studies in Development, Environment and Security.

MIRIAM R. LOWI is Assistant Professor of Political Science at Trenton State College.

MYRON WEINER is Professor of Political Science at the Massachusetts Institute of Technology.

F. STEPHEN LARRABEE is Senior Policy Analyst at RAND Corporation.

STEPHEN VAN EVERA is Assistant Professor of Political Science at the Massachusetts Institute of Technology.

BARRY R. POSEN is Professor of Political Science at the Massachusetts Institute of Technology.

V.P. GAGNON, JR. is Visiting Fellow at the Peace Studies Program, Cornell University.

Acknowledgments

The editors gratefully acknowledge the assistance that has made this book possible. A deep debt is owed to all those at the Center for Science and International Affairs, Harvard University, who have played an editorial role at *International Security*. Special thanks go to Mera Kachgal at CSIA and to Sally Gregg at MIT Press for their invaluable help in preparing this volume for publication.

Part I:
Rethinking Security

Introduction | *Sean Lynn-Jones and Steven E. Miller*

The East-West confrontation that dominated the international security agenda during the Cold War has largely receded from view. Revealed in its wake is a different set of dangers, not really new but previously overshadowed by Cold War preoccupations. Hence, while the end of the Cold War has changed the threats to international security, the field of security studies still has a full agenda of practical and intellectual problems. Indeed, the changes in the international system are making this agenda richer, more varied, and more challenging, much as the post-1945 changes in the international system stimulated new thinking about strategy after World War II. No longer will the field of international security be overwhelmingly fixated on how to deter the Soviet Union or how to reduce the risk of nuclear war between the superpowers. The newly revealed agenda is broader in its focus, giving much greater attention to previously neglected sources of conflict.

This volume examines three such potential threats to peace: environmental problems, including access to scarce resources and population pressures; international migration; and nationalism. These issues are global in scope, persistent in nature, and potent in their implications. It is tragically clear that they can give rise to political dispute and to violent conflict. The essays collected here provide both conceptual analysis and empirical assessment of the environment, migration, and nationalism as sources of conflict. They reflect and exemplify the broadening of security studies to embrace a more diverse agenda than that which dominated the Cold War Era.[1]

I. Rethinking Security

Even during the Cold War, there were voices that sought to call attention to a wider agenda of security concerns, encompassing more than the military preoccupations of the East-West conflict. This volume opens with one such essay. In "Redefining Security," Richard Ullman criticizes the "excessively narrow" and "excessively military" conception of national security that predominated in the United States during the Cold War. This conception, Ullman argues,

---

1. See, for example, Jessica Tuchman Mathews, "Redefining Security," *Foreign Affairs*, Vol. 68, No. 2 (Spring 1989), pp. 162–177; Neville Brown, "Climate, Ecology and International Security," *Survival*, Vol. 31, No. 6 (November/December 1989), pp. 519–532; Nicholas Eberstadt, "Population Change and National Security," *Foreign Affairs*, Vol. 70, No. 3 (Summer 1991), pp. 115–131; Sam C. Sarkesian, "The Demographic Component of Strategy," *Survival*, Vol. 31, No. 6 (November/December 1989), pp. 549–564; and Barry Buzan, "New Patterns of Global Security in the 21st Century," *International Affairs*, Vol. 67, No. 3 (July 1991), pp. 431–451.

produces two unfortunate effects: an undue militarization of U.S. foreign policy; and a neglect of other challenges to national well-being. In contrast, embrace of a wider conception of security leads to different conclusions about both problems and remedies. Polities and policies governed by a less narrow definition of security will be concerned not only with military threats, but with other problems that threaten, directly or indirectly, to degrade the quality of life for the national community; such problems would include, he suggests, demographic pressures, uncertain access to important resources, and adverse environmental trends such as deforestation. A government that is properly fulfilling its responsibility for the security of its citizens should, Ullman urges, address the full range of threats to their well-being, not only the military threats.

Nor are the appropriate remedies necessarily military in nature. Accumulating national stockpiles of key resources or providing foreign assistance aimed at curbing rapid population growth or preventing environmental damage may represent the most sensible or effective responses to these nonmilitary threats to national security. But, Ullman notes, whereas there is wide political support for enormous investments in military power, there is little consensus in support of large public expenditures to address these less direct, more diffuse, nonmilitary threats to national security. Consequently, governments tend to spend vast sums of money to address remote military threats but relative pittances in preparation for more likely natural disasters or other potential (and in some cases, predictable) degradations to the quality of national life.

Understanding and adopting a wider conception of national security is important not least, Ullman concludes, because this would contribute to a political climate that would permit more resources to be devoted to tackling the wider array of nonmilitary threats. And that matters, he believes, because some of these nonmilitary threats—such as population growth and environmental degradation—are growing more dangerous and less tractable with the passage of time.

This article, first published in 1983, is probably now more topical and more resonant with the current policy agenda than when it first appeared.

II. Environmental Issues and International Security

Recent years have witnessed an explosion of attention to and concern about environmental problems. They have become much more salient in public discourse, more prominent in media coverage, more visible and important in political deliberations; and environmental issues have become a significant factor in international politics.[2] There is now wide awareness of the environmental degradations that can attend human activity and the threats these can pose to human welfare.

Not all environmental problems and issues are matters of relevance to international security.[3] The causes of environmental degradation are fundamentally economic and demographic; the remedies often have to do with industrial adaption, internal regulation, or international cooperation, touching on matters far removed from questions of force and conflict. Fat books are written on international environmental politics that contain little or no mention of military matters, force, violence, and conflict, focusing instead on institutions, negotiations, and the need and prospects for international cooperation.[4] There is no reason to assume that all environmental issues will inherently raise security concerns.

Nevertheless, environmental problems can be a source of political conflict between states and can contribute to violence within and between states. The essays collected in this section explore the linkage between environmental problems and conflict. In the first offering, "On the Threshold: Environmental Changes as Causes of Acute Conflict," Thomas Homer-Dixon provides an extensive overview and analysis of this connection, self-consciously crafted as a set of hypotheses about the ways in which major environmental problems may cause violent conflict. He identifies seven such problems: greenhouse warming, stratospheric ozone depletion, acid deposition, deforestation, degradation of agricultural land, overuse and pollution of water supplies, and depletion of fish stocks.

Homer-Dixon focuses on two questions. First, what social effects are produced by environmental change? Second, how might these social effects cause conflict? In answer to the first, Homer-Dixon highlights four possible social effects of environmental degradation: reduced agricultural production, declining economic performance, the displacement of populations, and the disruption of communities and institutions. It is easy to imagine how growing hunger and poverty, the destruction of communal relations, the relocation of large

---

2. The internationalization of environmental concerns is extensively documented, for example, in Peter M. Haas, Robert O. Keohane, and Marc A. Levy, eds., *Institutions for the Earth: Sources of Effective International Environmental Protection* (Cambridge, Mass.: The MIT Press, 1993).
3. This point is more fully developed in Sean Lynn-Jones, "International Security Studies after the Cold War: An Agenda for the Future," November 20, 1992.
4. A case in point is Haas, Keohane, and Levy, eds., *Institutions for the Earth*.

numbers of impoverished people, and the collapse or erosion of legitimate authority or of established social relations could create conditions in which conflict is likely. Homer-Dixon is careful to point out, however, that conflict is not the inevitable result of such developments. Much will depend on the capacity of states to adapt and respond to the social and economic problems that arise from environmental change, and this capacity will vary considerably from state to state and from region to region. Homer-Dixon suggests that the developing world may be particularly vulnerable to the social consequences of environmental degradation because those states have fewer technical, financial, and institutional resources to devote to containing or coping with those consequences. Hence, in cases where the prospects for effective adaption to environmental degradation are poor, it is reasonable to expect conflicts borne of scarcity, relative deprivation, or ethnic, racial, or cultural strife exacerbated by scarcity and relative deprivation.

Where "On the Threshold" provides a conceptual approach to the issue, the subsequent three essays offer empirical examinations of the environment-conflict connection. Peter Gleick surveys the ways in which one particularly important, and often scarce, resource—fresh water—can become a source of conflict. He notes that access to water has often been an objective of military action, and that this could be even more true in the future if and as fresh water becomes increasingly scarce relative to demand. In arid regions of the world, notably in the Middle East, fresh water is a crucial strategic resource, control of which is a matter of high politics, international tension, and occasional conflict. Water can also serve as an instrument of war, as states upstream can manipulate shared river basins to the detriment of other riparian states; further, dams, desalination plants, and irrigation systems can be targets in war, or water supplies of enemies can be poisoned. Since water is an essential necessity of life, disruption of access to adequate supplies can have dramatic political and strategic impact.

Gleick notes that water disputes more often produce political friction than violent conflict and more often result in international negotiation and cooperation than military action. He also identifies a number of legal and institutional means of attempting to reduce the risk of water-related conflicts and to provide for fair and reasonable international management of rivers and other transboundary water resources. Still, he concludes that "recent disturbing examples of water-related conflicts, the apparent willingness to use water-supply systems as targets and tools of war, and growing disparities among nations between water availability and demand make it urgent that we work to reduce the probability and consequences of water-related conflict."

In "Bridging the Divide," Miriam Lowi provides a more detailed case study of the role on water in one specific political setting: the Arab-Israeli conflict. She describes Israel's increasingly problematic situation with respect to supplies of fresh water, the importance to Israel of water from the disputed West Bank, and the problems and frictions that derive from Israel's water policies on the West Bank. The problem of water, she argues, will be one of the "thorniest" to resolve in the Middle East peace negotiations. Further, the general political tensions and absence of settlement on other major issues in the Middle East impedes resolution of the water question. On the other hand, should progress toward peace in the Middle East continue, this could open up "vast possibilities" for functional cooperation in the management of water. But, Lowi warns in conclusion, in the absence of political settlement, "the alternative is likely to be increasing scarcity and war."

Finally, in "Environmental Scarcities and Violent Conflict: Evidence from Cases," Thomas Homer-Dixon reports on the results of a project intended to provide evidence about hypotheses on the link between the environment and conflict by generating a series of detailed case studies. These cases examined the impact of scarcity caused by depletion, degradation, population growth, and resource maldistribution, focusing particularly on forests, water, fisheries, and cropland.

The evidence is mixed. Not all hypotheses linking environmental scarcity to violent conflict find strong support in the empirical record. For example, scarcities of renewable resources such as forests and croplands do not appear to be a major cause of resource-related wars. But in general, there is considerable evidence that in a number of places, in a number of ways, with respect to a number of hypotheses, environmental scarcity does contribute to conflict. Environmentally-caused migrations, for example, appear to be a potent source of conflict. In addition, environmental distress can place tremendous stress on social and political institutions, which can cause the breakdown of political order. As Homer-Dixon observes, "Environmental scarcity has insidious and cumulative social impacts, such as population movement, economic decline, and the weakening of states. These can contribute to diffuse and persistent sub-national violence." In response to such pressures, Homer-Dixon suggests, states may become more authoritarian or they may fragment and collapse; either outcome can produce deleterious consequences and increase the risk of conflict. These points may be particularly germane to China, which will probably face mounting scarcity problems across a number of its regions. All told, Homer-Dixon concludes that environmental scarcity does cause violent conflict, that this is likely to be a larger problem in the future than in the past because the problem of scarcity will "rapidly worsen," and that therefore the environment as a source of conflict must be prominent on the agenda of security scholars.

III. Migration and International Security

Seduced by economic opportunity or driven by economic privation, impelled by persecution, civil violence, or war, fleeing rapacious governments or forced to flee by ruthless governments, dislocated by natural disaster, environmental distress, or political calamity, large numbers of human beings routinely flood across international borders—often unwanted in either country of origin or country of destination. In an age when ghastly scenes of Rwandan refugees in Zaire haunt television screens, when the question of immigration is a major electoral issue in politically important states like California and Florida, when resentment of immigrants and opposition to immigration has become widespread in many advanced industrial states, and when the problem of coping with refugees regularly and urgently presses itself on the international agenda, it should be clear that the problem of migration is a highly visible and significant factor in internal and international politics, raising a host of political, economic, and social problems.

What are the implications of migration for international security? The two essays gathered in this section provide some answers. In "Security, Stability, and International Migration," Myron Weiner offers an analytic overview of the security problems that can be caused by international migration and of the links between migration and violent conflict. He notes, in fact, that there is a double connection, since migration is properly regarded "both as cause and as consequence of international conflict."

Weiner identifies three broad categories of problems that can be posed by migration. First, forced migration (in effect, the purposeful creation of refugees) can be employed by governments as an instrument of policy. It can be a weapon against internal targets, including unwanted minorities, political rivals, dissidents, or any other self-defined undesirables. It can also be an instrument of foreign policy, a means of putting pressure on, undermining, or bargaining with neighboring states. As Weiner observes, "Forced emigration can be an instrument by which one state seeks to destabilize another, force recognition, stop a neighboring state from interfering in its internal affairs, prod a neighboring state to provide aid or credit in return for stopping the flow, or extend its own political and economic interests or those of a dominant ethnic group through colonization or decolonization."

Second, migration can be threatening to both the population-sending and the population-receiving country. With respect to the former, for example, refugees and emigrants may work to undermine or overthrow the regime in their home countries; this can include using the host country as a base for taking up arms or engaging in terrorism against the government from which they fled. On the other hand, refugees and immigrants can destabilize host countries, changing ethnic balances, causing or exacerbating social and economic problems, disrupting political arrangements and cultural identities.

A third category of problems arises from the possible responses of states to the flow of unwanted people onto their territory. These responses may include strenuous efforts to close off borders, which can become a source of contention between neighboring states. But the use of armed force to prevent or reverse migration (generally by altering conditions in the population-sending country) is also a possibility; the intervention by India in the Pakistani civil war of 1971 is a vivid example.

Complementing Weiner's overview of this issue is Stephen Larrabee's essay, "Down and Out in Warsaw and Budapest: Eastern Europe and East-West Migration." It examines the migration issue in a specific case, Europe, and in a specific context, the emergence of a post–Cold War order in Europe which, for the first time in many decades, allows people living in the eastern half of Europe the possibility to move freely. The result, from 1989 onwards, was an enormous increase in migration from east to west in Europe. Larrabee suggests that pressures for east-to-west migration could intensify still further if economic problems in the east intensify, should political disorder emerge or persist in the countries of the eastern half of the continent, or should conflict erupt (especially in the former Soviet Union); this would subject Europe to a still larger flood of migration than that experienced over the past half-decade.

Larrabee notes the problems, tensions, and frictions that have been caused by migration in Europe. These include, in the first instance, internal problems: housing shortages, stresses on social welfare systems, higher unemployment, increases in crime and, in general, greater social tension. These are bad enough, but they often lead further to hostility and violence toward foreigners, mounting opposition to immigration and to the provision of benefits to immigrants, and to the rise of nationalist, xenophobic, or even racist sentiments and parties.

These developments, in turn, can lead to friction and tension between what Larrabee terms migrant-exporting and migrant-importing countries.

In short, migration often is, as Weiner suggests, a matter of "high international politics." It can be a foreign policy instrument and a foreign policy problem. In several ways, it can be a source of political dispute and violent conflict. Accordingly, it is sure to have a place on the post–Cold War security agenda.

IV. Nationalism and International Security

Many hoped that the end of the Cold War would usher in a new era of international peace and cooperation, at least in Europe if not more widely. So far these hopes have been disappointed, confounded by a cruel and festering war in the former Yugoslavia and the flaming of violence in various locales in the former Soviet Union. Wars usually have complex origins that belie efforts to identify a single cause, but it appears that one of the primary culprits undermining peace in Europe is nationalism.

Indeed, the collapse of communism in Central and Eastern Europe produced not the end of history but the return of nationalism. The re-emergence of nationalism in the Balkans and within the republics of the Soviet Union will affect the prospects for international and civil conflict in those regions, and hence will have a major impact on the European order that emerges from the rubble of the Cold War. More broadly, in numerous places around the globe, from Kashmir and Sri Lanka to Quebec and Northern Ireland, the power of nationalism in human affairs and its potential to contribute to violence is regularly demonstrated. It appears to be one of the primal forces in world politics.

Yet the connections between nationalism and war are not well understood.[5] If nationalism is as important, and as dangerous, as it appears to be, then it is imperative to better understand this potential source of conflict. How does nationalism arise and what are its main consequences? What different categories of it exist and which are dangerous? When and how does it create conflict and war?

---

5. There is an extensive literature on nationalism, but remarkably few works assess its international impact. For a recent exception, see James Mayall, *Nationalism and International Society* (Cambridge: Cambridge University Press, 1990).

In "Hypotheses on Nationalism and War," Stephen Van Evera explores possible answers to these questions, providing an inventory of hypotheses about the link between nationalism and war. He notes that the effects of nationalism are quite varied: "Some types of nationalism are far more dangerous than other types, all types of nationalism are more dangerous under some conditions than under others, and nationalism can even dampen the risk of war under some conditions." Van Evera endeavors to sort out when nationalism has what effects, suggesting criteria that amount to a "nationalism danger-scale."

The framework he creates is built around four attributes of nationalist movements. First, has the nationalist movement attained statehood or not? Stateless nationalisms raise greater risks of conflict because accommodating their demands for statehood involves large, disruptive changes. Second, if national brethren are scattered across multiple states, does the nationalist ideology accept the fact of diaspora or does it wish to unify the nation within the boundaries of a single state? And if the latter, is this to be accomplished peacefully through immigration or more aggressively via expansion? Diaspora-annexing nationalisms are the most dangerous because their approach causes territorial conflict with others. Third, is the nationalist ideology tolerant or hegemonistic toward other nationalities? Hegemonistic nationalisms (such as interwar Nazi nationalism) usually operate on a presumption of racial, cultural, or political superiority and arrogate to themselves rights and powers that they deny to others. Hegemonic nationalisms are, Van Evera suggests, the most dangerous of all, having contributed to some of the great cataclysms of the twentieth century. Finally, does the nationalist movement respect or oppress minorities within its state or claimed state? Oppressive nationalisms can easily produce violence and war. Van Evera concludes that if these four attributes are benign, then nationalism poses little danger; but if they are malign, then "violence between nationalism and its neighbors is inevitable."

Van Evera also devotes attention to the factors which determine whether nationalism assumes its benign or malign form. These include such variables as the balance of power and will between the nationalist movement and the state it is challenging, the separation or intermingling of nationalities, the legitimacy and defensibility of the borders of the claimed state, the past and present behavior toward one another of intermingled nationalities, as well as the self-image and perception of others harbored by the nationalist movement. Van Evera emphasizes that some combinations of these factors are conducive to the benign incarnations of nationalism; others incline nationalisms toward the malign path.

Where Van Evera examines nationalism as a cause of war, Barry Posen explores the reverse: war as a cause of nationalism. Seeking to explain the growth, spread, and varying intensity of nationalism in Europe during the nineteenth century, he suggests that the rise of the mass army during and after the French revolution constitutes one important cause. The mass army, whose proven military effectiveness made it desirable or even necessary for major powers, raised new problems for states attempting to create it. One was the need to mobilize large numbers of men from the civilian population, who must be willing to confront the horrors of war and the risk of death. As Posen notes, nationalism increases "the ability of states to mobilize the creative energies and the spirit of self-sacrifice of millions of soldiers."

The mass army is also harder to command and control than its smaller predecessors, because large numbers of units and individuals will be dispersed widely across the battlefield (dispersal was also a result of the fact that advances in military technology made the tight battlefield formations of earlier eras too dangerous). In the mass army, therefore, combat effectiveness depends very heavily on the loyalty and motivation of the troops. Again, nationalism is part of the solution of this problem, because the soldier driven by a strong patriotism will be more loyal and motivated than one who is not so driven. For these reasons, he argues, states "act purposefully to produce nationalism because of its utility in mass mobilization warfare."

Posen explores the plausibility of this argument by tracing the relationship between nationalism and the development of military power in France and Prussia between 1750 and 1914—the period in which nationalism emerged and became a powerful, and occasionally pernicious, force in European politics. He concludes that there is evidence that states and leaders understand nationalism to be a potent military resource, that nationalism is "purveyed by states for the express purpose of improving their military capabilities," that leaders "use nationalism to mobilize public support for military preparation and sacrifices."

In contrast to Posen, who sees nationalism as a response to and a military asset in the international competition between states, V.P. Gagnon, Jr., in "Ethnic Nationalism and International Conflict: The Case of Serbia," argues that ethnic nationalism is an asset in the competition for power *within* states. Hence, while he shares with Posen the premise that nationalism is an instrument that can be manipulated by political elites, Gagnon identifies a different purpose that is served by such manipulation: the preservation of domestic power by self-interested individuals and political elites. The core of his argument is that "violent conflict along ethnic cleavages is provoked by elites in order to create a domestic political context where ethnicity is the only politically relevant identity." By so doing, challenged elites can "fend off domestic challengers who seek to mobilize the population against the status quo." This interpretation is important because it suggests that ethnic nationalist conflict is caused not by ancient (though long-repressed) ethnic hatreds and ineluctable social forces, but is intentionally provoked by leaders and elites seeking to advance their own domestic political fortunes. In Gagnon's analysis, both nationalism and external conflict are caused by domestic political dynamics.

Gagnon illustrates his argument by reconstructing the rise of ethnic nationalism and ethnic conflict in the former Yugoslavia. In his interpretation, the conflagration that has torn Yugoslavia apart and subjected its people to endless horrors has been the product of an intentional strategy by a conservative Serbian elite seeking to retain power in a country in which Serbs were not a majority and in a period in which dramatic reform and democratization were sweeping across Eastern Europe. Strongly challenged by the forces of reform, the Serbian leadership whipped up Serbian nationalism and provoked ethnic conflict within Yugoslavia as part of their effort to maintain their hold on power. Their original goal was an authoritarian Yugoslavia ruled by themselves, but when this proved impossible they preferred a greater Serbia ruled by them to a Yugoslavia ruled by others—and hence, as Gagnon puts it, they "resorted to destroying the old multi-ethnic Yugoslavia and creating on its ruins a new enlarged Serbian state with a large majority of Serbs in which they could use appeals to Serbian nationalism as a means of defining political interests."

Taken together, these three essays provide multiple perspectives on the sources of nationalism and the ways in which it contributes to causing or intensifying violent conflict. If the early years of the post–Cold War era are any indication of what is to come, coping with the consequences of nationalism will be a continuing challenge.

V. Conclusion

The Cold War superimposed on the international security agenda a political and conceptual framework that simplified most issues while magnifying some and obscuring others. That framework is a thing of the past and, as the essays in this volume demonstrate, its powerful and convenient simplifications are no longer useful or relevant. Further, the magnified obsessions of the Cold War— the superpower nuclear balance, the NATO-Warsaw Pact conventional balance, the Soviet-American rivalry in the Third World—no longer dominate, while once-obscured issues, including those examined in these pages, have come to the fore.

To the disappointment of many, the first half-decade of the post–Cold War era has made abundantly clear that the end of the East-West conflict does not mean the end of rivalry, conflict, violence, intervention, war, genocide, or disorder. Much as the risks, dangers, crises and conflicts of the Cold War were the understandable preoccupation of that earlier age, so are the sources and effects of (as well as possible solutions to) these continuing troubles coming to occupy center stage in contemporary political and intellectual deliberations on international security. The essays collected in this volume reflect this evolving agenda. We believe that they offer thoughtful and provocative discussion of several important issues that appear to be enduring sources of potential conflict in the new international system.

Redefining Security | *Richard H. Ullman*

Since the onset of the Cold War in the late 1940s, every administration in Washington has defined American national security in excessively narrow and excessively military terms. Politicians have found it easier to focus the attention of an inattentive public on military dangers, real or imagined, than on nonmilitary ones; political leaders have found it easier to build a consensus on military solutions to foreign policy problems than to get agreement on the use (and, therefore, the adequate funding) of the other means of influence that the United States can bring to bear beyond its frontiers.

Even the Carter Administration, which set out self-consciously to depart from this pattern, found in its later years that the easiest way to deflect its most potent domestic critics was to emphasize those aspects of the dilemmas it faced that seemed susceptible to military solutions and to downplay those that did not. Jimmy Carter's failure to win reelection may suggest not that his political instincts in these respects were faulty but merely that his conversion was neither early nor ardent enough.

Just as politicians have not found it electorally rewarding to put forward conceptions of security that take account of nonmilitary dangers, analysts have not found it intellectually easy. They have found it especially difficult to compare one type of threat with others, and to measure the relative contributions toward national security of the various ways in which governments might use the resources at their disposal.

The purpose of this paper is to begin to chip away at some of these analytical problems. It proceeds from the assumption that defining national security merely (or even primarily) in military terms conveys a profoundly false image of reality. That false image is doubly misleading and therefore doubly dangerous. First, it causes states to concentrate on military threats and to ignore other and perhaps even more harmful dangers. Thus it reduces their total security. And second, it contributes to a pervasive militarization of international relations that in the long run can only increase global insecurity.

Richard H. Ullman, Professor of International Affairs at Princeton University's Woodrow Wilson School of Public and International Affairs, spent the 1982–83 academic year as a visiting member of the Institute for Advanced Study.

International Security, Summer 1983 (Vol. 8, No. 1)

Security versus What?

One way of moving toward a more comprehensive definition of security may be to ask: what should we be willing to give up in order to obtain more security? how do we assess the tradeoffs between security and other values? The question is apposite because, of all the "goods" a state can provide, none is more fundamental than security. Without it, as the 17th-century philosopher Thomas Hobbes observed in a passage often cited but endlessly worth recalling:

there is no place for Industry, because the fruit thereof is uncertain: and consequently no Culture of the Earth, no Navigation, nor use of the commodities that may be imported by Sea; no commodious Building; no Instruments of moving and removing such things as require much force, no Knowledge of the face of the Earth; no account of Time; no Arts; no Letters; no Society; and which is worst of all, continuall feare, and danger of violent death; And the life of man, solitary, poore, nasty, bruitish, and short.[1]

For Hobbes it did not much matter whether threats to security came from within or outside one's own nation. A victim is just as dead if the bullet that kills him is fired by a neighbor attempting to seize his property as if it comes from an invading army. A citizen looks to the state, therefore, for protection against both types of threat.

Security, for Hobbes, was an absolute value. In exchange for providing it the state can rightfully ask anything from a citizen save that he sacrifice his own life, for preservation of life is the essence of security. In this respect, Hobbes was extreme. For most of us, security is not an absolute value. We balance security against other values. Citizens of the United States and other liberal democratic societies routinely balance security against liberty. Without security, of course, liberty—except for the strongest—is a sham, as Hobbes recognized. But we are willing to trade some perceptible increments of security for the advantages of liberty. Were we willing to make a Hobbesian choice, our streets would be somewhat safer, and conscription would swell the ranks of our armed forces. But our society would be—and we would ourselves feel—very much more regimented.

The tradeoff between liberty and security is one of the crucial issues of our era. In virtually every society, individuals and groups seek security against

---

1. *The Leviathan* (1651), Part I, Ch. XIII.

the state, just as they ask the state to protect them against harm from other states. Human rights and state security are thus intimately related. State authorities frequently assume—sometimes with justification—that their foreign enemies receive aid and sustenance from their domestic opponents, and vice versa. They often find it convenient, in any case, to justify the suppression of rivals at home by citing their links to enemies abroad.

The most profound of all the choices relating to national security is, therefore, the tradeoff with liberty, for at conflict are two quite distinct values, each essential to human development. At its starkest, this choice presents itself as: how far must states go, in order to protect themselves against adversaries that they regard as totalitarian, toward adopting totalitarian-like constraints on their own citizens? In the United States it is a tension that arises every day in the pulling and hauling between police and intelligence agencies and the Constitution. At a practical level, the choices become: what powers do we concede to local police? to the F.B.I.? to the C.I.A. and the other arms of the "intelligence community"?

Other security choices may seem equally vexing if they are not equally profound. One is the familiar choice between cure and prevention. Should the U.S. spend a (large) sum of money on preparations for military intervention in the Persian Gulf in order to assure the continued flow of oil from fragile states like Saudi Arabia, or should it be spent instead on nonmilitary measures—conservation, alternate energy sources, etc.—that promise substantially (although not rapidly) to reduce American dependence upon Persian Gulf oil? A second choice involves collaboration with regimes whose values are antithetic to America's own. Should the United States government forge a relationship of greater military cooperation with the Republic of South Africa, and risk racial conflict in its cities at home? Or should it continue to treat South Africa as an international outlaw and perhaps enhance domestic racial harmony—an important characteristic of a secure society—at the cost of enabling the Soviet navy to pose a greater potential challenge to the safety of the sea lanes around Africa upon which so much vital cargo flows? A third choice involves military versus economic assistance to poor countries. Should U.S. policy aim at strengthening Third World governments against the military threats that they assert they perceive to come from the Soviet Union and its allies, or at helping their citizens develop greater self-reliance so as, perhaps, ultimately to produce more healthful societies with lower rates of birth and thus relieve the rising pressure on global resources? Finally, many choices juxtapose international and domestic priorities. If a stretched national budget cannot afford both increased outlays for military forces and for a more effective criminal justice system at home, programs that create work opportunities for poor inner-city teenagers, or measures to improve the quality of the air we breathe and the water we drink, which expenditures enhance "security" more?

The tradeoffs implied in these and many other, similar questions are not as profound as that between security and liberty. But they are nevertheless capable of generating conflicts of values—between alternate ways of viewing national security and its relationship to what might be called global security.

There is, in fact, no *necessary* conflict between the goal of maintaining a large and powerful military establishment and other goals such as developing independence from Persian Gulf oil, promoting self-sustaining development in poor countries, minimizing military reliance on repressive governments, and promoting greater public tranquility and a more healthful environment at home. All these objectives could be achieved if the American people chose to allocate national resources to do so. But it is scarcely likely that they—or their Congressional representatives—will choose to make all the perceived sacrifices that such large governmental programs entail.

Indeed, the present Administration, supported by Congressional majorities, has embarked upon a substantial buildup of military spending while at the same time reducing outlays—and perceptible concern—for the other objectives listed here. Such policies are not merely neglectful of what some writers have called the "other dimensions" of security. They sometimes create conditions—increased worldwide arms expenditures, heightened intra-regional confrontations, and greater fragility rather than resilience in Third World governments—that make the world a more dangerous rather than a safer place. To use an image from the theory of games, there is a real danger that the policy choices of present and future U.S. administrations will place us on a square on the game board in which *all* the players are worse off. In other words, the game may well not be "zero-sum," making the United States and some other nations more secure, or richer, while yet others are left less well off. Instead, it might be "negative-sum," making all the nations perceptibly less secure, with fewer disposable assets to spend on welfare rather than on military forces.

To make this point is not to argue that a well-armed Soviet Union increasingly confident of its abilities to project military power at long distances poses no potential threat to American security. Clearly it does. Nor is it necessarily to argue (although I would do so) that much of what appears threatening about recent Soviet behavior has its origins in Soviet responses to American policies and force deployments. That is a topic for a separate discussion.[2] But it is to argue that the present U.S. Administration—and, to a substantial degree, its predecessors—has defined national security in an excessively narrow way. It happens also (as will be suggested later) to be a politically quite expedient way.

A Redefinition of Threats

In addition to examining security tradeoffs, it is necessary to recognize that security may be defined not merely as a goal but as a consequence—this means that we may not realize what it is or how important it is until we are threatened with losing it. In some sense, therefore, security is defined and valorized by the threats which challenge it.

We are, of course, accustomed to thinking of national security in terms of military threats arising from beyond the borders of one's own country. But that emphasis is doubly misleading. It draws attention away from the non-military threats that promise to undermine the stability of many nations during the years ahead. And it presupposes that threats arising from outside a state are somehow more dangerous to its security than threats that arise within it.

A more useful (although certainly not conventional) definition might be: a threat to national security is an action or sequence of events that (1) threatens drastically and over a relatively brief span of time to degrade the quality of life for the inhabitants of a state, or (2) threatens significantly to narrow the range of policy choices available to the government of a state or to private, nongovernmental entities (persons, groups, corporations) within the state. Within the first category might come the spectrum of disturbances and disruptions ranging from external wars to internal rebellions, from blockades and boycotts to raw material shortages and devastating "natural" disasters such as decimating epidemics, catastrophic floods, or massive and pervasive droughts. These are for the most part fairly obvious: in their presence any observer would recognize that the well-being of a society had been drastically impaired.

The second category is perhaps less obviously apposite. In considering it,

---

2. There is no better place to begin that discussion than Robert Jervis, *Perception and Misperception in International Politics* (Princeton, N.J.: Princeton University Press, 1976), chapter 3.

it may be helpful to reflect on the way in which the threat from Nazi Germany to the United States was discussed in the years immediately preceding American entry into World War II—or, indeed, the way the threat from the Soviet Union has been viewed throughout most of the postwar era. Death and physical destruction are, of course, one realization of the threat. They represent "degradation of the quality of life" in its most extreme form, and they would be an inevitable result of war—even a war from which the United States emerged victorious.

But suppose war had not come. Suppose Hitler's Germany or Stalin's Russia had asserted domination over Western Europe and, perhaps, other parts of the globe as well. The conquerors would have organized those societies in a manner that almost certainly would substantially have closed them to the United States. That, of course, would have meant fewer opportunities for American traders and investors. But so, also, would there have been fewer opportunities for unfettered intellectual, cultural, and scientific exchange. And the extinction of civil and political liberty in countries which shared our devotion to those values would have made it more difficult to assure their preservation in an isolated and even besieged United States. In a very large number of ways, the range of options open to the United States government, and to persons and groups within American society, would have been importantly diminished.

It is easy to think of degradation of the quality of life or a diminution of the range of policy choices as "national security" problems when the source of these undesirable conditions is a large, powerful, antagonistic state such as Nazi Germany or Stalin's U.S.S.R. And it is even (relatively) easy to organize responses to such clear and present dangers. But it is much more difficult to portray as threats to national security, or to organize effective action against, the myriads of other phenomena, some originating within a national society, many coming from outside it, which also kill, injure, or impoverish persons, or substantially reduce opportunities for autonomous action, but do so on a smaller scale and come from sources less generally perceived as evil incarnate. Interruptions in the flow of critically needed resources or, indeed, a dwindling of the available global supply; terrorist attacks or restrictions on the liberty of citizens in order to combat terrorism; a drastic deterioration of environmental quality caused by sources from either within or outside a territorial state; continuing violence in a major Third World state chronically unable to meet the basic human needs of large numbers of its citizens; urban conflict at home perhaps (or perhaps not) fomented by the presence of large numbers of poor immigrants from poor nations—all these either degrade the quality of life and/or reduce the range of policy options available to governments and private persons.

For a leader trying to instil the political will necessary for a national society to respond effectively to a threat to its security, a military threat is especially convenient. The "public good" is much more easily defined; sacrifice can not only be asked but expected; particular interests are more easily coopted or, failing that, overridden; it is easier to demonstrate that "business as usual" must give way to extraordinary measures; dissent is more readily swept aside in the name of forging a national consensus. A convenient characteristic of military threats to national security is that their possible consequences are relatively apparent and, if made actual, they work their harm rapidly. Therefore, they are relatively noncontroversial.[3]

The less apparent a security threat may be—whether military or nonmilitary—the more that preparations to meet it are likely to be the subject of political controversy. The American and the Soviet military establishments are symbiotically allied in the effort to coax resources from their respective political chiefs. Each regularly dramatizes (and surely exaggerates) the threat posed by the other. The effects of such arguments within the Kremlin are not easy to document, but the evidence suggests that they are often persuasive. So are they generally persuasive for American Congressmen anxious to demonstrate to their constituents that they are "pro-" national security. The contrast with the generally unenthusiastic reception given to programs aimed at aiding poor countries, ameliorating the disaffection of poor persons at home, halting environmental degradation, stockpiling strategically important materials, or other such measures is striking but scarcely surprising. Proponents of such programs in fact frequently do justify them on the ground that they promote national security. But because their connection to security is often not immediately apparent, opponents find it easy to reject or simply ignore such arguments, if not to refute them.[4]

---

3. This is not to say that there are not recriminations following wars or military crises. Indeed, the governments that lead nations when war is thrust upon them—or when they initiate war themselves—are often subject to pillory. It may be alleged that their complacence allowed their nations' defenses to atrophy to a point where their military forces no longer deterred attack. Or they may be accused of recklessness that brought on a needless and expensive war. But while the war is still in prospect, or while it is actually underway, there are too seldom any questions of leaders' abilities to command the requisite resources from their perceptibly threatened countrymen.

4. The same is true, it should be noted, about some "ordinary" foreign threats. In 1975 a

Preparing for Catastrophe

A comparison between American society's preparations for two events, each carrying relatively low risks but each posing the threat of catastrophically high costs, is instructive. One is nuclear war between the United States and the Soviet Union. The other is a large earthquake along the San Andreas fault that runs much of the length of the state of California. Nuclear war would undoubtedly result in many more casualties and much greater damage, but a major earthquake along the San Andreas fault, and the gigantic tidal wave that would likely follow it, might well kill or seriously injure hundreds of thousands of persons and cause billions of dollars of damage to property. Certainly it would be devastating to regional, if not national, security. Seismologists say that the probability of such an earthquake occurring within half a century is relatively high, from 2 to 5 percent in any one year.[5] The odds that large-scale nuclear war will occur cannot be so confidently calculated, but they are surely much smaller.

Every year the United States government spends many billions of dollars to build up nuclear forces whose purpose, at least according to strategic theory, is to make nuclear war between the U.S. and the U.S.S.R. less likely. Americans regard that as a proper function of government. So, also, do most Americans probably regard the construction of shelters and other facilities that might reduce the damage caused by nuclear war should it occur. But administrations in Washington or in likely target states and municipalities habitually spend very much less—indeed, quite small sums—on such measures, and they spend even less on measures that might reduce the damage from a catastrophic earthquake.[6]

---

majority of Senators and members of Congress did not believe that the presence of Soviet-supported Cuban troops in Angola posed a significant threat to U.S. security, and legislated limits on potential American involvement. Three years earlier they imposed a cutoff on U.S. bombing of targets in Cambodia and North Vietnam on the supposition that continued bombing would no longer (if it ever did) promote U.S. security. For a discussion of these Congressional curbs on the President's ability to commit American military resources, see Thomas M. Franck and Edward Weisband, *Foreign Policy By Congress* (New York: Oxford University Press, 1979), esp. pp. 13–23 and 46–57.

5. For a recent authoritative study, see *An Assessment of the Consequences and Preparations for a Catastrophic California Earthquake: Findings and Actions Taken* (Washington: Federal Emergency Management Agency, 1980). For a summary of current estimates, see Richard A. Kerr, "California's Shaking Next Time," *Science*, Vol. 215 (January 22, 1982), pp. 385–387.

6. The Federal Emergency Management Agency's (FEMA) fiscal year 1983 appropriation for civil defense was $147,407,000; for "comprehensive emergency preparedness planning" for

How can we explain these discrepancies? Regarding so-called "passive" defenses against nuclear weapons (shelters and the like, as distinguished from "active" defenses such as missiles to shoot down missiles), one explanation is that the task seems too daunting, a quixotic effort given the size of the attack the Soviet Union could launch. When scores of millions might be killed, the prospect of saving tens of millions—as, indeed, a large-scale effort at civil defense might make possible—seems heartening only to the most zealous student of what has come to be called "comparative recovery rates" between the U.S. and the U.S.S.R. And the cost of such a shelter program would be enormous, very expensive insurance against a catastrophic but very unlikely risk. Yet there is little doubt that it could (within these macabre limits) be made effective.[7]

Against earthquakes, of course, shelters can offer little protection. The danger to life and property along the San Andreas fault comes because many hundreds of thousands of California residents have individually made decisions to locate their homes and businesses there. In their view, the advantages of cost or location outweigh the disadvantages of exposure to the risk of major catastrophe. They might increase their own and their families' chances for survival by strengthening existing buildings or replacing them with more resistant structures. But the probability is that, owing to the geologic properties of the San Andreas fault, an earthquake there would be so severe that for many structures such measures would be ineffective. In such a situation governmental authorities can do little but monitor, warn, and make sure that emergency facilities are on hand for the moment when

---

earthquakes it was $3,120,000. California's total budgeted expenditure for earthquake safety for fiscal year 1983 was $13,391,000. For a detailed breakdown, see State of California, Seismic Safety Commission, *Annual Report to the Governor and the Legislature for July 1981–June 1982* (Sacramento: August 1982), pp. 16–21.

7. The "classic" appeal for a large U.S. civil defense program, based upon hypothesized comparative U.S. and Soviet recovery rates, is T.K. Jones and W. Scott Thompson, "Central War and Civil Defense," *Orbis*, Vol. 22, No. 3 (Fall 1978), pp. 681–712. For a more recent discussion, see Robert Scheer, *With Enough Shovels: Reagan, Bush and Nuclear War* (New York: Random House, 1982), pp. 104–119.

The enormous cost is one principal argument against a large-scale U.S. civil defense program. But another relates to strategic doctrine. A civil defense program that promises to offer effective protection might in a crisis invite an enemy first-strike attack. The adversary, so this reasoning runs, would read large-scale civil defenses as indicating that we ourselves were prepared to initiate nuclear war. It would therefore strike at the first sign that we were beginning to move our population into shelters, as we surely would during a severe international crisis. Thus we enhance stability by not opting for civil defenses: the other side knows that since our population is exposed, *we* would not be likely to initiate nuclear war, and the incentives for *them* to strike preemptively are thereby reduced.

a devastating quake occurs. Alas, while federal and state agencies currently monitor seismic events, they have done relatively little actually to prepare for the predicted disaster. Yet there is no doubt that, should it occur, the consequences would be extraordinarily dire.[8]

It scarcely needs stating that there are vast differences between the threats to "national security" posed by nuclear weapons and those posed by catastrophic natural disasters. Nuclear wars, after all, originate in human minds: other minds may therefore initiate actions to affect the adversary's calculations of costs and benefit, of risks and reward. Behind earthquakes and floods are no minds. They cannot be deterred. But their potential damage can be substantially reduced by the application of foresight and the expenditure of resources. Indeed, the probability that an incremental expenditure on protection against earthquakes or floods will be effective is surely very much greater than the probability that a comparable incremental expenditure will enhance deterrence against nuclear war. Yet Americans and their elected representatives are prepared to acquiesce in—indeed, in some instances they show enthusiasm for—vast programs of weapons acquisition which, in the name of forestalling nuclear war, have given the United States enough nuclear weapons to exterminate the world's population several times over. But the polity is ill-equipped to make resource allocations that, dollar for dollar, would contribute at least as much to "security" as would the acquisition of the additional nuclear weapons upon which the present Administration seeks to spend many billions of dollars.

The example of protection against earthquakes raises other interesting points of comparison. While some community measures are useful, risk aversion against such disasters is very largely in the hands of individuals. Individuals can also affect at least to some limited extent the degree to which they will be at risk in the event of nuclear war. They can choose not to live in the vicinity of likely nuclear targets, and householders can provide themselves with substantial protection against fallout and at least some protection against blast effects. But the pattern of a Soviet nuclear attack—and, therefore, the location of likely danger—is very much more difficult to predict than the danger zone of a major earthquake. And the opportunity costs to a citizen of choosing to live in a place so remote that injury from nuclear

---

8. The FEMA study cited above (note 5) estimates that the likely damage from the most probable (but far from the most destructive) major earthquake on the San Andreas fault might be $17 billion, but it indicates that the figure might be low by a factor as high as three (p. 22).

weapons effects are likely to be minimal are very much greater than the costs of choosing not to live near the San Andreas fault or another area of similarly great seismic instability, whose locations are all well known. In addition, protection against nuclear weapons effects is much more a community matter than is protection against earthquakes. Particularly is this true for residents of multiple-family urban dwellings. Only communities can afford to construct the deep, strong shelters that would offer city residents even a remote chance of surviving a nearby nuclear explosion.[9]

The other nonmilitary security measures discussed thus far in this paper are almost all considerably farther than protection against earthquakes toward the community end of a spectrum running from the individual to the national community.[10] Economic assistance to poor countries, programs to reduce dependence upon Persian Gulf oil, military relations with repressive regimes, efforts to combat air and water pollution, stockpiling of scarce resources, all require either governmental allocation of resources or governmentally framed policies and regulations. Like the acquisition and deployment of military forces, they all depend upon organization to be effective; in a polity like the United States, the impetus for such organization must come from government, the ultimate wielder of carrots and sticks.

Indirect Threats: Conflicts over Territory and Resources

At the root of most of the violent conflicts in history has been competition for territory and resources. The coming decades are likely to see a diminution in the incidence of overt conflict over territory: the enshrinement of the principle of national self-determination has made the conquest of peoples distinctly unfashionable. But conflict over resources is likely to grow more intense as demand for some essential commodities increases and supplies

---

9. The most authoritative generally available projection of the effects of a variety of types of Soviet nuclear attacks on the United States is *The Effects of Nuclear War* (Washington, D.C.: Congress of the United States, Office of Technology Assessment, 1979).

10. It should be noted that the currently preferred mode of *avoiding* nuclear war (as distinguished from diminishing the likely effects of nuclear war) is at the far end of this spectrum: the maintenance of a *deterrent* nuclear striking force is preeminently a national responsibility—one, incidentally, beyond the grasp of all but the wealthiest nation-states. Other modes of avoiding war, such as negotiation and disarmament, are also endeavors which only duly legitimate national authorities, as distinguished from sub-national groupings or private individuals, can undertake. Earthquakes differ from nuclear war in that they cannot be either deterred or forestalled. But societies can protect against their effects. That is why, despite obvious differences, the comparison with nuclear war as a threat to societal security seems instructive.

appear more precarious. These conflicts will also have their territorial aspects, of course, but the territory in contention is likely either to be unpopulated or only sparsely populated. Much of it will be under water—oil-rich portions of the continental shelves. Those parts above water will be the ostensible prizes, often isolated or barren islands whose titles carry with them exclusive rights to exploit the riches in and under the surrounding seas.

Such struggles over resources will often take the form of overt military confrontations whose violent phases will more likely be short, sharp shocks rather than protracted wars. In most instances they will involve neighboring states—Chile and Argentina, Iraq and Iran, Greece and Turkey, Morocco and Algeria, China and Vietnam, and many others. Most will be in the Third World. None is likely to involve the United States, although American firms—oil companies and other resource-extracting enterprises—may well be caught up on either side of a particular dispute. Thus, if national security is defined in conventional ways this country's national security is not likely to be directly affected by such disputes.[11]

Their indirect impact upon American national security is likely to be large, however. Supplies of essential commodities will be at least temporarily disrupted. Local regimes may fall, their places taken by successors often less friendly to the United States. Outside powers hostile to American interests, such as the Soviet Union or Cuba, may intervene to support local clients, placing pressure on Washington to launch (or at least organize) counter-interventions. In some quite plausible scenarios Washington might intervene to protect local clients whether or not Moscow or Havana were involved. Those circumstances that might lead to a direct confrontation of Soviet and American forces are, of course, the ones most dangerous to U.S. national security. Luckily, they are also the least likely.

"Resource wars" (as some call them) have figured prominently in dooms-day forecasts for more than a decade. But they are only one way—and not the most important way—in which resource issues will impinge upon national security in coming years. It will not require violent conflict for resource scarcities to affect the well-being—and the security—of nations on every rung of the development ladder. In considering ways in which such scarcities

---

11. For a discussion of the kinds and scope of disputes that are likely to arise, see Ruth W. Arad and Uzi B. Arad, "Scarce Natural Resources and Potential Conflict," in Arad et al., *Sharing Global Resources*, 1980s Project/Council on Foreign Relations (New York: McGraw-Hill, 1979), pp. 25–104.

might affect national security, analysts should distinguish those that arise from expansion of demand from those arising from restrictions on supply.

THREATS FROM RISING WORLDWIDE DEMAND

Behind expanding demand, of course, lies the continuing rapid growth in the world's population. Specialists note that the rate of population growth has not yet overtaken that of the globe's capacity to feed, house, and care for its people.[12] But that capacity is sorely strained. Moreover, global mechanisms for distributing or for managing resources are not effective enough to prevent local catastrophic failures or to prevent the consumption of some crucial renewable resources at greater-than-replacement rates. Those resources include tropical forests and other sources of fuelwood, fish stocks, the ozone layer surrounding the earth, and the global supply of clean air and water. Moreover, these problems are interconnected. Here is but one example: As Third World villagers cut down more and more forests in their search for fuelwood, the denuded land left behind is prey to erosion. Rains carry topsoil away, making the land unfit for cultivation. The topsoil, in turn, silts up streams in its path. Meanwhile, the fuel-short villagers substitute dung (which otherwise they would use for fertilizer) for the wood they can no longer obtain, further robbing the soil of nutrients and bringing on crop failures. Unable to sustain themselves on the land, many join the worldwide migration from the countryside into the cities.[13]

That migration—caused by many factors—has given rise to an explosive growth in the population of most Third World cities. Many are ringed by shantytowns containing millions of squatters, a high proportion of them unemployed, malnourished, and living in squalor. Under the weight of these enormous numbers municipal services break down and the quality of life for all but the very rich suffers drastically. Such cities are forcing grounds for criminality and violence. Some suffer a breakdown of governmental authority and become virtually unmanageable. Others are governable only by increasingly repressive means that lead, in turn, to a decline in the perceived legitimacy of the regime in power. Especially is this the case in nations that

---

12. See the tables in the statistical annexes to Roger D. Hansen et al., *U.S. Foreign Policy and the Third World: Agenda 1982*, Overseas Development Council (New York: Praeger Publishers, 1982), esp. tables B-8 and C-1.
13. For a discussion that brings out the seamless nature of this problem, see Lester R. Brown, "World Population Growth, Soil Erosion, and Food Security," *Science*, Vol. 214 (November 27, 1981), pp. 995–1002.

are marked by ethnic or religious divisions. When the resources of a nation are severely strained, those at the bottom of a social hierarchy are quick to imagine—often with justification—that those who govern distribute the benefits at their disposal in ways that favor some groups at the expense of others.

There is a widespread assumption that these are the circumstances from which revolutions are born. In fact, there is little evidence that any recent revolution except perhaps the one in Iran has had urban roots. Although rapid population growth and its attendant miseries have certainly given rise to conflicts, particularly along communal lines, the governing authorities in most Third World countries have been able to contain them. Rather than forging links among urban (and rural) dispossessed persons, recent arrivals in Third World cities have tended to be overwhelmingly preoccupied with retaining (and, if possible, expanding) whatever economic niches they have been able to carve for themselves. They have thus far provided few recruits for those who would organize revolutions, nor much in the way of troubled waters in which outside powers might fish.[14]

First World governments and peoples might be advised not to take too much comfort from this record. Although the consequences of explosive Third World population growth and rapid urbanization have not yet been felt much beyond their countries of origin, the strains on fragile political structures will not ease before the end of the century, if then: the would-be workers who will seek employment in the swollen cities of the Third World during the 1990s have already been born. Even if these strains do not give rise to revolutions (and, perhaps, to foreign interventions), they are likely to make Third World governments more militantly confrontational in their relations with the advanced, industrialized states. And they will produce multifold other pressures on the rich nations. For the United States, the most directly felt pressure is that of would-be immigrants, some coming through lawful channels, most coming illegally. The pressure is especially severe—and probably increasing—from Mexico, but it comes from all over the Caribbean and Central American region and from other continents as well. As population growth in the poor countries hobbles economic development, the

---

14. For a thorough survey of extant social science research on Third World urban growth and its relationship to political instability, see the unpublished paper by Henry Bienen, "Urbanization and Third World Stability," Research Program in Development Studies, Woodrow Wilson School, Princeton University, December 1982.

gap in living standards between them and the rich countries is likely to continue to widen, and resentment of the rich—rich nations and rich persons—will continue to grow. So will pressures for immigration. The image of islands of affluence amidst a sea of poverty is not inaccurate. This image has given rise to doomsday scenarios in which, several decades from now, the poor will threaten the rich with nuclear war unless the rich agree to a massive redistribution of wealth.[15] But even if these scenarios do not eventuate (and the superior destructive capabilities of the rich make such *denouements* unlikely), the pressure engendered by population growth in the Third World is bound to degrade the quality of life, and diminish the range of options available, to governments and persons in the rich countries.

This paper is not the place for detailed discussion of ways to slow population growth in the Third World, to help Third World countries absorb their multitudes of new citizens, and to introduce order into their processes of urban development. It is sufficient to say that most such ways involve transfers of resources and expertise to Third World countries. The record of the United States in these areas is generally abysmal: among the O.E.C.D. nations it is near the bottom of the league tables with regard to official development aid calculated on a per capita basis. Only in population programs has the U.S. made a respectable effort.[16] But U.S. programs to assist other nations to solve their population problems are increasingly coming under attack from the "right-to-life" movement in this country, many of whose supporters are in the forefront of those pressing for large increases in military spending. They, and the opponents of economic assistance in general, may someday pay a significant price for their arbitrarily narrow definition of national security.

THREATS FROM THE SUPPLY SIDE

Population growth dominates the problem of rising worldwide demand for resources. Moreover, overall demand is rising even more rapidly than population growth figures alone would indicate. Many developing countries

---

15. For a prototypical example, see Robert L. Heilbroner, *An Inquiry into the Human Condition* (New York: W.W. Norton, 1975), esp. pp. 42–45. For a provocative variation, see McGeorge Bundy, "After the Deluge, the Covenant," *Saturday Review/World*, August 24, 1975, pp. 18–20, 112–114.

16. For the O.E.C.D. rankings, see Hansen, *Agenda 1982*, table F-8 and figure F-18. For population programs, see Dana Lewison, "Sources of Population and Family Planning Assistance," *Population Reports*, Vol. 11, No. 1 (January–February 1983).

contain growing "modern" sectors, enclaves of affluence and higher living standards that enjoy the same wasteful consumption patterns of the industrialized world. That imposes yet additional strains on world resources. By contrast, no single factor dominates the problem of constraints on resource supplies. A crucial distinction is whether the resource in question is renewable, like forests or fish stocks or feedgrains, or nonrenewable, like (preeminently) oil. A second crucial distinction is whether the resource is becoming increasingly scarce through "normal" depletion or through efforts by governments (or, indeed, private persons) artificially to restrict supplies by means of boycotts, embargoes, cartel agreements, recovery limitations, and the like. Supply constraints are most injurious when they are sudden. For virtually every raw material there are substitutes with properties sufficiently similar so that replacement is possible. But whether or not replacement can take place without painful disruption depends upon whether the shortage in supply of the original item was foreseen adequately far in advance to make possible smooth adjustment.

The United States is in a particularly fortunate position. Study after study in recent years has concluded that oil is the only commodity whose sudden cutoff would have a drastic effect on national welfare or on economic activity. Indeed, the same applies in large measure to all of the advanced industrialized market-economy states. Since most produce a considerably smaller proportion of their domestic oil consumption than the United States, most would find an oil cutoff even more disruptive.[17] But other essential imported materials for them, as for the United States, either come from highly reliable suppliers—like-minded states—or from a sufficiently diverse range of suppliers so that a boycott by one or more would not impose really serious harm.[18] Regarding foodstuffs, the O.E.C.D. countries are for the most part well provided for. Collectively they produce large agricultural surplusses.[19]

---

17. See David A. Deese and Joseph S. Nye, eds., *Energy and Security* (Cambridge, Mass.: Ballinger, 1981), esp. pp. 131–228 and appendix B, "Worldwide Production and Use of Crude Oil."
18. See the well-documented discussion in Arad, "Scarce Natural Resources," pp. 32–59. For a widely cited earlier statement, see Stephen D. Krasner, "Oil is the Exception," *Foreign Policy*, No. 14 (Spring 1974), pp. 68–84. John E. Tilton, *The Future of Nonfuel Minerals* (Washington: The Brookings Institution, 1977), reaches the same conclusions.
19. A concise survey of global patterns of food production and consumption is in Paul R. Ehrlich, Anne H. Ehrlich, and John P. Holdren, *Ecoscience: Population, Resources, Environment* (San Francisco: W.H. Freeman, 1977), pp. 284–297. For a current accounting by a U.S. Agriculture Department official, see Terry N. Barr, "The World Food Situation and Global Grain Prospects," *Science*, Vol. 214 (November 27, 1981), pp. 1087–1095.

Individual O.E.C.D. states that import a high proportion of their domestic food consumption—Japan is the most important—need not worry about major disruptions of supply because their purchasing power will give them first claim on world markets.

The problem is much more serious for Third World states. Many are not able to feed themselves and find it difficult to pay for imported foodstuffs, a difficulty compounded since 1973 by the rising cost of the oil they also must import.[20] Food is indeed a weapon that can be wielded against them—although the industrialized states are most unlikely to employ it. The much more serious danger they face is their acute vulnerability to natural disasters that may cripple their own food production or substantially reduce the supply (and therefore raise the price) of foodstuffs on the world market. As population growth brings more mouths to feed, the situations of many Third World states are likely to grow more and more precarious.

Demand and supply are always related, of course. One approach to the resource problem is slowing the growth of demand by slowing the growth of population. But supply-side measures are equally necessary. When the too-rapid exploitation of renewable resources is viewed as a supply problem, the solution seems to lie in creating mechanisms for effective regulation of the rate at which fish are caught, forests are cut, seed crops are harvested for food, and effluents are released into streams and emissions into the atmosphere. Sometimes the nation-state is the appropriate arena for such regulatory activity. In other instances, international mechanisms ("regimes," in the current academic jargon) are required. Such measures are likely to be really effective, however, only when they are combined with efforts to slow the growth of demand. Moreover, as noted earlier, increasing demand for many commodities is a product not merely of population growth, but of rising affluence. And rising affluence is often not accompanied by rising sensitivity to the need for resource management, and the appropriate technical and political skills to make management possible.

As indicated above, one way to cope with depleting supplies of any commodity is to find substitutes for it. That applies even to some renewable resources—although not, of course, to clean air and water. It applies more obviously to nonrenewable resources. For minerals and fuels, a sensible strategy is to create stockpiles that make it possible to cope with short-run

---

20. See Deese and Nye, *Energy and Security*, pp. 229–58.

interruptions of supply while developing substitutes to cope with long-run inevitable depletion.

These are scarcely difficult principles to grasp. What is difficult is to persuade governments to allocate funds to put the principles into practice. Especially for powerful countries like the United States that are used to getting their way in the world, it seems easier to arouse the political will to respond to a supply disruption with military means than to forestall the disruption in the first place by fostering alternate sources of supply, or by developing substitutes for the resource whose supply is threatened.

Assessing Vulnerability

In every sphere of policy and action, security increases as vulnerability decreases.[21] At the most basic level of individual survival, this is a law of nature, seemingly as well understood by animals as by humans. At that level it is a reflexive response. Reducing vulnerability becomes a matter of policy, rather than of reflex action, when it seems necessary to calculate the costs and benefits involved. How much security do we buy when we expend a given increment of resources to reduce vulnerability? That is a difficult question even in relatively simple situations, such as a householder stockpiling a commodity against the possibility of a disruption in accustomed channels of supply. At the level of the community, rather than the individual, it becomes very much more difficult: different members assess risks differently, and they may well be differently damaged by a disrupting event. An investment in redundancy that seems worthwhile to one family may seem excessively costly to another. Neither will know which is correct unless the crunch actually comes. And even then they might disagree. They might experience distress differently.

---

21. Some might argue that this is not the case in the strategic nuclear relationship between the United States and the Soviet Union, and that it is the knowledge within each government that its society is highly vulnerable to nuclear attacks by the other that keeps it from ever launching such an attack itself. Security is thus a product of vulnerability. This argument has considerable force as a logical construct. Yet, not surprisingly, neither superpower is content to act upon it. As technological developments seem to make possible the limitation of damage from at least some forms of nuclear attack, each pursues them for fear that the other will secure a momentary advantage. We are therefore faced with the worst of situations, in which one or the other may be unduly optimistic regarding the degree to which it might limit damage to its own society if it were to strike first. Decreased vulnerability *accurately* assessed may well enhance security even in strategic nuclear relations; misleadingly assessed it may bring disaster.

At the level discussed in this paper, where states are the communities involved and where the problems are for the most part considerably more complicated than a simple disruption in an accustomed channel of supply, the relationship between decreased vulnerability and increased security is formidably difficult to measure. Consider even the relatively simple measure of adding crude oil to the U.S. Strategic Petroleum Reserve, the (for the most part) underground stockpile whose purpose is to make it possible for the nation to ride out a cutoff in deliveries from one or more major foreign oil suppliers. We know, of course, the cost of buying and storing a given increment of crude oil. But until mid-1981 the government of Saudi Arabia (the world's major exporter of oil) took the position that U.S. stockpiling of oil was an unfriendly act. It claimed that it maintained high levels of oil production to provide immediate benefits—"moderate" prices—to Western (and other) consumers, not to make it possible for Washington to buy insurance against the day when the Saudi leadership might want to cut production so as, say, to influence U.S. policy toward Israel. Successive administrations in Washington have regarded the retention of Saudi good will as something close to a vital American interest, on both economic and strategic grounds. They therefore dragged their feet on filling the Strategic Petroleum Reserve.[22]

Who can say with assurance that those administrations were wrong? Who could measure—before the event—the effects of putting Saudi noses out of joint? It may well have been that even so seemingly modest a measure as adding to the oil stockpile would ripple through Saudi and Middle Eastern politics in such a manner as ultimately to bring about just that calamity against which the stockpile is intended to offer insulation, that is, a production cutback. Moreover, being finite in size, the stockpile may not offer sufficient insulation against a protracted deep cutback. But, by the same token, who can be sure that even if the reserve remains unfilled (its level is still far below the total originally planned[23]), and even if the United States takes other additional measures to mollify the Saudis, an event will not occur

---

22. See, e.g., Walter S. Mossberg, "Kowtowing on the Oil Reserve," *The Wall Street Journal*, May 14, 1980, p. 20, and Sheilah Kast, "Filling Our Strategic Oil Reserve," *Washington Star*, February 9, 1981, the latter quoting Secretary-of-State-designate Alexander M. Haig, Jr., as calling the Saudi position "oil blackmail."
23. The Energy Information Administration's *Monthly Energy Review* (Washington: U.S. Department of Energy) presents a running tally of the size of the Strategic Petroleum Reserve. For a technical account of how the reserve is maintained, see Ruth M. Davis, "National Strategic Petroleum Reserve," *Science*, Vol. 213 (August 7, 1981), pp. 618–622. See also Deese and Nye, *Energy and Security*, pp. 326–328, 399–403.

that will trigger a supply disruption in any case? If that occurs, the nation would clearly be better off if it possessed a healthy reserve of stored oil, even one insufficient to cushion the entire emergency.

Ever since the OPEC embargoes of 1973–74, Western governments have been extremely sensitive to any hint of a further cutoff of oil or, for that matter, of other, less critically needed resources. It is not surprising that many analysts both in Washington and in other NATO capitals interpreted the Soviet invasion of Afghanistan at the end of 1979 not simply as Moscow's ruthless effort to handle a local political dilemma but as the start of a Soviet march toward the Persian Gulf. Since then, both the Carter and the Reagan Administrations have regarded raising a robust combined-arms military force earmarked for Gulf contingencies—the so-called Rapid Deployment Force— as the most appropriate and, not so coincidentally, also the politically most saleable response to the threat of instability in the Gulf.

Yet there is wide agreement among specialists that additional overt Soviet border-crossing aggression in the Middle East is an unlikely contingency. Far more likely is the coming to power in a major oil-producing state like Saudi Arabia of a militantly anti-Western regime that might restrict production. Against such an eventuality the Rapid Deployment Force offers little insurance, for there would be great resistance in Congress and in the public at large to any Presidential use of American forces for intervention in the turbulent internal politics of the region.

It requires a long and more relaxed view to deemphasize military intervention as an instrument of policy, however. And a longer view is much more possible under conditions of reduced vulnerability. Then the occupant of the Oval Office would be more likely to feel that he really has the option of allowing the politics of regions like the Middle East to run their course. Were the United States less vulnerable to interruptions in the supply of the region's oil, administrations might find they had a wider range of options for pursuing other interests, such as protecting communication routes or the independence of Israel. Communications routes, for instance, can be protected at many points. And the American commitment to Israel would cost less if the U.S. were not simultaneously supplying some of Israel's enemies with the most potent weapons in its inventory and then giving the Israelis additional weapons to offset them.

As this paper has suggested, many of the conditions that may most affect U.S. security have their origins in circumstances that have little or nothing to do with the rivalry between the United States and the Soviet Union. Yet many of them, if not managed, have the potential to give rise to crises between the superpowers as one or the other intervenes to secure resources or to support its clients in a domestic or regional conflict in the Third World. For crisis prevention, if for no other reasons, political leaders in Washington—and in Moscow, too—should pay heed to these conditions.[24]

There are, of course, other reasons. To the extent that the quality of life in the United States is degraded by resource scarcities and by the deterioration in the quality of life beyond its borders, Americans should be concerned. That is but the counsel of prudence. Focussing attention on these "other dimensions of security" will require political leadership of the highest order, however. Morever, it will require far greater consensus than now exists regarding what is to be done.

The absence of consensus is, indeed, a formidable obstacle. There is no agreement within the American policy community regarding ways of coping with resource scarcities or with the problems of poverty and explosive population growth in the Third World. The Administration currently in Washington is ideologically commited to market solutions in virtually every sphere of policy. Thus, rather than develop government stockpiles of oil and other scarce resources it prefers to leave the task to private entities. Indeed, so opposed is the Reagan Adminstration to governmentally directed resource management that it has even encouraged the depletion of the largest oil stockpile it itself owns, the oilfields set aside as so-called Naval Petroleum Reserves.[25]

The same is true for investments in alternate energy sources. The Adminstration has drastically reduced federal allocations for energy research and development of all sorts. Nuclear fusion, solar energy, unconventional oils—all have had their appropriations sliced. (Only the Clinch River breeder reactor, a project in the home state of the Republican Senate majority leader, has been spared.)[26] Not surprisingly, in an economic climate marked by both recession and high interest rates, the private sector shows few signs of acting upon the Administration's preferences, ideologically congenial though they

---

24. For an excellent discussion of the genesis and prevention of superpower crises, see Alexander L. George, *Managing U.S.–Soviet Rivalry: Problems of Crisis Prevention* (Boulder, Colo.: Westview Press, 1983).

25. Richard Corrigan, "Three Bowls of Oil," *National Journal*, December 5, 1981, p. 2167.

26. See these articles by Richard Corrigan, the *National Journal*'s energy correspondent: "The Next Energy Crisis: A Job for the Government or the Free Market?," June 20, 1981, pp. 1106–1109; "On Energy Policy, the Administration Prefers to Duck, Defer and Deliberate," July 18, 1981, pp. 1280–1283; and "Down for the Count," May 22, 1982, p. 919.

may be. Despite bargain prices, there has been little stockpiling of commodities. And, with a worldwide oil glut, the private sector has shown no inclination to invest in energy alternatives.

Opponents of the Administration's position assert that, regardless of the economic climate, the marketplace is incapable of adequately discounting scarcity. Therefore, they argue, the intervention of a single, authoritative actor—by definition, the federal government—is required to build up stockpiles and to fund research and development activities that are not likely to pay off within commercially acceptable timeframes.[27]

Measuring Security

That intervention will necessarily give rise to what appear to be inefficiencies. They will appear so because it will be possible to compare the costs of resources stockpiled, or developed by new production techniques, with the costs for the same or similar commodities bought on the market. Usually—unless there has been an intervention of a different sort, such as an embargo by suppliers—the costs of stockpiles or substitutes will be higher. It is easy to quantify these so-called inefficiencies. And once quantified, they are easy to decry. On the other hand, it is much more difficult to assign a weight to the security that the community may have purchased by sustaining them.

It is at least as difficult, however, to assign a weight to the quantity of security that the community purchases by a given investment in military hardware or in manpower. A missile or a tank or an infantry battalion that never enter combat are like commodities purchased for a stockpile. They also are inefficiencies. Yet we less often look at military purchases that way. We do, of course, incessantly decry "waste and inefficiency" in the armed services and in the defense industries. But we usually mean that better management could have purchased comparable military capability for less money. Rarely do we ask whether the possession of that particular capablity is in itself "efficient."

That is not to say that we do not often compare military with nonmilitary expenditures. Indeed, such comparisons are a staple of political discourse. Someone points out that for the price of, say, one Navy F-14 fighter it would be possible to build a certain number of daycare centers or black-lung clinics

---

27. Corrigan, "Energy Policy," *National Journal*, July 18, 1981, p. 1283.

for the mining towns of Appalachia. And we know that, unlike the F-14, the centers or clinics would be "used" (indeed, we hope the F-14 will never enter combat). Moreover, we know quite precisely how much welfare we purchase with a childcare center or a clinic. We can quantify it in terms of children attending (and mothers working) or patients treated. But at that point the comparison between guns and butter ends. We can weigh American forces against Soviet forces, and we can compare the capabilities of one weapons system against another. But we cannot really quantify the security we buy with the funds we spend on an F-14 or, indeed, on an entire carrier task group. We assume that the task group will deter hostile actions by unfriendly nations. But it may be that a smaller American Navy will deter them equally well, and a carrier air wing minus one F-14 may be fully capable of meeting all the threats that ever come against it.[28]

This discussion has sought to show that we generally think about—and, as a polity, dispose of—resource allocations for military and for nonmilitary dimensions of security in quite different ways. Regarding military forces, although analysts and interest groups may have their own ideas about such issues as the appropriate size of the American fleet or the composition of its air wings, there is general agreement on the principle that there must in the end be a single, authoritative determination, and that such a determination can come only from the central government of the polity. Because we acknowledge that there is no marketplace in which we can purchase military security (as distinguished from some of its components), we would not look to private individuals or firms or legislators or regional governments to make such a determination, even though we might disagree with the determination that the federal government makes.

By contrast, as indicated above, there is no consensus about the need for

---

28. Part of the difficulty of comparing guns and butter may arise from the fact that polities demand different orders of satisfaction from the evaluation of the two. Regarding daycare centers or clinics, officials often feel satisfied when they can certify that services of a given quality have in fact been delivered. They seldom feel it necessary to ask whether their delivery has really enhanced the welfare of the community, the nation, or the world: they regard the question as either self-evident or as impossible to answer. But publics have come to demand more of accountings for military expenditures. After Israel's sweeping victories in Lebanon in 1982 it was not enough to ascertain that the American-armed Israeli forces had decisively defeated the Soviet-armed Syrians and Palestinians, nor even that the campaign had vastly enhanced Israel's short-run security. Observers asked—and regarded the question as entirely appropriate— whether it had really enhanced Israel's long-run security.

For a discussion of assessing the benefits of welfare programs, see Alice M. Rivlin, *Systematic Thinking for Social Action* (Washington: The Brookings Institution, 1971), pp. 46–63.

a single, authoritative determination regarding the nonmilitary dimensions of security. The polity as a whole is therefore much more responsive to allegations that a given investment in, say, a commodity stockpile is "inefficient" than it is responsive to the same allegation regarding a given investment in military forces. Moreover, the alleged inefficiency is far more easily demonstrated. The situation is similar regarding measures for coping with the other problems mentioned in this paper: rapid population growth, explosive urbanization, deforestation, and the like. Here, also, the current American Adminstration—and much of the public—is committed to "efficient" marketplace solutions rather than to solutions involving international regimes or governmentally sponsored transfers of resources.

Changing the Consensus

Because of these preconceptions regarding the appropriate role of governmental authority both in defining problems and in proposing solutions, the tendency of American political leaders to define security problems and their solutions in military terms is deeply ingrained. The image of the President as Commander in Chief is powerful. When in this role he requests additional funds for American military forces the Congress and the public are reluctant to gainsay him. When he requests funds for economic assistance to Third World governments, he is much more likely to be disputed even though he may contend that such expenditures also provide the United States with security.

Altering that pattern will require a sustained effort at public education. It is not an effort that administrations themselves are likely to undertake with any real commitment, particularly in times when the economy is straightened and when they find it difficult enough to find funds for the military goals they have set for themselves. The agents for any change in public attitudes are therefore likely to be nongovernmental.

Over the past decade or so a vast array of public interest organizations have begun to put forward alternate conceptions of national security. Nearly all are devoted to particular issues—limiting population growth, enhancing environmental quality, eradicating world hunger, protecting human rights, and the like. Some are overt lobbies expressly seeking to alter political outcomes. Others devote themselves to research and educational activities, but are equally concerned with changing governmental behavior. Jointly they have succeeded in substantially raising public awareness of the vulnerability of the society to a variety of harms nonmilitary in nature, and of the limitations of military instruments for coping with many types of political problems.

One should not overestimate the achievements of these nongovernmental organizations, however. Awareness on the part of a substantial informed minority is one thing. Embodying it in public policy is a very much larger step. A society's consciousness changes only gradually—usually with the change of generations. The likelihood is that for the foreseeable future the American polity will continue to be much more willing to expend scarce resources on military forces than on measures to prevent or ameliorate the myriad profoundly dislocating effects of global demographic change. Yet those effects are likely to intensify with the passage of time. Problems that are manageable today may prove far less tractable in the future. And while political will and energy are focussed predominately on military solutions to the problems of national security, the nonmilitary tasks are likely to grow ever more difficult to accomplish and dangerous to neglect.

Part II:
Environmental Issues
and International Security

On the Threshold

Environmental Changes as Causes of Acute Conflict

Thomas F. Homer-Dixon

$\mathbf{A}$ number of scholars have recently asserted that large-scale human-induced environmental pressures may seriously affect national and international security.[1] Unfortunately, the environment-security theme encompasses an almost unmanageable array

Thomas F. Homer-Dixon is an Assistant Professor at University College, University of Toronto, and Coordinator of the College's Peace and Conflict Studies Program. He is co-director of an international research project on Environmental Change and Acute Conflict sponsored jointly by his Program and the American Academy of Arts and Sciences.

This article is an abridged version of a paper prepared for the Global Environmental Change Committee of the Social Science Research Council and for a conference on "Emerging Trends in Global Security" convened by York University in October, 1990. The full paper is available from the author. Portions have appeared in "Environmental Change and Economic Decline in Developing Countries," *International Studies Notes*, Vol. 16, No. 1 (Winter 1991), pp. 18–23; "Environmental Change and Human Security," *Behind the Headlines*, Vol. 48, No. 3 (Toronto: Canadian Institute for International Affairs, 1991); and "Environmental Change and Violent Conflict," American Academy of Arts and Sciences, Occasional Paper No. 4 (June 1990). For their helpful comments, the author is grateful to Peter Cebon, William Clark, Daniel Deudney, Darya Farha, Peter Gleick, Ernst Haas, Fen Hampson, Roger Karapin, Jill Lazenby, Vicki Norberg-Bohm, Ted Parson, George Rathjens, James Risbey, Richard Rockwell, Thomas Schelling, Eugene Skolnikoff, Martha Snodgrass, Janice Stein, Urs Thomas, Myron Weiner, and Jane Willms. Financial support for research and writing was received from The Royal Society of Canada, the Donner Canadian Foundation, and the Social Sciences and Humanities Research Council of Canada.

1. See, for example, Janet Welsh Brown, ed., *In the U.S. Interest: Resources, Growth, and Security in the Developing World* (Boulder, Colo.: Westview, 1990); Neville Brown, "Climate, Ecology and International Security," *Survival*, Vol. 31, No. 6 (November/December 1989), pp. 519–532; Peter Gleick, "Climate Change and International Politics: Problems Facing Developing Countries," *Ambio*, Vol. 18, No. 6 (1989), pp. 333–339; Gleick, "The Implications of Global Climatic Changes for International Security," *Climatic Change*, Vol. 15, No. 1/2 (October 1989), pp. 309–325; Ronnie Lipschutz and John Holdren, "Crossing Borders: Resource Flows, the Global Environment, and International Security," *Bulletin of Peace Proposals*, Vol. 21, No. 2 (June 1990), pp. 121–33; Jessica Tuchman Mathews, "Redefining Security," *Foreign Affairs*, Vol. 68, No. 2 (Spring 1989), pp. 162–177; Norman Myers, "Environment and Security," *Foreign Policy*, No. 74 (Spring 1989), pp. 23–41; Michael Renner, *National Security: The Economic and Environmental Dimensions*, Worldwatch Paper No. 89 (Washington, D.C.: Worldwatch Institute, 1989); and Arthur Westing, ed., *Global Resources and International Conflict: Environmental Factors in Strategic Policy and Action* (Oxford: New York, 1986). For a skeptical perspective, see Daniel Deudney, "The Case Against Linking Environmental Degradation and National Security," *Millennium*, Vol. 19, No. 3 (Winter 1990), pp. 461–476.

International Security, Fall 1991 (Vol. 16, No. 2)
© 1991 by the President and Fellows of Harvard College and of the Massachusetts Institute of Technology.

of sub-issues, especially if we define "security" broadly to include human physical, social, and economic well-being.[2]

We can narrow the scope of this research problem by focusing on how environmental change affects *conflict*, rather than security, but still the topic is too vast. Environmental change may contribute to conflicts as diverse as war, terrorism, or diplomatic and trade disputes. Furthermore, it may have different causal roles: in some cases, it may be a proximate and powerful cause; in others, it may only be a minor and distant player in a tangled story that involves many political, economic, and physical factors. In this article, I accept the premise that environmental change may play a variety of roles as a cause of conflict, but I bound my analysis by focusing on *acute* national and international conflict, which I define as conflict involving a substantial probability of violence.

How might environmental change lead to acute conflict? Some experts propose that environmental change may shift the balance of power between states either regionally or globally, producing instabilities that could lead to war.[3] Or, as global environmental damage increases the disparity between the North and the South, poor nations may militarily confront the rich for a greater share of the world's wealth.[4] Warmer temperatures could lead to contention over new ice-free sea-lanes in the Arctic or more accessible resources in the Antarctic.[5] Bulging populations and land stress may produce waves of environmental refugees[6] that spill across borders with destabilizing effects on the recipient's domestic order and on international stability. Countries may fight over dwindling supplies of water and the effects of upstream pollution.[7] In developing countries, a sharp drop in food crop production could lead to internal strife across urban-rural and nomadic-sedentary cleavages.[8] If environmental degradation makes food supplies increasingly tight,

---

2. Readers interested in a careful argument for an expanded notion of security that includes environmental threats to national well-being should see Richard Ullman, "Redefining Security," *International Security*, Vol. 8, No. 1 (Summer 1983), esp. pp. 133 and 143.
3. For example, see David Wirth, "Climate Chaos," *Foreign Policy*, No. 74 (Spring 1989), p. 10.
4. Robert Heilbroner, *An Inquiry into the Human Prospect* (New York: Norton, 1980), pp. 39 and 95; William Ophuls, *Ecology and the Politics of Scarcity: A Prologue to a Political Theory of the Steady State* (San Francisco: Freeman, 1977), pp. 214–217.
5. Fen Hampson, "The Climate for War," *Peace and Security*, Vol. 3, No. 3 (Autumn 1988), p. 9.
6. Jodi Jacobson, *Environmental Refugees: A Yardstick of Habitability*, Worldwatch Paper No. 86 (Washington, D.C.: Worldwatch Institute, 1988).
7. Peter Gleick, "Climate Change," p. 336; Malin Falkenmark, "Fresh Waters as a Factor in Strategic Policy and Action," in Westing, *Global Resources*, pp. 85–113.
8. Peter Wallensteen, "Food Crops as a Factor in Strategic Policy and Action," Westing, *Global Resources*, pp. 151–155.

exporters may be tempted to use food as a weapon.[9] Environmental change could ultimately cause the gradual impoverishment of societies in both the North and South, which could aggravate class and ethnic cleavages, undermine liberal regimes, and spawn insurgencies.[10] Finally, many scholars indicate that environmental degradation will "ratchet up" the level of stress within national and international society, thus increasing the likelihood of many different kinds of conflict and impeding the development of cooperative solutions.[11]

Which of these scenarios are most plausible and why? In the following pages, I review some reasons for the current salience of environmental issues, and I note several examples of good research on links between environmental change and acute conflict. I then suggest a preliminary analytical framework that lays out a research agenda for exploring the issue. Using this framework, and drawing on the literature of conflict theory, I suggest hypotheses about the likely links between environmental change and acute conflict.

I propose that poor countries will in general be more vulnerable to environmental change than rich ones; therefore, environmentally induced conflicts are likely to arise first in the developing world. In these countries, a range of atmospheric, terrestrial, and aquatic environmental pressures will in time probably produce, either singly or in combination, four main, causally interrelated social effects: reduced agricultural production, economic decline, population displacement, and disruption of regular and legitimized social relations. These social effects, in turn, may cause several specific types of acute conflict, including scarcity disputes between countries, clashes between ethnic groups, and civil strife and insurgency, each with potentially serious repercussions for the security interests of the developed world.

I do not hypothesize that the causal links between these variables will be tight or deterministic. As anti-Malthusians have argued for nearly two centuries, numerous intervening factors—physical, technological, economic, and social—often permit great resilience, variability, and adaptability in human-environmental systems.[12] I identify a number of these factors in this article;

---

9. Ibid., p. 146–151.
10. Ted Gurr, "On the Political Consequences of Scarcity and Economic Decline," *International Studies Quarterly*, Vol. 29, No. 1 (March 1985), pp. 51–75.
11. "The disappearance of ecological abundance seems bound to make international politics even more tension ridden and potentially violent than it already is. Indeed, the pressures of ecological scarcity may embroil the world in hopeless strife, so that long before ecological collapse occurs by virtue of the physical limitations of the earth, the current world order will have been destroyed by turmoil and war." Ophuls, *Ecology*, p. 214.
12. In his classic formulation, the economist Thomas Malthus claimed that severe human

in particular, I examine whether free-market mechanisms may permit developing countries to minimize the negative impacts of environmental degradation. But I suggest that, as the human population grows and environmental damage progresses, policymakers will have less and less capacity to intervene to keep this damage from producing serious social disruption, including conflict.

These hypotheses should be thoroughly tested using both historical and contemporary data at the regional and societal levels. There is great need for empirical research by students of security affairs.

The Recent Salience of Environmental Issues

While the last decades have seen increasing environmental damage around the globe, for the most part this change has progressed incrementally rather than abruptly. Several factors explain the sudden attention recently given the issue. First, with the waning of the ideological and military confrontation between the superpowers, a space for other issues has opened in public discourse in Western societies. Second, public and media awareness of global environmental change was catalyzed in North America by the particularly hot and dry summer of 1988.[13] These two factors are principally circumstantial. But there is a third factor at work: during the last decade there has been a genuine shift in the scientific community's perception of global environmental problems. The environmental system, in particular the earth's climate, used to be regarded as relatively resilient and stable in the face of human insults. But now it is widely believed to have multiple local equilibria that are not highly stable.[14] In 1987, for example, geochemist Wallace Broecker reflected on recent polar ice-core and ocean-sediment data: "What these

hardship was unavoidable, because human population grows geometrically when unconstrained, while food production can only grow arithmetically. Thomas Malthus, *An Essay on the Principle of Population* (New York: Penguin, 1970 [1798]), pp. 70–71.

13. See Stephen Schneider in *Global Warming: Are We Entering the Greenhouse Century?* (San Francisco: Sierra Club, 1989), chapter 7.

14. The development of chaos theory has contributed to this understanding. A chaotic system has nonlinear and feedback relationships between its variables that amplify small perturbations, thereby rendering accurate prediction of the system's state increasingly difficult the further one tries to project into the future. In chaos (not to be confused with randomness), deterministic causal processes still operate at the micro-level and, although the system's state may not be precisely predictable for a given point in the future, the boundaries within which its variables must operate are often identifiable. See James Crutchfield, J. Doyne Farmer, and Norman Packard, "Chaos," *Scientific American*, Vol. 255, No. 6 (December 1986), pp. 46–57; James Gleick, *Chaos: Making of a New Science* (New York: Viking, 1987).

records indicate is that Earth's climate does not respond to forcing in a smooth and gradual way. Rather, it responds in sharp jumps which involve large-scale reorganization of Earth's system. . . . We must consider the possibility that the main responses of the system to our provocation of the atmosphere will come in jumps whose timing and magnitude are unpredictable."[15]

A paradigm-shattering example of such nonlinear or "threshold" effects in complex environmental systems was the discovery of the Antarctic ozone hole in the mid-1980s.[16] The hole was startling evidence of the instability of the environmental system in response to human inputs, of the capacity of humankind to significantly affect the ecosystem on a global scale, and of our inability to predict exactly how the system will change.

This altered perception of the nature of the environmental system has percolated out of the scientific community into the policymaking community.[17] It may also be influencing the broader public's view of environmental problems. Scientists, policymakers, and laypeople are beginning to interpret data about environmental change in a new light: progressive, incremental degradation of environmental systems is not as tolerable as it once was, because we now realize that we do not know where and when we might cross a threshold and move to a radically different and perhaps highly undesirable system.

As compared to the first two factors accounting for the renewed salience of environmental issues, this one is not at all circumstantial; it is rooted in a maturing understanding of natural systems and the global damage humans

---

15. Wallace Broecker, "Unpleasant Surprises in the Greenhouse?" *Nature*, Vol. 328, No. 6126 (July 9, 1987), pp. 123–126. See also James Gleick, "Instability of Climate Defies Computer Analysis," *New York Times*, March 20, 1988, p. 30. William Clark has made a similar point about interlinked physical, ecological, and social systems: "Typically in such systems, slow variation in one property can continue for long periods without noticeable impact on the rest of the system. Eventually, however, the system reaches a state in which its buffering capacity or resilience has been so reduced that additional small changes in the same property, or otherwise insignificant external shocks, push the system across a threshold and precipitate a rapid transition to a new system state or equilibrium." See William Clark, *On the Practical Implications of the Carbon Dioxide Question* (Laxenburg, Austria: International Institute of Applied Systems Analysis, 1985), p. 41.

16. J.C. Farman, B.G. Gardiner, and J.D. Shanklin, "Large Losses of Total Ozone in Antarctica Reveal Seasonal ClO$_x$/NO$_x$ Interaction," *Nature*, Vol. 315, No. 6016 (May 16, 1985), pp. 207–210. Significant depletion of stratospheric ozone over Antarctica began in the 1970s, but was not identified until the 1980s because ozone-measuring satellites had been programmed to discard anomalous results. See Schneider, *Global Warming*, p. 226.

17. See, for example, the speeches on the floor of the U.S. Senate by Senators Nunn, Gore and Wirth, June 28, 1990, *Congressional Record—Senate*, pp. S8929–S8937.

are inflicting on these systems. This understanding is likely to endure, as will strong concern about the environment. Over the next fifty years there will be no shortage of increasingly ominous environmental data to interpret through this new paradigm. Even if there are no dramatic, nonlinear shifts in the ecosystem (though their probability may be quite high), environmental problems will remain prominent on our scientific, policy, and public agendas.

Recent Research on Environmental Change and Conflict

Although there is an old and rich body of thought on the social impacts of environmental change,[18] the literature on the specific connections between environmental change and acute conflict is surprisingly thin. Here I briefly review several important studies.

Angus MacKay examines the relationship between climate change and civil violence in the kingdom of Castile (much of modern-day Spain).[19] During the fifteenth century, there were numerous well-documented episodes of popular unrest in Castile, and some seem to have been produced directly by climate-induced food shortages. In March of 1462, for instance, rioters rampaged through Seville after floods forced the price of bread beyond the means of the poor. Usually, however, the causal connections were more complex. An important intervening factor was the fabric of religious and social beliefs held by the people and promoted by preachers, especially those beliefs

---

18. Discussions of the relationship between environment and society date back to the classical Greeks. In the early twentieth century, many explanations tended towards a simplistic "environmental determinism" that gave little regard to the role in human-environmental systems of feedback loops, human adaptability, and social institutions. See, for instance, Ellsworth Huntington, *Civilization and Climate* (New Haven: Yale University Press, 1915). This perspective has seen something of a resurgence in recent decades; see, for example, Margaret Biswas and Arit Biswas, eds., *Food, Climate and Man* (New York: Wiley, 1979). A survey of some of the best modern literature is William Clark, "The Human Dimensions of Global Change," in Committee on Global Change (U.S. National Committee for the IGBP), *Toward an Understanding of Global Change: Initial Priorities for U.S. Contributions to the International Geosphere-Biosphere Program (IGBP)* (Washington, D.C.: National Academy Press, 1988), pp. 134–213. On the social impact of climate change, see Robert Kates, Jesse Ausubel, and Mimi Berberian, eds., *Climate Impact Assessment: Studies of the Interaction of Climate and Society*, Scientific Committee on Problems of the Environment (SCOPE) No. 27 (New York: Wiley, 1985).

19. Angus MacKay, "Climate and Popular Unrest in Late Medieval Castile," in T.M. Wigley, M.J. Ingram, and G. Farmer, *Climate and History: Studies in Past Climates and Their Impact on Man* (Cambridge: Cambridge University Press, 1981), pp. 356–376. For other historical case studies of climate-society interaction, see Hubert Lamb, *Weather, Climate and Human Affairs* (London: Routledge, 1988).

attributing weather fluctuations to the sin of someone in the community.[20] MacKay thus argues against a simplistic "stimulus-response" model of environment-conflict linkages and instead for one that allows for "culturally mediated" behavior.

Addressing a modern conflict, William Durham has analyzed the demographic and environmental pressures behind the 1969 "Soccer War" between El Salvador and Honduras.[21] Because of the prominence in this conflict of previous migration from El Salvador to Honduras, and because of the striking evidence of population growth and land stress in the two countries (most notably in El Salvador), a number of analysts have asserted that the Soccer War is a first-class example of an ecologically driven conflict.[22] A simple Malthusian interpretation does seem to have credibility when one looks at the aggregate data.[23] But Durham shows that changes in agricultural practice and land distribution—to the detriment of poor farmers—were more powerful inducements to migration than sheer population growth. Land scarcity developed not because there was too little to go around, but because of "a process of competitive exclusion by which the small farmers [were] increasingly squeezed off the land" by large land owners.[24] Durham thus contends that ecologists cannot directly apply to human societies the simple, density-dependent models of resource competition they commonly use to study asocial animals: a distributional component must be added, because human behavior is powerfully constrained by social structure and the resource access it entails.[25]

20. Anger over food scarcity was sometimes turned against Jews and *conversos* (Jews who had converted to Christianity after Iberian pogroms in the late fourteenth century), and sometimes against small shopkeepers who were accused of the "sins" of creating shortages and overpricing food.

21. William Durham, *Scarcity and Survival in Central America: The Ecological Origins of the Soccer War* (Stanford, Calif.: Stanford University Press, 1979).

22. For instance, see Paul Ehrlich, Anne Ehrlich, and John Holdren, *Ecoscience: Population, Resources, Environment* (San Francisco: Freeman, 1977), p. 908.

23. El Salvador was the most densely populated country in the Western Hemisphere (190 people per square kilometer in 1976; compare India at 186), with a population growth rate of 3.5 percent per year (representing a doubling time of about twenty years). Most of the country had lost its virgin forest, land erosion and nutrient depletion were severe, and total food production fell behind consumption in the mid-50s. Per capita farmland used for basic food crops fell from 0.15 hectares in 1953 to 0.11 hectares in 1971.

24. Durham, *Scarcity and Survival*, p. 54.

25. The importance of variables intervening between population density and conflict is emphasized in Nazli Choucri, ed., *Multidisciplinary Perspectives on Population and Conflict* (Syracuse, N.Y.: Syracuse University Press, 1984); see also Jack Goldstone, *Revolution and Rebellion in the Early Modern World* (Berkeley, Calif.: University of California Press, 1991).

Others have analyzed environment-conflict linkages in the Philippines.[26] Although the country has suffered from serious internal strife for many decades, its underlying causes may be changing: population displacement, deforestation, and land degradation appear to be increasingly powerful forces driving the current communist-led insurgency.[27] Here, too, the linkages between environmental change and conflict are complex, involving numerous intervening variables, both physical and social. The Filipino population growth rate of 2.5 percent is among the highest in Southeast Asia. To help pay the massive foreign debt, the government has encouraged the expansion of large-scale lowland agriculture. Both factors have swelled the number of landless agricultural laborers. Many have migrated to the Philippines' steep and ecologically vulnerable uplands where they have cleared land or established plots on previously logged land. This has set in motion a cycle of erosion, falling food production, and further clearing of land. Even marginally fertile land is becoming hard to find in many places, and economic conditions are often dire for the peasants.[28] Civil dissent is rampant in these peripheral areas, which are largely beyond the effective control of the central government.

While these studies are commendable, a review of all of the recent work on environmental change and conflict reveals a number of difficulties, some methodological and some conceptual. First, researchers often emphasize human-induced climate change and ozone depletion to the neglect of severe terrestrial and aquatic environmental problems such as deforestation, soil degradation, and fisheries depletion. Second, much of the recent writing on the links between environmental change and conflict is anecdotal. These pieces do not clearly separate the "how" question (how will environmental change lead to conflict?) from the "where" question (where will such conflict occur?). I address the "how" question in the following sections of this article.

---

26. See especially Gareth Porter and Delfin Ganapin, Jr., *Resources, Population, and the Philippines' Future: A Case Study*, WRI Paper No. 4 (Washington, D.C.: World Resources Institute [WRI], 1988).

27. Other works on the Philippines used in this article are Gary Hawes, "Theories of Peasant Revolution: A Critique and Contribution from the Philippines," *World Politics*, Vol. 42, No. 1 (January 1990), pp. 261–298; Gregg Jones, *Red Revolution: Inside the Philippine Guerrilla Movement* (Boulder, Colo.: Westview, 1989); World Bank, *Philippines: Environment and Natural Resource Management Study* (Washington, D.C.: World Bank, 1989).

28. Leonard notes that, around the planet, population growth, inequitable land distribution, and agricultural modernization have caused huge numbers of desperately poor people to move to "remote and ecologically fragile rural areas" or to already overcrowded cities. See Jeffrey Leonard, "Overview," *Environment and the Poor: Development Strategies for a Common Agenda* (New Brunswick, N.J.: Transaction, 1989), p. 5.

Third, environmental-social systems are hard to analyze. They are characterized by multiple causes and effects and by a host of intervening variables, often linked by interactive, synergistic, and nonlinear causal relations. Empirical data about these variables and relations are rarely abundant. Although the underlying influence of environmental factors on conflict may be great, the complex and indirect causation in these systems means that the scanty evidence available is always open to many interpretations. Furthermore, understanding environmental-social systems involves specifying links across levels of analysis usually regarded as quite independent.[29]

Fourth, the prevailing "naturalistic" epistemology and ontology of social science may hinder accurate understanding of the links between physical and social variables within environmental-social systems.[30] In particular, it may be a mistake to conjoin, in causal generalizations, types of physical event with types of intentional social action.[31] Fifth, researchers must acquire detailed knowledge of a daunting range of disciplines, from atmospheric science and agricultural hydrology to energy economics and international relations theory.

Sixth and finally, the modern realist perspective that is often used to understand security problems is largely inadequate for identifying and explaining the links between environmental change and conflict. Realism focuses on states as rational maximizers of power in an anarchic system; state behavior is mainly a function of the structure of power relations in the system.[32] But this emphasis on states means that theorists tend to see the world as divided into territorially distinct, mutually exclusive countries, not broader environmental regions or systems. Realism thus encourages scholars to deemphasize transboundary environmental problems, because such prob-

---

29. For example, researchers might need to be able to show how countless individual actions affect global climate variables (thus moving "up" through several levels of analysis), and how, in turn, these global variables influence conflict behavior (thereby moving back "down" to group and individual behavior).

30. A naturalistic view of social science holds that there is no qualitative difference between the domains of investigation of the natural and social sciences, suggesting that the procedures used for research and explanation can be basically the same in both domains.

31. For over three decades, issues surrounding intentionality and causal generalization have been the subject of heated debate in philosophy of mind, language, and science. For the purposes of this article, however, I treat as unproblematic causal generalizations that include physical and social variables.

32. My comments here principally refer to the influential "neorealist" school. See in particular Kenneth Waltz, *Theory of International Politics* (Reading, Mass.: Addison-Wesley, 1979); and Robert Gilpin, *War and Change in World Politics* (Cambridge: Cambridge University Press, 1981).

lems often cannot be linked to a particular country, and do not have any easily conceptualized impact on the structure of economic and military power relations between states. Realism induces scholars to squeeze environmental issues into a structure of concepts including "state," "sovereignty," "territory," "national interest," and "balance of power." The fit is bad, which may lead theorists to ignore, distort, and misunderstand important aspects of global environmental problems.

Mapping Causes and Effects

This article proposes a research agenda to guide the study of environmental change and acute conflict. Before we can formulate plausible hypotheses, however, we need a clear analytical framework, such as suggested by Figure 1. This and subsequent figures in this article provide the basis for a detailed causal-path analysis of the links between environmental change and conflict. Such an analysis can help bring some order into the profusion of predictions concerning these issues, and it can also help researchers address several of the impediments to research mentioned above.[33]

Figure 1 suggests that the total effect of human activity on the environment in a particular ecological region is mainly a function of two variables: first, the product of total population in the region and physical activity per capita, and second, the vulnerability of the ecosystem in that region to those particular activities. Activity per capita, in turn, is a function of available physical resources (which include nonrenewable resources such as minerals, and renewable resources such as water, forests, and agricultural land) and ideational factors, including institutions, social relations, preferences, and beliefs.[34] The figure also shows that environmental effects may cause social effects that in turn could lead to conflict. For example, the degradation of agricultural land might produce large-scale migration, which could create

---

33. Most notably, it can help them gauge the causal power of distant environmental forces, identify potentially important interactions of simultaneous environmental problems, specify intervening variables, and identify causal links across levels of analysis.
34. Over short and medium terms, activity per capita is also a function of the economy's current capital stock, which reflects the society's prevailing level and type of technological development. Over the long term, we can assume that a society's technology is a result of two components of Figure 1: certain ideational factors (most importantly, beliefs about the nature of physical reality held by particular knowledge-oriented groups in the society) and available physical resources. I use the adjective "ideational" to emphasize that factors such as institutions, social relations, and beliefs are products of the human mind.

Figure 1.   Environmental Change and Acute Conflict.

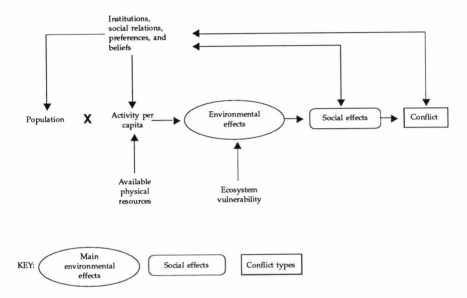

ethnic conflicts as migratory groups clash with indigenous populations. There are important feedback loops from social effects and conflict to the ideational factors and thence back to activity per capita and population. Thus, ethnic clashes arising from migration could alter the operation of a society's markets and thereby its economic activity.[35]

---

35. Numerous writers, especially those considering the social impact of climate change, have generated similar diagrams. See in particular the excellent survey article by Richard Warrick and William Riebsame entitled "Societal Response to CO_2-Induced Climate Change: Opportunities for Research," *Climatic Change,* Vol. 3, No. 4 (1981), pp. 387–428. Two points should be noted about Figure 1: First, there are many ways it could be made more accurate, but at the cost of greater complexity. For example, there are feedback loops from social effects and conflict to environmental effects. The diagrams in this article highlight what I believe are the variables and causal linkages most important to our discussion. Second, each variable in Figure 1 aggregates many sub-variables. For instance, "activity per capita" encompasses sub-variables ranging from the extent of cattle ranching to the rate of automobile use. Consequently, an arrow in Figure 1 may represent either a positive or a negative correlation, depending on the specific sub-variables considered. In Figures 2–4, which identify more specific variables, all arrows represent positive correlations.

To clarify the research agenda, we can divide the "how" question (how will environmental change lead to conflict?) into two independent questions. First, what are the important social effects of environmental change? Second, what types of acute conflict, if any, are most likely to result from these social effects? The first question asks about the nature of the arrow in Figure 1 between "environmental effects" and "social effects," while the second asks about the arrow between "social effects" and "conflict."

My focus on these two causal linkages does not deny the importance of the other variables and linkages in the figure. We must be aware of the role of population growth, demographic structure, and patterns of population distribution.[36] And we must understand the effect of the ideational factors at the top of the diagram. This social and psychological context is immensely broad and complex. It includes patterns of land distribution (as in the Soccer War); family and community structure; the economic and legal incentives to consume and produce goods, including the system of property rights and markets; perceptions of the probability of long-run political and economic stability; historically rooted patterns of trade and interaction with other societies (as with debt and export relations between the Philippines and the North); the distribution of coercive power within and among nations; the form and effectiveness of institutions of governance; and metaphysical beliefs about the relationship between humans and nature (as in medieval Castile).

Without a full understanding of these intervening factors we cannot begin to grasp the true nature of the relationships between human activity, environmental change, social disruption, and conflict.[37] These factors largely determine the vulnerability and adaptability of a society when faced with environmental stresses. There is historical evidence that certain societies have technological, institutional, or cultural characteristics that make them very

---

36. Experts vigorously dispute the effects of population growth on the environment, economic well-being, and social organization. Julian Simon is optimistic in *The Ultimate Resource* (Princeton: Princeton University Press, 1981); Paul and Anne Ehrlich reiterate their well-known pessimism in *The Population Explosion* (London: Hutchinson, 1990). The question is surveyed by Geoffrey McNicoll in "Consequences of Rapid Population Growth: An Overview and Assessment," *Population and Development Review,* Vol. 10, No. 2 (June 1984), pp. 177–240.

37. Recognition of the role of these factors distinguishes simplistic environmental determinism from sophisticated accounts of the nature of the environmental threat posed to humankind. Perhaps the most extreme example of the former in the environmental-security literature is Brown, "Climate, Ecology and International Security," pp. 523–524. Brown implies that climate change was an important and relatively proximate cause of social upheaval in Europe in the 1840s, imperial expansion between 1850 and 1940, the Cold War, and the 1974 Ethiopian coup.

resilient to such pressures.[38] Not only do we need to identify the thresholds beyond which given societies cannot effectively respond, we need to determine why some societies respond better than others.

Figure 1 clarifies these aspects of our research agenda. If we wish to understand a society's capacity to prevent severe social disruption (where the preventive action could be either mitigation of, or adaptation to, the environmental stress), we need to understand the arrows between the ideational factors at the top of the figure and "population," "activity per capita," and "social effects" along the main spine of the figure. If we wish to understand a society's propensity toward conflict (given certain social effects due to the environmental stress), we need to understand the arrow between the ideational factors and "conflict." When sufficiently advanced, this research should help identify key intervention points where policymakers might be able to alter the causal processes linking human activity, environmental degradation, and conflict. These interventions will fall into two general categories: those that seek to prevent negative social effects and those that seek to prevent the conflict that could result from these social effects. In the following pages I refer to these as "first-stage" and "second-stage" interventions.

THE RANGE OF ENVIRONMENTAL PROBLEMS

Developing countries are likely to be affected sooner and more severely by environmental change than rich countries. By definition, they do not have the financial, material, or intellectual resources of the developed world; furthermore, their social and political institutions tend to be fragile and riven with discord. It is probable, therefore, that developing societies will be less able to apprehend or respond to environmental disruption.[39]

Seven major environmental problems (the "environmental effects" in Figure 1) might plausibly contribute to conflict within and among developing countries: greenhouse warming, stratospheric ozone depletion, acid deposition, deforestation, degradation of agricultural land, overuse and pollution

---

38. Social vulnerability and adaptability have been the focus of much research and thought. See Warrick and Riebsame, "Societal Response." On the conditions and variables that determine vulnerability, see Diana Liverman, "Vulnerability to Global Environmental Change," in Roger Kasperson, et al., eds., *Understanding Global Environmental Change: The Contributions of Risk Analysis and Management*, report of an international workshop at Clark University, October 11–13, 1989 (Worcester, Mass.: Clark University, 1989), pp. 32–33.
39. Gurr, "Political Consequences of Scarcity," pp. 70–71.

of water supplies, and depletion of fish stocks.[40] These problems can all be crudely characterized as large-scale human-induced problems, with long-term and often irreversible consequences, which is why they are often grouped together under the rubric "global change."[41] However, they vary greatly in spatial scale: the first two involve genuinely global physical processes, while the last five involve regional physical processes, although they may appear in locales all over the planet. These seven problems also vary in time scale: for example, while a region can be deforested in only a few years, and severe ecological and social effects may be noticeable almost immediately, human-induced greenhouse warming will probably develop over many decades[42] and may not have truly serious implications for humankind for half a century or more after the signal is first detected. In addition, some of these problems (for instance, deforestation and degradation of water supplies) are much more advanced than others (such as greenhouse warming and ozone depletion) and are already producing serious social disruption. This variance in tangible evidence for these problems contributes to great differences in our certainty about their ultimate severity. The uncertainties surrounding greenhouse warming, for example, are thus far greater than those concerning deforestation.[43]

---

40. I have left off this list a number of environmental problems. Declining biodiversity, for example, might contribute to acute conflict (by weakening agricultural productivity over the long term), but even more indirectly than the seven environmental stresses discussed here. Increased dumping of toxic wastes in the South, and accidents in the South involving subsidiaries of Northern companies (such as the Bhopal tragedy), will probably do no more than strain economic and diplomatic relations, although such incidents could lead to sporadic, localized violence. Perceptions of environmental damage or potential damage (whether or not the perceptions are justified) might also induce tensions; for instance, the siting of a nuclear plant close to an international border could lead to protests in neighboring countries. However, it seems unlikely that such perceptions by themselves could cause widespread conflict.

41. Readers interested in technical background on these problems should consult *World Resources 1990–91* (New York: Oxford University Press, 1990) and *World Resources 1988–89* (New York: Basic Books, 1988). This publication, produced biennially by the World Resources Institute (WRI) in collaboration with the United Nations Environment Programme and other organizations, is widely regarded as the most accessible, accurate, and comprehensive source for information on global change issues. The more popular *State of the World* report published annually by the Worldwatch Institute is useful but sometimes selective and tendentious.

42. However, as Broecker has pointed out, nonlinear or threshold effects in the atmospheric system could produce a sudden shift of the *climate* to a new equilibrium by altering, for example, the direction of major ocean currents such as the Gulf Stream. Broecker, "Unpleasant Surprises in the Greenhouse?" p. 124.

43. However, the uncertainties remain substantial for deforestation. See Vaclav Smil, *Energy, Food, Environment: Realities, Myths, Options* (Oxford, U.K.: Oxford University Press, 1987), pp. 231–237.

Many of these problems are causally interrelated. For instance, acid deposition damages agricultural land, fisheries, and forests. Greenhouse warming may contribute to deforestation by moving northward the optimal temperature and precipitation zones for many tree species, by increasing the severity of windstorms and wildfires, and by expanding the range of pests and diseases.[44] The release of carbon from these dying forests would reinforce the greenhouse effect. The increased incidence of ultraviolet radiation due to the depletion of the ozone layer will probably damage trees and crops, and it may also damage the phytoplankton at the bottom of the ocean food chain.[45]

Finally, when we consider the social effects of environmental change, especially of climate change, we should be especially aware of changes in the incidence of "extreme" environmental events. Social impacts result "not so much from slow fluctuations in the mean, but from the tails of the distribution, from extreme events." While a two-to-three degree celsius mean global warming might not seem too significant for agricultural production, it may produce a large increase in crop-devastating droughts, floods, heat waves, and storms.[46]

FOUR PRINCIPAL SOCIAL EFFECTS

Environmental degradation may cause countless often subtle changes in developing societies. These range from increased communal cooking as fuelwood becomes scarce around African villages, to worsened poverty of Filipino coastal fishermen whose once-abundant grounds have been destroyed by trawlers and industrial pollution. Which of the many types of social effect might be crucial links between environmental change and acute conflict? This is the first part of the "how" question. To address it, we must use both the best knowledge about the social effects of environmental change and the best knowledge about the nature and causes of social conflict.

---

44. WRI, et al., *World Resources 1990–91*, p. 111.

45. Robert Worrest, Hermann Gucinski, and John Hardy, "Potential Impact of Stratospheric Ozone Depletion on Marine Ecosystems," in John Topping, Jr., ed., *Coping with Climate Change: Proceedings of the Second North American Conference on Preparing for Climate Change* (Washington, D.C.: The Climate Institute, 1989), pp. 256–262.

46. T.M.L. Wigley, "Impact of Extreme Events," *Nature*, Vol. 316, No. 6024 (July 11, 1985), pp. 106–107. Since the probability distributions for most climate variables describe a bell curve, Wigley calculates that a shift in the mean by one standard deviation would change a 1-in-20-year extreme to one that occurs on average 1 year in 4, while the 1-in-100-year extreme would become a 1-in-11-year event.

In thus working from both ends towards the middle of the causal chain, I hypothesize that four principal social effects may, either singly or in combination, substantially increase the probability of acute conflict in developing countries: decreased agricultural production, economic decline, population displacement, and disruption of legitimized and authoritative institutions and social relations. These effects will often be causally interlinked, sometimes with reinforcing relationships. For example, the population displacement resulting from a decrease in agricultural production may further disrupt agricultural production. Or economic decline may lead to the flight of people with wealth and education, which in turn could eviscerate universities, courts, and institutions of economic management, all of which are crucial to a healthy economy.

AGRICULTURAL PRODUCTION. Decreased agricultural production is often mentioned as potentially the most worrisome consequence of environmental change,[47] and Figure 2 presents some of the causal scenarios frequently proposed by researchers. This illustration is not intended to be exhaustive: the systemic interaction of environmental and agricultural variables is far more complex than the figure suggests.[48] Moreover, no one region or country will exhibit all the indicated processes: while some are already clearly evident in certain areas, others are not yet visible anywhere.

The Philippines provides a good illustration of deforestation's impact, which can be traced out in the figure. Since the Second World War, logging and the encroachment of farms have reduced the virgin and second-growth forest from about sixteen million hectares to 6.8–7.6 million hectares.[49] Across the archipelago, logging and land-clearing have accelerated erosion, changed regional hydrological cycles and precipitation patterns, and decreased the land's ability to retain water during rainy periods. The resulting flash floods have damaged irrigation works while plugging reservoirs and irrigation channels with silt. These factors may seriously affect crop production. For ex-

---

47. See, for example, Lester Brown, "Reexamining the World Food Prospect," in Worldwatch Institute, *State of the World 1989* (New York: Norton, 1989), pp. 41–58.
48. Useful discussions of these systems include World Commission on Environment and Development (commonly known as the Brundtland Commission), "Food Security: Sustaining the Potential," in *Our Common Future* (Oxford: Oxford University Press, 1987), chapter 5, pp. 118–146; WRI, et al., *World Resources 1988–89*, pp. 18–21, 51–68, and especially 215–234, 271–284; WRI, et al., *World Resources 1990–91*, pp. 5–6, 83–100; United Nations Food and Agriculture Organization (FAO), *The State of Food and Agriculture 1989* (Rome: FAO, 1989), pp. 65–74.
49. Porter and Ganapin, *Resources, Population, and the Philippines' Future*, p. 24. These authors call this "perhaps the most rapid destruction of forest reserves in the world." The figures cited refer to adequately stocked forested land, and are approximate.

Figure 2. Possible Effects of Environmental Change on Agricultural Production.

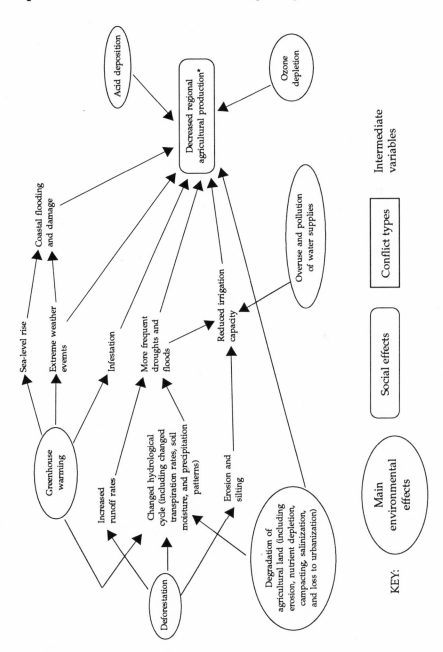

ample, when the government of the Philippines and the European Economic Community commissioned an Integrated Environmental Plan for the still relatively unspoiled island of Palawan, the authors of the study found that only about half of the 36,000 hectares of irrigated farmland projected within the Plan for 2007 will actually be irrigable because of the hydrological effects of decreases in forest cover.[50]

Figure 2 also highlights the importance of the degradation and decreasing availability of good agricultural land, problems that deserve much closer attention than they usually receive. Currently, total global cropland amounts to about 1.5 billion hectares. Optimistic estimates of total arable land on the planet, which includes both current and potential cropland, range from 3.2 to 3.4 billion hectares, but nearly all the best land has already been exploited. What is left is either less fertile, not sufficiently rainfed or easily irrigable, infested with pests, or harder to clear and work.[51]

For developing countries during the 1980s, cropland grew at just 0.26 percent a year, less than half the rate of the 1970s. More importantly, in these countries arable land per capita dropped by 1.9 percent a year.[52] In the absence of a major increase in arable land in developing countries, experts expect that the world average of 0.28 hectares of cropland per capita will decline to 0.17 hectares by the year 2025, given the current rate of world population growth.[53] Large tracts are being lost each year to urban encroachment, erosion, nutrient depletion, salinization, waterlogging, acidification, and compacting. The geographer Václav Smil, who is generally very conservative in his assessments of environmental damage, estimates that two to three million hectares of cropland are lost annually to erosion; perhaps twice as much land goes to urbanization, and at least one million hectares are abandoned because of excessive salinity. In addition, about one-fifth of the

50. Christopher Finney and Stanley Western, "An Economic Analysis of Environmental Protection and Management: An Example from the Philippines," *The Environmentalist*, Vol. 6, No. 1 (1986), p. 56.

51. Experts generally describe a country as "land scarce" when 70 percent or more of the arable land is under production. In Asia about 82 percent of all arable land is cultivated. See WRI, et al., *World Resources 1990–91*, p. 5.

52. Nafis Sadik, *The State of the World Population 1990* (New York: United Nations Population Fund, 1990), p. 8.

53. WRI, et al., *World Resources 1990–91*, p. 87. Nearly 73 percent of all rural households in developing countries are either landless or nearly landless. Using this figure, Leonard estimates that "935 million rural people live in households that have too little land to meet the minimum subsistence requirements for food and fuel. These data exclude China, which could add as many as 100–200 million more people to the category." See Leonard, "Overview," p. 13.

world's cropland is suffering from some degree of desertification.[54] Taken together, he concludes, the planet will lose about 100 million hectares of arable land between 1985 and 2000.[55]

Figure 2 also depicts some of the effects that greenhouse warming and climate change may have on agricultural production.[56] Coastal cropland in countries such as Bangladesh and Egypt is extremely vulnerable to storm surges. Such events could become more common and devastating, because global warming will cause sea levels to rise and might intensify storms. The greenhouse effect will also change precipitation patterns and soil moisture; while this may benefit some agricultural regions, others will suffer. Many plants grow faster and larger in a warm environment rich in carbon dioxide, and they often use water more efficiently.[57] But optimistic estimates of greatly increased crop yields have usually been based on laboratory experiments under ideal growing conditions. In addition, these estimates have ignored the influence on yields of more frequent extreme climate events (especially droughts and heat waves), increased pest infestation, and the decreased nutritional quality of crops grown in a carbon dioxide–enriched atmosphere.

ECONOMIC DECLINE. If we are interested in environment-conflict linkages, perhaps the most important potential social effect of environmental degra-

---

54. Experts give "desertification" a variety of meanings. In general, it implies a complex syndrome of very low soil productivity, poor rain-use efficiency by vegetation, and consequent adverse changes in the hydrological cycle. It can therefore encompass several of the variables identified in Figure 2. See Michel Verstraete, "Defining Desertification: A Review," *Climatic Change*, Vol. 9, No. 1/2 (August/October 1986), pp. 5–18.

55. Smil gives a startling account of the situation in China. From 1957 to 1977 the country lost 33.33 million hectares of farmland (30 percent of its 1957 total), while it added 21.2 million hectares of largely marginal land. He notes that "the net loss of 12 million hectares during a single generation when the country's population grew by about 300 million people means that per capita availability of arable land dropped by 40 per cent and that China's farmland is now no more abundant than Bangladesh's—a mere one-tenth of a hectare per capita!" See Smil, *Energy, Food, Environment*, pp. 223 and 230.

56. There is scientific debate about the likely magnitude, rate, and timing of greenhouse warming and about its climatic, ecological, and social impacts. The current consensus is summarized in the reports prepared by Working Groups I and II of the Intergovernmental Panel on Climate Change (IPCC) under the auspices of the World Meteorological Organization and the United Nations Environment Programme. The complete report of Working Group I has been published as J.T. Houghton, G.J. Jenkins, and J.J. Ephraums, eds., *Climate Change: The IPCC Scientific Assessment* (Cambridge: Cambridge University Press, 1990). For a thorough assessment of climate change and agriculture, see M.L. Parry, T.R. Carter, and N.T. Konijn, eds., *The Impact of Climatic Variations on Agriculture*, Volume 1: *Assessments in Cool Temperate and Cold Regions*; Volume 2: *Assessments in Semi-arid Regions* (Dordrecht, Netherlands: Kluwer, 1989).

57. See R.A. Warrick, R.M. Gifford, and M.L. Parry, "CO_2, Climatic Change and Agriculture: Assessing the Response of Food Crops to the Direct Effects of Increased CO_2 and Climatic Change," in Bert Bolin, et al., eds. *The Greenhouse Effect, Climatic Change, and Ecosystems*, SCOPE No. 29 (New York: Wiley, 1986), pp. 393–474.

dation is the further impoverishment it may produce in developing societies. In Figure 3, I suggest some key causal processes. The figure shows that economic productivity may be influenced directly by environmental disruption, or indirectly via other social effects such as decreased agricultural production. While few developing countries will exhibit all causal links indicated in Figure 3, most will exhibit some.

A great diversity of factors might affect wealth production. For example, increased ultraviolet radiation caused by ozone depletion is likely to raise the rate of disease in humans and livestock,[58] which could have serious economic results. Logging for export markets may produce short-term economic gain for the country's elite, but increased runoff can damage roads, bridges, and other valuable infrastructure, while the extra siltation reduces the transport and hydroelectric capacity of rivers. As forests are destroyed, wood becomes scarcer and more expensive, and it absorbs an increasing share of the household budget for the poor families that use it for fuel.[59]

Agriculture is the source of much of the wealth generated in developing societies. Food production soared in many regions over the last decades because the green revolution more than compensated for inadequate or declining soil productivity;[60] but some experts believe this economic relief will be short-lived. Jeffrey Leonard writes: "Millions of previously very poor families that have experienced less than one generation of increasing wealth due to rising agricultural productivity could see that trend reversed if environmental degradation is not checked."[61] Damage to the soil is already producing a harsh economic impact in some areas.[62]

Gauging the actual economic cost of land degradation is not easy. Current national income accounts do not incorporate measures of resource depletion: "A nation could exhaust its mineral reserves, cut down its forests, erode its soils, pollute its aquifers, and hunt its wildlife to extinction—all without

---

58. Janice Longstreth, "Overview of the Potential Health Effects Associated with Ozone Depletion," in Topping, *Coping with Climate Change*, pp. 163–167.

59. The FAO estimates that up to 2.5 billion people in the developing world will face acute fuelwood shortages by the year 2000. FAO, *Fuelwood Supplies in the Developing Countries*, FAO Forestry Paper No. 42 (Rome: FAO, 1983).

60. The term "green revolution" refers to the dramatic gains in crop output in the developing countries from the 1960s into the 1980s due to higher-yielding grains and the intensive use of irrigation, chemical fertilizers, and pesticides.

61. Leonard, *Environment and the Poor*, p. 27.

62. For a case study of Indonesia, see Robert Repetto, "Balance-Sheet Erosion—How to Account for the Loss of Natural Resources," *International Environmental Affairs*, Vol. 1, No. 2 (Spring 1989), pp. 103–137.

Figure 3. **Possible Effects of Environmental Change on Economic Productivity in Developing Countries.**

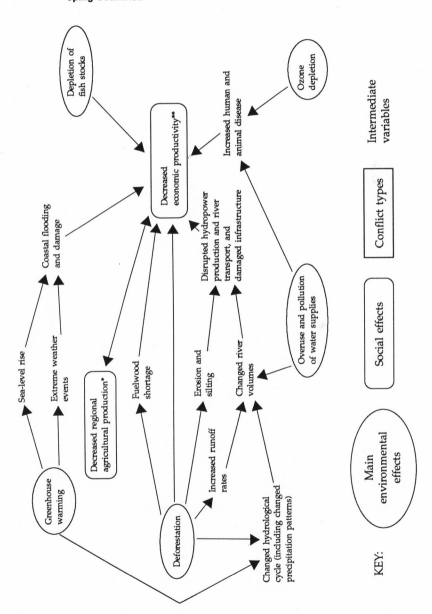

*See Figures 2 and 4.
**See Figure 4.

affecting measured income."[63] The inadequacy of measures of economic productivity reinforces the perception that there is a policy trade-off between economic growth and environmental protection; this perception, in turn, encourages societies to generate present income at the expense of their potential for future income.[64]

POPULATION DISPLACEMENT. Some commentators have suggested that environmental degradation may produce vast numbers of "environmental refugees."[65] Sea-level rise may drive people back from coastal and delta areas in Egypt; spreading desert may empty Sahelian countries as their populations move south; Filipino fishermen may leave their depleted fishing grounds for the cities. The term "environmental refugee" is somewhat misleading, however, because it implies that environmental disruption could be a clear, proximate cause of refugee flows. Usually, though, environmental disruption will be only one of many interacting physical and social variables, including agricultural and economic decline, that ultimately force people from their homelands. For example, over the last three decades, millions of people have migrated from Bangladesh to neighboring West Bengal and Assam in India. While detailed data are scarce (in part because the Bangladeshi government is reluctant to admit there is significant out-migration), many specialists believe this movement is a result, at least in part, of shortages of adequately fertile land due to a rapidly growing population. Flooding, caused by deforestation in watersheds upstream on the Ganges and Brahmaputra rivers, might also be driving people from the area.[66] In the future, this migration could be aggravated by rising sea-levels coupled with extreme weather events (both perhaps resulting from climate change).

DISRUPTED INSTITUTIONS AND SOCIAL RELATIONS. The fourth social effect especially relevant to the connection between environment change and acute conflict is the disruption of institutions and of legitimized, accepted, and

---

63. Robert Repetto, "Wasting Assets: The Need for National Resource Accounting," *Technology Review,* January 1990, p. 40.

64. Repetto carefully analyzes soil types, cropping practices, logging, and erosion rates in upland areas of Java. Applying a 10 percent discount rate to the future stream of lost income, Repetto calculates the total economic cost of one year of erosion to be $481 million; this is about 40 percent of the annual value of upland cropland production. He writes: "Nearly 40 cents in future income is sacrificed to obtain each dollar for current consumption." He also estimates that off-site costs, including the higher expense of clearing waterways and irrigation channels of silt, come to $30–$100 million a year. Repetto, "Balance-Sheet Erosion," pp. 129–132.

65. E.g., Jacobson, *Environmental Refugees.*

66. Lester Brown and John Young, "Feeding the World in the Nineties," in Worldwatch Institute, *State of the World: 1990* (New York: Norton, 1990), p. 61.

authoritative social relations. In many developing societies, the three social effects described above are likely to tear this fabric of custom and habitual behavior. A drop in agricultural output may weaken rural communities by causing malnutrition and disease, and by encouraging people to leave; economic decline may corrode confidence in the national purpose, weaken the tax base, and undermine financial, legal, and political institutions; and mass migrations of people into a region may disrupt labor markets, shift class relations, and upset the traditional balance of economic and political authority between ethnic groups.

The Capacity of Developing Countries to Respond: First-Stage Interventions

Can developing countries respond to environmental problems effectively enough to avert these negative social effects? The aggregate data on world food production might give us reason for optimism. Between 1965 and 1986, many developing regions suffered serious environmental problems, including erosion, salinization, and loss of land to urbanization. Yet global cereal production increased at 3 percent a year, meat and milk output increased 2 percent annually, while the rate for oil crops, vegetables, and pulses was 2.5 percent.[67] At the regional level, increased food production kept ahead of population growth, except in Africa, and local shortfalls were alleviated by exports from developed countries with huge surpluses. We might therefore conclude that developing countries have sufficient capacity, with intermittent assistance from Northern grain exporters, to respond to environmental problems.

But aggregate figures hide significant disparities in food availability among and within developing countries.[68] Moreover, these figures are becoming less promising than they once were: many developing countries have already reaped most of the green revolution's potential benefit, and the rate of increase in global cereal production has declined by over 40 percent since the 1960s.[69] For three successive years—from 1987 through 1989—estimated

---

67. WRI, et al., *World Resources 1988–89*, p. 52.
68. In 1985, for example, average caloric intake was insufficient for health, growth, and productive work in eight countries in Asia, and six in Latin America and the Caribbean. Ibid., p. 53.
69. From 1962–72, global cereal production increased at an annual rate of 3.7 percent; from 1972–82, at 2.5 percent; and from 1982–86, at 2.1 percent. See Pierre Crosson and Norman Rosenberg, "Strategies for Agriculture," *Scientific American*, Vol. 261, No. 3 (September 1989), p. 130.

global cereal consumption exceeded production.[70] Bumper grain crops were again harvested in 1990, but carry-over stocks can be depleted rapidly, and we remain within one or two years of a global food crisis.

Over the long term, the capacity of developing countries to respond effectively to the consequences of environmental change on agriculture will depend on the complex interactions within each society of the factors indicated in Figure 1. Of particular importance are the society's prevailing land-use practices, land distribution, and market mechanisms within the agricultural sector.[71] Market factors are especially relevant today as numerous developing countries are relinquishing state control over the marketplace, reducing government spending, and removing impediments to foreign investment. Economists often contend that—in a market economy with an efficient price mechanism—environmentally induced scarcity will encourage conservation, technological innovation, and resource substitution. Julian Simon, in particular, displays an unwavering faith in the capacity of human ingenuity to overcome scarcity when spurred by self-interest.[72] Many economists point to the success of the green revolution, which was often driven by market forces; it involved both new technologies and the substitution of petroleum resources (in the form of fertilizer) for inadequate or degraded nutrients in the soil. This argument supports the policies for market liberalization and "structural adjustment" currently promoted by international financial and lending institutions, such as the International Monetary Fund and World Bank. Below, however, I suggest why these policies will not be an effective response to environmental scarcity in the future.

CORNUCOPIANS AND NEO-MALTHUSIANS

Experts in environmental studies now commonly use the labels "cornucopian" for optimists like Simon and "neo-Malthusian" for pessimists like Paul and Anne Ehrlich.[73] Cornucopians do not worry much about protecting the stock of any single resource, because of their faith that market-driven human ingenuity can always be tapped to allow the substitution of more abundant

---

70. FAO, *The State of Food and Agriculture 1989*, p. 13.
71. For a thorough review, see Piers Blaikie and Harold Brookfield, *Land Degradation and Society* (London: Methuen, 1987).
72. Simon, *The Ultimate Resource*. Population growth, by Simon's analysis, is not necessarily a bad thing; in fact, it may be helpful because it increases the labor force and the pool of potential human ingenuity. See also Ester Boserup, *The Conditions of Agricultural Growth: The Economics of Agrarian Change Under Population Pressure* (Chicago: Aldine, 1965).
73. Ehrlich, Ehrlich, and Holdren, *Ecoscience*; Ehrlich and Ehrlich, *The Population Explosion*.

resources to produce the same end-use service. Simon, for example, writes: "There is no physical or economic reason why human resourcefulness and enterprise cannot forever continue to respond to impending shortages and existing problems with new expedients that, after an adjustment period, leave us better off than before the problem arose."[74] Neo-Malthusians are much more cautious. For renewable resources, they often distinguish between resource "capital" and its "income": the capital is the resource stock that generates a flow (the income) that can be tapped for human consumption and well-being. A "sustainable" economy, using this terminology, is one that leaves the capital intact and undamaged so that future generations can enjoy an undiminished income stream.[75]

Historically, cornucopians have been right to criticize the idea that resource scarcity places fixed limits on human activity. Time and time again, human beings have circumvented scarcities, and neo-Malthusians have often been justly accused of "crying wolf." But in assuming that this experience pertains to the future, cornucopians overlook seven factors.

First, whereas serious scarcities of critical resources in the past usually appeared singly, now we face multiple scarcities that exhibit powerful interactive, feedback, and threshold effects. An agricultural region may, for example, be simultaneously affected by degraded water and soil, greenhouse-induced precipitation changes, and increased ultraviolet radiation. This makes the future highly uncertain for policymakers and economic actors; tomorrow will be full of extreme events and surprises. Furthermore, as numerous resources become scarce simultaneously, it will be harder to identify substitution possibilities that produce the same end-use services at costs that prevailed when scarcity was less severe. Second, in the past the scarcity of a given resource usually increased slowly, allowing time for social, economic, and technological adjustment. But human populations are much larger and activities of individuals are, on a global average, much more resource-intensive than before. This means that debilitating scarcities often develop much more quickly: whole countries may be deforested in a few

---

74. Simon, *The Ultimate Resource*, p. 345.
75. For example, if average topsoil creation on farmed land is about 0.25 millimeters per year (or about 3.25 tons/hectare), then to be sustainable, agriculture should not, on average, produce soil loss greater than this amount. According to neo-Malthusians, such a limit on human activity should rarely be breached: topsoil is a resource essential to human well-being; human beings cannot create it themselves; and petroleum-based substitutes such as fertilizers and pesticides are only short-term remedies.

decades; most of a region's topsoil can disappear in a generation; and critical ozone depletion may occur in as little as twenty years. Third, today's consumption has far greater momentum than in the past, because of the size of the consuming population, the sheer quantity of material consumed by this population, and the density of its interwoven fabric of consumption activities. The countless individual and corporate economic actors making up human society are heavily committed to certain patterns of resource use; and the ability of our markets to adapt may be sharply constrained by these entrenched interests.

These first three factors may soon combine to produce a daunting syndrome of environmentally induced scarcity: humankind will face multiple resource shortages that are interacting and unpredictable, that grow to crisis proportions rapidly, and that will be hard to address because of powerful commitments to certain consumption patterns.

The fourth reason that cornucopian arguments may not apply in the future is that the free-market price mechanism is a bad gauge of scarcity, especially for resources held in common, such as a benign climate and productive seas. In the past, many such resources seemed endlessly abundant; now they are being degraded and depleted, and we are learning that their increased scarcity often has tremendous bearing on a society's well-being. Yet this scarcity is at best reflected only indirectly in market prices. In addition, people often cannot participate in market transactions in which they have an interest, either because they lack the resources or because they are distant from the transaction process in time or space; in these cases the true scarcity of the resource is not reflected by its price.

The fifth reason is an extension of a point made earlier: market-driven adaptation to resource scarcity is most likely to succeed in wealthy societies, where abundant reserves of capital, knowledge, and talent help economic actors invent new technologies, identify conservation possibilities, and make the transition to new production and consumption patterns. Yet many of the societies facing the most serious environmental problems in the coming decades will be poor; even if they have efficient markets, lack of capital and know-how will hinder their response to these problems.

Sixth, cornucopians have an anachronistic faith in humankind's ability to unravel and manage the myriad processes of nature. There is no *a priori* reason to expect that human scientific and technical ingenuity can always surmount all types of scarcity. Human beings may not have the mental capacity to understand adequately the complexities of environmental-social systems. Or it may simply be impossible, given the physical, biological, and social laws governing these systems, to reduce all scarcity or repair all environmental damage. Moreover, the chaotic nature of these systems may keep us from fully anticipating the consequences of various adaptation and intervention strategies.[76] Perhaps most important, scientific and technical knowledge must be built incrementally—layer upon layer—and its diffusion to the broader society often takes decades. Any technical solutions to environmental scarcity may arrive too late to prevent catastrophe.

Seventh and finally, future environmental problems, rather than inspiring the wave of ingenuity predicted by cornucopians, may instead reduce the supply of ingenuity available in a society. The success of market mechanisms depends on an intricate and stable system of institutions, social relations, and shared understandings (the ideational factors in Figure 1). Cornucopians often overlook the role of *social* ingenuity in producing the complex legal and economic climate in which *technical* ingenuity can flourish. Policymakers must be clever "social engineers" to design and implement effective market mechanisms.[77] Unfortunately, however, the syndrome of multiple, interacting, unpredictable, and rapidly changing environmental problems will increase the complexity and pressure of the policymaking setting. It will also generate increased "social friction" as elites and interest groups struggle to protect their prerogatives. The ability of policymakers to be good social engineers is likely to go *down*, not up, as these stresses increase.

Population size and growth are key variables producing the syndrome of environmental scarcity I have described. While sometimes population growth does not damage the environment, often this growth—in combination with prevailing social structures, technologies, and consumption patterns—makes environmental degradation worse. During the 1970s and early 1980s, family size dropped dramatically in many countries from six or seven children to three or four. But family planners have discovered that it is much more

---

76. On chaotic processes, see footnote 14. Our technological interventions might increase the probability of dramatic threshold effects in environmental-social systems. For example, the cultural ecologist Roy Rappaport notes that our quest for higher crop yields has produced "some of the most delicate and unstable ecosystems ever to have appeared on the face of the earth." Roy Rappaport, "The Flow of Energy in an Agricultural Society," *Scientific American*, Vol. 225, No. 3 (September 1971), p. 126.

77. Development experts dispute the extent to which such social engineering is possible. On the determinants of the "social capability" to seize opportunities for economic growth, see James Bradford De Long, "The 'Protestant Ethic' Revisited: A Twentieth Century Look," *The Fletcher Forum of World Affairs*, Vol. 13, No. 2 (Summer 1989), pp. 229–241.

difficult to convince parents to forgo a further one or two children to bring family size down to replacement rate. As a result, the growth rates of some of the world's most populous countries—including India and China—are hardly declining at all.[78] India's rate has leveled off at around 2.1 percent (17.9 million people) per year, China's at around 1.3 percent (14.8 million) per year. These developments have recently led the United Nations to increase its mid-range estimate of the globe's population when it stabilizes (predicted to occur towards the end of the twenty-first century) from 10.2 to 11 billion, which is over twice the size of the planet's current population.[79]

Consequently, many countries will have to keep boosting their agricultural production by 2 to 4 percent per year well into the next century to avoid huge food imports.[80] But, for the seven reasons discussed above, the social and technical engineers in these countries might not be able to supply the ever-increasing ingenuity required over this extended period. In particular, in many developing countries the effects of land scarcity and degradation are likely to become much more evident as the potential gains from green revolution technologies are fully realized. Unfortunately, there is no new generation of agricultural technologies waiting in the wings to keep productivity rising. Genetic engineering may eventually help scientists develop nitrogen-fixing, salinity-resistant, and drought-resistant grains, but their widespread use in the developing world is undoubtedly decades in the future.

Although we must be careful not to slip into environmental determinism, when it comes to the poorest countries on this planet we should not invest too much faith in the potential of human ingenuity to respond to multiple,

---

78. Sadik, *The State of World Population 1990;* Griffith Feeney, et al., "Recent Fertility Dynamics in China: Results from the 1987 One Percent Population Survey," *Population and Development Review,* Vol. 15, No. 2 (June 1989), pp. 297–321.

79. Demographers have long assumed that developing countries would pass through a "demographic transition" similar to that exhibited by currently developed countries in the nineteenth and twentieth centuries, during which a decline in death rate was eventually followed by a compensating decline in birth rate. This transition is thought to have resulted from increased material prosperity and certain social changes, such as higher literacy rates and the emancipation of women. However, if some developing countries cannot maintain a steady growth in social and economic prosperity, their demographic transition may be in doubt.

80. Assuming that the necessary foreign exchange or financial aid is available, such imports might seem a reasonable way to compensate for Southern shortfalls, even over an extended period. However, a dependence on agricultural areas in the North will make importers vulnerable to vagaries of climate, economics, and politics in the exporting countries. As the redundancy of food-growing regions is reduced, the likelihood of a sudden and severe global shortfall increases.

interacting, and rapidly changing environmental problems once they have become severe. The most important of the seven factors above is the last: growing population, consumption, and environmental stresses will increase social friction. This will reduce the capacity of policymakers in developing countries to intervene as good social engineers in order to chart a sustainable development path and prevent further social disruption. Neo-Malthusians may underestimate human adaptability in *today's* environmental-social system, but as time passes their analysis may become ever more compelling.[81]

Types of Conflict

It seems likely that first-stage policy interventions will not be fully successful in preventing the four principal social effects posited above. We therefore turn to the second part of the "how" question: if agricultural production drops, if developing societies slide further into poverty, if large numbers of people are forced from their homelands, and if institutions and social relations are disrupted, what kinds of conflict are likely to develop? At present, we can bring only limited empirical evidence to bear on this question. This may be partly because environmental and population pressures have not yet passed a critical threshold of severity in many developing countries; also, there has been little case-study research on environment-conflict linkages. In what follows, therefore, I propose some further hypotheses for testing.

THREE THEORETICAL PERSPECTIVES ON CONFLICT

Three types of theory on the nature and etiology of social conflict—one each at the individual, group, and systemic levels of analysis—are particularly important in light of the four general social effects identified.

Frustration-aggression theories use individual psychology to explain civil strife, including strikes, riots, coups, revolutions, and guerrilla wars. They

---

81. While I contend that cornucopian policies are unlikely to prove successful in the long run, their failure will occur in different ways and at different rates in different societies. Notably, some rapidly industrializing societies—such as Thailand, South Korea, and Indonesia—seem to have successfully shaped their social, economic, and political structures to promote the production of material wealth. As this development is often at stunning cost to the environment, it represents in part a massive conversion of current and future ecological wealth to current economic wealth, in the form of physical and intellectual capital and materials for consumption. This wealth may give these countries greater ability to respond and adapt to environmental change, thus weakening the force of the fifth factor above. But the other six factors will still have force, which suggests that these societies are only postponing the crisis, not escaping it.

suggest that individuals become aggressive when they feel frustrated by something or someone they believe is blocking them from fulfilling a strong desire. An important subset of these theories suggests that this frustration and aggression can be caused by relative deprivation, when people perceive a widening gap between the level of satisfaction they have achieved (often defined in economic terms) and the level they believe they deserve.[82]

Group-identity theories use social psychology to help explain conflicts involving nationalism, ethnicity, and religion. The focus is on the way groups reinforce their identities and the "we-they" cleavages that often result. Individuals may have a need for a sense of camaraderie or "we-ness" that can be satisfied in a group when it discriminates against or attacks another group; similarly, a person's sense of self-worth may be strengthened when his or her group's status is enhanced relative to that of other groups. By attacking outside groups, leaders may try to exploit these needs in order to increase their political power within their own groups, but this behavior makes divisions between groups deeper and more acrimonious.[83]

Structural theories, which are often grounded in the assumptions of microeconomics and game theory, explain conflicts that arise from the rational calculations of actors in the face of perceived external constraints. The structure of an actor's social situation is the perceived set of possible interactions with other actors and the perceived likely outcomes of these interactions. This structure is determined by physical factors such as number of actors, resource limits, and barriers to movement or communication; by social factors such as shared beliefs and understandings, rules of social interaction, and the set of power relations between actors; and by psychological factors such as the beliefs and preferences of other actors.[84]

---

82. John Dollard, et al., *Frustration and Aggression* (New Haven: Yale University Press, 1939); Leonard Berkowitz, *Aggression: A Social Psychological Analysis* (New York: McGraw-Hill, 1962). On relative deprivation, see James Davies, "Toward a Theory of Revolution," *American Sociological Review*, Vol. 6, No. 1 (February 1962), pp. 5–19; Ted Gurr, *Why Men Rebel* (Princeton, N.J.: Princeton University Press, 1970); and Ted Gurr and Raymond Duvall, "Civil Conflict in the 1960s: A Reciprocal Theoretical System with Parameter Estimates," *Comparative Political Studies*, Vol. 6, No. 2 (July 1973), pp. 135–169.

83. See M. Sherif, *Group Conflict and Cooperation: Their Social Psychology* (London: Routledge and Kegan Paul, 1966); Henri Tajfel, ed., *Differentiation between Social Groups* (London: Academic Press, 1978); Henri Tajfel, *Human Groups and Social Categories: Studies in Social Psychology* (Cambridge: Cambridge University Press, 1981); Edward Azar and John Burton, *International Conflict Resolution: Theory and Practice* (Sussex, U.K.: Wheatsheaf, 1986); Lewis Coser, *The Functions of Social Conflict* (London: Free Press, 1956); Donald Horowitz, *Ethnic Groups in Conflict* (Berkeley: University of California Press, 1985).

84. As Alexander Wendt notes, the view of structure as constraint is only one of three possible

General structural theories suggest that external constraints can encourage or even compel actors to engage in conflict.[85] Domestic structural theories hold that civil strife will be more likely if there are well-organized groups within a society that can quickly articulate, channel, and coordinate discontent. These theories suggest that insurgency is a function of the "opportunity structure" that confronts groups challenging the authority of elites. This opportunity structure depends on the relative power and resources of challenger and elite groups, on the power of groups that might ally themselves with challenger or elite groups, and on the costs and benefits that groups believe they will accrue through different kinds of collective action in support of or in opposition to elite groups.[86]

Drawing on these theories, I hypothesize that severe environmental degradation will produce three principal types of conflict. These should be considered ideal types: they will rarely, if ever, be found in pure form in the real world.

SIMPLE SCARCITY CONFLICTS. Simple scarcity conflicts are explained and predicted by general structural theories. They are the conflicts we would expect when state actors rationally calculate their interests in a zero-sum or negative-sum situation such as might arise from resource scarcity.[87] We have seen such conflicts often in the past; they are easily understood within the realist paradigm of international relations theory, and they therefore are likely to receive undue attention from current security scholars. In Figure 4, I propose that simple scarcity conflicts may arise over three types of resource

---

positions on the issue. Structure can also be thought of as generating the actors rather than constraining them, or structure and actor can be seen as dialectically related—that is, as Anthony Giddens suggests, generating but not reducible to each other. Alexander Wendt, "The Agent-Structure Problem," *International Organization*, Vol. 41, No. 3. (Summer 1987), pp. 335–370; Anthony Giddens, *The Constitution of Society: Outline of the Theory of Structuration* (Cambridge, U.K.: Polity Press, 1984).

85. Those scholars who emphasize such constraints usually also acknowledge the causal importance of internal factors, such as the actor's particular interests and beliefs. By stressing power relations almost exclusively, perhaps Waltz comes closest to presenting a purely structural theory of international behavior and war. De Mesquita contends that the geographic proximity of actors is an important structural determinant of international conflict, while Choucri and North emphasize differences in states' resource endowments. See Waltz, *Theory of International Politics*; Bruce Bueno de Mesquita, *The War Trap* (New Haven: Yale University Press, 1981); and Nazli Choucri and Robert North, *Nations in Conflict* (San Francisco: Freeman, 1975).

86. See in particular Doug McAdam, *Political Process and the Development of Black Insurgency, 1930–1970* (Chicago: University of Chicago Press, 1982); and Charles Tilly, *From Mobilization to Revolution* (Reading, Mass.: Addison-Wesley, 1978).

87. The adjective "simple" does not mean "unimportant." Rather, it distinguishes this type of conflict from others that involve psychological and social processes more complex than those posited by rational-choice theorists.

Figure 4. Types of Conflict likely to Arise from Environmental Change in the Developing World.

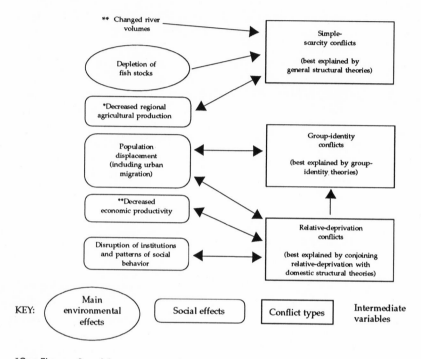

*See Figures 2 and 3.
**See Figure 3.

in particular: river water, fish, and agriculturally productive land. These renewable resources seem particularly likely to spark conflict because their scarcity is increasing rapidly in some regions, they are often essential for human survival, and they can be physically seized or controlled. There may be a positive feedback relationship between conflict and reduced agricultural production: for example, lower food supplies caused by environmental change may lead countries to fight over irrigable land, and this fighting could further reduce food supplies.

The current controversy over the Great Anatolia Project on the Euphrates River illustrates how simple scarcity conflicts can arise. By early in the next century, Turkey plans to build a huge complex of twenty dams and irrigation systems along the upper reaches of the Euphrates.[88] This $21 billion project, if fully funded and built, would reduce the average annual flow of the Euphrates within Syria from 32 billion cubic meters to 20 billion.[89] The water that passes through Turkey's irrigation systems and on to Syria will be laden with fertilizers, pesticides, and salts. Syria is already desperately short of water, with an annual water availability of only about 600 cubic meters per capita.[90] Much of the water for its towns, industries, and farms comes from the Euphrates, and the country has been chronically vulnerable to drought. Furthermore, Syria's population growth rate, at 3.7 percent per year, is one of the highest in the world, and this adds further to the country's demand for water.

Turkey and Syria have exchanged angry threats over this situation. Syria gives sanctuary to guerrillas of the Kurdish Workers Party (the PKK), which has long been waging an insurgency against the Turkish government in eastern Anatolia. Turkey suspects that Syria might be using these separatists to gain leverage in bargaining over Euphrates River water. Thus in October, 1989, then Prime Minister Turgut Ozal suggested that Turkey might impound the river's water if Syria did not restrain the PKK. Although he later retracted the threat, the tensions have not been resolved, and there are currently no high-level talks on water sharing.[91]

GROUP-IDENTITY CONFLICTS. Group-identity conflicts are explained and predicted by group-identity theories. Such conflicts are likely to arise from the large-scale movements of populations brought about by environmental change. As different ethnic and cultural groups are propelled together under circumstances of deprivation and stress, we should expect intergroup hostility, in which a group would emphasize its own identity while denigrating, discriminating against, and attacking outsiders. The situation in the Bangladesh-Assam region may be a good example of this process; Assam's ethnic

---

88. Alan Cowell, "Water Rights: Plenty of Mud to Sling," *New York Times*, February 7, 1990, p. A4; "Send for the Dowsers," *The Economist*, December 16, 1989, p. 42.
89. On January 13, 1990, Turkey began filling the giant reservoir behind the Ataturk Dam, the first in this complex. For one month Turkey held back the main flow of the Euphrates River, which cut the downstream flow in Syria to about a quarter of its normal rate.
90. Peter Gleick, "Climate Change and International Politics," pp. 333–339.
91. The issue of Euphrates water is entwined with concerns about territorial integrity and relations with ethnic minorities. Consequently, although water scarcity is a source of serious tensions between Syria and Turkey, and may trigger interstate violence in the future, this dispute is not a pure example of a simple-scarcity conflict. As suggested above, pure examples may be impossible to find.

strife over the last decade has apparently been provoked by migration from Bangladesh.[92]

As population and environmental stresses grow in developing countries, migration to the developed world is likely to surge. "The image of islands of affluence amidst a sea of poverty is not inaccurate."[93] People will seek to move from Latin America to the United States and Canada, from North Africa and the Middle East to Europe, and from South and Southeast Asia to Australia. This migration has already shifted the ethnic balance in many cities and regions of developed countries, and governments are struggling to contain a xenophobic backlash. Such racial strife will undoubtedly become much worse.

RELATIVE-DEPRIVATION CONFLICTS. Relative-deprivation theories indicate that as developing societies produce less wealth because of environmental problems, their citizens will probably become increasingly discontented by the widening gap between their actual level of economic achievement and the level they feel they deserve. The rate of change is key: the faster the economic deterioration, it is hypothesized, the greater the discontent. Lower-status groups will be more frustrated than others because elites will use their power to maintain, as best they can, access to a constant standard of living despite a shrinking economic pie. At some point, the discontent and frustration of some groups may cross a critical threshold, and they will act violently against other groups perceived to be the agents of their economic misery or thought to be benefiting from a grossly unfair distribution of economic goods in the society.

Relative-deprivation theories are often contrasted with domestic structural theories of civil strife, but, as suggested by Figure 4, these points of view can be usefully combined. The emphasis of domestic structural theories on the "opportunity structure" that confronts potential challenger groups is important, because a principal social effect of environmental change in developing countries is likely to be the disruption of institutions and of regular and legitimized social relations. Thus, environmental problems may not only increase the frustration and anger within developing societies (by increasing relative deprivation), but by disrupting institutions and social relations, they may also open up structural opportunities for challenger groups to act on

---

92. Myron Weiner, "The Political Demography of Assam's Anti-Immigrant Movement," *Population and Development Review,* Vol. 9, No. 2 (June 1983), pp. 279–292.
93. Ullman, "Redefining Security," p. 143.

their grievances and overthrow existing authority. Doug McAdam contends that *"any* event or broad social process that serves to undermine the calculations and assumptions on which the political establishment is structured occasions a shift in political opportunities."[94]

The relative-deprivation and domestic-structural perspectives together tell us that severe civil strife is likely when: 1) there are clearly defined and organized groups in a society; 2) some of these groups regard their level of economic achievement, and in turn the broader political and economic system, as wholly unfair; and 3) these same groups believe that all peaceful opportunities to effect change are blocked, yet regard the balance of power within the society as unstable; that is, they believe there are structural opportunities for overthrowing authority in the society.[95]

Figure 4 reflects these two theoretical perspectives: I hypothesize that decreased economic productivity and disrupted institutions will jointly contribute to relative-deprivation conflicts. I again suggest that positive feedbacks may operate: relative-deprivation conflicts may cause further economic decline and institutional dislocation. In addition, the figure reflects the idea that the arrival of refugees in an area, even if the event does not reduce total economic productivity, will probably result in a dilution of existing resources and aggravate a sense of deprivation in the indigenous population. This stress may also manifest itself as inter-ethnic tension. Thus causal arrows point from population displacement to relative-deprivation conflicts and from these conflicts to group-identity conflicts.[96]

The probability of civil strife is also strongly influenced by whether challenger groups have the organizational and leadership capacity to provide themselves with adequate information and coordination. Leaders are impor-

---

94. McAdam, *Political Process*, p. 41.
95. A wealth of literature exists on the theoretical and empirical relationships between economic deprivation and civil strife. Mark Lichbach provides a survey in "An Evaluation of 'Does Economic Inequality Breed Political Conflict?' Studies," *World Politics*, Vol. 41, No. 4 (July 1989), pp. 431–470.
96. Population displacement into urban areas may be of particular importance. Many cities in developing countries are already surrounded by sprawling squatters' settlements rife with disease, crime, and violence. Whether these poor millions will be a source of civil strife remains to be seen. Ullman suggests that modern revolutions have rarely started in cities, because recent arrivals in urban areas are usually too preoccupied with retaining and expanding their economic niches to join revolutionary organizations. See Ullman, "Redefining Security," p. 142. But urban masses may not remain so quiescent in the future. Heavy urban subsidization in many developing countries of food, transport, and other amenities indicates that governments believe there is a real threat of unrest in the cities.

tant in causing the members of a challenger group to believe that the group's situation should and can be changed. McAdam calls this a group's "cognitive liberation." Leaders define the categories through which challenger groups see their situations and themselves. By developing and exploiting a particular view of the "social good," leaders can shift the preferences of the members of a challenger group so they come to view their situation as illegitimate and intolerable, thus increasing their sense of relative deprivation. In addition, by altering group members' self-perceptions, their understandings of the nature of power, and their assumptions about the possible means to achieve change, leaders can change the perceived opportunity structure.

This theoretical perspective on civil strife can be applied to the Filipino situation. The insurgency is motivated by the relative deprivation of the landless agricultural laborers and poor farmers displaced to the uplands where they try to eke out a living from the failing land; it exploits the structural opportunities provided by the crumbling of the central government's authority in the country's hinterland; and it is facilitated by the creative leadership of the cadres of the New People's Army (NPA) and the National Democratic Front (NDF). These revolutionary groups shape the peasants' understandings of their situation, focus their discontent, and assist them in extracting concessions from landlords. Gary Hawes points out that the rationality of Filipino peasants must be understood within their own world of meaning, which includes a strong commitment to family and community. The NDF has sought to build on this world of meaning to create "a national community linked not by kinship, but by something analogous, a commitment to a vision of a better future for all those who are exploited."[97]

Assessing the prospect for civil strife arising from environmental degradation in a particular society requires a thorough understanding of the society's social relations and institutions; its class, ethnic, religious, and linguistic structure; the culture of leadership in these groups and in the society as a whole; and the beliefs about the social good that motivate challenger and elite groups.[98] Since analysis must be so specific to each case, we cannot hope for more than rough, probabilistic generalizations about the relationship between environmental degradation, economic decline, and civil strife.

---

97. Hawes, "Theories of Peasant Revolution," pp. 297–298.
98. In technical terms, we need to use the techniques of anthropology, ethno-methodology, and interpretivism to develop a detailed "internal" understanding of these societies. See Clifford Geertz, *The Interpretation of Cultures* (New York: Basic Books, 1973).

CONFLICT OBJECTIVES AND SCOPE

Table 1 compares some attributes of the principal types of acute conflict that I hypothesize may result from environmental change. The table lists the objectives sought by actors involved in these conflicts (which are, once again, ideal types). There is strong normative content to the motives of challenger groups involved in relative-deprivation conflicts: these groups believe the distribution of rewards is unfair. But such an "ought" does not necessarily drive simple-scarcity conflicts: one state may decide that it needs something another state has, and then try to seize it, without being motivated by a strong sense of unfairness or injustice.

Table 1 also shows that the scope of conflict can be expected to differ. Although relative-deprivation conflicts will tend to be domestic, we should not underestimate their potentially severe international repercussions. The correlation between civil strife and external conflict behavior is a function of the nature of the regime and of the kind of internal conflict it faces. For example, highly centralized dictatorships threatened by revolutionary actions, purges, and strikes are especially prone to engage in external war and belligerence. In comparison, less centralized dictatorships are prone to such behavior when threatened by guerrilla action and assassinations.[99] External aggression may also result after a new regime comes to power through civil strife: regimes borne of revolution, for example, are particularly good at mobilizing their citizens and resources for military preparation and war.[100]

While environmental stresses and the conflicts they induce may encourage the rise of revolutionary regimes, other results are also plausible: these pres-

Table 1. Comparison of Conflict Types.

Conflict Type	Objective Sought	Conflict Scope
Simple scarcity	Relief from scarcity	International
Group identity	Protection and reinforcement of group identity	International or domestic
Relative deprivation	Distributive justice	Domestic (with international repercussions)

99. Jonathan Wilkenfeld, "Domestic and Foreign Conflict Behavior of Nations," *Journal of Peace Research*, Vol. 5 (1968), pp. 56–69.
100. See Theda Skocpol, "Social Revolutions and Mass Military Mobilization," *World Politics*, Vol. 40, No. 2 (January 1988), pp. 147–168.

sures might overwhelm the management capacity of institutions in developing countries, inducing praetorianism[101] or widespread social disintegration. They may also weaken the control of governments over their territories, especially over the hinterland (as in the Philippines). The regimes that do gain power in the face of such disruption are likely to be extremist, authoritarian, and abusive of human rights.[102] Moreover, the already short time horizons of policymakers in developing countries will be further shortened. These political factors could seriously undermine efforts to mitigate and adapt to environmental change. Soon to be the biggest contributors to global environmental problems, developing countries could become more belligerent, less willing to compromise with other states, and less capable of controlling their territories in order to implement measures to reduce environmental damage.

If many developing countries evolve in the direction of extremism, the interests of the North may be directly threatened. Of special concern here is the growing disparity between rich and poor nations that may be induced by environmental change. Robert Heilbroner notes that revolutionary regimes "are not likely to view the vast difference between first class and cattle class with the forgiving eyes of their predecessors." Furthermore, these nations may be heavily armed, as the proliferation of nuclear and chemical weapons and ballistic missiles continues. Such regimes, he asserts, could be tempted to use nuclear blackmail as a "means of inducing the developed world to transfer its wealth on an unprecedented scale to the underdeveloped world."[103] Richard Ullman, however, argues that this concern is overstated. Third world nations are unlikely to confront the North violently in the face of the "superior destructive capabilities of the rich."[104] In light of the discussion in this article, we might conclude that environmental stress and its attendant social disruption will so debilitate the economies of developing countries that they will be unable to amass sizeable armed forces, conven-

---

101. "Praetorian" is a label used by Samuel Huntington for societies in which the level of political participation exceeds the capacity of political institutions to channel, moderate, and reconcile competing claims to economic and political resources. "In a praetorian system, social forces confront each other nakedly; no political institutions, no corps of professional political leaders are recognized or accepted as the legitimate intermediaries to moderate group conflict." Samuel Huntington, *Political Order in Changing Societies* (New Haven: Yale University Press, 1968), p. 196.
102. Ophuls notes that ecological scarcity "seems to engender overwhelming pressures toward political systems that are frankly authoritarian by current standards." Ophuls, *Ecology*, p. 163.
103. Heilbroner, *Inquiry*, pp. 39 and 95. These North-South disputes would be the international analogues of domestic relative-deprivation conflicts.
104. Ullman, "Redefining Security," p. 143.

tional or otherwise. But the North would surely be unwise to rely on impoverishment and disorder in the South for its security.

SECOND-STAGE INTERVENTIONS

Many factors could break the causal links between the four main social effects of environmental change and the three types of conflict hypothesized above. Some of these factors could be open to intentional manipulation by policymakers. Focusing first on domestic conflict, it appears that regime repressiveness is a critical variable. For instance "semi-repressive" regimes may be more vulnerable to insurgency induced by income inequality than are either highly repressive or democratic regimes. In semi-repressive societies, dissident groups can develop relatively strong organizations, but opportunities to engage in effective and nonviolent forms of political action are blocked.[105]

Another key variable is the perceived legitimacy of the regime, that is, its perceived fairness, appropriateness, and reasonableness. Seymour Martin Lipset shows that this variable mediates the relationship between economic crisis and political instability: economic crisis must first lead to a crisis of legitimacy before widespread civil strife can occur.[106] A perception that the political and economic system is legitimate will moderate a citizen's sense of relative deprivation and will hinder the mass mobilization of discontent. Through various techniques of persuasion and distraction, policymakers may be able to sustain a perception of legitimacy even in the face of environmentally induced economic decline.

Finally, we must not forget the role of *politics* in shaping a society's response to social stress. For example, analyzing variance in the effects of the depression on European societies in the 1930s, Ekkart Zimmermann and Thomas Saalfeld emphasize the explanatory power of coalitions between politically powerful groups such as agrarian classes, labor, the bourgeoisie/business class, and the state. Whether stabilizing coalitions form, in spite of economic stress, is influenced by a host of factors, including political culture, the nature and extent of socioeconomic cleavage, the "channels and proce-

---

105. Edward Muller and Mitchell Seligson, "Inequality and Insurgency," *American Political Science Review*, Vol. 81, No. 2 (June 1987), pp. 425–452.
106. See Seymour Martin Lipset, *Political Man: The Social Bases of Politics* (Garden City, N.Y.: Doubleday, 1959), pp. 77–83; and Mitchell Seligson and Edward Muller, "Democratic Stability and Economic Crisis: Costa Rica, 1978–83," *International Studies Quarterly*, Vol. 31, No. 3 (September 1987), pp. 301–326.

dures" for political bargaining and, as emphasized above, political leadership.[107]

Several variables might offer opportunities for second-stage policy intervention to prevent war. The spread of liberal democracy in the developing world might reduce the chance that environmental stress (and its social effects) will cause interstate conflict.[108] Similarly, increased trade between states could increase their economic interdependence and thereby strengthen disincentives to engage in conflict.[109] Also important are the nature and rate of change of power relations among states; these relations may be affected by environmental degradation, yet they may also be open to independent manipulation by political leaders. Numerous scholars of international affairs, especially those of the realist school, have claimed that shifting power relations can prompt war. Robert Gilpin and others suggest that war may be started by a dominant state suffering declining power, while A.F.K. Organski and Jacek Kugler contend the initiator will usually be a weaker state gaining in power and challenging the hegemon.[110] Whichever view is more accurate, these theories suggest that statesmen might hold in check the risk of interstate conflict despite the effects of environmental change, if they can keep power relations among states relatively stable.

Conclusions

This article sets out a research agenda for studying the links between environmental change and acute conflict. Given current theories and data, we probably cannot go much further than the preliminary analysis offered here. Case studies of specific societies focused on the "where" question—where are the different kinds of environmentally derived conflict most likely to

---

107. Ekkart Zimmermann and Thomas Saalfeld, "Economic and Political Reactions to the World Economic Crisis of the 1930s in Six European Countries," *International Studies Quarterly*, Vol. 32, No. 3 (September 1988), p. 326.
108. The argument that democracies are less inclined to war is often traced to Kant. For a thorough discussion, see Michael Doyle, "Liberalism and World Politics," *American Political Science Review*, Vol. 80, No. 4 (December 1986), pp. 1151–1170. This kind of second-stage intervention may be particularly difficult because environmental change may reduce the prospects for success of democratic regimes.
109. See Richard Rosecrance, *The Rise of the Trading State* (New York: Basic Books, 1986).
110. Gilpin, *War and Change in World Politics*, pp. 94 and 191; A.F.K. Organski and Jacek Kugler, *The War Ledger* (Chicago: University of Chicago Press, 1980); and Jack Levy, "Research Note: Declining Power and the Preventive Motivation for War," *World Politics*, Vol. 40, No. 1 (October 1987), pp. 82–107.

occur?—will help us test our hypotheses about *how* environmental change might contribute to conflict.

Such research will also reveal important things about real societies in the real world. We must in particular look for intervening variables—including institutions, technologies, and market mechanisms—that humankind might influence in order to change the course of environmental-social systems. We may learn that there are real opportunities for intervention; hardship and strife are not preordained. But it seems likely that, as environmental degradation proceeds, the size of the potential social disruption will increase, while our capacity to intervene to prevent this disruption decreases. It is therefore not a reasonable policy response to assume we can intervene at a late stage, when the crisis is upon us. Developing countries, in concert with the North, should act now to address the forces behind environmental degradation.

Water and Conflict | *Peter H. Gleick*

Fresh Water
Resources and International Security

$\mathbf{F}$resh water is a fundamental resource, integral to all ecological and societal activities, including food and energy production, transportation, waste disposal, industrial development, and human health. Yet fresh water resources are unevenly and irregularly distributed, and some regions of the world are extremely water-short. As we approach the twenty-first century, water and water-supply systems are increasingly likely to be both objectives of military action and instruments of war as human populations grow, as improving standards of living increase the demand for fresh water, and as global climatic changes make water supply and demand more problematic and uncertain. This article outlines the links between water and conflict, and presents some of the issues and information that make it possible to assess when and where water-related conflicts are most likely to occur. Tools for reducing the risks of such conflicts are also presented, together with recommendations for policymakers.

Where water is scarce, competition for limited supplies can lead nations to see access to water as a matter of national security. History is replete with examples of competition and disputes over shared fresh water resources. Below, I describe ways in which water resources have historically been the objectives of interstate conflict and how they have been used as instruments of war. Next, I explain why the maldistribution of fresh water together with current trends in population and development suggest that water is going to be an increasingly salient element of interstate politics, including violent conflict. Complicating the analysis are the incompleteness of the data, and growing uncertainties about the role of global climatic change in altering

Peter H. Gleick is director of the Global Environment Program at the Pacific Institute for Studies in Development, Environment, and Security, in Oakland, California.

This article is modified and updated from Occasional Paper No. 1, "Water and Conflict," of the project "Environmental Change and Violent Conflict" of the American Academy of Arts and Sciences, Cambridge, Massachusetts and the University of Toronto (September 1992). Helpful comments on earlier versions were provided by Jeffrey Boutwell, Fen Hampson, Haleh Hatami, John Holdren, Tad Homer-Dixon, Miriam Lowi, Irving Mintzer, Laura Reed, the late Roger Revelle, and Arthur Westing. Financial support for different portions of this work has been provided to the Pacific Institute by the Joyce Mertz-Gilmore, New-Land, and Compton Foundations, and by the Ploughshares and Rockefeller Brother Funds.

International Security, Vol. 18, No. 1, (Summer 1993), pp. 79–112
© 1993 by the President and Fellows of Harvard College and the Massachusetts Institute of Technology.

water supply and demand. Nevertheless, policymakers should be more aware of potential conflicts arising over, or exacerbated by, water issues, and the ways in which international bodies could either mitigate or avoid some possible conflicts.

How might we predict when and where such conflicts could arise? Many rivers, lakes, and ground water aquifers are shared by two or more nations. This geographical fact has led to the geopolitical reality of disputes over shared waters, including the Nile, Jordan, and Euphrates rivers in the Middle East; the Indus, Ganges, and Brahmaputra in southern Asia; and the Colorado, Rio Grande, and Paraná in the Americas. I suggest several quantitative indices for measuring the vulnerability of states to water-related conflict. Bearing in mind the uncertainties of such indices, tensions appear especially likely in parts of southern and central Asia, central Europe, and the Middle East, where the history of water-related conflicts already extends back 5000 years.

Identifying potential trouble areas does little good if we have no tools for mitigating the problem. International law for resolving water-related disputes must play an important role, and I outline here recent advances in developing principles for managing internationally shared water resources. Their strengths and shortcomings are also assessed, together with their ability to deal with the kinds of uncertainties that will increasingly dominate interstate disputes over water. Not all water resources disputes will lead to violent conflict; indeed most lead to negotiations, discussions, and non-violent resolutions. But in certain regions of the world, such as the Middle East and southern and central Asia, water is a scarce resource that has become increasingly important for economic and agricultural development. In these regions, water is evolving into an issue of "high politics," and the probability of water-related violence is increasing. Policymakers and the military should be alert to the likelihood of violent conflict over water, and to the possible changes in both international water law and regional water treaties that could be implemented to minimize the probability and consequences of such conflicts over this essential and irreplaceable resource.

Environment, Resources, and International Security

"Ecological" or "environmental" security has become one of the most controversial and stimulating issues in the field of international security studies today. The relationships between the environment and international conflict and cooperation are drawing attention at many levels, from the military to the political, from the local to the global. While the concept of non-military aspects to "security" is not new, it has gained substantial attention in the last five years, largely as a result of the burgeoning interest in international environmental issues and the waning of the Cold War. Several new and dramatic environmental threats with international political implications have now been recognized, among them abuse and degradation of essential goods and services, such as those provided by the ozone layer and our global climate, and the growing inequities among nations in resource use. This situation has led, in turn, to a lively debate about the need for new definitions of security that explicitly incorporate environmental concerns.[1]

Implicit in this argument is the notion that local or regional instability, arising from a combination of environmental, resource, and political factors, may escalate to the international level and may become violent. Thus, it is imperative to clarify the terms of debate, and to identify and analyze those cases in which environmental variables threaten security.

There is some controversy over the role that resources and environmental problems play in affecting international security, but much of the argument stems from different definitions of "security" and from disagreement over the applicability of specific methods of analysis and conflict resolution to problems with environmental roots.[2] For the purposes of this article, threats

---

1. The earliest references to national "security" included concerns about economic issues, the strength of domestic industry, and the "proper correlation of all measures of foreign and domestic policy." For a brief history of definitions of national security, see Joseph J. Romm, "Defining National Security," Council on Foreign Relations Occasional Paper (New York: Council on Foreign Relations, forthcoming 1993). In their book, *The Ecological Perspective on Human Affairs with Special Reference to International Politics* (Princeton: Princeton University Press, 1965), Harold and Margaret Sprout identified the environment as one factor that influences a nation's foreign policy. For discussion of the principal points in the on-going debate, see Peter H. Gleick, "Environment, Resources, and International Security and Politics," in Eric Arnett, ed., *Science and International Security: Responding to a Changing World* (Washington, D.C.: American Association for the Advancement of Science, 1990), pp. 501–523; Peter H. Gleick, "Environment and Security: Clear Connections," *The Bulletin of the Atomic Scientists*, Vol. 47, No. 3 (April 1991), pp. 17–21; Jessica Tuchman Mathews, "Redefining Security," *Foreign Affairs*, Vol. 68, No. 2 (Spring 1989), pp. 162–177; Richard H. Ullman, "Redefining Security," *International Security*, Vol. 8, No. 1 (Summer 1983), pp. 129–153; Arthur H. Westing, ed., *Global Resources and International Conflict: Environmental Factors in Strategic Policy and Action* (Oxford: Oxford University Press, 1986). Definitional issues are discussed by Thomas F. Homer-Dixon, "On the Threshold: Environmental Changes as Causes of Acute Conflict," *International Security*, Vol. 16, No. 2 (Fall 1991), pp. 76–116.
2. These issues are reviewed in far more depth by Gleick, "Environment, Resources and International Security and Politics"; Gleick, "Environment and Security: Clear Connections"; Homer-Dixon, "On the Threshold"; and Daniel Deudney, "Environment and Security: Muddled Thinking," *The Bulletin of the Atomic Scientists*, Vol. 47, No. 3 (April 1991), pp. 22–28.

to security include resource and environmental problems that reduce the quality of life and result in increased competition and tensions among sub-national or national groups. In the more extreme cases, this can lead to violent conflicts, though not all security threats have violent components to them. While this approach encompasses a broader range of problems than conventional international security analysis, there is little doubt that re-sources and environmental concerns are playing an increasingly important role in international politics, and even in war. Examples abound: preparations for the 1992 UN Conference on Environment and Development (UNCED) included especially controversial and high-level international negotiations about the role of environment and development in trade, foreign aid, and other international arrangements; the international treaty to protect the ozone layer involved both developed and developing countries, and produced un-precedented agreement for strong actions on product development, trade in goods and information, and compensation for poorer countries;[3] environ-mental issues have played a large role in the negotiations and debate over the free trade agreement between the United States and Mexico; and the recent Persian Gulf War had deep and pervasive environmental and resource roots.

This broader conception of security has gained considerable acceptance by the policy and military communities in the last few years,[4] and the 1992 presidential election in the United States elevated policymakers to the highest levels of government who understand the clear connections among the en-vironment, interstate politics, and international security. The focus of security analysts must now be *when* and *where* resource-related conflicts are most

---

3. "The Vienna Convention for the Protection of the Ozone Layer, March 22, 1985," Final Act (Nairobi, Kenya: United Nations Environment Programme [UNEP]); "The Montreal Protocol on Substances That Deplete the Ozone Layer, September 16, 1987"; Final Act (Nairobi, Kenya: UNEP); and the London Revisions to the Montreal Protocol, June 1990, whose text can be found in "Report of the Second Meeting of the Parties to the Montreal Protocol on Substances that Deplete the Ozone Layer," UNEP/OzL. Pro. 2/3, June 29, 1990 (London: UNEP). The complete texts of all of these can be found together in Richard E. Benedick, *Ozone Diplomacy*, World Wildlife Fund and the Conservation Foundation (Cambridge: Harvard University Press, 1991).
4. For example, see President Gorbachev's speech, "Reality and Guarantees for a Secure World," published in English in *Moscow News*, supplement to issue No. 39 (3287), 1987; the statement by Secretary of State James A. Baker 3d on January 30, 1989, *New York Times*, January 31, 1989, p. 1; and comments by Senators Sam Nunn, Albert Gore, and Timothy Wirth, *Congressional Record*, June 28, 1990, S8929–8943. Environmental security was also a central topic of discussion among military analysts at the National War College, National Defense University symposium, "From Globalism to Regionalism—New Perspectives on American Foreign and Defense Policies," November 14–15, 1991.

likely to arise, not *whether* environmental concerns can contribute to instability and conflict. There are many possible levels and scales of conflict: regional disputes at the village level, disputes within national political subdivisions, border disputes between two nations, or frictions involving many nations that may not share borders. These conflicts may be political or economic; and they may be diplomatic or violent. Recent experience suggests that conflicts are more likely to occur on the local and regional level and in developing countries where common property resources may be both more critical to survival and less easily replaced or supplemented.[5] Still, however, environmental threats to security will be affected by the economic, cultural, and sociopolitical factors at work in a given country or region.

The Geopolitics of Shared Water Resources

There is a long history of water-related disputes, from conflicts over access to adequate water supplies to intentional attacks on water systems during wars. Water and water-supply systems have been the roots and instruments of war. Access to shared water supplies has been cut off for political and military reasons. Sources of water supply have been among the goals of military expansionism. And inequities in water use have been the source of regional and international frictions and tensions. These conflicts will continue—and in some places grow more intense—as growing populations demand more water for agricultural, industrial, and economic development. While various regional and international legal mechanisms exist for reducing water-related tensions, these mechanisms have never received the international support or attention necessary to resolve many conflicts over water. Indeed, there is growing evidence that existing international water law may be unable to handle the strains of ongoing and future problems.[6] In addition to improving international law in this area, efforts by UN and international aid agencies to ensure access to clean drinking water and adequate sanitation

---

5. Thomas F. Homer-Dixon, "Environmental Change and Violent Conflict," Occasional Paper No. 4, American Academy of Arts and Sciences, Cambridge, Mass., and the University of Toronto (1990); Ronnie Lipschutz and John P. Holdren, "Crossing Borders: Resource Flows, the Global Environment, and International Security," *Bulletin of Peace Proposals*, Vol. 21, No. 2 (1990), pp. 121–133; Gleick, "Environment and Security: Clear Connections."

6. Recent events such as the destruction of the Peruca dam in the former Yugoslavia, the controversy between Hungary and Slovakia over the Gabcikovo dam on the Danube, and the continuing water disputes throughout the Middle East suggest the limited influence of international water law when other political interests are paramount.

can reduce the competition for limited water supplies and the economic and social impacts of widespread waterborne diseases. In regions with shared water supplies, third-party participation in resolving water disputes, either through UN agencies or regional commissions, can also effectively end conflicts.

Interstate conflicts are caused by many factors, including religious animosities, ideological disputes, arguments over borders, and economic competition. Although I argue here that resource and environmental factors are playing an increasing role in such disputes, it is difficult to disentangle the many intertwined causes of conflict.[7] This section identifies several classes of water-related disputes and presents brief historical examples of each. These classes are not completely unrelated; in some regions water may play multiple roles in contributing to regional conflicts. These categories do, however, provide a useful way to think about not only how conflicts over water may arise, but also how they may be prevented.

WATER RESOURCES AS MILITARY AND POLITICAL GOALS

The focus of recent academic international security analysis has been "geopolitics" or "realpolitik," which stresses the concept of power politics as the root of conflict. Even at this level of analysis, the role of resources as a goal of military action is acknowledged, if the resources are a defining factor in the power of a nation.[8] The drive to possess or control another country's oil has often been a goal of military action in the twentieth century, including Japanese actions in World War II, the conflict over the Falkland Islands, and the recent Persian Gulf War. Although non-renewable resources such as oil and other minerals are more typically the focus of traditional international security analyses, even water can fit into this framework if water provides a source of economic or political strength. Under these conditions, ensuring access to water provides a justification for going to war, and water-supply systems can become a goal of military conquest.[9]

The characteristics that make water likely to be a source of strategic rivalry are: (1) the degree of scarcity, (2) the extent to which the water supply is shared by more than one region or state, (3) the relative power of the basin

---

7. Gleick, "Environment, Resources, and International Security and Politics."
8. Ronnie D. Lipschutz, *When Nations Clash: Raw Materials, Ideology and Foreign Policy* (New York: Ballinger Publishing Co., 1989).
9. Malin Falkenmark, "Fresh waters as a factor in strategic policy and action," in Westing, *Global Resources and International Conflict*, pp. 85–113.

states, and (4) the ease of access to alternative fresh water sources. Perhaps the clearest example of a region where fresh water supplies have had strategic implications is the Middle East.[10]

The Middle East region, with its many ideological, religious, and geographical disputes, is also extremely arid. Even those parts of the Middle East with relatively extensive water resources, such as the Nile, Tigris, and Euphrates river valleys, are coming under increasing population, irrigation, and energy pressures. And every major river in the region crosses international borders.

As far back as the seventh century BC, Ashurbanipal of Assyria seized control of water wells as part of his strategy of desert warfare against Arabia.[11] In modern times, the most pressing water conflicts in this region have centered on control of the Jordan River basin. This region has seen intense interstate conflict since the establishment of Israel in 1948, and the riparian dispute over the Jordan River is an integral part of the ongoing conflict. Although by international standards the Jordan is a small river, its basin is shared by several antagonistic nations (Jordan, Syria, Israel, and Lebanon) with extremely volatile political and military dynamics, and there are few alternative sources of water. One of the factors directly contributing to the 1967 War was the attempt by members of the Arab League in the early 1960s to divert the headwaters of the Jordan River away from Israel.[12] Israeli Premier Levi Eshkol declared that, "water is a question of life for Israel," and that therefore "Israel would act to ensure that the waters continue to flow";[13] in the 1967 Arab-Israeli War, Israel occupied much of the headwaters of the Jordan River, ensuring a more reliable water supply and denying Jordan a significant fraction of its available water. Today, approximately forty percent of the ground water upon which Israel is now dependent—and more than thirty-three percent of its total sustainable annual water yield—originates in

---

10. See, for example, Thomas Naff and Ruth Matson, *Water in the Middle East, Conflict or Cooperation?* (Boulder: Westview Press, 1984); and Miriam R. Lowi, "The Politics of Water Under Conditions of Scarcity and Conflict: The Jordan River and Riparian States" (Ph.D. dissertation, Department of Politics, Princeton University, Princeton, New Jersey, 1990).

11. M.S. Drower, "Water-Supply, Irrigation, and Agriculture," in C. Singer, E.J. Holmyard, and A.R. Hall, ed., *A History of Technology* (New York: Oxford University Press, 1954).

12. Lowi, "The Politics of Water," see especially Chapter 5. Also see Miriam Lowi, "Transboundary Resource Disputes: The Case of West Bank Water," *International Security*, Vol. 18, No. 1 (Summer 1993), pp. 113–138.

13. British Broadcasting Corporation, "Summary of World Broadcasts," Part 4, the Middle East: "Eshkol's statements to foreign correspondents," January 18, 1965, No. 1761, p. A/1; "Levi Eshkol's speech at Tiberias," January 21, 1965, No. 1764, p. A/1. See Lowi, "The Politics of Water," Chapter 5.

the territories occupied in the 1967 War.[14] Indeed, almost the entire increase in Israeli water use since 1967 derives from the waters of the West Bank and the upper Jordan River.

The Nile River is also an international river of tremendous regional importance and the control of the Nile is increasingly contentious, as water demands in the region soar. The Nile flows through some of the most arid regions of northern Africa and is vital for agricultural production in Egypt and the Sudan. Ninety-seven percent of Egypt's water comes from the Nile River, and more than ninety-five percent of the Nile's runoff originates outside of Egypt, in the other eight nations of the basin: the Sudan, Ethiopia, Kenya, Rwanda, Burundi, Uganda, Tanzania, and Zaire. A treaty signed in 1959 resolved a number of important issues, but was negotiated and signed by only two nations, Egypt and the Sudan,[15] raising the possibility that additional water development in other upstream nations could reduce the supply available to Egypt and greatly increase tensions in this arid region. Egypt is extremely vulnerable to intentional reductions in the flow of the Nile, although Egypt has by far the stronger position militarily and has indicated its willingness to intervene with force to prevent any disruption of flow. In 1979, President Anwar Sadat said, "the only matter that could take Egypt to war again is water."[16] More recently, Egypt's foreign minister, Boutros Boutros-Ghali (now secretary general of the United Nations), said "the next war in our region will be over the waters of the Nile, not politics."[17] While these statements partly reflect political rhetoric, they also give an indication of the importance of the Nile to Egypt.

WATER-RESOURCE SYSTEMS AS INSTRUMENTS OF WAR

Although the usual instruments of war are military weapons of destruction, the use of water and water-resources systems as both offensive and defensive weapons also has a long history. In political conflicts that escalate to military aggression, water-resource systems have regularly been both the targets and the tools of war. While fresh water resources are renewable, in practice they

---

14. Lowi, "The Politics of Water," p. 342.
15. "Agreement Between the United Arab Republic and the Republic of Sudan for the Full Utilization of the Nile Waters," Cairo, November 8, 1959. The treaty allocated the presumed flow of the river and established an international commission between the two countries to negotiate additional issues and disputes.
16. Cited by Joyce Starr in "Water Wars," *Foreign Policy*, No. 82 (Spring 1991), pp. 17–30.
17. This statement has been widely cited. See, e.g., Tim Walker, "The Nile Struggles to Keep Up the Flow," *Sunday Nation* (Nairobi), January 10, 1988, p. 11.

are finite, poorly distributed, and often subject to substantial control by one nation or group. In such circumstances, the temptation to use water for political or military purposes may prove irresistible. Even the perception that access to fresh water could be used as a political tool by another nation may lead to violence.

When Sennacherib of Assyria destroyed Babylon in 689 BC as retribution for the death of his son, he purposefully destroyed the water-supply canals to the city.[18] Nebuchadnezzar of Babylon later used a system of canals in the defense of the city:

To strengthen the defenses of Babylon, I had a mighty dike of earth thrown up, above the other, from the banks of the Tigris to that of the Euphrates 5 bern long and I surrounded the city with a great expanse of water, with waves on it like the sea.[19]

In this century, hydroelectric dams were bombed during World War II, and the centralized dams on the Yalu River serving North Korea and China were attacked during the Korean War.[20] Similarly, Iran claimed to have blacked out large portions of Iraq in July 1981 by bombing a hydroelectric station in Kurdistan.[21] Irrigation water-supply systems in North Vietnam were bombed by the United States in the late 1960s. When Syria tried to stop Israel in the 1950s from building its National Water Carrier, an aqueduct to provide water to southern Israel, fighting broke out across the demilitarized zone, and when Syria tried to divert the headwaters of the Jordan in the mid-1960s, Israel used force, including air strikes against the diversion facilities to prevent their construction and operation.[22] These military actions contributed to the tensions that led to the 1967 War.

Most recently, dams, desalination plants, and water-conveyance systems were targeted by both sides during the 1991 Persian Gulf War. Most of Kuwait's extensive desalination capacity was destroyed by the retreating Iraqis, and in mid-1992, the Iraqis were still suffering severe problems rebuilding Baghdad's modern water supply and sanitation system, which had intentionally been destroyed during the war.[23] In early 1993, it was reported

---

18. Drower, "Water-Supply, Irrigation, and Agriculture."
19. Quoted in Drower, "Water-Supply, Irrigation, and Agriculture."
20. Amory B. Lovins and L. Hunter Lovins, *Brittle Power: Energy Strategy for National Security* (Andover, Mass.: Brick House Publishing, 1982), p. 69.
21. "Iran Says It Bombed Iraqi Hydroelectric Plant," *New York Times,* July 20, 1981, p. A2.
22. See, for example, Naff and Matson, *Water in the Middle East.*
23. "Iraq's Water Systems Still in Shambles," *U.S. Water News,* Vol. 8, No. 10 (1992), p. 2.

that Saddam Hussein was poisoning and draining the water supplies of southern Shiite Muslims in his efforts to quell the opposition to his government.[24] And in late January 1993, the Peruca dam, the second largest dam in the former Yugoslavia, was intentionally destroyed in the civil war there.[25] As water supplies and delivery systems become increasingly valuable in water-scarce regions, their value as military targets also increases.

A strange twist on this problem surfaced in 1986, when North Korea announced plans to build the Kumgansan hydroelectric dam on a tributary of the Han River upstream of South Korea's capital, Seoul. This raised fears in South Korea that the dam could be used as a tool to disrupt its water supply or to upset the ecological balance of the area, or that it could even be used as an intentional offensive weapon in the event of hostilities. South Korean military analysts predicted that the deliberate destruction of the dam by the North could be used as a military weapon to flood Seoul and that the sudden release of the entire contents of the dam would raise the level of the Han River as it passes through Seoul by over 50 meters, enough to destroy most of the city. A formal request to halt construction was made to the North Korean government, and South Korea built a series of levees and check dams above Seoul to try to mitigate possible impacts.[26]

In the Middle East, hydroelectric and agricultural developments on the Euphrates River have been the source of considerable international concern. This river flows from the mountains of southern Turkey through Syria to Iraq before emptying into the Persian Gulf. Both Syria and Iraq depend heavily on the Euphrates River for drinking water, irrigation, industrial uses, and hydroelectricity, and view any upstream development with concern. In 1974, Iraq threatened to bomb the al-Thawra dam in Syria; it massed troops along the border, alleging that the flow of water to Iraq had been reduced by the dam. More recently, Turkey has implemented an ambitious water-supply scheme to increase its hydroelectricity production and to irrigate an additional two million hectares of land. In 1990, Turkey finished construction of the Atatürk Dam, the largest of the twenty-one dams proposed for the

---

24. "New Repression of Iraqi Shiites Reported," *Boston Globe*, February 28, 1993, p. 4, reporting on a story in the British paper *Observer*.

25. Laura Silber, "Battle to avert Croat dam disaster," *Financial Times*, January 30/31, 1993, p. 2.

26. Susan Chira, "North Korea Dam Worries the South," *New York Times*, November 30, 1986, p. 3. Noel Koch, "North Korean Dam Seen as Potential 'Water Bomb'," *Washington Post/San Francisco Chronicle*, September 30, 1987, "Briefing," p. 3. North Korea denied any military intentions, but construction on the dam was halted in the late 1980s and the project remains on hold.

Grand Anatolia Project, and interrupted the flow of the Euphrates for a month to partly fill the reservoir. Despite advance warning from Turkey of the temporary cutoff, Syria and Iraq both protested that Turkey now had a water weapon that could be used against them. Indeed, in mid-1990, Turkish President Turgut Ozal threatened to restrict water flow to Syria to force it to withdraw support for Kurdish rebels operating in southern Turkey. While Turkish politicians later disavowed this threat, Syrian officials argue that Turkey has already used its power over the headwaters of the Euphrates for political goals and could do so again.[27] When the Turkish projects are complete, the flow of the Euphrates River to Syria could be reduced by up to 40 percent, and to Iraq by up to 80 percent.[28]

It is sometimes only a short step from capability to implementation. The ability of Turkey to shut off the flow of the Euphrates, even temporarily, was noted by political and military strategists at the beginning of the Persian Gulf conflict.[29] In the early days of the war, there were behind-the-scenes discussions at the United Nations about using Turkish dams on the Euphrates River to deprive Iraq of a significant fraction of its fresh water supply in response to its invasion of Kuwait.[30] While no such action was ever taken, the threat of the "water weapon" was again made clear.

Resource Inequities and the Impacts of Water Developments

There are growing tensions between rich and poor nations due to inequitable distribution and use of resources. While most of the attention of political scientists interested in the links between resources and interstate conflict has focused on non-renewable mineral resources such as rare metals and oil, some renewable resources such as water also suffer great maldistribution and may pose comparable risks to international peace in the future. Unlike

27. Alan Cowell, "Water Rights: Plenty of Mud to Sling," *New York Times*, February 7, 1990, p. A4.
28. This estimate comes from Professor Thomas Naff of the University of Pennsylvania and is cited in "Water Wars in the Middle East," *The Economist*, May 12, 1990, pp. 54–59.
29. See Peter Schweizer, "The Spigot Strategy," *New York Times* op-ed, November 11, 1990.
30. These closed-door discussions were described to the author by the ambassador of a member nation of the U.N. Security Council under the condition that he remain anonymous. See also the statement of the Minister of State of Turkey, Kamran Inan, at the Conference on Transboundary Waters in the Middle East: Prospects for Regional Cooperation, Ankara, Turkey, September 3, 1991. At that meeting, Minister Inan stated that Turkey would never use water as a means of political pressure and noted that it had declined to do so during the Gulf War.

rare metals, water is quite difficult to redistribute economically. Unlike oil, water has no substitutes.

In some regions, water availability is coming up against the limits of minimum water requirements—the so-called "water barrier" defined by Malin Falkenmark.[31] Falkenmark identifies levels of water availability below which serious constraints to development will arise. Falkenmark sets this level at between 1000 and 2000 people for every million cubic meters of water per year. In fast-growing semi-arid nations and regions, limits to supply will eventually be reached, despite efforts to reduce waste and to redirect priorities. While there is no doubt that great improvements in the efficiency of water use can be made throughout the world, as can trade-offs between water-consumptive and water-efficient sectors, these actions only push back the barrier, they do not eliminate it.

As a result, some countries could eventually reach an absolute limit on the type and extent of industrial development due solely to constraints on the availability of fresh water. How fast these limits are reached depends on three factors: (1) the absolute availability of water; (2) the population needing to be supplied; and (3) the level of development desired, as measured by both the need for water and the efficiency with which water is used. Such limits will contribute to tensions between water-poor and water-rich nations and could be the source of future conflict.

Other hydrologic conditions may contribute to regional tensions. Enormous human suffering occurs because of the lack of satisfactory water for health and sanitation. Despite great efforts during the International Drinking Water Supply and Sanitation Decade of the 1980s, 1.3 billion people are still without access to safe, clean water, and over 1.7 billion are without access to appropriate sanitation facilities.[32] By 2000, 900 million more people will have been born in regions without these essential services.

These conditions are directly responsible for the severe impact of waterborne diseases around the world, including dysentery, malaria, cholera, and the parasitic diseases rampant in parts of Africa and Asia. These diseases can explode in intensity in regions that lack sanitation services and clean water for drinking. In 1990, 71,000 cases of cholera were reported to the

---

31. Malin Falkenmark, "Fresh Water—Time for A Modified Approach," *Ambio*, Vol. 15, No. 4 (1986), pp. 194–200.
32. Joseph Christmas and Carel de Rooy, "The Decade and Beyond: At a Glance," *Water International*, Vol. 16, No. 3 (Urbana, Illinois: International Water Resources Association, 1991), pp. 127–134.

World Health Organization; none came from Latin America, which had been free of cholera since the mid-1800s. One year later, in 1991, cholera exploded in the region, with over 390,000 cases reported in fourteen Latin American countries alone, and over 590,000 cases worldwide.[33] This epidemic is clear evidence of the shortfall in provision of water, sanitation, and health services in the poorest areas of the Americas.

Lack of progress in providing safe drinking water and sanitation services during the 1980s was due in large part to population growth, the substantial and growing debt burden carried by developing countries, and the lack of industrial and intellectual infrastructure for building and maintaining sanitation and water-supply projects. Unless there is a renewed effort on the part of the richer nations to fill these gaps, the world's water-related health burden will rise.

Similar inequities exist in the use of water for energy production and for irrigation. Two percent of global hydroelectricity comes from Africa, which has 12 percent of the world's population; in contrast, nearly 30 percent comes from North America, with only 6 percent of the world's population.[34] Only nine countries in Africa irrigate more than 10 percent of their cropland; over sixty countries worldwide fall into this category. In Africa as a whole, only six percent of cropland is irrigated; worldwide the total is close to 16 percent. In fact, nearly twenty nations in Africa have effectively *no* irrigation supply systems at all.[35] Differences in the level and quality of water development are not always the result of shortages in water availability, but of access to capital, technology, and know-how,[36] and the inefficiency of governmental

33. The updated 1991 cholera data come from a personal communication with Dr. S.J. Siméant of the World Health Organization in Geneva. See also Pan American Health Organization, "Mortality Due to Intestinal Infectious Diseases in Latin America and the Caribbean, 1965–1990," and "Cholera Situation in the Americas: An Update," *Epidemiological Bulletin*, Vol. 12, No. 3 (1991), pp. 1–13.
34. U.S. Department of Energy, *International Energy Annual*, DOE/EIA-0219(90) (Washington, D.C.: Energy Information Administration, 1990).
35. Food and Agriculture Organization, *FAO Production Yearbook 1990*, FAO Statistical Series, Vol. 44, No. 99 (Paris: Food and Agriculture Organization of the United Nations, 1990). These data are for 1989. For a summary of cropland use by region and country see Table E.1 in Peter H. Gleick, ed., *Water in Crisis: A Guide to the World's Fresh Water Resources* (New York: Oxford University Press, 1993).
36. For example Professor Charles Okidi, from Moi University in Kenya, pointed out that there are only four Ph.D-level hydrologists in all of Kenya to work on problems of water supply, sanitation, hydroelectricity, and hydroclimatology. Charles Okidi, "Environmental Stress and Conflicts in Africa: Case Studies of African International Drainage Basins," paper prepared for the Project on Environmental Change and Acute Conflict, American Academy of Arts and Sciences and the University of Toronto (May 1992).

organizations in many developing nations in implementing effective agricultural or energy policies.

What is the link between these water-resource problems and conflict? In most cases, resource inequities will lead to more poverty, shortened lives, and misery, but not directly to violent conflict. But in some cases, these resource gaps will increase the likelihood of international disputes, create refugees who cross borders, and decrease the ability of a nation to resist economic and military activities by neighboring countries.

Conflicts over sources of irrigation water may become particularly severe, given the urgent demands to increase food production to meet both current needs and expected increases in population. Even where arable land suitable for irrigation exists, political or physical constraints may hinder any expansion of irrigation. In northern Africa, for example, the Sudan is considered one of the few nations with great potential for increased irrigation: there is sufficient arable land and there is, in theory, sufficient water in the Nile. In reality, however, withdrawing additional water from the Nile would require that the Sudan renegotiate or abrogate the treaty it signed in 1959 with Egypt.[37]

Similarly, many major hydroelectric projects are multi-national. Occasionally a dam is built by a smaller nation that then sells excess electricity to a larger neighbor. The Itaipú Dam on the Paraná River, for example, was built jointly by Brazil and Paraguay, although almost all of the hydroelectric benefits go to Brazil. Changes in electricity needs of the region may require difficult renegotiation of the present agreement. In addition, some subsidiary effects of the dam, such as changes in the timing and magnitude of downstream flows, caused disputes between Brazil and Argentina, which wanted to build its own dam on the Paraná that would have affected the operation of the Itaipú dam. A compromise agreement was ultimately reached after some tense negotiations, permitting the construction of the Yacyreta dam by Argentina. The Kariba Dam, one of the largest in Africa, is built on the Zambezi River on the border of Zambia and Zimbabwe, and dam operation has sometimes been difficult to coordinate. Situations like these can promote cooperation and peace. But they may also be the source of conflict where

---

37. Peter H. Gleick, "Climate Changes, International Rivers, and International Security: The Nile and the Colorado," in Robert Redford and Terrill J. Minger, editors, *Greenhouse Glasnost* (New York: The Ecco Press, 1990), pp. 147–165; Peter H. Gleick, "The Vulnerability of Runoff in the Nile Basin to Climatic Changes," *The Environmental Professional*, Vol. 13, No. 1 (1991), pp. 66–73.

there are gross inequities in energy use. When disputes arise over the distribution of electricity, or for other reasons, conflicts for these hydroelectric resources are a distinct possibility.

OTHER LINKS BETWEEN CONFLICT AND WATER DEVELOPMENTS

Water-related conflicts may also arise over the secondary impacts of water development schemes such as irrigation facilities, hydroelectric developments, and flood-control reservoirs. Major water developments often lead to displacement of large local populations, adverse impacts on downstream water users and ecosystems, changes in control of local resources, and economic dislocations. These impacts may, in turn, lead to disputes among ethnic or economic groups, between urban and rural populations, and across borders. Table 1 lists some of the most severe population displacements caused by the construction of dams and reservoirs worldwide.

There are many examples of local and regional water disputes. In South Africa in 1990, for example, a pro-apartheid council cut off water to the Wesselton township of 50,000 blacks following their protest over miserable sanitation and living conditions.[38] Zimbabwe recently reported that its output of ethanol, which is mixed with gasoline to reduce the country's fuel imports, has dropped because the severe African drought has crippled sugar cane production.[39] This has a direct impact on Zimbabwe's economic strength, and may affect its ability to maintain both domestic and regional stability. Violent conflicts have arisen over water allocations in India, most recently in early 1992 following a court decision to allocate the waters of the Cauvery River between the states of Karnataka and Tamil Nadu. The Cauvery River originates in Karnataka, but the greatest use of the water is in Tamil Nadu, before it flows to the Bay of Bengal. Over fifty people were reported killed in riots in Karnataka following the allocation of additional water to Tamil Nadu.[40]

These examples mostly involve regional political borders, but they are little different from the kinds of disputes that can be international. Indeed, some of the regional resource disputes within what was the Soviet Union must now be considered international due to the changing political status of the

38. Rodney Pinder, "50,000 Blacks Deprived of Water" Reuters Press/*San Francisco Chronicle*, October 24, 1990, p. A-11.
39. "Drought reduces output of ethanol," *The Herald* (Harare), February 24, 1992. p. 1.
40. Marcus Moench, 1992, personal communication with author.

Table 1.   Populations Displaced as a Consequence of Dam Construction.

Dam	Countries	Installed Capacity (MW)	Area of Reservoir (km²)	Number of People Displaced	Date Completed[a]
Sanmenxia	China			870,000	1960
Maduru Oya	Sri Lanka		64	200,000	1983
Aswan	Egypt, Sudan	1,815	6,500	120,000	1970
Mangla	Pakistan	600		110,000	1967
Kaptai	Bangladesh		777	100,000	1962
Damodar (4 projects)	India			93,000	1959
Nanela	Pakistan			90,000	1967
Tarbela	Pakistan	1,750	243	86,000	1976
Akasombo	Ghana	882	9,000	80,000	1965
Kossou	Ivory Coast		1,700	75,000	1972
TVA (about 20 projects)	United States			60,000	1930s on
Kariba	Zambia, Zimbabwe	1,266	5,100	50,000–57,000	1959
Gandhi Sagar	India			52,000	
Itaparica	Brazil	1,500		50,000	1988
Kainji	Nigeria			42,000–50,000	1968
Ataturk (Southeast Anatolia Project)	Turkey			40,000	1991
Bhakra	India	450		36,000	1963
Lam Pao	Thailand		400	30,000	1970
Keban	Turkey	1,360	675	30,000	1974
Mython (Jharkh)	India	200		28,030	1955
Kedong Ombo	Java, Indonesia			27,000	1992
Nam Pong	Thailand		20	25,000–30,000	1965
Tucurui	Brazil	4,000	2,430	23,871	1984
Upper Pampanga	Phillippines			14,000	1973
Ruzizi II	Rwanda, Zaire	40		12,600	
Manantali	Mali	200		10,000	
Salvajina	Colombia		22	10,000	1985
Brokopondo	Suriname			5,000	1971
Caracol	Mexico			5,000	1986
Batang Ai	Sarawak, Borneo	92	85	3,000	
Nam Ngum	Laos			3,000	1971
Netzahualcoyotl	Mexico			3,000	1964

NOTE:
a. Approximate date of completion. Blanks in the table mean this information is not available.
SOURCE: Compiled by Cynthia Chiang. See Peter H. Gleick, ed., *Water in Crisis: A Guide to the World's Water Resources* (New York: Oxford University Press, 1993).

former republics. The destruction of the Aral Sea from overuse of the Amu Dar'ya and Syr Dar'ya rivers was once was an internal Soviet matter; now the problem affects five independent nations.

The impacts of some water developments involve more than one nation from the beginning. The construction of the Aswan High Dam by Egypt led to flooding and dislocation of populations in the Sudan. The construction of the Farakka Barrage on the Ganges in India affected water conditions and availability in Bangladesh. The construction of several major irrigation projects in the southwestern United States led to the serious degradation of Colorado River water quality delivered to Mexico and an intense political dispute that was ultimately resolved through diplomatic negotiations.[41] In 1992, a serious political dispute arose between Hungary and Czechoslovakia over the construction and operation of the Gabcikovo/Nagymaros project on the Danube River. In May 1992, Hungary abrogated a 1977 treaty with Czechoslovakia governing construction of the project, complaining of possible severe environmental damage, but Czechoslovakia continued construction unilaterally, completing the Gabcikovo dam and diverting the Danube out of its bed into a canal inside of the Slovakian republic. This prompted massive public protests in both Hungary and Slovakia, rumors of military actions, Hungarian appeals to the International Court of Justice, consultation with the Conference on Security and Cooperation in Europe (CSCE), and the intervention of the European Community Commission. As of early 1993, the risk of violent conflict appears to have decreased as other political mechanisms have come into play, particularly the participation of European Community negotiators, but the relationship between the parties remains very tense.[42]

Conflicts in regions with other simmering tensions, such as the Middle East, have been contained less successfully than in regions with few other political disputes. The major dam developments in Turkey, as part of the Grand Anatolia Project, have caused growing, and so far unresolved, tensions among Turkey, Syria, and Iraq. In addition, the construction of a large dam on the Han River, discussed earlier, adds another layer to the long-standing dispute between North and South Korea.

---

41. Peter H. Gleick, "The Effects of Future Climatic Changes on International Water Resources: The Colorado River, the United States, and Mexico," *Policy Sciences*, Vol. 21, No. 1 (February 1988), pp. 23–39.

42. During the height of the dispute, as Slovakia began to divert the Danube, there were rumors of military maneuvers. Nicholas Denton, "Hungarians furious over work on dam," *Financial Times*, October 26, 1992, p. 3. The controversy was complicated by the presence of a large ethnic Hungarian minority in Slovakia near the construction site, by Slovakia's claim that the project is essential to its "energy security and economic well-being," by disputes over navigation rights on the Danube, and by the participation of Austrian banks and construction companies on the project. Nicholas Denton, "Hungary backed by Germany over dam," *Financial Times*, October 27, 1992, p. 3.

Future Conflicts over Water

Nations fight for access to water, use water as a tool and weapon in battle, and target the water facilities of enemies. While water resources have rarely been the sole cause of conflict, fresh-water resources are becoming more valuable in many regions, and the likelihood of water-induced conflicts is thus increasing. In arid and semi-arid areas of the world, where water is already a vital resource, conflicts over access and possession are likely to worsen.

In addition to the threats of scarcity caused by growing populations and changing levels of development, there is a new danger posed by the so-called "greenhouse effect."[43] The preceding discussion has assumed that total water availability in the future will not change, and will be subject only to natural variations in flow. But in fact, future climatic changes effectively make obsolete all our old assumptions about the behavior of water supply. Perhaps the greatest certainty about future climatic changes is that the future will not look like the past. We may not know precisely what it will look like, but changes are coming, and by the turn of the century, many of these changes will already be apparent.

Global climatic change will affect water availability in many ways, although the precise nature of such changes is still obscure.[44] Our challenge is to identify those cases in which conflicts are likely to be exacerbated and to work to reduce the probability and consequences of those conflicts.

Despite many remaining scientific uncertainties, the outlines of important water resource changes can now be seen. The clearest threat posed by climatic change is the increase in both evaporative losses and water demands caused by higher average temperatures. Even without changes in precipitation, water availability can decrease by 10 percent or more simply owing to average temperature increases of 2 to 3°C, well within the range of expected changes over the next few decades.[45] These effects are independent of the increased

---

43. Peter H. Gleick, "The implications of global climatic changes for international security," *Climatic Change*, Vol. 15, No. 1–2, (October 1989), pp. 309–325.
44. For more detail on the science of climate change, see the report of the Intergovernmental Panel on Climate Change, *Climate Change: The IPCC Scientific Assessment* (Cambridge, U.K.: Cambridge University Press, 1990).
45. See the summary of climate and water issues in Peter H. Gleick, "Climate Change, Hydrology, and Water Resources," *Review of Geophysics*, Vol. 27, No. 3 (1989), pp. 329–344. For details on future climate conditions, including a discussion of the uncertainties, see Table 4.1 from Stephen H. Schneider, Linda Mearns, and Peter H. Gleick, "Climate-Change Scenarios for

demands from both human users and natural ecosystems that will occur at the same time.[46]

In addition to temperature changes, annual precipitation changes of 10 to 25 percent may occur, and even larger fluctuations may occur on a monthly basis. These shifts are more than enough to cause serious problems in some places, and some benefits in others, with concomitant impacts on local populations. Regions subject to droughts and water competition may benefit from increases in rainfall or suffer from decreases in rainfall. Areas vulnerable to periodic floods may suffer from climate-induced increases in runoff or benefit from reductions in peak flows. Regions dependent on hydroelectricity for a substantial fraction of their energy production may suffer from reductions in reservoir levels that result from prolonged shortages, and the associated economic stresses such energy losses will bring.

Climate impact information combined with data on per-capita water availability and supply reveals that certain regions are highly vulnerable. A recent review of climate changes estimated by large-scale climate models (so-called "general circulation models" or "GCMs") for the Middle East shows both the uncertain nature of the changes and the possibility that the climate changes will be severe. For the region of the Jordan and Litani Rivers, three different climate models estimate that precipitation could change by an amount between −14 and +48 percent.[47] For the region of the Nile, comparable changes are possible. Using estimates of plausible changes in temperature and precipitation derived from large-scale global climate models, some studies suggest that runoff in the Nile basin as a whole could decrease by 25 percent.[48] While short-term changes in flow of this magnitude are manageable, a long-term decrease of this magnitude could be catastrophic.

In some regions flooding may be a more severe problem than droughts. Floodplains, river deltas, and mountainous areas are particularly vulnerable to increases in flow. The risk of flooding depends on the intensity of storms,

Impact Assessment," in Robert L. Peters and Thomas E. Lovejoy, eds., *Global Warming and Biological Diversity* (New Haven: Yale University Press, 1992), pp. 38–55.

46. Estimates of evaporative losses as a function of temperature come from Richard Wetherald and Sykuro Manabe, "Influence of Seasonal Variation upon the Sensitivity of a Model Climate," *Journal of Geophysical Research*, Vol. 86 (C2), (1981), pp. 1194–1204; and Mikhail I. Budyko, *The Earth's Climate: Past and Future*, International Geophysics Series, Vol. 29 (New York: Academic Press, 1982).

47. Stephen Lonergan, "Climate Warming, Water Resources, and Geopolitical Conflict: A Study of Nations Dependent on the Nile, Litani and Jordan River Systems," Operational Research and Analysis Establishment, ORAE Paper No. 55 (Ottawa: National Defence, 1991).

48. Gleick, "The Vulnerability of Runoff in the Nile Basin."

the level of floodplain development, geomorphology, and the extent of physical protection such as levees and dams. If estimates of increased intensity of monsoons are correct, southern Asia, including Bangladesh, Bhutan, Cambodia, and Laos, will be particularly vulnerable to flooding.[49] Other regions that already suffer from severe periodic floods include central Sudan, eastern India, Turkey, Congo, and Guyana.

Perhaps the most important effect of climatic change on water resources will be a great increase in the overall uncertainty associated with water management and supply. Rainfall, runoff, and storms are all natural events with a substantial random component to them; in the language of hydrologists, they are "stochastic." In many ways, therefore, the science of hydrology is the science of estimating the probabilities of certain types of events. But these estimates are almost always done assuming that climate is stationary—i.e., variable but unchanging over the long term. Indeed, hydrologists and water managers have few analytical tools with which they can incorporate future changes of uncertain magnitude.

Recent studies of the effects of future climatic changes suggest that present methods of water allocation, dam and turbine operation, and the inflexible setting of delivery priorities may leave international rivers open to significant water supply and quality problems.[50] Yet no organizations or agencies responsible for shared international river management have yet indicated a willingness to consider changing operating rules to improve their ability to handle possible climatic changes. For example, increased flexibility on the timing of hydroelectricity generation and deliveries of water to users of the Colorado River (shared by seven states of the United States and by Mexico) could reduce the risks of shortages there.[51] Adding to this problem is the fact that many water data are still classified as secret by national governments. Changes in flow could therefore be perceived and misinterpreted by

---

49. Schneider, Mearns, and Gleick, "Climate Change Scenarios."
50. Gretta Goldenman, "International River Agreements in the Context of Climatic Change," Pacific Institute for Studies in Development, Environment, and Security (Berkeley, Calif.: Pacific Institute, 1989); Linda Nash and Peter H. Gleick, "The Sensitivity of Streamflow in the Colorado Basin to Climatic Changes," *Journal of Hydrology*, Vol. 125 (July 1991), pp. 221–241; Linda Nash and Peter H. Gleick, "The Sensitivity of Streamflow and Water Supply in the Colorado Basin to Climatic Changes" (Washington, D.C.: U.S. Environmental Protection Agency, 1993); Peter H. Gleick, "Effects of Climate Change on Shared Fresh Water Resources," in Irving M. Mintzer, ed., *Confronting Climate Change: Risks, Implications and Responses* (Cambridge, U.K.: Cambridge University Press, 1992), pp. 127–140.
51. Nash and Gleick, "The Sensitivity of Streamflow and Water Supply."

downstream nations as intentional manipulations rather than geophysical events, thereby provoking conflict.

We thus see growing pressures on both the supply of and demand for water resources because of global climate changes. Unless we can anticipate where these pressures will be the most severe, and where conflicts may arise, we will be condemned to react to outbreaks of actual conflict, rather than able to act to prevent them or reduce their probability. It is crucial, therefore, to try to anticipate where and when water-related conflicts will occur. Despite the unpredictable and uncertain nature of resource disputes, the next section explores how one might evaluate a country's vulnerability to water-resource problems or reliance on disputed supplies.

Indices of Water-Resources Vulnerability

Water-resources vulnerability is a function of many things, including economic and political conditions, water availability, and the extent to which a source of water supply is shared. Although they should be considered rough, some quantitative indices that look at several of these factors suggest "regions at risk."[52] Countries where such indicators suggest that the risk of conflict may be high might also be regions where creative regional cooperation or the intervention of international organizations would be particularly valuable.

Table 2 measures the ratio of annual water demand (withdrawals) to annual renewable water availability (supply). Countries whose present water withdrawals exceed one-third of their total renewable supply are listed. In these countries, shortages could result from limited overall water supply or high water demands: either situation can lead to a conflict over water with neighboring or relatively water-rich countries. As the data in Table 2 indicate, twenty-one countries use more than one-third of their renewable supply, with nine of them already forced to import additional fresh water, pump ground water at a non-renewable rate, or desalinate non-potable sources at

---

52. A similar series of regional indices of water resource vulnerability for the United States was developed using measures of supply, demand, dependence on hydroelectricity, overpumping of ground water, and hydrologic variability. See Peter H. Gleick, "Vulnerability of Water Systems," in Paul E. Waggoner, ed., *Climate Change and U.S. Water Resources* (New York: John Wiley and Sons, 1990), pp. 223–240. Such indices are not meant to be definitive. In many regions of the world, water resource data are limited or unreliable, making the quantification of these indices difficult. For some of the measures, more detailed regional data, or data on a seasonal basis rather than on an annual average basis, would be valuable.

Table 2. Ratio of Water Demand to Supply by Country.

Country	Water Withdrawals as a Percentage of Renewable Supply[a]	Country	Water Withdrawals as a Percentage of Renewable Supply[a]
Libya	374	Belgium	72
Qatar	174	Cyprus	60
United Arab Emirates	140	Tunisia	53
Yemen	135	Afghanistan	52
Jordan	110	Pakistan	51
Israel	110	Barbados	51
Saudi Arabia	106	Iraq	43
Kuwait	>100	Madagascar	41
Bahrain	>100	Iran	39
Egypt	97	Morocco	37
Malta	92		

NOTE:

a. These data are for the late 1980s and show the percentage of water used annually compared to the annually renewable supply of water including river flows from other countries. Nine countries use more than 100 percent of available supply, which means that these countries partly depend on water imports, non-renewable ground water, or desalination of brackish or salt water.

SOURCES: United Nations Environment Programme, "The State of the World Environment in 1991," *Climate Change: Need for Global Partnership* (Nairobi, Kenya: United Nations, 1991); World Resources Institute, *World Resources 1990–91: A Guide to the Environment* (New York: Oxford University Press, 1990); and Professor Thomas Naff, personal communication (1992).

great expense. All nine of these are in the Middle East, a region where political and resource tensions are already high.

A second quantitative indicator, which takes into account growing populations, is shown in Table 3. This Table lists those countries where annual per capita water availability in 1990 falls below 1,000 cubic meters per person, or will do so by 2025.[53] As described earlier, this level of water availability is typically considered the minimum per-capita water requirement for an efficient, industrialized nation. For many of the countries in Table 3, annual availability falls below 250 cubic meters per person, suggesting significant water scarcity and stress. No developed country uses this little water. Even Israel, which has done a great deal to increase its water-use efficiency and

---

53. Falkenmark, "Fresh water."

Table 3. Per Capita Water Availability Today and in 2025 (cubic meters/person/year).ª

Country	Per Capita Water Availability 1990	Projected Per Capita Water Availability 2025
Africa		
Algeria	750	380
Burundi	660	280
Cape Verde	500	220
Comoros	2,040	790
Djibouti	750	270
Egypt	1,070	620
Ethiopia	2,360	980
Kenya	590	190
Lesotho	2,220	930
Libya	160	60
Morocco	1,200	680
Nigeria	2,660	1,000
Rwanda	880	350
Somalia	1,510	610
South Africa	1,420	790
Tanzania	2,780	900
Tunisia	530	330
North and Central America		
Barbados	170	170
Haiti	1,690	960
South America		
Peru	1,790	980
Asia/Middle East		
Cyprus	1,290	1,000
Iran	2,080	960
Israel	470	310
Jordan	260	80
Kuwait	<10	<10
Lebanon	1,600	960
Oman	1,330	470
Qatar	50	20
Saudi Arabia	160	50
Singapore	220	190
United Arab Emirates	190	110
Yemen	240	80
Europe		
Malta	80	80

NOTE:

a. Some hydrologists have identified 1000 cubic meters per person per year as a minimum water requirement for an efficient, moderately industrialized nation. The countries listed here are those that either in 1990 or in 2025 will fail to meet this level of fresh water availability. The change between 1990 and 2025 is due solely to increases in population.

SOURCES: Computed from United Nations population data and estimates. Population and water availability data come from World Resources Institute, *World Resources 1991–92* (New York: Oxford University Press, 1991).

minimize water-intensive development, uses over 400 m³/person/year.[54] Note that most of the water-limited nations are located in Africa and Asia; few nations in Europe, the Pacific, or the Americas face these constraints. Over the next few decades, some of these countries will begin to see limits to their economic development because of the limited availability of water. Ethiopia, Kenya, Rwanda, Tanzania, and Burundi, all listed in Table 3, are all part of the Nile Basin and are likely to want to increase their utilization of Nile waters, at the ultimate expense of Egypt. Libya, Yemen, and many countries in the Persian Gulf (Saudi Arabia, Qatar, United Arab Emirates, and Kuwait) are pumping ground water resources at rates faster than they are being replenished by rainfall. These countries are vitally dependent on ground water and on desalination fueled by inexpensive oil and gas, and they may exhaust ground water supplies early in the next century, at the risk of severe economic dislocations.

An index that measures the extent to which water supplies are shared, and hence potentially vulnerable to competing interests, is shown in Table 4. This table lists those nations with a large fraction of their total water supply originating outside of their borders and under the control of other nations. The best example of this is Egypt, which is entirely dependent on the Nile River for its water, ninety-seven percent of which originates outside of Egypt's border. Thirty other nations receive more than one-third of their surface water across national borders.[55] This suggests that frictions and tensions over water may arise in parts of Europe (Hungary, Germany, Austria, Belgium, the Czech Republic, and Slovakia) and in Asia (Cambodia, Bangladesh, and Pakistan), where water is controlled by neighboring countries.

A fourth measure of vulnerability to hydrologic conditions is a high dependence on hydroelectricity as a fraction of total electrical supply. Table 5 lists those nations that use hydroelectricity to provide more than 50 percent of their total electrical demand. For nations that rely on hydroelectricity for 50 percent of their total energy supply, military actions against hydroelectric

---

54. All countries, including Israel, can do more to reduce waste of water and thus extend the amount of water available for other use. In addition, most data on water use do not differentiate between water withdrawn and water *consumed*. Better data on water consumption are needed.
55. These data precede the breakup of the Soviet Union and Yugoslavia. Many major rivers in these regions cross the borders of the newly formed political states. When the political status of these regions becomes clearer, it will be possible to recalculate the number of nations receiving significant fractions of water from sources originating outside of their political boundaries.

Table 4. Dependence on Imported Surface Water.

Country	Percent of Total River Flow Originating Outside of Border[a]	Country	Percent of Total River Flow Originating Outside of Border[a]
Egypt	97	Iraq	66
Hungary	95	Albania	53
Mauritania	95	Uruguay	52
Botswana	94	Germany	51
Bulgaria	91	Portugal	48
Netherlands	89	Yugoslavia	43
Gambia	86	Bangladesh	42
Cambodia	82	Thailand	39
Romania	82	Austria	38
Luxembourg	80	Pakistan	36
Syria	79	Jordan	36
Congo	77	Venezuela	35
Sudan	77	Senegal	34
Paraguay	70	Belgium	33
Czechoslovakia	69	Israel[b]	21
Niger	68		

NOTES:

a. Using average annual river flows originating outside national borders.

b. Although only 21 percent of Israel's water comes from outside current borders, a significant fraction of Israel's fresh water supply comes from disputed lands, complicating the calculation of the origin of surface water supplies. This percentage would be affected by a political settlement of the Middle East conflict.

SOURCES: These data come from many sources compiled by the World Resources Institute, *World Resources, 1991–92* (New York: Oxford University Press, 1991).

dams, the intentional alteration of flows that cross borders, and any changes in climate that affect water availability would all be strongly felt. Once again, the countries of the Nile basin appear highly vulnerable, as are portions of west Africa and South America.

Combining the index of hydroelectric dependence with the index of dependence on water originating outside of national borders provides some measure of the vulnerability of a nation's energy supply to outside intervention. Nations that show up on both lists—Congo, Paraguay, Uruguay, Albania, and Austria—are especially at risk and may be worthy of more attention.

Table 5. Hydroelectric Production, by Continent and Country.[a]

Region	Hydroelectric Production as a Percent of Total Electricity Generation 1987	Region	Hydroelectric Production as a Percent of Total Electricity Generation 1987
Africa	**17.4**	**North and Central America**	**17.9**
Angola	74.2		
Burundi	96.3	Canada	63.7
Cameroon	97.2	Costa Rica	98.3
Central African Republic	80.4	El Salvador	54.2
		Haiti	71.1
Congo	99.1	Honduras	81.1
Cote D'Ivoire	58.6	Panama	70.0
Ethiopia	80.2		
Gabon	77.1		
Ghana	98.3	**Asia**	**17.5**
Kenya	72.7		
Madagascar	53.6	Afghanistan	60.8
Malawi	97.6	Laos	95.5
Mali	79.4	Nepal	95.2
Rwanda	97.7	N. Korea (DPRK)	58.0
Tanzania	69.8	Sri Lanka	80.4
Uganda	98.3		
Zaire	97.4		
Zambia	99.6	**Europe**	**18.7**
		Albania	87.2
South America	**75.2**	Austria	70.9
		Iceland	94.0
Bolivia	74.3	Norway	99.5
Brazil	91.7	Switzerland	60.2
Chile	77.7		
Colombia	72.3		
Ecuador	80.7	**Oceania**	**20.9**
Paraguay	99.8		
Peru	77.8	Fiji	81.4
Suriname	70.3	New Zealand	72.9
Uruguay	77.6		

NOTE:
a. For all countries with 50 percent or more of total electricity supplied by hydroelectricity.

SOURCE: United Nations Statistical Office, *Energy Statistics Yearbook 1987* (New York: United Nations Publications, 1989).

Reducing the Risks of Water-Related Conflicts

How can we reduce the risks of water-related conflict? International law and international institutions must play a leading role. There have already been some attempts to develop international law protecting the environment, but almost all of these focus on attempting to limit the environmental impacts of conflicts and war; few efforts have been made to address the equally important problem of limiting the use of the environment as an instrument of conflict, preventing conflicts over access to resources, or averting military responses to the consequences of environmental damages, such as population displacements.

An example of such an effort is the Environmental Modification Convention of 1977, negotiated under the auspices of the United Nations, which states, in part, that "each State Party to this Convention undertakes not to engage in military or any other hostile use of environmental modification techniques having widespread, long-lasting or severe effects as the means of destruction, damage or injury to any other State Party" (Article I.1).

In 1982 the United Nations General Assembly promulgated the World Charter for Nature, supported by over 110 nations, which states that "nature shall be secured against degradation caused by warfare or other hostile activities" (Article V) and that "military actions damaging to nature shall be avoided" (Article XX).

The 1977 Bern Geneva Convention on the Protection of Victims of International Armed Conflicts (additional to the Geneva Conventions of 1949), declares that "it is prohibited to employ methods or means of warfare which are intended, or may be expected, to cause widespread, long-term and severe damage to the natural environment" (Article XXXV.3) and that "care shall be taken in warfare to protect the natural environment against widespread, long-term and severe damage. This protection includes a prohibition of the use of methods or means of warfare which are intended or may be expected to cause such damage to the natural environment and thereby to prejudice the health or survival of the population" (Article LV.1).

Such agreements and statements, however, carry little weight in the international arena when politics, economics, and other factors are considered more important. One of their greatest limitations is the lack of enforcement teeth. Until the ideals expressed by these agreements are considered true facets of international law and behavior, and until enforcement mechanisms are included, they will remain ineffective.

International water law and institutions have important roles to play despite the fact that no satisfactory water law has been developed that is acceptable to all nations. Developing such agreements is difficult because of the many intricacies of interstate politics, national practices, and other complicating political and social factors. For nations sharing river basins, factors affecting the successful negotiation and implementation of international agreements include whether a nation is upstream, downstream, or sharing a river as a border, the relative military and economic strength of the nation, and the availability of other sources of water supply.

PRINCIPLES OF INTERNATIONAL LAW
In the last few decades, however, international organizations have attempted to derive more general principles and new concepts governing shared fresh water resources. The International Law Association's Helsinki Rules of 1966 (since modified) and the work of the International Law Commission of the United Nations are among the most important examples. In 1991, the International Law Commission completed the drafting and provisional adoption of thirty-two articles on the Law of the Non-Navigational Uses of International Watercourses.[56] Among the general principles set forth are those of equitable utilization, the obligation not to cause harm to other riparian states, and the obligation to exchange hydrologic and other relevant data and information on a regular basis. Some of these principles are described below. Questions still remain, however, about their relative importance and means of enforcement.[57] In particular, defining and quantifying "equitable utilization" of a shared water supply remains one of the most important and difficult problems facing many nations. Similar problems remain in determining the implications of severe variability; for example, how to share shortages and who should bear the costs of protecting against floods.

EQUITABLE UTILIZATION. The principle of equitable utilization means that each basin state is entitled to a reasonable and equitable share in the beneficial use of shared water. It contrasts with the so-called "Harmon Doctrine," which holds that a nation can use the water within its borders without restriction, even if that use substantially injures a neighbor. While some upstream na-

---

56. UN International Law Commission, *Report of the International Law Commission on the Work of Its Forty-Third Session* (New York: United Nations, 1991).
57. Goldenman, "International River Agreements"; Stephen McCaffrey, "Water, Politics, and International Law," in Gleick, ed., *Water in Crisis* (New York: Oxford University Press, 1993).

tions still cite the Harmon Doctrine, almost all river treaties signed in the last 100 years reject this practice and restrict the freedom of action of upstream nations. "Equitable" does not mean equal use. Rather it means that a large variety of factors, including population, geography, availability of alternative resources, and so on, can be considered during negotiations over the allocation of water rights. One region where the concept of equitable utilization needs to be applied is the disputed territories of the West Bank of the Jordan River. Disagreements between the Israeli and Palestinian populations over the sources, control, and allocation of scarce surface and ground water are contributing to the conflict there. Quantifying the equitable distribution of these resources, while fraught with technical and political difficulties, would go a long way toward reducing tensions there.

PREVENTION OF SIGNIFICANT HARM TO OTHER STATES. Another principle of the Law on Non-Navigational Uses of International Watercourses, though perhaps subordinate to the principle of equitable utilization, is the obligation not to cause significant harm to other states through actions to international watercourses. Often the maxim, "sic utere tuo ut alienum non laedas"—use your property in a way not to injure others—is cited. This principle says that a state is responsible for preventing actions within its borders that would harm the activities or property of another state. As sometimes applied, however, this principle permits harmful actions but requires compensation or mitigation as acceptable alternatives to avoidance. A major complication in applying this principle is the difficulty in quantifying downstream environmental and economic impacts and in determining the extent of responsibility for those impacts resulting from upstream activities. The dispute between Hungary and Slovakia over the Gabcikovo/Nagymaros project on the Danube arose in part because of Hungary's perception that the project would lead to significant environmental damage in Hungary. Particularly worrisome was the possibility of contamination of one of the largest untapped ground water supplies in the region. The unwillingness of Slovakia to redesign the project or to do a complete environmental assessment led Hungary to abrogate the 1977 agreement with Czechoslovakia to construct the project.

OBLIGATION TO NOTIFY AND INFORM. Both the Helsinki Rules and the International Law Commission recommendations state that nations have an obligation to notify and inform other nations of any activities on shared watercourses that will affect them. Such notification permits the affected state to negotiate mitigation or to protest and, perhaps, modify or prevent the action. One recent application of this principle was Turkey's closure of the Atatürk Dam on the Euphrates River in 1991 in order to fill the reservoir behind the dam. Prior to taking action, Turkey notified the downstream nations of this closure, which effectively reduced the flow in the river to zero for approximately one month. Although both Syria and Iraq complained, Turkey's obligation to notify under the principles of international water law was met.

OBLIGATION TO SHARE DATA. The obligation to share data is reaching widespread acceptance, but there are still several regions of the world where some basic water-resources data are considered classified and are withheld from neighboring nations. For example, many data on river flows in India are considered state secrets. Similarly, Israel classifies as secret some water supply and use data, particularly data from the disputed territories. Releasing all water-resources data, and setting up a mechanism to ensure wide access to those data, would help reduce tensions in the Middle East over water.[58] Unless all basin states share hydrologic data, no satisfactory agreements on allocations, responses during shortages, and flood management and planning can be reached. International organizations, such as those under the umbrella of the United Nations or scientific associations, should actively encourage the collection and open sharing of water-resource data.

COOPERATIVE MANAGEMENT OF INTERNATIONAL RIVERS. The International Law Commission is considering adoption of a "principle of participation" that affirms the duty of all basin states to participate in the development, use, and protection of shared water resources. Such participation would generally take the form of a joint basin commission empowered to negotiate disputes and resolve questions of resource allocation. Establishing such a commission does not ensure successful or effective management, in part because nations only reluctantly grant decisionmaking power to multinational bodies. Other problems arise if the commission does not include *all* affected participants. One example is the Nile commission—the Permanent Joint Technical Committee—set up by the 1959 treaty between the Sudan and Egypt, which does not include the other seven riparian nations along the Nile. While these other nations have played only a small part in the hydropolitics of the region in the past, several are now beginning to view the

---

58. Peter H. Gleick, "Reducing the risks of conflict over fresh water resources in the Middle East," in Hillel Shuval and Jad Isaac, eds., *Proceedings of the First Israeli-Palestinian International Academic Conference on Water Resources,* December 10–13, 1992, Zurich, Switzerland (Netherlands: Elsevier Publishers, forthcoming 1993).

waters of the Nile as an important resource for their future development. Their exclusion from the 1959 Treaty complicates the debate now underway.

OBLIGATION TO RESOLVE DISPUTES PEACEFULLY. The Charter of the United Nations requires that nations resolve all disputes, not just those over water resources, without resorting to force. Because international shared water resources have been the source of violent conflicts in the past, international negotiations over water law devote considerable time and effort to identifying non-violent approaches to resolving disputes. When combined with the principle of cooperative management, this often leads to the suggested creation of joint basin management commissions with the authority to receive and investigate complaints, and to offer findings to the governments of the affected parties. Recourse is sometimes made to the International Court of Appeals in The Hague, as in the Hungarian-Slovakian dispute over the Gabcikovo project described above, but unless both parties agree to accept The Hague's jurisdiction, this mechanism has limited success. In the case of Gabcikovo, Czechoslovakia rejected the jurisdiction of the International Court of Appeals and other means of dispute resolution were sought.

TREATIES

Until now, individual water treaties covering river basins have been more effective, albeit on a far more limited regional basis, than the broader principles described above. International treaties concerning shared fresh water resources extend back centuries and there are hundreds of international river treaties covering everything from navigation to water quality to water rights allocations. For example, freedom of navigation was granted to a monastery in Europe in the year 805, and a bilateral treaty on the Weser River, which today flows through Germany into the North Sea, was signed in 1221.[59] Such treaties have helped reduce the risks of water conflicts in many areas, but some of them are beginning to fail as changing levels of development alter the water needs of regions and nations. The 1959 Nile River Treaty, the 1977 Agreement on Sharing of the Ganges Waters (now expired, but still observed), and some limited bilateral agreements on the Euphrates between Iraq and Syria, and between Iraq and Turkey, are good examples of treaties now under pressure because of changes in the political and resource condi-

---

59. Food and Agriculture Organization, *Systematic Index of International Water Resources Treaties, Declarations, Acts and Cases by Basin,* Legislative Study No. 15 (Rome: Food and Agriculture Organization of the United Nations, 1978). This index is irregularly updated.

tions of the region. India and Nepal agreed by a December 1991 treaty to go forward on hydroelectric, irrigation, and flood control projects that have been pending for many decades. Yet this agreement does not include Bangladesh, which will certainly be affected by any changes in the flows of the Ganges, and which may claim to have been deprived of its equitable share of the benefits of the Ganges, or to have been appreciably harmed by the projects.[60]

To make both regional treaties and broader international agreements over water more flexible, detailed mechanisms for conflict resolution and negotiations must be developed, basic hydrologic data must be acquired and completely shared with all parties, flexible rather than fixed water allocations are needed, and strategies for sharing shortages and apportioning responsibilities for floods need to be developed before shortages become an important factor. For example, both the 1944 Colorado River treaty between the United States and Mexico and the 1959 Nile River treaty between Egypt and the Sudan allocate fixed quantities of water, based on assumptions about the total average flows of each river. However, mistaken estimates of average flows, or future climatic changes that could alter flows, would make this type of rigid allocation ripe for disputes. Proportional sharing agreements, if they include agreements for openly sharing all hydrologic data, can help to reduce the risk of conflicts over water, and modifications to these treaties should be undertaken by their signatories now, before such changes become evident.

In sum, existing institutions appear sufficient to design and implement the kinds of conflict resolution mechanisms described above, but some major improvements in them are needed. The UN has played an important role, through the International Law Commission, in developing guidelines and principles for internationally shared watercourses, but it should continue to press for the adoption and application of the principles in water-tense regions such as the Middle East, central and southern Asia, and parts of Europe. Similarly, bilateral or multilateral river treaties have been effective in the past, but they should consistently include all affected parties, they should include a joint management committee empowered to negotiate disputes, and they should be flexible enough to adapt to long-term changes in hydrologic conditions, such as those that may result from global climatic change. Finally, as disputes over shared ground water resources become far more important

---

60. McCaffrey, "Water, Politics, and International Law."

and common in the future, international ground water law and principles must be better developed.

Conclusions

Water already contributes to conflicts among nations, and future conflicts over water are increasingly likely. Nations fight over access to water resources in some regions of the world and use water and water-supply systems as instruments of war, while growing populations and development are increasing the competition for limited water supplies, and many countries depend on sources of supply that are under the control of other nations.

Human needs for water are growing. Many countries in the Middle East and elsewhere already use water at a rate faster than natural processes can replenish it, leading to falling ground water levels, reliance on expensive desalination projects, and imports of water across borders. Oddball schemes that would have been laughed at a few decades ago are now being implemented or seriously considered, including the importation of water in tankers, pipelines thousands of kilometers long, or the diversion of icebergs from the polar regions.

Global climatic changes will increase the demand for water for human and industrial uses, change irrigation requirements, and alter in unpredictable ways the availability and quality of fresh water resources. Countries or regions that use a significant fraction of their total available supply are vulnerable to slight changes in flow or water quality. Countries or regions with considerable dependence on irrigation water or hydroelectricity are vulnerable to changes in flow and the vagaries of a changing climate.

The Middle East and the Persian Gulf exhibit many vulnerabilities to water-related conflict, as do certain countries of Africa, Europe, and southern and central Asia. Given the high level of political conflict already evident in some of these areas, and the inability of nations in these regions to reach agreements on water sharing, future water-related disputes appear inevitable. Conflicts over the Nile, the Jordan, the Euphrates, the rivers of Central Asia, and the Ganges/Brahmaputra river systems appear increasingly likely because of growing competition for limited water resources, or because of disputes over the ownership and the right to use the resource. Disputes may also arise because of the contamination of shared water by upstream parties on the Colorado, the Rhine, and the Mekong; because of the complications of managing multiple interests in a river, such as with the Danube, the

Mekong, the Niger, and the Zambezi; or because of the difficulty of rationally sharing hydroelectric generation on international rivers, such as the Zambezi and the Paraná.

Water-related disputes are more likely to lead to political confrontations and negotiations than to violent conflict. But recent disturbing examples of water-related conflicts, the apparent willingness to use water-supply systems as targets and tools of war, and growing disparities among nations between water availability and demand make it urgent that we work to reduce the probability and consequences of water-related conflict. Hydrologists and water-resources specialists must begin to collect and more widely disseminate data on the supply and use of shared water resources, and on ways of reducing inefficient uses of water. International legal experts must better understand the links among natural resource needs, national sovereignty, and water rights. And academic and military scholars need to better understand the threats of conflict arising from a wide range of resource and environmental problems, and to hone the tools for preventing those conflicts.

Bridging the Divide | *Miriam R. Lowi*

Transboundary Resource Disputes and the Case of West Bank Water

"It appears equally clear that along with other outstanding issues of the Palestine dispute—compensation, repatriation, Jerusalem, boundaries—there is a fifth element, water, which must be considered as we approach a final settlement."
—U.S. Department of State Position Paper, May 4, 1953.[1]

At the second round of Middle East peace talks, held in Moscow in January 1992, the participants agreed to the formation of working groups on five substantive issues of mutual concern—refugees, the environment, economic development, arms control, and water resources. Established within the framework of the multilateral track of the peace process, these working groups were to meet separately, but simultaneously with the bilateral negotiating teams. The implicit objective was that each would draw inspiration from the other; in other words, progress, in the form of agreements, for example, at the "technical" level would have positive repercussions at the political level, and vice versa.

To date, the water resources working group has met twice: in Vienna in May 1992, and in Washington in September 1992. The discussions have not gone far beyond agreement on the obvious: that there is not enough water in the region, that consumption demand is growing, that water quality has been deteriorating rapidly. Lengthy discussions have taken place on the problem of data collection, and the parties have agreed that under more favorable political conditions, it would be important to share data. There it stands.

Miriam Lowi is a visiting fellow at the Center for Energy and Environmental Studies, Princeton University.

An earlier version of this article was commissioned by the American Academy of Arts and Sciences—University of Toronto, Peace and Conflict Studies Program, for their joint project on "Environmental Change and Acute Conflict." The final version of this article was written at the Center for Energy and Environmental Studies, Princeton University. The author wishes to thank these institutions for their support, and the following individuals for their helpful comments on earlier drafts: Jeffrey Boutwell, David Brooks, Rex Brynen, Sharif Elmusa, Abdellah Hammoudi, Thomas Homer-Dixon, John Kolars, Charles Lawson, Zachary Lockman, Henry Lowi, Thomas Naff, Susan Ossman, Avrum Udovitch, Aaron Wolf, and the participants at the Water Resources Workshop, University of Toronto (June 15–17, 1991).

1. *Foreign Relations of the United States*, Vol. 9, No. 604, pp. 1185–88.

International Security, Vol. 18, No. 1, (Summer 1993), pp. 113–138
© 1993 by the President and Fellows of Harvard College and the Massachusetts Institute of Technology.

In the five working groups, significant headway has been impeded by the "high politics" conflict. Both sides, but especially the Arabs, have been reluctant to enter into binding agreements, even on seemingly technical matters, in the absence of a political settlement on the core issue of dispute: the future status of the territories occupied by Israel in June 1967. This is not surprising, given the history of the dispute over the Jordan waters and the various efforts to resolve it.

This paper considers the linkage between "low politics" and "high politics" in conflict resolution, as it relates to resource scarcity, resource dependence, and the Arab-Israeli conflict, and especially with the issue of water in the Jordan River basin.[2] More specifically, I focus on Israel's dependence on the subterranean water supply of the West Bank and its effects on the prospects for a political settlement in the region.[3]

---

2. Until recently, the linkages between resource scarcity and national security concerns attracted little interest in the social sciences. But see Sara Hoagland and Susan Conbere, "Environmental Stress and National Security," Center for Global Change, University of Maryland, February 1991; Thomas Homer-Dixon, "On the Threshold: Environmental Changes as Causes of Acute Conflict," *International Security*, Vol. 16, No. 2 (Fall 1991), pp. 76–116; R. Lipschutz, "Sustainable Resource Management and Global Security," *Resources and Security Working Paper*, No. 5 (Berkeley, Calif.: Pacific Institute, October 26, 1989); Miriam R. Lowi, *Water and Power: The Politics of a Scarce Resource in the Jordan River Basin* (Cambridge: Cambridge University Press, 1993); Jessica Tuchman Matthews, "Redefining Security," *Foreign Affairs*, Vol. 68, No. 2 (Spring 1989); Harold and Margaret Sprout, "Environmental Factors in the Study of International Politics," *Journal of Conflict Resolution*, Vol. 1, No. 4 (1957), pp. 309–328; Richard H. Ullman, "Redefining Security," *International Security*, Vol. 8, No. 1 (Summer 1983), pp. 129–153. Moreover, the notion of environmental degradation of renewable resources such as water is only slowly being recognized as a potential source of conflict. Often a result of rapid population growth, over-exploitation of local resources, and external climatic phenomena, environmental stresses pose increasing challenges to traditional concepts of security. In the domestic arena, environmental degradation and societal unrest may result from demand for a resource exceeding its supply; Ted Gurr, "On the Political Consequences of Economic Scarcity and Decline," *International Studies Quarterly*, Vol. 29 (1985), pp. 51–75. Thomas Naff makes a similar argument with regard to water resources in the Kingdom of Jordan: "Testimony before the House Committee on Foreign Affairs: Subcommittee on Europe and the Middle East," *The Middle East in the 1990s: Middle East Water Issues* (Washington, D.C., June 26, 1990). At the international level, as well, patterns of resource use within or among countries, or a dwindling of the available regional or global supply of the resource, could result in competition, conflict, and threats to security. See, for example, Nazli Choucri and R. North, *Nations in Conflict* (San Francisco: W.H. Freeman, 1975); Geoffrey Kemp, "Scarcity and Strategy," *Foreign Affairs*, Vol. 56, No. 2 (January 1978); Ronnie Lipschutz, *When Nations Clash: Raw Materials, Ideology and Foreign Policy* (New York: Ballinger, 1989); Arthur H. Westing, ed., *Global Resources and International Conflict: Environmental Factors in Strategic Policy and Action* (Oxford: Oxford University Press, 1986).

3. The case of West Bank water is only one element of the water dispute in the Jordan-Yarmouk basin. Other conflicts include the utilization of the Yarmouk River, the question of a Mediterranean–Dead Sea or a Red Sea–Dead Sea canal, and the exploitation of groundwater south of the Dead Sea.

I begin by sketching the availability of water resources in Palestine/Israel and the extent of their utilization. I demonstrate the degree to which Israel is dependent upon water that originates in occupied territory. A brief overview is then provided of the importance of both water resources and the West Bank in Israeli security thinking. Following that, I outline Israel's West Bank water policies and some of the effects they have had on the physical, social, and economic environment of the territory. Next, in an effort to relate the issue of water resources more directly to the current Middle East peace process, I discuss the various lessons that can be learned from the history of the Jordan waters dispute about conflict resolution in the Israeli-Arab-Palestinian arena. Finally, I discuss a variety of possible arrangements for sharing and managing water resources in the basin, if and when a political settlement has been reached.

The Jordan River Basin

The Jordan Basin is an elongated valley in the central Middle East. Draining some 18,300 square kilometers, it extends from Mount Hermon in the north to the Dead Sea in the south, and lies within the pre–June 1967 boundaries of Israel, Jordan, Lebanon, and Syria. Its waters, which originate in rainfall and in rivers and streams of the riparian states, drain the land east and west of the Jordan Valley. Precipitation in the basin ranges from over 1000 mm/yr (millimeters per year) in the north to less than 50 mm/yr in the south, but averages less than 200 mm/yr on both sides of the Jordan River.[4] Much of the basin, therefore, is arid or semi-arid, and requires irrigation water for agricultural development. (See Table 1.)

While the basin extends into four states, about eighty percent of it is located in present-day Israel, Jordan, and the West Bank. It is these lands that are the most dependent upon its waters. The political conflict in the region has, since its inception, been intertwined with a dispute over access to the water resources of the Jordan basin.[5] Prior to the 1967 War, the water dispute engaged the four basin states. Since June 1967, when at least one of the

---

4. Moshe Inbar and Jacob Maos, "Water Resource Planning and Development in the Northern Jordan Valley," *Water International*, Vol. 9, No. 1 (1984), p. 19.
5. For a study of the Jordan waters conflict from its inception until the present day, see Lowi, *Water and Power*.

Table 1. Jordan Basin: Principal Surface Waters.

River	Source	Direction	Political control	Discharge (mcm/yr)[a]
Hasbani	Lebanon	South to Upper Jordan River	Lebanon Israel post-82	138
Banias	Syria	South to Upper Jordan River	Syria pre-67 Israel post-67	121
Dan	Israel	"	Israel	245
Upper Jordan		South to Lake Tiberias	Israel	650
Lower Jordan		South to Dead Sea	Israel/Jordan	1200[b]
Yarmouk	Syria	Southwest to Lower Jordan	Syria/Jordan/Israel	450

NOTES:
a. These figures represent average flow under "normal" climatic conditions and prior to extractions for irrigation and development. Discharge figures for the Upper and Lower Jordan include the contributions of tributaries and other sources. In this article, million cubic meters (mcm) is used as the standard measure of water volume. One cubic meter of water equals 1,000 kilograms in weight, or one metric ton.
b. This figure represents the flow into the Dead Sea until the early 1950s, prior to the inception of development schemes in the basin. Today, the flow is no more than 100 mcm per annum. Moreover, the waters of the Jordan River below Lake Tiberias are of poor quality. They are highly saline and cannot be used for most agricultural purposes. Over the years, this portion of the river has become little more than a drainage ditch.
SOURCE: Compiled by author from Charles T. Main, Inc., *The Unified Development of the Water Resources of the Jordan Valley Region* (Boston: Charles T. Main, Inc., 1953).

upstream states, Syria, lost its superior riparian position to Israeli forces, the water dispute has engaged Israel, Jordan, and the West Bank.[6]

The West Bank, so named because of its location relative to the Jordan River, covers an area of 5584 square kilometers, or 5946 square kilometers if one includes East Jerusalem.[7] It borders the Negev Desert to the south, the

6. Syria, however, has retained its upstream status on the Yarmouk and so is party to discussions concerning Yarmouk River water.
7. Thomas Naff, "The Jordan Basin: Political, Economic, and Institutional Issues," in Guy LeMoigne, Shawki Barghouti, Gershon Feder, Lisa Garbus, and Mei Xie, eds., *Country Experiences with Water Resources Management: Economic, Institutional, Technological and Environmental Issues*, World Bank Technical Paper No. 175 (Washington, D.C.: The World Bank, 1992), p. 115.

coastal plain to the west, the Galilee to the north, and the Jordan River and the Kingdom of Jordan to the east. The territory comprises hilly regions in the north, west, and center, valley lands in the east, and desert in the southeast.

Water Resources and their Utilization

Israel's overall water inventory is limited, unevenly distributed, and subject to rather high, climatically determined fluctuations. The country has a Mediterranean climate, varying from semi-arid in the north to arid in the south. More than one-half the area of the country receives an annual average of less than 200 millimeters of rain.[8]

Israel's water resources are unfavorably located in relation to its main areas of demand. Water is most plentiful in the north and northeast, but the densest concentrations of population, industry, and irrigable land are in the center of the country and in the coastal plain. There are also timing problems with the distribution of water. Streamflow and storm-water runoff are at their peak during the winter months, whereas consumption peaks at the height of the irrigation season in July and August. Moreover, drought years and even successions of drought years are not at all uncommon. Finally, the extent of stream flow available to Israel is small. The annual volume of the Upper Jordan River at the northern tip of Lake Tiberias, Israel's largest exploitable body of surface water, represents less than one-third of the country's total demand. In contrast, approximately three-fifths of the country's total renewable water potential—that is, 1200 mcm out of 1900 mcm—originates from groundwater, located in three principal aquiferous formations.[9] The coastal plain aquifer and the more abundant Yarqon-Taninim aquifer (also called the "mountain" or "western" aquifer) in the mountainous north-

8. M. Jacobs and Y. Litwin, "A Survey of Water Resources Development, Utilization and Management in Israel," in V.T. Chow, et al., eds., *Water for the Human Environment*, vol. 2 (Chicago: Proceedings of the First World Congress on Water Resources, September 24–28, 1973), pp. 231–232; Jehoshua Schwarz, "Israeli Water Sector Review: Past Achievements, Current Problems, and Future Options," in Le Moigne, et al., *Country Experiences*, p. 129.
9. Groundwater refers to that part of rainfall that seeps into the ground and, upon reaching the water table, moves as subterranean flow. Much of the groundwater appears as the perennial flow in springs and wadis (seasonal streams). Where the geological formations are favorable, groundwater may be obtained as a source of supply by pumping from wells. In order to be considered a gain in total water resources, the supply from groundwater thus obtained must be so located that it would not be recoverable from the springs and wadis.

east and center of geographic Palestine provide the bulk of the groundwater supply.[10] (See Table 2.)

Because of the rapid increase in population and the marked expansion of irrigated area since 1949, demands on the limited resources of the country have been great. By 1989, Israel's population had quadrupled in size, while irrigated area increased sevenfold. Total water consumption increased more than eight-fold.[11] Since the mid-1970s, in fact, consumption of fresh water has exceeded the country's sustainable annual water yield—the fixed quantity of water available on a yearly basis. And the prospects for the development of yet unexploited conventional fresh water resources remain extremely limited.[12]

Table 2. Israel: Renewable Fresh Water Resources (1984/85).

Source	Quantity (mcm/yr)
River flow	
Upper Jordan	580
Yarmouk	100–125
Groundwater	1205
Floodwater	15
Wastewater	30–110
Losses	(60)
Total	1870–1970

SOURCE: Compiled by author from Associates for Middle East Research Data Base (Philadelphia: University of Pennsylvania); Schwarz, *Water Sector Review*; Arnon Sofer, *Neharot shel Eish* (Rivers of Fire) (Tel. Aviv: Am Oved Publishers, 1992).

10. Jacobs and Litwin, *Survey of Water Resources Development*, pp. 226–227.

11.

	Population	Irrigated area	Water consumption (mcm/yr)
1949	1,059,000	30,000 ha.	230
1977	3,575,000	186,500 ha.	1660
1989	4,200,000	217,000 ha.	1950

Itzhak Galnoor, "Water Policymaking in Israel," in Hillel I. Shuval ed., *Water Quality Management under Conditions of Scarcity* (New York: Academic Press, 1980), p. 289; Schwarz, *Israeli Water Sector Review*, p. 130.

12. Indeed, it is only through recycling wastewater that net additions can be achieved. Jacobs and Litwin, *Survey of Water Resources Development*, p. 231; Yaacov Vardi, "National Water Re-

During the basin-wide drought conditions of the 1980s, supply constraints intensified considerably. Israeli consumption of water in agriculture had to be reduced for the first time in 1986.[13] Since then, the government has been forced to cut back the sector's allocation on two occasions, in order to satisfy urban and industrial demand. While the cutback was a mere ten percent in 1986, it was thirty-seven percent in 1990. Given supply constraints and population growth projections, these trends toward increasing scarcity are bound to continue.[14]

Israel's 1991 population of 4.4 million is expected to reach 6.4 million in the year 2000.[15] According to one source, the consumption of water in Israel, including the Golan Heights and Jewish settlements on the West Bank, was 2100–2200 mcm per year in 1991, while the total renewable fresh water supply was about 1950 mcm.[16] Moreover, demand for fresh water is expected to increase by thirty percent: it will reach 2800–2900 mcm between the years 2015 and 2020. However, supply projections for Israel—excluding the Occupied Territories—for the year 2010, for example, do not exceed 2060 mcm.[17] (See Table 3.)

In the absence of additional sources of surface water, groundwater tends to be over-exploited, thereby diminishing its quality and threatening its future availability. Since in any given year the sustainable annual yield is a fixed quantity, excess withdrawals by over-pumping or depletion of underground reserves constitute an overdraft that could cause irreversible damage. Over-pumping lowers the water table, increasing the danger of salt water infiltration. When the reserve of underground flow sinks below a certain level in the coastal aquifer, the interface, or dividing line, between fresh and sea water is drawn upward and causes salination.[18] Israel has been over-pumping groundwater sources since 1970; some hydrologists maintain that

sources Planning and Development in Israel–the Endangered Resource," in Shuval, *Water Quality Management under Conditions of Scarcity*, p. 42; Schwarz, *Israeli Water Sector Review*, p. 133.

13. *Jerusalem Post*, March 24, 1986, p. 1.

14. Joyce R. Starr, "Water Wars," *Foreign Policy*, No. 82 (Spring 1991), p. 25; United States Department of State, Bureau of Intelligence and Research, *Geographic Notes*, No. 13 (March 1, 1991), p. 5.

15. Schwarz, *Israeli Water Sector Review*, p. 130.

16. Associates for Middle East Research, Data Base.

17. Ibid.

18. Itzhak Galnoor, "Water Planning: Who Gets the Last Drop?" in Raphaella Bilski, Itzhak Galnoor, Dan Inbar, Yohanan Manor, and Gabriel Sheffer, eds., *Can Planning Replace Politics? The Israeli Experience* (The Hague: Martinus Nijhoff Publishers, 1980), pp. 141–142.

Table 3. Population, Water Supply and Demand Projections.

	Israel	West Bank	Jordan
Population			
1990	4.6 million[a]	1.8 million[b]	3.2 million
2020	6.7	4.7	9.8
Water Supply			
1985	1950 mcm[c]	650 mcm	900 mcm
Drought[d]	1600[e]	450–550	700–750
2010	2060		
Water Demand			
1987–91	2100 mcm[a]	125 mcm[f]	800 mcm
2020	2800	530	1800

NOTES:
a. Includes Jewish settlements in Occupied Territories and Golan Heights.
b. Arab population of West Bank and Gaza Strip.
c. This figure includes about 520 mcm of groundwater originating in the West Bank.
d. Average annual supply of water during drought conditions of 1980s.
e. This figure includes some portion of groundwater originating in the West Bank.
f. Demand for water by the Arab population of the West Bank alone.
SOURCE: Associates for Middle East Research Data Base.

since 1980, 200 mcm have been over-pumped on an annual basis. Indeed, the deteriorating quality of the water supply has become a cause of growing concern.[19]

The critical point about the groundwater sources upon which the state of Israel is dependent is their location and direction of flow. Of the three main aquifer groups, only one is located in Israel proper, beneath the coastal plain. This is the second most abundant of the three main aquifer groups. The remaining two originate in occupied territory. The Yarqon-Taninim aquifer—the most abundant—extends from north to south, along the western foothills of the West Bank. Its natural recharge flows west across the Green Line (the 1949 United Nations Armistice Demarcation line) into Israel's coastal plain. The least abundant—those aquifer groups in the northern part of the West Bank—drain an area across the Green Line as well, and discharge into the Bet She'an and Jezre'el Valleys. Both the western and northern basins can

19. Interview by author with a spokesman for Mekorot, Israel's National Water Authority, Tel-Aviv, June 15, 1986; Fred Pearce, "Wells of Conflict on the West Bank," *New Scientist* (June 1, 1991), p. 37.

be tapped from either side of the Green Line. However, only five percent of the combined recharge area of the two water tables is located in Israel proper.[20] Another group of aquifers, the smallest of the West Bank water tables, forms the eastern drainage basin. Its water does not traverse the Armistice Demarcation line and hence cannot be exploited outside the territory. Its flow discharges into the Jordan Valley.[21] (See Table 4). Thus, about 475 mcm, or forty percent of Israel's sustainable annual supply of groundwater, and one-quarter of its total renewable fresh water supply, originate in occupied territory.

The water resources of the West Bank consist of surface run-off and groundwater. There is considerable variation in published discharge figures, which range from a total of about 650 mcm per annum to as much as 900 mcm.[22] No matter which of the figures one considers, what is significant about total availability is that the consumption of water by the Arab population of the West Bank in the 1980s has not been allowed to exceed 125 mcm, or 14–18 percent of total availability.[23] Hence, the remainder, between 525–775 mcm minus what is lost to evaporation or surface run-off before it can be utilized, represents the quantity that can be exploited by the non-Arab population, and/or beyond the territory of the West Bank.

Until the mid-1960s, agriculture on the West Bank—then under Jordanian jurisdiction—was mostly rainfed.[24] The limited irrigated agriculture that did

---

20. Declassified document on West Bank water, provided to author by the Department of State, Government of the United States (n.d.).

21. Jehoshua Schwarz, "Water Resources in Judea, Samaria, and the Gaza Strip," in Daniel Elazar, ed., *Judea, Samaria, and Gaza: Views on the Present and the Future* (Washington, D.C.: American Enterprise Institute for Public Policy Research, 1982), pp. 88–91.

22.

Source	Surface run-off	Groundwater	Total
Naff			650 mcm
Schwarz	105–165 mcm	580 mcm	685–745
USG		850	
Dakkak	176	724	900

Ibrahim Dakkak, "al-Siyaasa al-Ma'iya f'il Difa al-Gharbiya al-Muhtala" (Water Policy on the Occupied West Bank) *Shu'un Filastiniyah*, Vol. 126 (May 1982), p. 38, based on *West Bank Hydrology* (London: Rofe and Raffety Consulting Engineers, 1965), p. 15; Naff, *Jordan Basin*, p. 115; Schwarz, "Water Resources in Judea," pp. 85, 90; Department of State document, p. 2.

23. Dakkak, *Water Policy*, pp. 38–39; David Kahan, *Agriculture and Water in the West Bank and Gaza* (Jerusalem: The West Bank Data Base Project, 1983), p. 25; Shawkat Mahmoud, "al-Zira'a w-al-Miyaa f-il-Dafa al-Gharbiya taht al-Ihtilaal al-Isra'ili" (Agriculture and Water on the West Bank under the Israeli Occupation), *Samed al-Iqtisadi*, Vol. 6, No. 52 (November–December 1984), p. 19; Schwarz, "Water Resources in Judea," p. 91.

24. On West Bank agriculture, see Kahan, *Agriculture and Water*, pp. 6–23. Precipitation on the West Bank ranges from 800 millimeters per annum in the Judean hills to 400–500 millimeters in the foothills. It diminishes rapidly as one moves eastward toward the Jordan River and the

exist was largely dependent upon spring water. Only a few wells were sunk, and those were primarily for household consumption. Nonetheless, by June 1967, the total output of wells on the western slopes and in the Jordan Valley was 38 mcm.[25]

Water and the West Bank in Israeli Security Thinking

The establishment of the state of Israel was, to a considerable degree, the product of the Zionist movement's concerns for the security and survival of world Jewry. European Zionists of the late nineteenth century argued that Jews would continue to be persecuted until they constituted a majority in a territory over which they held sovereign control. Hence, the answer to what was referred to as the "Jewish Question" was the founding of a Jewish

Table 4. Principal Aquifers from which Israel Draws Water.

	Drainage Area	**Direction of Flow**	**Safe Yield[a]**
In Israel:			
Coastal plain	1800 sq. km.	West	240–300 mcm
In West Bank:			
Western basin	1600 sq. km.	West	335[b]
Northern basin	590	North	130–140

NOTES:

a. The remainder of about 430 mcm of groundwater (the difference between the total quantity of groundwater consumed by Israel and the safe yield of the principal aquifers) is drawn from a variety of other, smaller aquifers throughout the country, as well as from over-pumping the principal subterranean basins.

b. In February 1993, an Israeli geographer told this author that Israel now takes 390 mcm per annum from the western basin; in other words, the aquifer is over-exploited by at least 55 mcm per annum.

SOURCE: Associates for Middle East Research Data Base; Schwarz, "Water Resources in Judea," pp. 85–90.

Dead Sea. In the Jordan Valley, for example, precipitation ranges from 200 millimeters in the north to 50 millimeters in the south. Agriculture in the valley is possible only with irrigation. Efraim Orni and Elisha Efrat, *Geography of Israel* (Jerusalem: Israel Universities Press, 1971), p. 58.

25. Dakkak, *Water Policy*, pp. 41–42.

national home and the "ingathering of the exiles."[26] This position was given irreversible momentum with the rise of Nazism in central Europe in the 1930s and the subsequent extermination of six million Jews.

From the outset of the Zionist movement's endeavors, unrestricted access to water resources was perceived as a non-negotiable prerequisite for the survival of a Jewish national home. In fact, concerns for the economic viability of a Jewish state in arid Palestine prompted the World Zionist Organization to insist, at the Paris Peace Conference on February 3, 1919, that it was "of vital importance not only to secure all water resources already feeding the country, but also to be able to conserve and control them at their sources."[27] With that in mind, the Organization submitted a frontier claim to the conference that included the whole of the Jordan River basin and headwaters, as well as most of the Litani River.[28]

In addition to drawing a relationship between water resources and the economic viability of the Jewish state, the Zionist movement considered water to be important insofar as it was part of the "ideology of agriculture" in Zionist thought.[29] By working the land, Jews would be returning to *Eretz Yisrael* (the Land of Israel) in the most literal sense. Moreover, to Socialist Zionism, which dominated the movement from its inception through the 1930s, the "ideal man" is he who tills the land. And in keeping with socialist doctrine, he who tills the land has rights to it.

In time, however, agriculture—and by extension, water—became related to defense and defense imperatives. Not only was it essential to be on the land in order to lay claim to it, but also, to quote one Israeli interviewed: "Jews must work the land—all the land. Because if not, it will be occupied by Arabs. This would be the end of the Jewish state."[30] Agricultural development has remained a national goal, embodying a socially accepted value and dictated by ideology.

Water, because it is an essential ingredient of agriculture, was and continues to be important to Zionists and to the state of Israel. It has always been

---

26. Ben Halpern, *The Idea of the Jewish State* (Cambridge: Harvard University Press, 1969); Walter Laqueur, *A History of Zionism* (New York: Schocken Books, 1972).

27. "The Zionist Organization's Memorandum to the Supreme Council at the Peace Conference," in J. C. Hurewitz, *Diplomacy in the Near and Middle East*, Vol. 2 (Princeton: Van Nostrand, 1956), p. 48.

28. H.F. Frischwasser-Ra'anan, *The Frontiers of a Nation* (Westport, Conn.: Hyperion Press, 1955), p. 107. Nonetheless, the demands of the Zionists were not met.

29. Laqueur, *History of Zionism*.

30. Interview by author with an Israeli geomorphologist and expert on water development, Haifa, June 21, 1986.

linked in some fashion to their security-related concerns, whether of an ideological, economic, or political nature. The primacy of water resources in the continued survival of the Jewish state has been elucidated unequivocally by former Prime Minister Moshe Sharett:

Water for Israel is not a luxury; it is not just a desirable and helpful addition to our system of natural resources. *Water is life itself.* It is bread for the nation—and not only bread. Without large irrigation works we will not reach high production levels . . . to achieve economic independence. And without irrigation we will not create an agriculture worthy of the name . . . and without agriculture. . . . we will not be a nation rooted in its land, sure of its survival, stable in its character, controlling all opportunities of production with material and spiritual resource.[31]

THE SIGNIFICANCE OF THE WEST BANK

Since the Arab-Israeli War of June 1967, the continued occupation of the West Bank has remained, for the most part, basic to the official rhetoric with regard to the security of the state. In most government circles, retaining control over the territory has been perceived as the solution to the problem of Israel's geographic vulnerability. Within the pre-1967 boundaries, 67 percent of the population of the state of Israel and 80 percent of big industry are located in the narrowest portion of the country; the coastal plain is less than 14 kilometers wide in the north, just over 20 kilometers in the center, and about 30 kilometers in the south. In other words, not only is there no "strategic depth" between the Mediterranean Sea and the Green Line, but Israel is also strategically the most vulnerable precisely where it is economically and demographically the strongest.[32] Hence, the dominant view is that Israeli control of the West Bank enhances the state's capabilities. It offers strategic depth and provides a natural frontier, the Jordan River to the east, which could be more easily defended than could the Green Line, the Armistice Demarcation line of 1949. Moreover, by providing land for the "ingath-

---

31. Quoted in Michael Brecher, *Decisions in Israel's Foreign Policy* (New Haven, Conn.: Yale University Press, 1975), p. 184, from *Divrei Ha-Knesset*, Vol. 15 (November 30, 1953), pp. 270–271.
32. Michel Foucher, "Israël-Palestine: quelles frontières?" *Hérodote*, 2e–3e trimestres (1983), p. 111; Dan Horowitz, "The Israeli Concept of National Security and the Prospects of Peace in the Middle East," in Gabriel Sheffer, ed., *Dynamics of a Conflict: A Re-examination of the Arab-Israeli Conflict* (Highlands, N.J.: Humanities Press International, 1975), p. 251; Michael Mandelbaum, *The Fate of Nations: The Search for National Security in the Nineteenth and Twentieth Centuries* (Cambridge, U.K.: Cambridge University Press, 1988), p. 318.

ering of exiles," it serves the ideological interests of the state and affords the possibility of narrowing the margin of quantitative inferiority.

In addition, continued occupation of the West Bank guarantees the state control over vital water supplies that originate in the West Bank but are consumed, for the most part, in Israel.[33] This suggests why it is considered essential for Israel to control and determine the extent of utilization of this resource. It highlights the indisputable significance of the West Bank for the security and development concerns of the state, and exposes one of the major reasons why Israel will not easily relinquish control over the territory. In part because of the links between the water resources of the West Bank and the survival of the State of Israel, accepting an independent Palestinian state on the West Bank, and hence relinquishing control of the territory's resources, is interpreted by some as equivalent to an act of national suicide.[34] Without access to the rich groundwater supplies of the West Bank, Israel, in the worst case scenario, could be denied about 500 mcm of water per annum. A former Israeli water commissioner has referred to the water issue as a "time bomb" that would eventually demolish any political arrangements with regard to the future status of the Occupied Territories, unless they included a satisfactory solution to struggles for access to and control over water resources.[35] In the Arab-Israeli conflict, water resources and national security are thus intimately linked.

Israel's West Bank Water Policies

Israel's water resources are administered by the Israeli Water Commission, which is subject to the authority of the Minister of Agriculture. Two other institutions are part of the Water Commission Administration: Mekorot, Israel's national water authority, and Tahal, the Water Planning for Israel Company. Mekorot is responsible for the construction of irrigation and water supply projects, and Tahal for the overall planning and design of water

---

33. Thomas Stauffer, "The Price of Peace: The Spoils of War," *American-Arab Affairs*, No. 1 (Summer 1982), p. 45.
34. Consider the following statement made by the Likud party in its campaign literature before the Israeli election of November 1988: "Judea and Samaria boast 40 percent of Israel's available fresh water supply. . . . Water is our life. As such, it makes no sense to place it in the hands of those whose intentions toward us may not always be the kindest." Alan Cowell, "Next Flashpoint in Middle East: Water," *New York Times*, April 16, 1989.
35. Lea Spector, "Waters of Controversy: Implications for the Arab-Israel Peace Process" (New York: Foreign Affairs Dept., American-Jewish Committee, December 1980), p. 11.

development projects. Since July 1967, the water resources of the Occupied Territories have gradually been integrated into the Israeli water system, and now are under the direct control of the Water Commission.[36] The policy set forth by the commissioner allows West Bank Arabs a total consumption of 125 mcm per annum, plus limited growth in personal consumption.

Stringent measures have been adopted to ensure that this policy is respected. First, no wells can be drilled on the West Bank without permission from the Civil Administration, Tahal, and Mekorot. No Palestinian Arab individual or village has received permission to drill a new well for agricultural purposes since July 1967, nor to repair one that is close to an Israeli well.[37] Sinking wells on the mountain ridge, the location of the Yarqon-Taninim aquifer, is strictly forbidden to anyone but Mekorot.[38] Occasionally, permission is granted for the drilling of wells designed for household use. With regard to Arab requests, a former water commissioner, Meir Ben-Meir, has said: "If their demand is for drinking water, we must say yes. . . . We do say yes. But we are not going to stop irrigating our orchards so they can plant new ones."[39]

Second, for the agricultural activities of West Bank Arabs, only "existing uses" of water are recognized, and the term refers to uses which existed in 1967–68.[40] Thus, water allocations to Arab agriculture have remained at their 1968 level of 100 mcm, with a slight margin for growth. Third, the technology for deep-drilling and rock-drilling—which would be required in the western basin, at least—remains in Israeli hands. Fourth, West Bank Arabs are not allowed to use water for farming after four o'clock in the afternoon.[41] Fifth,

---

36. Uri Davis, Antonia Maks, and John Richardson, "Israel's Water Policies," *Journal of Palestine Studies*, Vol. 9, No. 2 (Winter 1980), p. 13; Jeffrey D. Dillman, "Water Rights in the Occupied Territories," *Journal of Palestine Studies*, Vol. 19, No. 1 (Autumn 1989), p. 54.
37. Meron Benvenisti, *The West Bank Data Project: A Survey of Israel's Policies* (Washington, D.C.: American Enterprise Institute for Public Policy Research and West Bank Data Base Project, 1984), p. 14; Dillman, "Water Rights," p. 56; House Committee on Foreign Affairs, *Middle East in the 1990s*, p. 187; Department of State document.
38. Kahan, *Agriculture and Water*, p. 28.
39. Ned Temko, "Water—Toughest Issue on West Bank," *Christian Science Monitor*, September 18, 1979.
40. Interview by author with Israeli water engineer, formerly with Tahal, Tel-Aviv, June 26, 1986.
41. House Committee on Foreign Affairs, *Middle East in the 1990s*, p. 187. This is a curious regulation. In hot, dry climates, the best times of day for irrigating during the hot seasons (six months per year) are early in the morning and late in the afternoon or evening; irrigating at night is not uncommon. At these times, there is significantly less evaporation than there is between 10 a.m. and 4 p.m., the hottest time of day. Moreover, there is less risk of destroying

strict limits are placed on the amount of water that can be pumped annually from each well. Meters fixed to wells monitor the amounts extracted. In 1983, the total quantity of well-water permitted to the Arab population did not exceed the 1967 level of 38 mcm.[42] Finally, whereas the water utilized by Jewish settlers is heavily subsidized by the state, West Bank Palestinians receive no subsidy at all.[43] They pay a higher price per cubic meter of water than do Jewish settlers. It has been estimated that in 1990, Palestinians were paying as much as six times more for water than were the settlers.[44]

ARAB AND ISRAELI USAGE OF WEST BANK WATER

While Palestinian Arabs have been prevented from sinking new wells for agriculture, Mekorot drilled thirty-six wells on the West Bank between July 1967 and 1989 for the domestic and irrigation needs of Jewish settlements. Of these, at least twenty are in the Jordan Valley and ten on the mountainous western fringe.[45] Unlike Arab wells, which rarely exceed depths of 100 meters, those drilled by Mekorot are between 200 and 750 meters deep.[46] Greater depths allow for superior output and water quality. While Arab extractions have remained fixed at their 1968 level of 38 mcm, Jewish settlements, in the early 1980s, were consuming close to 50 percent of the total amount of water pumped on the West Bank.[47] By 1987, the inequality of the distribution of water resources had sharpened yet further. *Le Monde* reported that West Bank Arabs were receiving barely more than 20 percent of the total volume of water pumped from the territory.[48]

---

plants and their roots. Intense watering turns soil to mud; and when hot sun beats down on mud, plants rot.

42. Interview by author with former deputy mayor of Jerusalem, June 8, 1986; Dakkak, "Water Policy," pp. 44, 60; Kahan, *Agriculture and Water*, p. 167; Mahmoud, "Agriculture and Water on the West Bank," p. 21. The total quantity of water available to West Bank Palestinians for agricultural, municipal and industrial consumption is about 125 mcm per annum. Of the approximately 100 mcm of water consumed in agriculture, only 38 mcm is pumped by the Palestinians directly from their wells.

43. House Committee on Foreign Affairs, *Middle East in the 1990s*, p. 187.

44. Thomas Naff, testimony before the House Committee on Foreign Affairs; ibid.

45. Department of State document.

46. Kahan, *Agriculture and Water*, p. 167; Mahmoud, "Agriculture and Water on the West Bank," p. 8; Department of State document.

47. Dakkak, "Water Policy," p. 42; Kahan, *Agriculture and Water*, pp. 165–167. The figure of 38 mcm pumped by the Palestinian population excludes extractions from approximately 300 fresh water springs and a small amount from the Jordan River, as well as the 2 mcm of well water that the Palestinians receive directly from Mekorot.

48. J.-P. Langellier, "Guerre de l'Eau en Cisjordanie," *Le Monde*, November 7, 1987.

At the end of the 1980s, Palestinians were receiving 16–17 percent of water that originates on the West Bank. (See Table 5.) The most recent statistics gauge Israel's usage, within Israel proper, of water from the West Bank aquifers at 560 mcm per annum, and Jewish settlements on the West Bank, with a total population of approximately 70,000 (excluding East Jerusalem), at an additional 40–50 mcm per annum. In contrast, the one million West Bank Palestinians are permitted a maximum of 125 mcm under the Israeli-imposed quota.[49] Moreover, it has been reported that, in their projections for the year 2000, the Israeli water authorities plan to allot some 150 mcm for the Arab population of the West Bank, who will then number well over one million, and 110 mcm for the expected 100,000 Israeli settlers. These figures represent a per capita water allocation that is ten times greater for Jewish settlers than for West Bank Palestinians.[50]

The total land area of the West Bank, excluding East Jerusalem, is about 560,000 hectares (an area roughly the size of Delaware). Of this, approximately one-third is cultivated.[51] (See Table 6.) Today, just under seven percent of the cultivated area of the West Bank is irrigated, in contrast to Israel, where 45–50 percent is irrigated.[52] In 1989, the cultivated area of Jewish

Table 5. Consumption of West Bank Water (1988–89).

Consumer	Population	Consumed (mcm/yr.)
Israelis (inside 'Green Line')	4,200,000	560
Settlers (excluding East Jerusalem)	70,000	40–50
West Bank Arabs	1,000,000	125

SOURCE: Compiled by author from Associates for Middle East Research Data Base; John Kolars, "The Course of Water in the Arab Middle East," *American-Arab Affairs*, No. 33 (Summer 1990); Department of State document.

49. John Kolars, "The Course of Water in the Arab Middle East," *American-Arab Affairs*, No. 33 (Summer 1990), pp. 66–67; Department of State document. Apparently, it was reported in the Israeli press in May 1990 that West Bank Palestinians were consuming only 12.5 percent of West Bank water, while Jews on the West Bank and inside Israel proper were consuming a total of 87.5 percent. House Committee on Foreign Affairs, *Middle East in the 1990s*, p. 187.
50. Department of State document.
51. Foucher, "Israël-Palestine," p. 118.
52. Department of State document; Dakkak, "Water Policy," p. 48, says that only four percent of the cultivated area of the West Bank is irrigated; Elisha Kally says seven percent in the West Bank–Gaza Strip in total. See also Kally, *A Middle East Water Plan under Peace* (The Armand

Table 6. West Bank: Cultivated and Irrigated Area by population (1989).

	Total (hectares)	Arabs	Jews
Land area	560,000		
Cultivated area	200,000	190,000 ha.	9,030 ha.
as % of total cult. area		95%	4.5%
Irrigated area	13,000	4,873 ha.	8,127 ha.
as % of tot. irrig. area		37%	62%
as % of own cult. area		2.5%	90%

SOURCE: Associates for Middle East Research Data Base; Department of State document; Foucher, "Israël-Palestine"; Kahan, *Agriculture and Water.*

settlements represented less than five percent (9,030 hectares) of the total cultivated area in the West Bank. However, as much as ninety percent of the Jewish cultivated area is irrigated.[53]

The most striking differential in water use can be found in the Jordan Valley. There, Jewish settlers who farm one-quarter of the cultivated area use 45 percent of the water consumed by agriculture in the valley. In contrast, Arab farmers with three times as much cultivated land consume only slightly more water (55 percent).[54]

Furthermore, Jewish settlers are said to consume four times more water per capita than do West Bank Arabs: about 300 liters per capita per day, as opposed to 76 liters.[55] According to one source, the Palestinian average in some areas of the West Bank has gone down since the beginning of the *intifada* to less than 44 litres per capita per day—"less than the United Nations reckons is necessary for maintaining minimal health standards."[56]

Hammer Fund for Economic Cooperation in the Middle East, Tel-Aviv University, March 1986), p. 8.
53. Kahan, *Agriculture and Water*, pp. 66–67. Department of State document. The latter maintains that by the late 1980s, almost seventy percent of the settlers' cultivated area was irrigated. The former claims that in the mid-1980s, the cultivated area of Jewish settlements was less than two percent of the total cultivated area.
54. Kahan, *Agriculture and Water*, p. 165.
55. House Committee on Foreign Affairs, *Middle East in the 1990s*, p. 187; Kolars, "Course of Water," p. 66. These figures are not significantly different from those of an Israeli source who has told this author that today (early 1993), Israeli Jews, including settlers on the West Bank, consume 100 cubic meters of water per person per year (equivalent to 273 liters per person per day), while West Bank and Gaza Strip Palestinians consume less than 30 cubic meters per person (82 liters per person per day).
56. House Committee on Foreign Affairs, *Middle East in the 1990s*, p. 187.

Effects of Israel's West Bank Policies

Israel's water policies and land acquisition and settlement strategies have caused significant changes to the West Bank economy and society.[57] Efforts have been made to integrate the Occupied Territories into the Israeli economy and to prevent the establishment of an independent economic infrastructure that could serve as the infrastructure for a Palestinian state.[58] Restructuring West Bank agriculture has facilitated the integration of this sector into the Israeli economy. Crop production, for example, is regulated by the Israeli authorities; Palestinian farmers are not permitted to grow crops that would compete with Israeli agriculture. Moreover, to sell their products in Israel, West Bank farmers must have permits, and those are highly restrictive and difficult to obtain.[59] As a result of these measures, farming has become increasingly unprofitable for many Palestinians, and food imports are constantly increasing.

Because of the declining profitability of agriculture, the loss of cultivated land to settlements, an increasingly saline water supply, a considerable portion of the Palestinian peasantry has abandoned agricultural activity. Many of those who left agriculture have joined the swelling ranks of the unemployed or work as unskilled day laborers inside the Green Line. In 1979, there were 75,000 Palestinians from the West Bank and Gaza Strip working in Israel. By 1988, there were more than 100,000 day laborers from the West Bank alone.[60]

---

57. On Israel's land acquisition and settlement strategies, see Abdul-ilah Abu Ayyash, "Israeli Planning Policy in the Occupied Territories," *Journal of Palestine Studies*, Vol. 11, No. 1 (Autumn 1981); Peter Demant, "Les implantations israéliennes dans les térritoires occupées," *Hérodote*, 2è-3è trimestres (1983), pp. 155–186; Alain Dieckhoff, *Les espaces d'Israël* (Paris: Fondations pour les Etudes de Défense Nationale, 1987); Elisha Efrat, *Geography and Politics in Israel since 1967* (London: Frank Cass, 1988); Baruch Kimmerling, *Zionism and Territory* (Berkeley: Institute of International Studies, University of California, 1983); Ibrahim Matar, "Settlements in the West Bank and Gaza Strip," *Journal of Palestine Studies*, Vol. 11, No. 1 (Autumn 1981). According to Alasdair Drysdale and Gerald H. Blake, *The Middle East and North Africa: A Political Geography* (New York: Oxford University Press), p. 304, conservative estimates hold that by 1982, Israel had appropriated 160,000 to 166,000 hectares of the West Bank's total land area of 587,000 hectares (including East Jerusalem), that is, almost 30 percent.
58. Efrat, *Geography and Politics*, p. 69.
59. Dillman, "Water Rights," p. 64; Kahan, *Agriculture and Water*; interview by author with World Bank water expert, Washington, D.C., April 11, 1991.
60. Abu Ayyash, "Israeli Planning Policy"; Demant, "Implantations israéliennes," p. 184; Efrat, *Geography and Politics*, p. 68; Foucher, "Israël-Palestine," p. 115. Also, in part because of the economy, an estimated 20,000 Arabs leave the territories annually. Drysdale and Blake, *Middle East and North Africa*, p. 305.

Israeli measures to control water development have had environmental effects on Palestinian agriculture. To take one example, where well-drilling for Jewish settlements is carried out in close proximity to Palestinian springs or wells, the result has frequently been a marked decline in the output of the springs and a lowering of the water level in the wells.[61] This is due largely to the fact that Mekorot has the technology to drill deep wells after extensive geological surveying, in contrast to Palestinian farmers who drill shallower wells in convenient locations.[62] The deeper the well (and the more geologically sound its location), the more abundant its water supply and the better equipped it is to resist contamination, salt-water encroachment, and the harsh effects of drought. In addition, when two wells are located within the effective radius of each other, the deeper one tends to milk the water supply of the shallower one. When this is coupled with absence or sparseness of rainfall, the shallower well is gradually sucked dry.

The problem of salinity is a very serious one. Jericho, in the Jordan Valley, is one of three principal areas of Palestinian irrigated agriculture. It is also the area in which competition with Israel over cultivable land and irrigation water is the most severe.[63] However, the increased salinity of Jericho's water supply—largely the result of the proximity of shallow wells to deeper wells—has substantially reduced the size of the annual banana crop. In fact, it has been reported that during the 1980s, the total cultivated area of the West Bank shrank by several tens of thousand hectares due to saline water, the confiscation of agricultural land, and the declining profitability of agriculture.[64]

Although figures vary considerably, the absolute limit on West Bank water use—that is, the sustainable annual yield minus what is lost to evaporation or surface run-off—is, according to one study, about 650 mcm per year.[65] However, it has been reported that in the spring of 1990, the combined water allocations for West Bank Arabs, Jewish settlers, and the amount reaching

---

61. Dakkak, "Water Policy," p. 44; Paul Quiring, "Israeli Settlements and Palestinian Rights, Part 2," *Middle East International* (October 1978), pp. 14–15; Temko, "Water—Toughest Issue"; Khalil Touma, "Bethlehem Plan Further Threatens Scarce Water Resources," *Al-Fajr* (Qatar), July 26, 1987, pp. 8–9; "Proposed Israeli Well will Deepen West Bank Water Crisis," *Al-Fajr*, July 5, 1987, p. 3; "Water Supply under Occupation," *Al-Awdah* English Weekly, October 12, 1987, pp. 19–23; United Nations, Committee on the Exercise of the Inalienable Rights of the Palestinian People, *Israel's Policy on the West Bank Water Resources* (New York: UN, 1980), pp. 13–15.
62. Department of State document.
63. Ibid.; Dillman, "Water Rights", p. 57.
64. Department of State document.
65. Naff, in House Committee on Foreign Affairs, *Middle East in the 1990s*, p. 187.

Israel was estimated at 807 mcm per year. This represents an annual water deficit of almost 200 mcm, due to the over-exploitation of the western and northeastern basins.[66]

By 1982, over-utilization had led to a drop in the water table at a rate of 0.3 to 0.4 meters per annum in the western basin and, according to some sources, of almost two meters in part of the northeastern basin.[67] This constitutes a grave potential danger to the continued intensive utilization of groundwater. Furthermore, overpumping will increase the salinity of the entire aquifer system of the West Bank, beginning in the coastal region and moving inland.[68]

Of the 200,000 hectares of cultivated land on the West Bank, in the early 1980s, roughly 13,000 were under irrigation. According to a report by Tahal, there remained approximately 53,500 hectares of potentially irrigable land. An additional 200 mcm of water would be required to bring this land under irrigation.[69] However, as the water resources of the territory are already almost fully committed, such development cannot take place. The Israeli water establishment contends that the West Bank suffers from acute water shortage, more so than does Israel proper.[70]

It is true that there is more irrigable land on the West Bank than water currently available for new uses. Hence, some analysts argue that the future development of the territory is "totally dependent upon imports of water from outside sources."[71] What is equally true, however, is that a large portion

---

66. Kolars, "Course of Water," p. 66. The following table demonstrates the extent of water deficit or surplus, as calculated by the author, given Kolars' figure of a combined allocation of roughly 807 mcm:

	Year	Total usable water	(Deficit)/surplus
Kolars	1990	615 mcm	(192) mcm/yr
Naff (House)*	1990		(150)
Schwarz	1982	685–745	(122)–(62)
State**	1990	850	43
Dakkak	1982	900	93

* House Committee on Foreign Affairs
** Department of State document

67. Department of State document; Schwarz, "Water Resources in Judea," pp. 92–93. The eastern water table, the smallest of the three West Bank aquifers, is the principal Palestinian water source and the only one that is not yet overused.
68. Department of State document.
69. Kahan, *Agriculture and Water*, pp. 20–23, 111.
70. Interview by author with an Israeli water engineer, formerly with Tahal, Tel-Aviv, June 26, 1986.
71. Kally, *Middle East Water Plan*, p. 5.

of the West Bank water supply is exploited beyond the territory's frontiers. Hence, if even part of what is currently tapped outside were made available to the local population, there would be the resources with which to irrigate the remaining irrigable land. Indeed, all of the West Bank's current and even anticipated future needs could be met if the waters of the western basin alone were available for local consumption.[72]

Nonetheless, it is important to remember that the waters of the western basin drain naturally toward Israel's coastal plain. They do not respect boundary markings nor Armistice Demarcation lines. Nor are there any clearly-defined international laws prohibiting the exploitation of groundwater across political frontiers.[73]

Resolving Riparian Dispute: Lessons from the Jordan Basin

The development of river basins as indivisible units, irrespective of political boundaries, has been advocated as optimal by planners, politicians, and jurists, and has been adopted as policy in multi-national agreements in several basins, including the Mekong (1957), Columbia (1961), and Senegal (1963).[74] Unitary basin-wide development is consistent with a functionalist approach to conflict resolution: the idea that on-going functional cooperation among adversaries and the creation of supra-national task-related organizations is the most promising avenue to achieving peace.[75]

---

72. Interview by author with water engineer, Tel-Aviv, June 26, 1986.
73. See Ludwik A. Teclaff and Albert E. Utton, *International Groundwater Law* (London/Rome/ N.Y.: Oceana Publications, 1981), pp. 1–75.
74. On the internationalization of river basins and its advantages, see C.B. Bourne, "The Development of International Water Resources: the Drainage Basin Approach," *The Canadian Bar Review*, Vol. 47, No. 1 (March 1969), pp. 62–82; A.H. Garretson, et al., eds., *The Law of International Drainage Basins* (Dobbs Ferry, N.Y.: Oceana Publications, 1967); Albert Lepawsky, "International Development of River Resources," *International Affairs*, Vol. 39 (1963), pp. 533–550; Ludwick A. Teclaff, *The River Basin in History and Law* (The Hague: Martinus Nijhoff, 1967).
75. Functionalists argue that the combination of wide sacrifices in national sovereignty, on-going functional cooperation, and the creation of supra-national task-related organizations creates a strong foundation for peaceful relations. According to David Mitrany, the architect of political functionalism, "Every activity organized in that way would be a layer of peaceful life," insofar as "economic unification would build up the foundation for political agreement." Mitrany, *A Working Peace System* (Chicago: Quadrangle Books, 1986 (Chicago: Quadrangle Books, 1986 [first published 1943]), pp. 48, 58, 97–98. An ever-widening range of interdependencies in economic, technical, and welfare areas would not only enmesh governments, but would also encourage actors to set aside their political differences. Functional integration would, it is argued, eventually spill over into more broadly-based regional peace.

On two occasions in the history of the conflict over the Jordan waters, the U.S. government responded to the acute need for resource development in the states of the Jordan-Yarmouk watershed by actively supporting functional, basin-wide projects. In both cases, the government hoped that the implementation of these projects would serve as catalysts to peace in the region.[76] As suggested by functionalist theory, the United States viewed regional development as a stepping-stone to regional peace, given that projects would require on-going multilateral cooperation in the use of water resources. It believed that solving water problems would provide the climate necessary for resolving larger inter-state conflicts. But both efforts fell short of their objectives.

In the first of these two cases, in 1953, a broad, regional plan was drawn up by an American engineering firm to use the water of the Jordan River basin for the irrigation and hydro-electric power needs of the four riparian states. President Eisenhower appointed Eric Johnston as his personal representative to secure agreement from the riparians to the Unified Plan. The mediation effort was conducted in four rounds of negotiation over a two-year period.

Throughout the negotiating process, there was constant disagreement over allocations of water and locations of storage sites, as well as conflicting views of rights, needs, and international legal precedents. Eventually, both sides admitted that the plan was acceptable on technical grounds. However, the League of Arab States was against it for political reasons; it could not agree to cooperate with and enhance the development of a state with which it was engaged in a protracted conflict that hinged on issues of identity, recognition, and territorial sovereignty. In 1955, the mediation effort came to a halt.

In the late 1970s, the U.S. government again tried to promote regional water development as a stepping-stone to regional peace. This time, the issue was the impounding of the Yarmouk River waters behind a proposed dam at Maqarin, so that Jordan could utilize the winter flow which, until then, had been "going to waste." The Carter administration announced that it would fund a large portion of the construction, if Jordan reached an understanding on water allocations with Syria, the upstream riparian, and with Israel, the downstream riparian.

---

76. For detailed analysis of these two episodes, see Lowi, *Water and Power,* chapters four and eight.

Over a three-year period, Philip Habib, then U.S. assistant secretary of state, shuttled among the three capitals trying to get an agreement. Again, there was constant haggling over allocations of water and locations of usage. Syria wanted to use Yarmouk water upstream before it flowed into the dam, and Israel wanted to be guaranteed a certain amount of water for the West Bank. In the meantime, Jordan's need for access to the Yarmouk waters was increasing; the country was facing severe water shortages. By 1981, the talks broke down. Syria would not approve the Maqarin Dam project since it would entail cooperation with Israel and would be located within reach of Israeli artillery. And Jordan would not approve the usage of Yarmouk water for Jewish settlements in occupied territory. As with the Unified Plan, the Maqarin project was laid to rest.[77]

On both occasions in the history of the Jordan waters conflict, the U.S. government did what the functionalists prescribe: it treated the highly-charged psychological environment in the central Middle East as an abstraction in its attempts to resolve some of the tensions in the region. However, the Arabs and Israelis could not do likewise. The possibility of sharing water in the Jordan basin could not be unlinked from the political conflict. Implicit in water use arrangements was formal acceptance of the other side and its rights as a political entity. Politics could not be bypassed, nor could ideological issues be neutralized.

These episodes suggest that states that are antagonists in the "high politics" of war and diplomacy are not likely to agree willingly to extensive collaboration in the sphere of "low politics," centered around economic and welfare issues. Hence, caution is warranted: one should not expect basin-wide solutions to the water problem to be effected while the larger "high politics" issues remain contentious. It may be that cooperation in water utilization requires, at the outset, the positive resolution of political conflict.[78]

Nonetheless, water sharing is sure to be one of the thorniest issues to resolve in any future negotiations. One Israeli analyst notes that: "The Arab

---

77. The idea to build a dam on the Yarmouk was revived once again in 1987, with the signing of a treaty between Syria and Jordan. The United States Department of State acted as mediator between Israel and Jordan from September 1989 to August 1990. The negotiations broke down, however, with the Iraqi invasion of Kuwait. Information on this project—the Unity (*al-Wahdah*) dam—derives from House Committee on Foreign Affairs, *Middle East in the 1990s*, as well as from personal interviews with U.S. government officials, Washington, D.C., April 1991. An Israeli source, very close to the negotiations, told this author that the negotiations were discontinued because of Israel's insistence on a guarantee of a specific quantity of water from the river.
78. These arguments are developed more fully in Lowi, *Water and Power*.

population in Judea and Samaria may have a claim to the waters that flow underground, and that is one-third of Israel's water supply. The Arabs could say that Israel is using their water."[79] The Palestinians will certainly demand a greater share of the water than they now have access to, while Israel will not voluntarily cede sizable portions of what it currently exploits from the West Bank.

Sharing the Waters of the West Bank

The resolution of the political conflict would open the way for resolving the water conflict. However, establishing a just distribution of West Bank water would entail many complicated issues. Below I outline a three-stage process by which these issues might be addressed and a reasonable and just allocation of West Bank water determined.[80] Such a process might be incorporated into a treaty, or proposed by a third-party mediator. It could be carried out under the auspices of a multilateral body such as the United Nations or the World Bank.

First, the parties might agree to form an independent, international panel of experts, and to abide by the results of its studies. Its task would be to evaluate with precision the status of water resources and the nature and extent of their utilization. It would collect data in order to determine the amount of water available for use from West Bank sources; the locations, directions of flow and destinations of the various bodies; and their rates of flow and migration. Included among the panel's tasks would be to determine the extent of water demand in Palestinian and Israeli areas by evaluating existing use patterns. To get an idea of changes to demand in the future, it may consider rates of population growth and projected changes in economic activities that could affect water consumption. The panel could also investigate the possibilities for meeting demand from alternate sources of a technological nature, such as desalinization, cloud-seeding, or sewage reclamation.

The second stage would involve deciding on water allocations from each aquifer based on the results of the studies conducted in the first stage of the

---

79. Interview by author with Israeli geographer and specialist on water resources, Haifa, June 22, 1986.
80. I am grateful to a World Bank expert for his lengthy discussion with me (Washington, D.C., April 11, 1991) on this issue.

process. Once the panel fixed the allocations, the West Bank population would have the right to pump to the extent of its quota from the specified aquifers, while leaving the remainder to flow freely across the border.

In the final stage, the international panel would establish a monitoring system to oversee allocations. This could include meters on wells and springs to gauge extractions, and international inspectors at extraction sites to supervise and scrutinize allocations and to record any obvious changes in flow patterns. In addition, the multilateral body might establish mechanisms for arbitration and the imposition of sanctions.

With peace in the Middle East, unitary basin-wide development of water resources under supra-national authority could also be reconsidered. Indeed, in terms of geography, economic efficiency, and human welfare, this represents the ideal solution to the satisfaction of competing needs and conflicting interests in an international river basin. Moreover, if it became apparent that the waters of the basin were insufficient for meeting the needs of the basin states, then, with a favorable political climate, it might be feasible to "import" water from outside. In recent years, the interest in this solution to water scarcity has inspired a variety of proposals. In the early 1980s, for example, Jordan considered the feasibility of a project to carry about 160 mcm of water through a pipeline from the Euphrates River in Iraq to the kingdom's northern plateau.[81] A Tel-Aviv University–Armand Hammer Fund project drew up a Middle East water-sharing plan that includes details for the transfer of Nile water to Israel, Jordan, the West Bank, and Gaza Strip, and the transfer of Litani water to Israel, Jordan, and the West Bank.[82] More recently, Turkey's president Turgut Ozal championed the concept of a "peace pipeline" that would transport water from two Turkish rivers, the Seyhan and Ceyhan, southward to Syria, Jordan, Saudi Arabia, and the other Gulf states.[83] And for the past year, a Canadian company has been trying to market a highly imaginative project: the transfer of as much as 250 mcm of water from Turkey to Israel in enormous containers—referred to as "Medusa bags"—that would be floated across the Mediterranean.

---

81. Interview by author with a former president of the Jordan Valley Authority, Amman, December 3, 1985; Selig A. Taubenblatt, "The Jordan River Basin Water Dilemma: A Challenge for the 1990s," in Joyce Starr and Daniel Stoll, eds., *The Politics of Scarcity: Water in the Middle East* (Boulder, Colo.: Westview, 1988).
82. Kally, *Middle East Water Plan*, pp. 20–50.
83. Cem Duna, "Turkey's Peace Pipeline," in Starr and Stoll, eds., *Politics of Scarcity*, pp. 119–124; Kolars, "Course of Water," p. 61; Starr, "Water Wars," pp. 28–29.

The resolution of protracted conflict would open up vast possibilities for functional cooperation. However, this must not be viewed as the entire solution to resource scarcity in adversarial settings. For, in addition to resolving their political disputes, the states of the central Middle East must take bold measures to curtail excessive and wasteful consumption of water, especially by their agricultural sectors.[84] This means that they must reconsider the size and importance of agriculture in their economies, revise the choice of crops grown, and phase out the production of water-intensive crops such as cotton, tomatoes, lettuce, bananas. Concurrently, they must adopt the most effective water-conservation technologies. There may be little justification for states that are between sixty and eighty percent desert and have high population growth rates to earmark as much as seventy percent of their water supply for agricultural sectors which, relative to the availability of water, are quite inefficient.[85] Such states may have no choice in the near future but to face the politically sensitive question of whether to take land out of agriculture.

Revamping agriculture does not require the end of regional political conflict. However, if conflict is not brought to an end, states in arid regions will be forced to continue to rely on, at best, sub-optimal solutions of a purely domestic and piecemeal nature. At worst, they may be tempted to adopt policies of an aggressive and imperialistic nature in response to the constraints posed by scarcity.[86] Given the stresses on water supplies in Israel, Jordan, the West Bank and Gaza Strip—among them, the absence of additional unexploited sources, population growth trends, and recurrent drought conditions—basin-wide arrangements for sharing and utilizing water are crucial for the long-term stability of the region. A political settlement of the Arab-Israeli conflict is the first step in that direction. The alternative is very likely to be increasing scarcity and war.

---

84. In Israel, for example, a country which is about sixty percent desert, water is consumed at the rate of 280–300 liters per capita per day. This rate is as high as that found in some advanced industrialized states. House Committee on Foreign Affairs, *Middle East in the 1990s*, p. 22.

85. In the last few years, Jordan's agricultural sector has been consuming about seventy-four percent of the water supply, down from over eighty percent in the early 1980s. Like Israel, it has been forced to take water out of agriculture to meet the domestic demand of a rapidly growing population. Kally, *Middle East Water Plan*, p. 14; Elias Salameh, "Jordan's Water Resources: Development and Future Prospects," *American-Arab Affairs*, No. 33 (Summer 1990), p. 74.

86. Choucri and North, *Nations in Conflict*.

Environmental Scarcities and Violent Conflict

Thomas F. Homer-Dixon

Evidence from Cases

Within the next fifty years, the planet's human population will probably pass nine billion, and global economic output may quintuple. Largely as a result, scarcities of renewable resources will increase sharply. The total area of high-quality agricultural land will drop, as will the extent of forests and the number of species they sustain. Coming generations will also see the widespread depletion and degradation of aquifers, rivers, and other water resources; the decline of many fisheries; and perhaps significant climate change.

If such "environmental scarcities" become severe, could they precipitate violent civil or international conflict? I have previously surveyed the issues and evidence surrounding this question and proposed an agenda for further research.[1] Here I report the results of an international research project guided by this agenda.[2] Following a brief review of my original hypotheses and the project's research design, I present several general findings of this research that led me to revise the original hypotheses. The article continues with an account of empirical evidence for and against the revised hypotheses, and it concludes with an assessment of the implications of environmentally induced conflict for international security.

Thomas F. Homer-Dixon is Assistant Professor of Political Science and Director of the Peace and Conflict Studies Program at the University of Toronto. From 1990 to 1993, he was co-director and lead researcher of the Project on Environmental Change and Acute Conflict.

Portions of this article have been drawn from Thomas Homer-Dixon, Jeffrey Boutwell, and George Rathjens, "Environmental Scarcity and Violent Conflict," *Scientific American*, February 1993; and from Homer-Dixon, "Environmental Scarcity and Global Security" *Headline Series* (New York: Foreign Policy Association, 1993). The author thanks the participants in the Project on Environmental Change and Acute Conflict, especially project co-directors Jeffrey Boutwell and George Rathjens. The Donner Canadian Foundation funded the article's preparation.

---

1. Thomas Homer-Dixon, "On the Threshold: Environmental Changes As Causes of Acute Conflict," *International Security*, Vol. 16, No. 2 (Fall 1991), pp. 76–116.
2. The three-year Project on Environmental Change and Acute Conflict brought together a team of thirty researchers from ten countries. It was sponsored by the American Academy of Arts and Sciences and the Peace and Conflict Studies Program at the University of Toronto.

International Security, Vol. 19, No. 1 (Summer 1994), pp. 5–40
© 1994 by the President and Fellows of Harvard College and the Massachusetts Institute of Technology.

In brief, our research showed that environmental scarcities are already contributing to violent conflicts in many parts of the developing world. These conflicts are probably the early signs of an upsurge of violence in the coming decades that will be induced or aggravated by scarcity. The violence will usually be sub-national, persistent, and diffuse. Poor societies will be particularly affected since they are less able to buffer themselves from environmental scarcities and the social crises they cause. These societies are, in fact, already suffering acute hardship from shortages of water, forests, and especially fertile land.

Social conflict is not always a bad thing: mass mobilization and civil strife can produce opportunities for beneficial change in the distribution of land and wealth and in processes of governance. But fast-moving, unpredictable, and complex environmental problems can overwhelm efforts at constructive social reform. Moreover, scarcity can sharply increase demands on key institutions, such as the state, while it simultaneously reduces their capacity to meet those demands. These pressures increase the chance that the state will either fragment or become more authoritarian. The negative effects of severe environmental scarcity are therefore likely to outweigh the positive.

General Findings

Our research was intended to provide a foundation for further work. We therefore focused on two key preliminary questions: does environmental scarcity cause violent conflict? And, if it does, how does it operate?

The research was structured as I proposed in my previous article. Six types of environmental change were identified as plausible causes of violent inter-group conflict:

- greenhouse-induced climate change;
- stratospheric ozone depletion;
- degradation and loss of good agricultural land;
- degradation and removal of forests;
- depletion and pollution of fresh water supplies; and
- depletion of fisheries.

We used three hypotheses to link these changes with violent conflict. First, we suggested that decreasing supplies of physically controllable environmental resources, such as clean water and good agricultural land, would provoke interstate "simple-scarcity" conflicts or resource wars. Second, we hypothesized that large population movements caused by environmental stress would induce "group-identity" conflicts, especially ethnic clashes. And third, we suggested that severe environmental scarcity would simultaneously increase economic deprivation and disrupt key social institutions, which in turn would cause "deprivation" conflicts such as civil strife and insurgency.

Two detailed case studies were completed for each of the three research hypotheses.[3] By selecting cases that appeared, *prima facie*, to show a link between environmental change and conflict, we sought to falsify the null hypothesis that environmental scarcity does not cause violent conflict. By carefully tracing the causal processes in each case, we also sought to identify how environmental scarcity operates, if and when it is a cause of conflict. The completed case studies were reviewed at a series of workshops of leading experts; in light of these findings, I revised the original hypotheses, identified common variables and processes across the cases, and examined the revised hypotheses in light of the case-study evidence. The project's conclusions were reviewed by a core team of experts. The following are four general findings of this research effort.

RESOURCE DEPLETION AND DEGRADATION

Of the major environmental changes facing humankind, degradation and depletion of agricultural land, forests, water, and fish will contribute more to social turmoil in coming decades than will climate change or ozone depletion.

When analysts and policymakers in developed countries consider the social impacts of large-scale environmental change, they focus undue attention on climate change and stratospheric ozone depletion.[4] But vast populations in the developing world are already suffering from shortages of good land, water, forests, and fish; in contrast, the social effects of climate change and ozone depletion will probably not be seen till well into the next century. If

---

3. On simple-scarcity conflicts, we examined water in the Jordan and Nile River basins and the Southern African region; on environmentally induced group-identity conflicts, we focused on Bangladesh-Assam and the Miskito Indians in Nicaragua; and on economic decline and civil strife, we studied the Philippines and China. Researchers in the project also investigated the 1989 conflict in the Senegal River basin, the 1969 Soccer War between El Salvador and Honduras, the rise of the Sendero Luminoso in Peru, migration and civil strife in Haiti, and migration from black homelands in South Africa.

4. For example, see David Wirth, "Climate Chaos," *Foreign Policy*, No. 74 (Spring 1989), pp. 3–22; and Neville Brown, "Climate, Ecology and International Security," *Survival*, Vol. 31, No. 6 (November/December 1989), pp. 519–532.

these atmospheric problems do eventually have an impact, they will most likely operate not as individual environmental stresses, but in interaction with other, long-present resource, demographic, and economic pressures that have gradually eroded the buffering capacity of some societies.

Mexico, for example, is vulnerable to such interactions. People are already leaving the state of Oaxaca because of drought and soil erosion. Researchers estimate that future global warming could decrease Mexican rainfed maize production up to forty percent. This change could in turn interact with ongoing land degradation, free trade (because Mexico's comparative advantage is in water-intensive fruits and vegetables), and the privatization of communal peasant lands to cause grave internal conflict.[5]

ENVIRONMENTAL SCARCITY

Environmental change is only one of three main sources of scarcity of renewable resources; the others are population growth and unequal social distribution of resources. The concept "environmental scarcity" encompasses all three sources.

Analysts often usefully characterize environmental problems as resource scarcities. Resources can be roughly divided into two groups: non-renewables, like oil and iron ore, and renewables, like fresh water, forests, fertile soils, and the earth's ozone layer. The latter category includes renewable "goods" such as fisheries and timber, and renewable "services" such as regional hydrological cycles and a benign climate.

The commonly used term "environmental change" refers to a human-induced decline in the quantity or quality of a renewable resource that occurs faster than it is renewed by natural processes. But this concept limits the scope of environment-conflict research. Environmental change is only one of three main sources of renewable-resource scarcity. The second, population growth, reduces a resource's per-capita availability by dividing it among more and more people.[6] The third, unequal resource distribution, concentrates a

---

5. Diana Liverman, "The Impacts of Global Warming in Mexico: Uncertainty, Vulnerability and Response," in Jurgen Schmandt and Judith Clarkson, eds., *The Regions and Global Warming: Impacts and Response Strategies* (New York: Oxford University Press, 1992), pp. 44–68; and Diana Liverman and Karen O'Brien, "Global Warming and Climate Change in Mexico," *Global Environmental Change*, Vol. 1, No. 4 (December 1991), pp. 351–364.
6. Peter Gleick provides a potent illustration of the effect of population growth on water scarcity in Table 3 of "Water and Conflict: Fresh Water Resources and International Security," *International Security*, Vol. 18, No. 1 (Summer 1993), p. 101.

resource in the hands of a few people and subjects the rest to greater scarcity.[7] The property rights that govern resource distribution often change as a result of large-scale development projects or new technologies that alter the relative values of resources.

In other words, reduction in the quantity or quality of a resource shrinks the resource pie, while population growth divides the pie into smaller slices for each individual, and unequal resource distribution means that some groups get disproportionately large slices.[8] Unfortunately, analysts often study resource depletion and population growth in isolation from the political economy of resource distribution.[9] The term "environmental scarcity," however, allows these three distinct sources of scarcity to be incorporated into one analysis. Empirical evidence suggests, in fact, that the first two sources are most pernicious when they interact with unequal resource distribution.

We must also recognize that resource scarcity is, in part, subjective; it is determined not just by absolute physical limits, but also by preferences, beliefs, and norms. This is illustrated by a debate about the role of population growth and resource scarcity as causes of the conflict between the Sandinista government and the Miskito Indians in Nicaragua.[10] Bernard Nietschmann argues that the Nicaraguan state's need for resources to sustain the country's economic and agricultural development caused environmental degradation to spread from the Pacific to the Atlantic coast of the country. As this happened, indigenous Miskitos in the east came into conflict with the central government. Sergio Diaz-Briquets responds that the Sandinistas expropriated Miskito lands because of ideology, not scarcity. The Atlantic coastal region was largely ignored by the Nicaraguan state under Somoza. Following the revolution, the Sandinistas had ample newly expropriated land to distribute to their followers; but the new government—guided by Marxism—saw the Miskitos as a backward people with a competing worldview and a precapitalist mode of production, whose land rightfully belonged to a state that was removing impediments to the historical progress of the working class.

---

7. The second and third types of scarcity arise only with resources that can be physically controlled and possessed, like fish, fertile land, trees, and water, rather than resources like the climate or the ozone layer.
8. Since population growth is often a main cause of a decline in the quality and quantity of renewable resources, it actually has a dual impact on resource scarcity, a fact rarely noted by analysts.
9. James Boyce, "The Bomb Is a Dud," *The Progressive,* September 1990, pp. 24–25.
10. Bernard Nietschmann, "Environmental Conflicts and Indigenous Nations in Central America," paper prepared for the Project on Environmental Change and Acute Conflict (May 1991); and Sergio Diaz-Briquets, "Comments on Nietschmann's Paper," ibid.

Figure 1. Resource Capture and Ecological Marginalization.

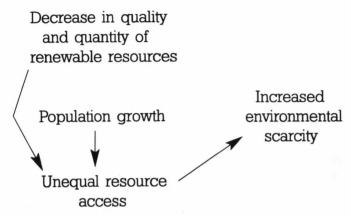

Decrease in quality
and quantity of
renewable resources

Population growth

Increased
environmental
scarcity

Unequal resource
access

Resource Capture: Resource depletion and population growth cause unequal resource access.

The gap between the two views can be bridged by noting that scarcity is partly subjective. Marxist ideology encouraged the Sandinistas to adopt a strategy of state-directed industrialization and resource-use; this led them to perceive resources as more scarce than had the Somoza regime.

INTERACTION OF SOURCES OF ENVIRONMENTAL SCARCITY

The three sources of environmental scarcity often interact, and two patterns of interaction are particularly common: "resource capture" and "ecological marginalization" (see Figure 1).

A fall in the quality and quantity of renewable resources can combine with population growth to encourage powerful groups within a society to shift resource distribution in their favor. This can produce dire environmental scarcity for poorer and weaker groups whose claims to resources are opposed by these powerful elites. I call this type of interaction "resource capture." Unequal resource access can combine with population growth to cause migrations to regions that are ecologically fragile, such as steep upland slopes, areas at risk of desertification, and tropical rain forests. High population densities in these areas, combined with a lack of knowledge and capital to

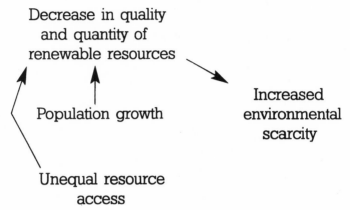

Decrease in quality
and quantity of
renewable resources

Population growth

Increased
environmental
scarcity

Unequal resource
access

Ecological Marginalization: Unequal resource access and population growth cause resource degradation and depletion.

protect local resources, causes severe environmental damage and chronic poverty. This process is often called "ecological marginalization."[11]

RESOURCE CAPTURE. Events in the Senegal River valley in 1989 illustrate resource capture. The valley demarcates the border between Senegal and Mauritania in West Africa. Senegal has fairly abundant agricultural land, but much of it suffers from high to severe wind and water erosion, loss of nutrients, salinization because of overirrigation, and soil compaction caused by intensification of agriculture.[12] The country has an overall population density of 38 people per square kilometer and a population growth rate of 2.8 percent; in 25 years the population will double.[13] In contrast, except for the Senegal Valley along its southern border and a few oases, Mauritania is

11. Jeffrey Leonard, "Overview," *Environment and the Poor: Development Strategies for a Common Agenda* (New Brunswick, N.J.: Transaction, 1989), p. 7. For a careful analysis of the interaction of population and land distribution in El Salvador, see chap. 2 in William Durham, *Scarcity and Survival in Central America: The Ecological Origins of the Soccer War* (Stanford, Calif.: Stanford University Press, 1979), pp. 21–62.

12. Global Assessment of Soil Degradation, *World Map on Status of Human-Induced Soil Degradation*, Sheet 2, Europe, Africa, and Western Asia (Wageningen, the Netherlands: United Nations Environment Programme [UNEP], International Soil Reference Centre, 1990).

13. Nafis Sadik, *The State of the World Population 1991* (New York: United Nations Population Fund, 1991), p. 24; World Resources Institute [WRI], *World Resources 1992–93* (New York: Oxford University Press, 1992), pp. 246 and 262.

largely arid desert and semiarid grassland.[14] Its population density is very low at about 2 people per square kilometer, but the growth rate is 2.9 percent. This combination of factors led the Food and Agriculture Organization (FAO) and two other organizations in a 1982 study to include both Mauritania and Senegal in their list of "critical" countries whose croplands cannot support their current and projected populations without a large increase in agricultural inputs, such as fertilizer and irrigation.[15]

Normally, the broad floodplains fringing the Senegal River support productive farming, herding, and fishing based on the river's annual floods. During the 1970s, however, the prospect of chronic food shortages and a serious drought encouraged the region's governments to seek international financing for the Manantali Dam on the Bafing River tributary in Mali, and the Diama salt-intrusion barrage near the mouth of the Senegal River between Senegal and Mauritania. These dams were designed to regulate the river's flow to produce hydropower, expand irrigated agriculture, and provide river transport from the Atlantic Ocean to landlocked Mali, which lies to the east of Senegal and Mauritania.

But the plan had unfortunate and unforeseen consequences. Anticipation of the new dams sharply increased land values along the river in areas where high-intensity agriculture would become feasible. The elite in Mauritania, which consists mainly of white Moors, then rewrote legislation governing land ownership, effectively abrogating the rights of black Africans to continue farming, herding, and fishing along the Mauritanian riverbank.[16]

---

14. Despite popular perception and the past claims of the United Nations Environment Programme, many experts now believe that the African Sahel (which includes southern Mauritania) is a robust ecosystem that does not exhibit extensive human-induced desertification. There is no clear southward march of the Sahara desert, and ecosystem recovery can be rapid if there is adequate rainfall and a reduction in grazing pressures. See "The Ebb and Flow of the Sahara," *New York Times*, July 23, 1991, p. B9. Overgrazing across the western Sahel, and the consequent migration of people from the region, appear to arise from the expansion of sedentary farming and population growth that together concentrate pastoralists on smaller areas of land (an example of ecological marginalization). In general, pastoralists are weak in the face of modern African states; state development since decolonization has often changed property rights at their expense. See Olivia Bennett, ed., *Greenwar: Environment and Conflict* (London: Panos, 1991), chap. 3, pp. 33–53.

15. G.M. Higgins, et al., *Potential Population Supporting Capacities of Lands in the Developing World*, Technical Report of Project INT/75/P13, "Land Resources of the Future," undertaken by the UN Food and Agriculture Organization (FAO) in collaboration with the International Institute for Applied Systems Analysis (IIASA) and the UN Fund for Population Activities (Rome, 1982), Table 3.5, p. 137.

16. Michael Horowitz, "Victims of Development," *Development Anthropology Network*, Bulletin of the Institute for Development Anthropology, Vol. 7, No. 2 (Fall 1989), pp. 1–8; and Horowitz, "Victims Upstream and Down," *Journal of Refugee Studies*, Vol. 4, No. 2 (1991), pp. 164–181.

There has been a long history of racism by white Moors in Mauritania towards their non-Arab, black compatriots. In the spring of 1989, the killing of Senegalese farmers by Mauritanians in the river basin triggered explosions of ethnic violence in the two countries. In Senegal, almost all of the 17,000 shops owned by Moors were destroyed, and their owners were deported to Mauritania. In both countries several hundred people were killed and the two nations nearly came to war.[17] The Mauritanian regime used this occasion to activate the new land legislation, declaring the Mauritanians who lived alongside the river to be "Senegalese," thereby stripping them of their citizenship; their property was seized. Some 70,000 of the black Mauritanians were forcibly expelled to Senegal, from where some launched raids to retrieve expropriated cattle. Diplomatic relations between the two countries have now been restored, but neither has agreed to allow the expelled population to return or to compensate them for their losses.

We see here the interaction of two sources of human-induced environmental scarcity: degradation of the land resource and population pressures helped precipitate agricultural shortfalls, which in turn encouraged a large development scheme. These factors together raised land values in one of the few areas in either country that offered the potential for a rapid move to high-intensity agriculture. A powerful elite then changed property rights and resource distribution in its own favor, which produced a sudden increase in resource scarcity for an ethnic minority, expulsion of the minority, and ethnic violence.

The water shortage on the occupied West Bank of the Jordan River offers a similar example of how population growth and excessive resource consumption can promote resource capture. While figures vary, Israel's average annual supply of renewable fresh water is about 1,950 million cubic meters (mcm).[18] Current Israeli demand, including that of settlements in the occupied territories and Golan Heights, exceeds this supply by about ten percent. The deficit is covered by overpumping aquifers. As a result, water tables in some parts of Israel and the West Bank have dropped. This can cause the

---

17. Jacques Belotteau, "Senegal-Mauritanie: les graves evenements du printemps 1989," *Afrique Contemporaine*, No. 152 (April 1989), pp. 41–42.

18. Miriam Lowi, "West Bank Water Resources and the Resolution of Conflict in the Middle East," Occasional Paper No. 1, Project on Environmental Change and Acute Conflict (September 1992); see also Lowi, "Bridging the Divide: Transboundary Resource Disputes and the Case of West Bank Water," *International Security*, Vol. 18, No. 1 (Summer 1993), pp. 113–138; and Natasha Beschorner, "Water and Instability in the Middle East," Adelphi Paper No. 273 (London: International Institute for Strategic Studies [IISS], Winter 1992/93).

exhaustion of wells and the infiltration of sea water from the Mediterranean.[19] Israel's population growth in the next thirty years, even without major immigration from the former Soviet Union, will probably cause the country's water demand to outstrip supply by at least forty percent.[20]

Over half of Israel's water comes from aquifers, and the rest from river flow, floodwater, and waste-water recycling. Two of the three main aquifers on which Israel depends lie principally underneath the West Bank, although their waters drain into Israel. About forty percent of the groundwater Israel uses (and therefore about a quarter of its sustainable supply) originates in occupied territory. To protect this important source, the Israeli government strictly limits water use by Jewish settlers and Arabs on the West Bank. But there is a stark differential in water access between the groups: on a per capita basis, settlers consume about four times as much as Arabs. Israel restricts the number of wells Arabs can drill in the territory, the amount of water Arabs are allowed to pump, and the times at which they can draw irrigation water. Since 1967, Arabs have not been permitted to drill new wells for agricultural purposes, although the Mekorot (the Israeli water company) has drilled more than thirty wells for settlers' irrigation.

Arab agriculture in the region has also suffered because some Arab wells have become dry or saline as a result of deeper Israeli wells drilled nearby. These Israeli water policies, combined with the confiscation of agricultural land for settlers as well as other Israeli restrictions on Palestinian agriculture, have encouraged many West Bank Arabs to abandon farming and move to towns.[21] Those who have done so have mostly become either unemployed or day laborers within Israel. The links between these processes and the recent unrest in the occupied territories are unclear; many political, economic, and ideological factors operate. But it seems reasonable to conclude that water scarcity and its consequent economic effects contributed to the grievances behind the *intifada* both on the West Bank and in Gaza.

---

19. There appears to be an impending crisis, for example, from salinization of aquifers beneath the Gaza Strip, where the pressure on water resources is "rapidly becoming intolerable"; Beschorner, "Water and Instability," pp. 14–15. The Gaza aquifers are connected to the coastal aquifer that is vital to Israel. Salinization can cause irreversible physical changes in aquifers; even if replenished with fresh water, their capacity is reduced. See Fred Pearce, "Wells of Conflict on the West Bank," *New Scientist*, June 1, 1991, pp. 37–38.
20. Lowi, "West Bank Water Resources," p. 34.
21. Since 1967, the irrigated area on the West Bank has dropped from 27 percent of the total cultivated area to 3.5–6 percent. Beschorner, "Water and Instability," pp. 14 and 78.

ECOLOGICAL MARGINALIZATION. The Philippines offers a good illustration of ecological marginalization. There, inequalities in access to rich agricultural lowlands combine with population growth to cause migration to easily degraded upland areas; erosion and deforestation contribute to economic hardship that spurs insurgency and rebellion.

Spanish and American colonial policies in the Philippines left behind a grossly unfair distribution of good cropland in lowland regions, an imbalance perpetuated since independence by a powerful landowning elite.[22] Since World War II, green-revolution technologies have greatly increased lowland production of grain for domestic consumption, and of cash crops such as sugar, coconut, pineapple, and bananas that help pay the country's massive external debt. This has raised demand for agricultural labor on large farms, but not enough to compensate for a population growth rate of 2.5 to 3.0 percent per annum. Together, therefore, inequalities in land access and growth in population have produced a surge in agricultural unemployment.

With insufficient rural or urban industrialization to employ this excess labor, there has been unrelenting downward pressure on wages.[23] Economically desperate, millions of poor agricultural laborers and landless peasants have migrated to shantytowns in already overburdened cities, such as Manila. Millions of others have moved to the least productive—and often most ecologically vulnerable—territories, such as steep hillsides.[24] In these uplands, settlers use fire to clear forested or previously logged land. They bring with them little knowledge or money to protect their fragile ecosystems, and their small-scale logging, production of charcoal for the cities, and slash-and-burn farming often cause horrendous environmental damage, particularly water erosion, landslides, and changes in the hydrological cycle.[25] This has set in motion a cycle of falling food production, the clearing of new plots,

---

22. The best cropland lies, for the most part, in the coastal plains of the archipelago's islands. Landowning and manufacturing elites are closely linked, and their relative economic power has actually grown since independence: the top 10 percent of the country's families controlled 37 percent of the nation's total income in 1985, up from 27 percent in 1956. See Richard Kessler, *Rebellion and Repression in the Philippines* (New Haven: Yale University Press, 1989), p. 18.
23. Using a standardized figure of 100 for 1972, average real wages dropped from 150 in the early 1950s to about 100 in 1980. Kessler, *Rebellion and Repression*, p. 26.
24. A full account can be found in Maria Concepción Cruz, et al., *Population Growth, Poverty, and Environmental Stress: Frontier Migration in the Philippines and Costa Rica* (Washington, D.C.: WRI, 1992).
25. World Bank, *Philippines: Environment and Natural Resource Management Study* (Washington, D.C.: World Bank, 1989). Erosion rates can exceed 300 tons per hectare per year, ten to twenty times the sustainable rate.

and further land degradation. There are few new areas in the country that can be opened up for agricultural production, so even marginally fertile land is becoming hard to find in many places, and economic conditions are often desperate for the peasants.[26]

The situation in the Philippines is not unique. Ecological marginalization occurs with striking regularity around the planet, affecting hundreds of millions of people in places as diverse as the Himalayas, Indonesia, Costa Rica, Brazil, and the Sahel.

SOCIAL AND TECHNICAL INGENUITY

Societies are more able to avoid turmoil if they can adapt to environmental scarcity so that it does not cause great suffering. Strategies for adaptation fall into two categories, and both depend on adequate social and technical ingenuity. First, societies can continue to rely on their indigenous resources but use them more sensibly and provide alternative employment to people who have limited resource access. For example, economic incentives like increases in resource prices and taxes can reduce degradation and depletion by encouraging conservation, technological innovation, and resource substitution. Family planning and literacy campaigns can ease population-growth induced scarcity. Land redistribution and labor-intensive rural industries can relieve the effects of unequal access to good cropland.

Second, the country might "decouple" itself from dependence on its own depleted environmental resources by producing goods and services that do not rely heavily on those resources; the country could then trade the products on the international market for the resources it no longer has at home. Such decoupling might, in fact, be achieved by rapidly exploiting the country's environmental resources and reinvesting the profits in capital, industrial equipment, and skills to permit a shift to other forms of wealth creation. For instance, Malaysia could use the income from over-logging its forests to fund a modern university system that trains electrical engineers and computer specialists for a high-technology industrial sector.

If either strategy is to succeed, a society must be able to supply enough ingenuity at the right places and times. Two kinds are key. Technical ingenuity is needed to develop, for example, new agricultural and forestry technologies that compensate for environmental loss. Social ingenuity is needed

---

26. Gareth Porter and Delfin Ganapin, Jr., *Resources, Population, and the Philippines' Future: A Case Study*, WRI Paper No. 4 (Washington, D.C.: World Resources Institute, 1988).

to create institutions and organizations that buffer people from the effects of scarcity and provide the right incentives for technological entrepreneurs. Social ingenuity is therefore often a precursor to technical ingenuity. The development and distribution of new grains adapted for dry climates and eroded soils, of alternative cooking technologies to compensate for the loss of firewood, and of water conservation technologies depend on an intricate and stable system of markets, legal regimes, financial agencies, and educational and research institutions.

In the next decades, the need for both technical and social ingenuity to deal with environmental scarcities will rise sharply. Population growth, rising average resource consumption, and persistent inequalities in access to resources ensure that scarcities will affect many environmentally sensitive regions with a severity, speed, and scale unprecedented in history. Resource-substitution and conservation tasks will be more urgent, complex, and unpredictable, driving up the need for technical ingenuity. Moreover, solving these problems through market and other institutional innovations (such as changes in property rights and resource distribution) will require great social ingenuity.

At the same time that environmental scarcity is boosting the demand for ingenuity, however, it may interfere with supply. Poor countries start at a disadvantage: they are underendowed with the social institutions—including the productive research centers, efficient markets, and capable states—that are necessary for an ample supply of both social and technical solutions to scarcity. Moreover, their ability to create and maintain these institutions may be diminished by the very environmental stress they need to address, because scarcity can weaken states, as we shall see, and it can engender intense rivalries between interest groups and elite factions.[27]

Evidence Bearing on the Hypotheses

The findings described above led me to revise the original three hypotheses by redefining the independent variable, "environmental scarcity." I narrowed the range of environmental problems that were hypothesized to cause conflict, so as to deemphasize atmospheric problems and focus instead on for-

---

27. For a full elaboration of the argument in this section, see Homer-Dixon, "The Ingenuity Gap: Can Developing Countries Adapt to Environmental Scarcity?" paper prepared for the Project on Environmental Change and Acute Conflict (March 1994).

ests, water, fisheries, and especially cropland. I expanded the scope of the independent variable to include scarcity caused by population growth and resource maldistribution as well as that caused by degradation and depletion. And I also incorporated into the variable the role of interactions among these three sources of scarcity.

Our research project produced the following empirical evidence bearing on the three hypotheses thus revised.

HYPOTHESIS 1: SIMPLE-SCARCITY CONFLICTS BETWEEN STATES
There is little empirical support for the first hypothesis that environmental scarcity causes simple-scarcity conflicts between states. Scarcities of renewable resources such as forests and croplands do not often cause resource wars between states. This finding is intriguing because resource wars have been common since the beginning of the state system. For instance, during World War II, Japan sought to secure oil, minerals, and other resources in China and Southeast Asia, and the 1991 Gulf War was at least partly motivated by the desire for oil.

However, we must distinguish between non-renewable resources such as oil, and renewable resources. Arthur Westing has compiled a list of twelve conflicts in the twentieth century involving resources, beginning with World War I and concluding with the Falklands/Malvinas War.[28] Access to oil or minerals was at issue in ten of these conflicts. Just five conflicts involved renewable resources, and only two of these—the 1969 Soccer War between El Salvador and Honduras, and the Anglo-Icelandic Cod War of 1972–73—concerned neither oil nor minerals (cropland was a factor in the former case, and fish in the latter). However, the Soccer War was not a simple-scarcity conflict between states; rather it arose from the ecological marginalization of Salvadorean peasants and their consequent migration into Honduras.[29] It is evidence in support, therefore, of our second and third hypotheses (below), but not for the first. And, since the Cod War, despite its name, involved very little violence, it hardly qualifies as a resource war.

States have fought more over non-renewable than renewable resources for two reasons, I believe. First, petroleum and mineral resources can be more

28. Arthur Westing, "Appendix 2. Wars and Skirmishes Involving Natural Resources: A Selection from the Twentieth Century," in Arthur Westing, ed., *Global Resources and International Conflict: Environmental Factors in Strategic Policy and Action* (Oxford: New York, 1986), pp. 204–210.
29. See Durham, *Scarcity and Survival*.

directly converted into state power than can agricultural land, fish, and forests. Oil and coal fuel factories and armies, and ores are vital for tanks and naval ships. In contrast, although captured forests and cropland may eventually generate wealth that can be harnessed by the state for its own ends, this outcome is more remote in time and less certain. Second, the very countries that are most dependent on renewable resources, and which are therefore most motivated to seize resources from their neighbors, also tend to be poor, which lessens their capability for aggression.

Our research suggests that the renewable resource most likely to stimulate interstate resource war is river water.[30] Water is a critical resource for personal and national survival; furthermore, since river water flows from one area to another, one country's access can be affected by another's actions. Conflict is most probable when a downstream riparian is highly dependent on river water and is strong in comparison to upstream riparians. Downstream riparians often fear that their upstream neighbors will use water as a means of coercion. This situation is particularly dangerous if the downstream country also believes it has the military power to rectify the situation. The relationships between South Africa and Lesotho and between Egypt and Ethiopia have this character.[31]

The Lesotho case is interesting. Facing critical water shortages, South Africa negotiated in vain with Lesotho for thirty years to divert water from Lesotho's mountains to the arid South African province of Transvaal. In 1986 South Africa gave decisive support to a successful military coup against Lesotho's tribal government. South Africa declared that it helped the coup because Lesotho had been providing sanctuary to guerrillas of the African National Congress. This was undoubtedly a key motivation, but within months the two governments reached agreement to construct the huge Highlands Water Project to meet South Africa's needs. It seems likely, therefore, that the desire for water was an ulterior motive behind South African support for the coup.[32]

---

30. Peter Gleick, "Water and Conflict," Occasional Paper No. 1, Project on Environmental Change and Acute Conflict (September 1992); and Gleick, "Water and Conflict: Fresh Water Resources and International Security," *International Security*, Vol. 18, No. 1 (Summer 1993), pp. 79–112.

31. In 1980, Egyptian President Anwar el-Sadat said, "If Ethiopia takes any action to block our right to the Nile waters, there will be no alternative for us but to use force"; quoted in Norman Myers, "Environment and Security," *Foreign Policy*, No. 74 (Spring 1989), p. 32. See also chap. 6, "The Nile River," in Thomas Naff and Ruth Matson, eds., *Water in the Middle East: Conflict or Cooperation?* (Boulder, Colo.: Westview, 1984), pp. 125–155.

32. "Pretoria Has Its Way in Lesotho," *Africa Report* (March–April, 1986), pp. 50–51; Patrick

However, our review of the historical and contemporary evidence shows that conflict and turmoil related to river water are more often internal than international. The huge dams that are often built to deal with general water scarcity are especially disruptive. Relocating large numbers of upstream people generates turmoil among the relocatees and clashes with local groups in areas where the relocatees are resettled. The people affected are often members of ethnic or minority groups outside the power hierarchy of their society, and the result is frequently rebellion by these groups and repression by the state. Water developments can also induce conflict over water and irrigable land among a country's downstream users, as we saw in the Senegal River basin.[33]

HYPOTHESIS 2: POPULATION MOVEMENT AND GROUP-IDENTITY CONFLICTS

There is substantial evidence to support the hypothesis that environmental scarcity causes large population movement, which in turn causes group-identity conflicts. But we must be sensitive to contextual factors unique to each socio-ecological system. These are the system's particular physical, political, economic, and cultural features that affect the strength of the linkages between scarcity, population movement, and conflict.

For example, experts emphasize the importance of both "push" and "pull" factors in decisions of potential migrants.[34] These factors help distinguish migrants from refugees: while migrants are motivated by a combination of push and pull, refugees are motivated mainly by push. Environmental scarcity is more likely to produce migrants than refugees, because it usually develops gradually, which means that the push effect is not sharp and sudden and that pull factors can therefore clearly enter into potential migrants' calculations.

Migrants are often people who have been weak and marginal in their home society and, depending on context, they may remain weak in the receiving society. This limits their ability to organize and to make demands. States play

---

Laurence, "A 'New Lesotho'?" *Africa Report* (January–February 1987), pp. 61–64; "Lesotho Water Project Gets Under Way," *Africa Report* (May–June 1988), p. 10. See also Charles Okidi, "Environmental Stress and Conflicts in Africa: Case Studies of African International Drainage Basins," paper prepared for the Project on Environmental Change and Acute Conflict (May 1992).
33. See Thayer Scudder, "River Basin Projects in Africa," *Environment*, Vol. 31, No. 2 (March 1989), pp. 4–32; and Scudder, "Victims of Development Revisited: The Political Costs of River Basin Development," *Development Anthropology Network*, Vol. 8, No. 1 (Spring 1990), pp. 1–5.
34. Astri Suhrke, "Pressure Points: Environmental Degradation, Migration, and Conflict," Occasional Paper No. 3, Project on Environmental Change and Acute Conflict (March 1993).

a critical role here: migrants often need the backing of a state (either of the receiving society or an external one) before they have sufficient power to cause conflict, and this backing depends on the region's politics. Without it, migration is less likely to produce violence than silent misery and death, which rarely destabilizes states.[35] We must remember too that migration does not always produce bad results. It can act as a safety valve by reducing conflict in the sending area. Depending on the economic context, it can ease labor shortages in the receiving society, as it sometimes has, for instance, in Malaysia. Countries as different as Canada, Thailand, and Malawi show the astonishing capacity of some societies to absorb migrants without conflict.

Even accounting for such contextual factors, events in Bangladesh and Northeast India provide strong evidence in support of the second hypothesis. In recent decades, huge numbers of people have moved from Bangladesh to India, producing group-identity conflicts in the adjacent Indian states. Only one of the three sources of environmental scarcity—population growth— seems to be a main force behind this migration. Even though Bangladesh's cropland is heavily used, in general it is not badly degraded, because the annual flooding of the Ganges and Brahmaputra rivers deposits nutrients that help maintain the fertility of the country's floodplains.[36] And while land distribution remains highly unequal, this distribution has changed little since an initial attempt at land reform immediately following East Pakistan's independence from the British.[37]

But the United Nations predicts that Bangladesh's current population of 120 million will nearly double, to 235 million, by the year 2025.[38] Cropland, at about 0.08 hectares per capita, is already desperately scarce. Population density is over 900 people per square kilometer (in comparison, population density in neigboring Assam is under 300 per square kilometer). Since virtually all of the country's good agricultural land has been exploited, population growth will cut in half the amount of cropland available per capita by 2025. Land scarcity and the brutal poverty and social turmoil it engenders have been made worse by flooding (perhaps aggravated by deforestation in

---

35. Ibid.
36. The relationship between flooding and soil fertility is ill-understood. See James Boyce, "Birth of a Megaproject: Political Economy of Flood Control in Bangladesh," *Environmental Management*, Vol. 14, No. 4 (July/August 1990), pp. 419–428, especially p. 424.
37. James Boyce, *Agrarian Impasse in Bengal: Institutional Constraints to Technological Change* (Oxford: Oxford University Press, 1987), p. 9.
38. Sadik, *The State of the World Population 1991*, p. 43.

the Himalayan watersheds of the region's major rivers); by the susceptibility of the country to cyclones; and by the construction by India of the Farakka Barrage, a dam upstream on the Ganges River.[39]

People have been moving around this part of South Asia in large numbers for centuries. But the movements are increasing in size. Over the last forty years, millions have migrated from East Pakistan or Bangladesh to the Indian states of Assam, Tripura, and West Bengal. Detailed data are scarce, since both India and Bangladesh manipulate their census data for political reasons, and the Bangladeshi government avoids admitting there is large out-migration, because the question causes friction with India. But by piecing together demographic information and experts' estimates, we concluded that migrants from Bangladesh have expanded the population of neighboring areas of India by 12 to 17 million, of which only 1 or 2 million can be attributed to migration induced by the 1971 war between India and Pakistan that created Bangladesh. We further estimate that the population of the state of Assam has been boosted by at least 7 million people, to its current total of 22 million.[40]

This enormous flux has produced pervasive social changes in the receiving regions. It has altered land distribution, economic relations, and the balance of political power between religious and ethnic groups, and it has triggered serious intergroup conflict. Members of the Lalung tribe in Assam, for instance, have long resented Bengali Muslim migrants: they accuse them of stealing the area's richest farmland. In early 1983, during a bitterly contested election for federal offices in the state, violence erupted. In the village of Nellie, Lalung people massacred nearly 1,700 Bengalis in one five-hour rampage.[41]

---

39. Controversy surrounds the question of whether Himalayan deforestation contributes to flooding; see Centre for Science and Environment (CSE), *Floods, Flood Plains, and Environmental Myths* (New Delhi: CSE, 1991), especially pp. 68–69. On the Farakka Barrage, Ashok Swain writes: "It has disrupted fishing and navigation [in Bangladesh], brought unwanted salt deposits into rich farming soil, affected agricultural and industrial production, changed the hydraulic character of the rivers and caused changes in the ecology of the Delta." See Swain, "Environmental Destruction and Acute Social Conflict: A Case Study of the Ganges Water Dispute," Department of Peace and Conflict Research, Uppsala University (November 1992), p. 24.

40. Sanjoy Hazarika, "Bangladesh and Assam: Land Pressures, Migration, and Ethnic Conflict," Occasional Paper No. 3, Project on Environmental Change and Acute Conflict (March 1993), p. 52–54.

41. "A State Ravaged," *India Today*, March 15, 1983, pp. 16–21; "Spillover Tension," *India Today*, March 15, 1983, pp. 22–23. The 1991 Indian Census showed that Assam's population growth rate has declined; the conflicts in Assam in the early 1980s appear to have encouraged many migrants from Bangladesh to go to West Bengal instead.

In Tripura, the original Buddhist and Christian inhabitants now make up less than 30 percent of the state's population. The rest are Hindu migrants from either East Pakistan or Bangladesh. This shift in the ethnic balance precipitated a violent insurgency between 1980 and 1988 that diminished only after the government agreed to return land to dispossessed Tripuris and to stop the influx of Bangladeshis. But, as the migration has continued, this agreement is in jeopardy.[42]

There are important features unique to this case. Within Bangladesh, key "push" factors include inheritance practices that divide cropland into smaller plots with each generation, and national and community water-control institutions that sharply limit agricultural output and keep peasants from gaining full benefit from some of the most fertile land in the world.[43] On the "pull" side, the standard of living in India is markedly better, and Indian politicians have often encouraged Bangladeshi migration to garner their votes. Furthermore, in the Ganges-Brahmaputra region, the concept of nation-state is often not part of the local culture. Many people think of the region as "greater Bengal," and state borders do not figure heavily in the calculations of some migrants, especially when there are receptive family, linguistic, and religious groups across the frontier. Finally, during the colonial period, the British used Hindus from Calcutta to administer Assam, and Bengali became the official language. As a result, the Assamese are particularly sensitive to their loss of political and cultural control in the state.

While such contextual factors are important, they cannot obscure the fact that land scarcity in Bangladesh, arising largely from population growth, has been a powerful force behind migration to neighboring regions and communal conflict there.[44]

HYPOTHESIS 3: ECONOMIC DEPRIVATION, INSTITUTIONAL DISRUPTION, AND CIVIL STRIFE

Empirical evidence partially supports the third hypothesis that environmental scarcity simultaneously increases economic deprivation and disrupts key

---

42. Hazarika, "Bangladesh and Assam," pp. 60–61.
43. Boyce, *Agrarian Impasse.*
44. See Shaukat Hassan, "Environmental Issues and Security in South Asia," Adelphi Paper No. 262 (London: IISS, Autumn 1991), pp. 42–43; P.C. Goswami, "Foreign Immigration into Assam," in B.L. Abbi, ed., *Northeast Region: Problems and Prospects of Development* (Chandigarh, India: Centre for Research in Rural and Industrial Development), pp. 35–59; and Susanta Dass, *Spotlight on Assam* (Chanderpur, India: Premier Book Service, 1989).

social institutions, which in turn causes "deprivation" conflicts such as civil strife and insurgency. Environmental scarcity does produce economic deprivation, and this deprivation does cause civil strife. But more research is needed on the effects of scarcity on social institutions.

Resource degradation and depletion often affect economic productivity in poor countries and thereby contribute to deprivation. For example, erosion in upland Indonesia annually costs the country's agricultural economy nearly half a billion dollars in discounted future income.[45] The Magat watershed on the northern Filipino island of Luzon—a watershed representative of many in the Philippines—suffers gross erosion rates averaging 219 tons per hectare per year; if the lost nutrients were replaced by fertilizer, the annual cost would be over $100 per hectare.[46] Dryland degradation in Burkina Faso reduces the country's annual gross domestic product by nearly nine percent annually because of fuelwood loss and lower yields of millet, sorghum, and livestock.[47]

Vaclav Smil has estimated the combined effect of environmental problems on China's economic productivity.[48] The main burdens he identifies are reductions in crop yields caused by pollution of water, soil, and air; higher human morbidity from air pollution; farmland loss because of construction and erosion; nutrient loss and flooding due to erosion and deforestation; and timber loss arising from poor harvesting practices. Smil calculates the current cost to be at least 15 percent of China's gross national product, and he is convinced that the toll will rise steeply in the next decades.[49] Although China's economy is booming, much of the new wealth is concentrated in the

---

45. Robert Repetto, "Balance-Sheet Erosion—How to Account for the Loss of Natural Resources," *International Environmental Affairs*, Vol. 1, No. 2 (Spring 1989), pp. 103–137.
46. This estimate does not include the economic costs of lost rooting depth and increased vulnerability to drought, which may be even larger. See Wilfrido Cruz, Herminia Francisco, and Zenaida Conway, "The On-Site and Downstream Costs of Soil Erosion in the Magat and Pantabangan Watersheds," *Journal of Philippine Development*, Vol. 15, No. 1 (1988), p. 88.
47. Ed Barbier, "Environmental Degradation in the Third World," in David Pearce, ed., *Blueprint 2: Greening the World Economy* (London: Earthscan, 1991), Box 6.8, p. 90.
48. Vaclav Smil, "Environmental Change as a Source of Conflict and Economic Losses in China," Occasional Paper No. 2, Project on Environmental Change and Acute Conflict (December 1992).
49. It is hard to judge gross economic activity in China and convert these figures into dollars. Perhaps because of this, the World Bank has not increased its estimates of per capita annual GNP in line with the rapid expansion of the Chinese economy. Smil suggests that the Bank's current annual figure of $370/capita may be too low by a factor of four. This judgment is supported by recent re-evaluations of China's GNP by the International Monetary Fund. See World Bank, *World Development Report, 1992* (New York: Oxford University Press, 1992), p. 218; and Steven Greenhouse, "New Tally of World's Economies Catapults China into Third Place," *New York Times*, May 20, 1993, p. A1.

coastal provinces, especially around Hong Kong; many other parts of the country remain terribly poor.

I originally hypothesized that scarcity would undermine a variety of social institutions. Our research suggests, however, that one institution in particular—the state—is most important. Although more study is needed, the multiple effects of environmental scarcity, including large population movements and economic decline, appear likely to weaken sharply the capacity and legitimacy of the state in some poor countries.

First, environmental scarcity increases financial and political demands on governments. For example, to mitigate the social effects of loss of water, soil, and forest, governments must spend huge sums on industry and infrastructure such as new dams, irrigation systems, fertilizer plants, and reforestation programs. Furthermore, this resource loss can reduce the incomes of elites directly dependent on resource extraction; these elites usually turn to the state for compensation. Scarcity also expands marginal groups that need help from government by producing rural poverty and by displacing people into cities where they demand food, shelter, transport, energy, and employment. In response to swelling urban populations, governments introduce subsidies that drain revenues, distort prices, and cause misallocations of capital, which in turn hinders economic productivity. Such large-scale state intervention in the marketplace can concentrate political and economic power in the hands of a small number of cronies and monopolistic interests, at the expense of other elite segments and rural agricultural populations.

Simultaneously, if resource scarcity affects the economy's general productivity, revenues to local and national governments will decline. This hurts elites that benefit from state largesse and reduces the state's capacity to meet the increased demands arising from environmental scarcity. A widening gap between state capacity and demands on the state, along with the misguided economic interventions such a gap often provokes, aggravates popular and elite grievances, increases rivalry between elite factions, and erodes the state's legitimacy.

Key contextual factors affect whether lower economic productivity and state weakening lead to deprivation conflicts. Civil strife is a function of both the level of grievance motivating challenger groups and the opportunities available to these groups to act on their grievances. The likelihood of civil strife is greatest when multiple pressures at different levels in society interact to increase grievance and opportunity simultaneously. Our third hypothesis says that environmental scarcity will change both variables, by contributing to economic crisis and by weakening institutions such as the state. But numerous other factors also influence grievance and opportunity.

Contrary to common belief, there is no clear correlation between poverty (or economic inequality) and social conflict.[50] Whether or not people become aggrieved and violent when they find themselves increasingly poor depends, in part, upon their notion of economic justice. For example, people belonging to a culture that inculcates fatalism about deprivation—as with lower castes in India—will not be as prone to violence as people believing they have a right to economic wellbeing. Theorists have addressed this problem by introducing the variable "relative deprivation."[51] But there is little correlation between measures of relative deprivation and civil conflict.[52]

Part of the problem is that analysts have commonly used aggregate data (such as GNP/capita and average educational levels) to measure individual deprivation.[53] In addition, more recent research has shown that, to cause civil strife, economic crisis must be severe, persistent, and pervasive enough to erode the legitimacy or moral authority of the dominant social order and system of governance. System legitimacy is therefore a critical intervening variable between rising poverty and civil conflict. It is influenced by the aggrieved actors' subjective "blame system," which consists of their beliefs about who or what is responsible for their plight.[54]

Serious civil strife is not likely to occur unless the structure of political opportunities facing challenger groups keeps them from effectively expressing their grievances peacefully, but offers them openings for violence against authority.[55] The balance of coercive power among social actors affects the

---

50. Some of the best studies of this question have focused on the relationship between poverty and urban violence in the United States. See William Ford and John Moore, "Additional Evidence on the Social Characteristics of Riot Cities," *Social Science Quarterly*, Vol. 51, No. 2 (September 1970), pp. 339–348; and Robert Jiobu, "City Characteristics and Racial Violence," *Social Science Quarterly*, Vol. 55, No. 1 (June 1974), pp. 52–64.
51. People are said to be relatively deprived when they perceive a widening gap between the level of satisfaction they have achieved (usually defined in economic terms) and the level they believe they deserve. Deprivation is said to be relative to some subjective standard of equity or fairness; the size of the perceived gap depends upon the beliefs about economic justice held by the individual. See Ted Gurr, *Why Men Rebel* (Princeton: Princeton University Press, 1970).
52. Steven Finkel and James Rule, "Relative Deprivation and Related Theories of Civil Violence: A Critical Review," in Kurt and Gladys Lang, eds. *Research in Social Movements, Conflicts, and Change* (Greenwich, Conn.: JAI, 1986), pp. 47–69.
53. Ibid.
54. These beliefs are grounded in historical and economic experience. See, for example, James Scott, *The Moral Economy of the Peasant: Rebellion and Subsistence in Southeast Asia* (New Haven: Yale University Press, 1976), pp. 1–11.
55. Homer-Dixon, "On the Threshold," pp. 105–106 and 109–111.

probability of success and, therefore, the expected costs and benefits of different actions by the state, its supporters, and challenger groups. A state debilitated by corruption, by falling revenues and rising demand for services, or by factional conflicts within elites will be more vulnerable to violent challenges by political and military opponents; also vital to state strength is the cohesiveness of the armed forces and its loyalty to civil leadership.[56]

Challengers will have greater relative power if their grievances are articulated and actions coordinated through well-organized, well-financed and autonomous opposition groups. Since grievances felt at the individual level are not automatically expressed at the group level, the probability of civil violence is higher if groups are already organized around clear social cleavages, such as ethnicity, religion, or class. These groups can provide a clear sense of identity and act as nuclei around which highly mobilized and angry elements of the population, such as unemployed and urbanized young men, will coalesce. Conversely, if economic crisis weakens challenger groups more than the state, or affects mainly disorganized people, it will not lead to violence.

Factors that can influence both grievance and opportunity include the leadership and ideology of challenger groups, and international shocks and pressures such as changes in trade and debt relations and in costs of imported factors of production such as energy.[57] The rapid growth of urban areas in poor countries may have a similar dual effect: people concentrated in slums can communicate more easily than those in scattered rural villages; this may reinforce grievances and, by reducing problems of coordination, also increase the power of challenger groups. Research shows, however, surprisingly little historical correlation between rapid urbanization and civil strife;[58] and the exploding cities of the developing world have been remarkably quiescent in recent decades. This may be changing: India has lately witnessed ferocious urban violence, often in the poorest slums, and sometimes directed at new

---

56. See Farrokh Moshiri, "Revolutionary Conflict Theory in an Evolutionary Perspective," in Jack Goldstone, Ted Gurr, and Farrokh Moshiri, eds., *Revolutions of the Late Twentieth Century* (Boulder, Colo.: Westview, 1991), pp. 4–36; and Goldstone, "An Analytical Framework," ibid., pp. 37–51.
57. For a review of some of these factors, see Jack Goldstone, "Theories of Revolution: The Third Generation," *World Politics*, Vol. 32, No. 3 (April 1980), pp. 425–453.
58. Wayne Cornelius, Jr., "Urbanization As an Agent in Latin American Political Instability: The Case of Mexico," *American Political Science Review*, Vol. 63, No. 3 (September 1969), pp. 833–357; and Abdul Lodhi and Charles Tilly, "Urbanization, Crime, and Collective Violence in 19th-Century France," *American Journal of Sociology*, Vol. 79, No. 2 (September 1973), pp. 296–318.

migrants from the countryside.[59] In Egypt, fundamentalist opposition to the government is located in some of the most desperate sectors of Cairo and other cities such as Asyut.

The Philippines provides evidence of the links between environmental scarcity, economic deprivation, and civil strife. The country has suffered from serious strife for many decades, usually motivated by economic stress.[60] Today, cropland and forest degradation in the uplands sharply exacerbates this economic crisis. The current upland insurgency—including guerrilla attacks and assaults on military stations—is motivated by the poverty of landless agricultural laborers and farmers displaced into the remote hills, where the central government is weak.[61] During the 1970s and 1980s, the communist New People's Army and the National Democratic Front found upland peasants receptive to revolutionary ideology, especially where coercive landlords and local governments left them little choice between rebellion and starvation. The insurgency has waned somewhat since President Marcos left, not because economic conditions have improved much in the countryside, but because the democratically elected central government is more legitimate and the insurgent leadership is ideologically rigid.

Contextual factors are key to a full understanding of this case. Property rights governing upland areas are, for the most part, either nonexistent or very unclear. Legally these areas are a public resource, and their "open access" character encourages in-migration. Yet many upland peasants find themselves under the authority of concessionaires and absentee landlords who have claimed the land. Neither peasants, nor concessionaires, nor landlords, however, have secure enough title to have incentive to protect the land from environmental degradation. Increasing external debt encouraged the Marcos government, under pressure from international financial agencies, to adopt draconian stabilization and structural adjustment policies. These caused an economic crisis in the first half of the 1980s, which boosted

---

59. Sanjoy Hazarika, "Week of Rioting Leaves Streets of Bombay Empty," *New York Times*, January 12, 1993, p. A3.
60. The Huk rebellion in the late 1940s and early 1950s provides some of the best evidence for the link between economic conditions (especially unequal land distribution) and civil strife in the Philippines. See Benedict Kerkvliet, *The Huk Rebellion: A Study of Peasant Revolt in the Philippines* (Quezon City, Philippines: New Day Publishers, 1979); and E.J. Mitchell, "Some Econometrics of the Huk Rebellion," *American Political Science Review*, Vol. 63, No. 4 (December 1969), pp. 1159–1171.
61. Celso Roque and Maria Garcia, "Economic Inequality, Environmental Degradation and Civil Strife in the Philippines," paper prepared for the Project on Environmental Change and Acute Conflict (1993).

agricultural unemployment, reduced opportunities for alternative employment in urban and rural industries, and gave a further push to migration into the uplands.[62]

Finally, the insurgents gained adherents because they built on indigenous beliefs and social structures to help the peasants define their situation and focus their discontent. The most successful rebellions in Filipino history have drawn on peasants' millenarian vision—rooted in their Catholicism—of "an idealized pre-Spanish condition of wholeness."[63] The current insurgency has been particularly potent because it mingles "the spiritual search for liberation and the political search for independence, into the overarching quest for Filipino identity."[64] This has provided peasants with an alternative moral system to the traditional patron-client relationship between peasants and landowners. The feudal norms imposed obligations on landowners, which gave peasants rudimentary economic security, but disintegrated with the commercialization of agriculture and the urbanization of elites in the early and mid-twentieth century.[65]

Causal processes like those in the Philippines can be seen around the planet: population growth and unequal access to good land force huge numbers of rural people into cities or onto marginal lands. In the latter case, they cause environmental damage and become chronically poor. Eventually these people may be the source of persistent upheaval, or they may migrate yet again, stimulating ethnic conflicts or urban unrest elsewhere.

The rise of the Sendero Luminoso rebellion in Peru can be attributed to a subsistence crisis caused, in part, by such a process of ecological marginalization.[66] The country's mountainous southern highlands are not suitable for farming. The hills are steep, and the soil is thin and dry. Nonetheless, during

---

62. Maria Concepción Cruz and Robert Repetto, *The Environmental Effects of Stabilization and Structural Adjustment Programs: The Philippines Case* (Washington, D.C.: World Resources Institute, 1992). See also Francisco Lara, Jr., "Structural Adjustments and Trade Liberalization: Eating Away Our Food Security," *PPI Research Papers* (Quezon City: Philippine Peasant Institute [PPI], 1991); and Robin Broad, *Unequal Alliance, 1979–1986: The World Bank, the International Monetary Fund, and the Philippines* (Quezon City: Ateneo de Manila University Press, 1988).
63. Kessler, *Rebellion and Repression*, pp. 24–25.
64. Ibid.
65. Ibid, pp. 16–19. See also Reynaldo Clemena Ileto, *Pasyon and Revolution: Popular Movements in the Philippines, 1840–1910* (Manila: Ateneo de Manila University Press, 1979).
66. Cynthia McClintock, "Why Peasants Rebel: The Case of Peru's Sendero Luminoso," *World Politics*, Vol. 37, No. 1 (October 1984), pp. 48–84; and McClintock, "Peru's Sendero Luminoso Rebellion: Origins and Trajectory," in Susan Eckstein, ed., *Power and Popular Protest: Latin American Social Movements* (Berkeley: University of California Press, 1989), pp. 61–101.

the colonial period, Indian peoples in the region were displaced onto hillsides when Spanish settlers seized richer valley lands. In the 1970s, the Velasco government undertook a sweeping land-redistribution program. But people in the highlands benefited little, because the government was reluctant to break up large agricultural enterprises that generated much of the country's export earnings.

Natural population growth and a lack of good land or jobs elsewhere boosted population densities in the southern highlands. The department of Ayacucho saw density increase from 8.1 people per square kilometer in 1940 to 12.1 in 1980. Cropland availability dropped below .2 hectare per capita.[67] These densities exceed sustainable limits, given the inherent fragility of the region's land and prevailing agricultural practices. Cropland has therefore been badly degraded by erosion and nutrient depletion.

Cynthia McClintock notes that, "if population increases while the soil deteriorates, food production per-capita can be expected to decline."[68] Wealth in the region is almost entirely derived from subsistence agriculture. Family incomes—already among the lowest in Peru—dropped sharply in real terms in the 1970s and 1980s; in 1980, per-capita income in the Peruvian highlands was 82 percent of the 1972 level. This poverty resulted in declining caloric intake; in 1980 people in the southern highlands had less than 70 percent of the daily requirement set by the FAO. In 1983, a drought made the subsistence crisis even worse, and production of the staple crop of potatoes fell by 40–50 percent.

While government policies were partly responsible for the long-term income decline in the Peruvian highlands, the particularly harsh drop in the southern region was a result of population pressures, poor land, and the lack of alternative sources of income. The peasants' sense of deprivation was increased by the land reform in the 1970s, which raised their expectations in vain. There is thus a strong correlation between areas suffering severe poverty and areas of Sendero Luminoso strongholds: "the sine-qua-non element" of these strongholds is "the subsistence crisis in the country's southern highlands during the early 1980s."[69]

In terms of contextual factors, Ayacucho offered special opportunities to insurgents. It is physically remote, which reduced the government's control,

---

67. McClintock, "Why Peasants Rebel," pp. 61 and 63.
68. Ibid., p. 63.
69. Ibid., p. 82.

and it has a major university that served as an organizational base for radicals that became the core of Sendero. The university's remoteness also meant that students were disproportionately from the peasantry, and could therefore return to their communities with ease; moreover, they were less likely to find professional jobs on graduation. The relative power of the government was also weakened, ironically, by the land reform, which caused large landowners to leave the region. The Velasco regime did not fill the vacuum with new political and security institutions, in part because an economic downturn later in the decade reduced the government's resources for the task.

McClintock believes that the poverty of these regions condemns the country to chronic, long-term turmoil. The government may be civilian, but is unlikely to be very democratic, and will confront "virtually constant revolutionary and criminal violence."

A COMBINED MODEL
There are important links between the processes identified in the second and third hypotheses. For example, although population movement is sometimes caused directly by scarcity, more often it arises from the greater poverty caused by this scarcity. Similarly, the weakening of the state increases the likelihood not only of deprivation conflicts, but of group-identity conflicts.

It is useful, therefore, to bring the hypotheses together into one model of environment-conflict linkages (Figure 2). Decreases in the quality and quan-

Figure 2.   Some Sources and Consequences of Environmental Scarcity.

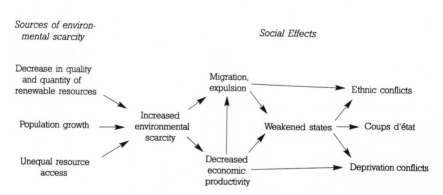

*Sources of environ-
mental scarcity*   *Social Effects*

Decrease in quality
and quantity of
renewable resources

Population growth ──▶ Increased
environmental
scarcity

Unequal resource
access

Migration,
expulsion ───────────────▶ Ethnic conflicts

Weakened states ──▶ Coups d'état

Decreased
economic ───────────────▶ Deprivation conflicts
productivity

Figure 3. Environmental Scarcity in the Philippines.

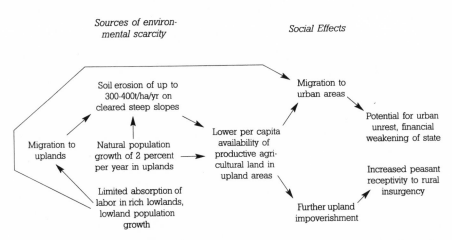

NOTE: The variables and linkages in Figure 3 map onto Figure 2, with the source of scarcity on the left and the forms of conflict on the right.

tity of renewable resources, population growth, and unequal resource access act singly or in various combinations to increase the scarcity, for certain population groups, of cropland, water, forests, and fish. This can reduce economic productivity, both for the local groups experiencing the scarcity and for the larger regional and national economies. The affected people may migrate or be expelled to new lands. Migrating groups often trigger ethnic conflicts when they move to new areas, while decreases in wealth can cause deprivation conflicts such as insurgency and rural rebellion. In developing countries, the migrations and productivity losses may eventually weaken the state which in turn decreases central control over ethnic rivalries and increases opportunities for insurgents and elites challenging state authority. Figure 3 shows how these linkages work in the Filipino case.

South Africa and Haiti illustrate this combined model. In South Africa, apartheid concentrated millions of blacks in some of the country's least productive and most ecologically sensitive territories, where population densities were worsened by high natural birth rates. In 1980, rural areas of the Ciskei homeland had 82 people per square kilometer, whereas the surrounding Cape Province had a rural density of 2. Homeland residents had little capital and few resource-management skills and were subject to corrupt and abusive local governments. Sustainable development in such a situation was impossible, and wide areas were completely stripped of trees for fuelwood, grazed down to bare dirt, and eroded of top soil. A 1980 report concluded that nearly 50 percent of Ciskei's land was moderately or severely eroded, and nearly 40 percent of its pasturage was overgrazed.[70]

This loss of resources, combined with a lack of alternative employment and the social trauma caused by apartheid, created a subsistence crisis in the homelands. Thousands of people have migrated to South African cities, which are as yet incapable of adequately integrating and employing these migrants. The result is the rapid growth of squatter settlements and illegal townships that are rife with discord and that threaten the country's move to democratic stability.[71]

In Haiti, the irreversible loss of forests and soil in rural areas deepens an economic crisis that spawns social strife, internal migration, and an exodus of "boat people." When first colonized by the Spanish in the late fifteenth century and the French in the seventeenth century, Haiti was treasured for its abundant forests. Since then, Haiti has become one of the world's most dramatic examples of environmental despoliation. Less than two percent of the country remains forested, and the last timber is being felled at four percent per year.[72] As trees disappear, erosion follows, worsened by the steepness of the land and by harsh storms. The United Nations estimates that at least 50 percent of the country is affected by topsoil loss that leaves the land "unreclaimable at the farm level."[73] So much soil washes off the slopes that the streets of Port-au-Prince have to be cleared with bulldozers in the rainy season.

Unequal land distribution was not a main cause of this catastrophe. Haiti gained independence in 1804 following a revolt of slaves and ex-slaves against

---

70. Francis Wilson and Mamphela Ramphele, *Uprooting Poverty: The South African Challenge* (New York: Norton, 1989); George Quail, et al., *Report of the Ciskei Commission* (Pretoria: Conference Associates, 1980), p. 73.
71. See Mamphela Ramphele and Chris McDowell, eds., *Restoring the Land: Environment and Change in Post-Apartheid South Africa* (London: Panos, 1991); and Chris Eaton, "Rural Environmental Degradation and Urban Conflict in South Africa," Occasional Paper of the Peace and Conflict Studies Program, University of Toronto, June 1992.
72. WRI, *World Resources, 1992–93*, p. 286.
73. Global Assessment of Soil Degradation, *World Map on Status of Human-Induced Soil Degradation*, Sheet 1, North and South America.

the French colonial regime. Over a period of decades, the old plantation system associated with slavery was dismantled, and land was widely distributed in small parcels.[74] As a result, Haiti's agricultural structure, unique to Latin America, has 73 percent of cropland in private farms of less than 4 hectares.[75]

But inheritance customs and population growth have combined to produce scarcity, as in Bangladesh. Land has been subdivided into smaller portions with each generation. Eventually the plots cannot properly support their cultivators, fallow periods are neglected, and greater poverty prevents investment in soil conservation. The poorest people leave for steeper hillsides, where they clear the forest and begin farming anew, only to exhaust the land in a few years.[76] Many peasants try to supplement their falling incomes by scavenging wood for charcoal production, which contributes to further deforestation.

These processes might have been prevented had a stable central government invested in agriculture, industrial development, and reforestation. Instead, since independence Haiti has endured a ceaseless struggle for power between black and mulatto classes, and the ruling regimes have been solely interested in expropriating any surplus wealth the economy generated. Today, over 60 percent of the population is still engaged in agriculture, yet capital is unavailable for agricultural improvement, and the terms of exchange for crop production favor urban regions.[77] The population growth rate has actually increased, from 1.7 percent in the mid-1970s to over 2 percent today: the UN estimates that the current population of 6.75 million will grow to over 13 million by 2025.[78] As the land erodes and the population grows, incomes shrink: agricultural output per capita has decreased ten percent in the last decade.[79]

Analysts agree that rising rural poverty has caused ever-increasing rural-rural and rural-urban migration. In search of work, agricultural workers move

---

74. Thomas Weil, et al., *Haiti: A Country Study* (Washington, D.C.: Department of the Army, 1982), pp. 28–33.
75. Anthony Catanese, "Haiti's Refugees: Political, Economic, Environmental," *Field Staff Reports*, No. 17 (Sausalito, Calif.: Universities Field Staff International, Natural Heritage Institute, 1990–91), p. 5.
76. Elizabeth Abbott, "Where Waters Run Brown," *Equinox*, Vol. 10, No. 59 (September/October 1991), p. 43.
77. Marko Ehrlich, et al., *Haiti: Country Environmental Profile, A Field Study* (Washington, D.C.: U.S. Agency for International Development, 1986), pp. 89–92.
78. WRI, *World Resources, 1992–93*, p. 246.
79. Ibid., p. 272.

from subsistence hillside farms to rice farms in the valleys. From there, they go to cities, especially to Port-au-Prince, which now has a population of over a million. Wealthier farmers and traders, and even those with slimmer resources, try to flee by boat.

These economic and migration stresses are undoubtedly contributing to civil strife. In the aftermath of the collapse of "Baby Doc" Duvalier's regime in 1986, the poor unleashed their vengeance on those associated with the regime, in particular on Duvalier's gangs of enforcers, the *tontons macoutes*. During his election campaign and his short tenure as president, Jean-Bertrand Aristide reportedly encouraged poor slum-dwellers to attack Haiti's elite. Fearful of uprisings, the current military regime has ferociously oppressed the country's poor and peasantry. Even if the present political stalemate is resolved, Aristide is returned to power, and international sanctions are lifted, Haiti will be forever bear the burden of its irreversibly ravaged environment, which may make it impossible to build a prosperous, just, and peaceful society.

THE CAUSAL ROLE OF ENVIRONMENTAL SCARCITY
Environmental scarcity often acts as a powerful long-term social stressor, but does it have any independent role as a cause of conflict? Many analysts assume that it is no more than a fully endogenous intervening variable linking political, economic, and social factors to conflict. By this view, environmental scarcity may be an important indicator that political and economic development has gone awry, but it does not merit, in and of itself, intensive research and policy attention at the expense of more fundamental political and economic factors.

But the cases reviewed here highlight three reasons why this view is wrong. First, as we saw in the Senegal and Jordan basins, environmental scarcity can itself be an important force behind changes in the politics and economics governing resource use. In both cases, scarcity caused powerful actors to increase in their own favor the inequities in the distribution of resources. Second, ecosystem vulnerability is often an important variable contributing to environmental scarcity, and this vulnerability is, at least in part, an independent physical factor: the depth of soils in the Filipino uplands and the vulnerability of Israel's aquifers to salt intrusion are not functions of human social institutions or behavior. Third, in many parts of the world—including regions of the Philippines, Haiti, Peru, and South Africa—environmental degradation has crossed a threshold of irreversibility. Even if enlightened social change removes the original political, economic, and cultural causes of the degradation, it will be a continuing burden on society. Once irreversible, in other words, environmental degradation becomes an exogenous variable.

Implications for International Security

Environmental scarcity has insidious and cumulative social impacts, such as population movement, economic decline, and the weakening of states. These can contribute to diffuse and persistent sub-national violence. The rate and extent of such conflicts will increase as scarcities worsen.

This sub-national violence will not be as conspicuous or dramatic as interstate resource wars, but it will have serious repercussions for the security interests of both the developed and the developing worlds. Countries under such stress may fragment as their states become enfeebled and peripheral regions are seized by renegade authorities and warlords. Governments of countries as different as the Philippines and Peru have lost control over outer territories; although both these cases are complicated, it is nonetheless clear that environmental stress has contributed to their fragmentation. Fragmentation of any sizeable country will produce large outflows of refugees; it will also hinder the country from effectively negotiating and implementing international agreements on collective security, global environmental protection, and other matters.

Alternatively, a state might keep scarcity-induced civil strife from causing its progressive enfeeblement and fragmentation by becoming a "hard" regime that is authoritarian, intolerant of opposition, and militarized. Such regimes are more prone to launch military attacks against neighboring countries to divert attention from internal grievances. If a number of developing countries evolve in this direction, they could eventually threaten the military and economic interests of rich countries.

A state's ability to become a hard regime in response to environmentally induced turmoil depends, I believe, on two factors. First, the state must have sufficient remaining capacity—despite the debilitating effects of scarcity—to mobilize or seize resources for its own ends; this is a function of the internal organizational coherence of the state and its autonomy from outside pressures. Second, there must remain enough surplus wealth in the country's ecological-economic system to allow the state, once it seizes this wealth, to pursue its authoritarian course. Consequently, the countries with the highest probability of becoming "hard" regimes, and potential threats to their neighbors, are large, relatively wealthy developing countries that are dependent on a declining environmental base and that have a history of state strength. Candidates include Indonesia and, perhaps, Nigeria.

Our research suggests that environmental pressures in China may cause the country's fragmentation.[80] This is not the received wisdom: most experts have been distracted by the phenomenal economic expansion in China's coastal areas; they have tended to project these trends onto the rest of the country and to neglect the dangers posed by resource scarcities.[81] The costs of misreading of the Chinese situation could be very high. China has over one-fifth of the world's population, a huge military with growing power-projection capability, and unsettled relations with some of its neighbors. The effects of Chinese civil unrest, mass violence, and state disintegration could spread far beyond its borders.

Chinese fertility rates peaked at the height of the cultural revolution between 1969 and 1972. Population growth will peak at about 17 million per year in the mid-1990s, as the babies born during the cultural revolution reach their reproductive years. In the late 1980s and early 1990s, specialists tempered their optimism about Chinese ability to bring population growth down to replacement rate.[82] Market liberalization in the countryside undermined the one-child policy. In rural areas state coercion seemed less effective, and peasants enriched by market reforms could more easily pay fines. In some provinces, therefore, it became common for families to have two or three children. The most recent evidence, however, suggests that Chinese authorities have renewed their commitment to controlling population growth. In response to often extremely coercive measures by low-level officials, fertility rates have fallen below two children per woman for the first time.[83] But

---

80. Smil, "Environmental Change as a Source of Conflict and Economic Losses in China"; Jack Goldstone, "Imminent Political Conflict Arising from China's Environmental Crises," Occasional Paper No. 2, Project on Environmental Change and Acute Conflict (December 1992).

81. See, for example, Barber Conable and David Lampton, "China: The Coming Power," *Foreign Affairs*, Vol. 72, No. 5 (Winter 1992/93), pp. 133–149. In their assessment of the pressures on contemporary China, the authors devote only half a sentence to demographic and environmental stresses.

82. Griffith Feeney, et al., "Recent Fertility Dynamics in China: Results from the 1987 One Percent Population Survey," *Population and Development Review*, Vol. 15, No. 2 (June 1989), pp. 297–321; Shanti Conly and Sharon Camp, "China's Family Planning Program: Challenging the Myths," *Country Study Series*, No. 1 (Washington, D.C.: Population Crisis Committee, 1992).

83. Nicholas Kristof, "China's Crackdown on Births: A Stunning, and Harsh, Success," *New York Times*, April 25, 1993, p. A1.

experts are not sure that this accomplishment can be sustained for long, and even if it is, China's population will continue to grow well into the next century.

Only two poor populous countries in the world have less arable land per capita than China: Egypt and Bangladesh. In fact, 300 million people in China's interior have even less arable land than the Bangladeshis. China has little scope to expand irrigated and arable land, although it might be able to increase the intensity of irrigation in some places. Consequently, continued population growth and loss of cropland mean that China will have 25 percent less arable land per capita by 2010. Moreover, the remaining land will often be of declining quality: every year the country loses as much nitrogen and phosphorous from soil erosion as it applies in inorganic fertilizer. Vaclav Smil notes that many experts and senior authorities in China are frightened by the environmental situation, believing the country has already crossed key thresholds of unsustainability. Grain is a constant preoccupation of the leadership, and imports even into rich areas may soon be necessary. Already, tens of millions of Chinese are trying to migrate from the country's interior and northern regions, where water and fuelwood are desperately scarce and the land is often badly damaged, to the booming coastal cities. Smil expects bitter disputes among these regions over migration and water sharing.

Jack Goldstone has estimated the consequences of these stresses for social stability. He notes that population and resource pressures led to widespread civil violence in China during the Ming and Qing dynasties.[84] The current regime recognizes that such pressures will cause mounting grievances in the worst-affected regions. "The rapidly growing population of the north and west cannot be fed and employed within those regions," Goldstone writes. "There is not sufficient land, nor sufficient water, to provide for the additional hundreds of millions that will be born in the next decades."[85] If large-scale migration out of the region is blocked, deprivation conflicts in the northwest are likely. Coupled with merchant and worker resistance in the major cities, they would probably lead to the fall of the central government. If the migration is diverted into China's southern countryside, deprivation and group-identity conflicts are likely to result there.

The only realistic policy is to permit movement to the wealthy coastal cities. Coastal areas must therefore be allowed to continue their rapid eco-

---

84. For a full analysis, see Jack Goldstone, *Revolution and Rebellion in the Early Modern World* (Berkeley: University of California Press, 1991).
85. Goldstone, "Imminent Political Conflicts Arising from China's Environmental Crises," p. 52.

nomic growth to absorb surplus labor. But, Goldstone argues, the Beijing government will have great difficulty maintaining economic and political control over this process. Economic liberalization helps to mobilize the population by dissolving long-standing social relations, and this weakens the Communist Party's ability to micro-manage Chinese society. Moreover, the Party is divided from the very non-Party elites that are rapidly expanding because of economic growth, including student, business, and professional groups. Further growth will depend on private domestic investment, which will encourage these elites, and also workers in private industry, to demand democratization and responsiveness of the regime. The Party has also been weakened by deep internal disagreements over the rate and degree of economic and political liberalization; suspicions about the reliability of the Army; and worker discontent that remains high throughout the country.

Divisions within the regime and among elites, combined with an increasingly mobilized population, create greater opportunities for challenges to central authority. But resource and population pressures force the regime to pursue policies, such as further economic liberalization, that only weaken it more. Goldstone believes that long-term stability would be more likely if China were to begin serious democratization soon, but he is not sanguine. Central authorities will probably refuse to recognize their loosening grip on the society, and this will eventually prompt secessionist movements in Moslem lands to the west and Tibet in the South. Sichuan may also seek independence. "Once the glue of unified communist rule dissolves, China may once again, as it has so often in its history following the fall of unifying dynasties, experience a decade or even century-long interregnum of warring among regional states."[86]

Conclusions

Our research shows that environmental scarcity causes violent conflict. This conflict tends to be persistent, diffuse, and sub-national. Its frequency will probably jump sharply in the next decades as scarcities rapidly worsen in many parts of the world. Of immediate concern are scarcities of cropland, water, forests, and fish, whereas atmospheric changes such as global warm-

---

86. Ibid., p. 54.

ing will probably not have a major effect for several decades, and then mainly by interacting with already existing scarcities.

The degradation and depletion of environmental resources is only one source of environmental scarcity; two other important sources are population growth and unequal resource distribution. Scarcity often has its harshest social impact when these factors interact. As environmental scarcity becomes more severe, some societies will have a progressively lower capacity to adapt. Of particular concern is the decreasing capacity of the state to create markets and other institutions that promote adaptation. The impact of environmental scarcity on state capacity deserves further research.

Countries experiencing chronic internal conflict because of environmental stress will probably either fragment or become more authoritarian. Fragmenting countries will be the source of large out-migrations, and they will be unable to effectively negotiate or implement international agreements on security, trade and environmental protection. Authoritarian regimes may be inclined to launch attacks against other countries to divert popular attention from internal stresses. Any of these outcomes could seriously disrupt international security. The social impacts of environmental scarcity therefore deserve concerted attention from security scholars.

Part III:
Migration and
International Security

Security, Stability, and International Migration

Myron Weiner

$\mathbf{M}$igration and refugee issues, no longer the sole concern of ministries of labor or of immigration, are now matters of high international politics, engaging the attention of heads of states, cabinets, and key ministries involved in defense, internal security, and external relations. Certainly the most dramatic high-politics event involving international migration in recent years was the exodus of East Germans to Austria through Czechoslovakia and Hungary in July and August 1989; it precipitated the decision of the German Democratic Republic to open its western borders, a massive migration westward followed by the fall of the East German government, and the absorption of East Germany by the Federal Republic of Germany. It was flight, not an invasion, that ultimately destroyed the East German state.[1]

Examples abound of migration flows—both of economic migrants affected by the push and pull of differentials in employment opportunities and income, and of refugees from the pushes of domestic turmoil and persecution—that have generated conflicts within and between states and have therefore risen to the top of the political agenda. Among these examples are the rise of right-wing anti-migrant political parties throughout Western Europe; the conflict between the United States and Great Britain over the forcible repatriation of refugees from Hong Kong; the U.S.-Israeli controversy over the settlement of Soviet Jews on the West Bank; the placement of Western migrants by Iraq at strategic locations in order to prevent air strikes; the anxieties in Western Europe over a possible influx of migrants from Eastern Europe and the former Soviet Union; a threat by Palestinian radicals that they would launch terrorist attacks against airlines that carried Soviet Jews to Israel; an

Myron Weiner is Ford International Professor in the Department of Political Science at the Massachusetts Institute of Technology. He was director of the Center of International Studies at MIT from 1987 to 1992.

For helpful comments on an earlier draft of this paper I am grateful to Rogers Brubaker, Karen Jacobsen, Robert Jervis, Stephen Krasner, Robert Lucas, Rosemarie Rogers, and Sharon Russell.

1. Timothy Garton Ash, "The German Revolution," *The New York Review of Books*, December 21, 1989, pp. 14–17, provides an informed eye-witness account of how the exodus of East Germans in the summer and fall of 1989 led to the dismantling of the Berlin Wall and the absorption of the East German state into West Germany.

International Security, Vol. 17, No. 3 (Winter 1992/93), pp. 91–126
© 1992 by the President and Fellows of Harvard College and the Massachusetts Institute of Technology.

invasion of Rwanda by armed Tutsi refugees in Uganda aimed at overthrowing the Hutu-dominated government; the successful defeat of the Kabul regime, after thirteen years of warfare, by the Afghan mujaheddin. One could go on, drawing examples from the daily press to make three points:

First, international migration shows no sign of abating. Indeed, with the end of the Cold War there has been a resurgence of violent secessionist movements that create refugee flows,[2] while barriers to exit from the former Soviet Union and Eastern Europe have been lifted. The breakup of empires and countries into smaller units has created minorities who now feel insecure.[3] Vast differentials in income and employment opportunities among countries persist, providing the push and pull that motivate economic migrants.[4] Environmental degradation, droughts, floods, famines, and civil conflicts compel people to flee across international borders.[5] And new global

---

2. On secessionist movements, see Allen Buchanan, *Secession: The Morality of Political Divorce from Fort Sumter to Lithuania and Quebec* (Boulder, Colo.: Westview Press, 1991). This otherwise excellent analysis by a political philosopher does not deal with the problem of minorities that remain in successor states.

3. Democratization and political liberalization of authoritarian regimes have enabled people to leave who previously were denied the right of exit. An entire region of the world, ranging from Central Europe to the Chinese border, had imprisoned those who sought to emigrate. Similar restrictions continue to operate for several of the remaining communist countries. If and when the regimes of North Korea and China liberalize, another large region of the world will allow its citizens to leave. See Alan Dowty, *Closed Borders: The Contemporary Assault on Freedom of Movement* (New Haven: Yale University Press, 1987), which provides a useful account of how authoritarian states engaged both in restricting exodus and in forced expulsions. For an analysis of the right to leave and return, see H. Hannum, *The Right to Leave and Return in International Law and Practice* (London: Martinus Nijhoff, 1987). As has happened twice before in this century, the breakup of an empire is producing large-scale ethnic conflict and emigration. With the withdrawal of Soviet power from Eastern Europe and the disintegration of the Soviet state itself, conflicts have erupted between Turks and Bulgarians in Turkey; Romanians and Hungarians in Transylvania; Armenians and Azeris in the Caucasus; Albanians, Croatians, Slovenians, Bosnians, and Serbs in former Yugoslavia; Slovaks and Czechs in Czechoslovakia; and among a variety of ethnic groups in Georgia, Moldova, Ukraine, and in the new states of Central Asia. There is a high potential for continued emigration of minorities among each of these states. See F. Stephen Larrabee, "Down and Out in Warsaw and Budapest: Eastern Europe and East-West Migration," *International Security*, Vol. 16, No. 4 (Spring 1992), pp. 5–33.

4. A long-term decline in the birth rate in advanced industrial countries combined with continued economic growth may lead employers to seek low-wage laborers from abroad. Transnational investment in manufacturing industries may reduce some manpower needs, but the demand for more workers in the service sector seems likely to grow, barring technological breakthroughs that would replace waiters, bus conductors, nurses, and household help. Employers in Japan, Singapore, and portions of the United States and Western Europe are prepared to hire illegal migrants, notwithstanding the objections of their governments and much of the citizenry. So long as employer demand remains high, borders are porous, and government enforcement of employer sanctions is limited, illegal migration seems likely to continue and in some countries to increase.

5. There have already been mass migrations within and between countries as a result of

networks of communication and transportation provide individuals with in-formation and opportunities for migration.[6]

Second, more people want to leave their countries than there are countries willing or capable of accepting them. The reluctance of states to open their borders to all who wish to enter is only partly a concern over economic effects. The constraints are as likely to be political, resting upon a concern that an influx of people belonging to another ethnic community may generate xenophobic sentiments, conflicts between natives and migrants, and the growth of anti-migrant right-wing parties.

Third, it is necessary to note that while the news media have focused on South/North migration and East/West migration, this focus is narrow and misleading. The movement of migrant workers from North Africa to Western Europe, migration from Asia and Latin America to the United States and Canada, and the increase in the number of people from the Third World and Eastern Europe claiming refugee status in the West represent simply one dimension of the global flows. Only a fraction of the world's seventeen million refugees are in the advanced industrial countries and only a small portion of global migration has flowed to Western Europe (where migrants total 5 percent of the population) or to the United States. Most of the move-ment has been from one developing country to another; the world's largest refugee flows have been in Africa, South Asia, Southeast Asia, and most recently in the Persian Gulf.[7] In South Asia alone, 35 to 40 million people

---

desertification, floods, toxic wastes (chemical contamination, nuclear reactor accidents, hazard-ous waste), and threats of inundation as a result of rising sea levels. According to one estimate, two million Africans were displaced in the mid-1980s as a result of drought. See Jodi L. Jacobson, *Environmental Refugees: A Yardstick of Habitability,* Worldwatch Paper No. 86 (Washington, D.C.: Worldwatch Institute, 1988).

6. Information concerning employment opportunities and changes in immigration and refugee laws is quickly transmitted to friends and relatives. Not only do many people in the Third World view the United States and Europe as potential places for migration, but differences and opportunities *within* the Third World are also becoming better known. Indonesians, for example, are seeking (illegal) employment in peninsular Malaysia, Sabah, and Sarawak. Malaysians and others are aware of opportunities in Singapore. Oil-rich Brunei attracts workers from Malaysia, the Philippines, Thailand, and Indonesia. Taiwan, Hong Kong, and South Korea export man-power, but also attract illegal immigrant workers drawn by their reputation for employment at high wages. Migrants continue to be attracted to the oil-producing countries of the Middle East. For one account of large-scale migration among Third World countries, see Michael Vatikiotis, "Malaysia: Worrisome Influx; Foreign Workers Raise Social, Security Fears," *Far Eastern Economic Review,* August 6, 1992, p. 21, which describes the concerns in Malaysia over the influx of an estimated one million migrants from Indonesia.

7. An estimated 5.5 million people from forty countries were temporarily or permanently displaced by the Gulf War. The largest single group was an estimated 1–1.5 million Yemenis who were forced to leave Saudi Arabia to return to Yemen. The other main displaced peoples

have crossed international borders within the region.[8] In the Middle East, wars and civil conflicts have led to large-scale population flows from Iraq, Kuwait, Israel, Saudi Arabia, Iran, and Lebanon. In Africa, civil wars and famines have produced some of the largest refugee populations to be found anywhere in the world.[9] Attention has been given by economists to the ways in which economic differentials between countries influence migration,[10] and by some political scientists to the ways in which conflicts within countries lead to refugee flows.[11] But little systematic comparative attention has been given to the ways in which international population movements create conflicts within and between states, that is, to population flows as an independent rather than as a dependent variable. A study of these effects is necessary to understand why states and their citizens often have an aversion to international migration even when there are economic benefits.

These features of population movements—a growth propelled by economic differentials, internal political disorder, and global networks of communication and transportation; the political as well as economic constraints on the admission of migrants and refugees; and the truly global character of migration—suggest the need for a security/stability framework for the study of international migration that focuses on state policies toward emigration and immigration as shaped by concerns over internal stability and international

---

were Kurds, Kuwaitis, Palestinians, and South Asians. See Elizabeth N. Offen, "The Persian Gulf War of 1990–91: Its Impact on Migration and the Security of States" (M.S. dissertation, Department of Political Science, MIT, June 1992).

8. For data on South Asia, including a description of the major bilateral flows that have led to conflict, see Myron Weiner, "Security, Migration, and Conflict," in *Defense Intelligence Journal* (forthcoming).

9. *World Refugee Survey, 1992* (Washington: D.C.: U.S. Committee for Refugees, 1992). The World Refugee Survey is the best single source for annual world-wide data on both refugees and internally displaced persons, with brief accounts by country of source and destination.

10. See Sidney Klein, ed., *The Economics of Mass Migration in the Twentieth Century* (New York: Paragon House, 1987); Brinley Thomas, *Migration and Economic Growth: A Study of Great Britain and the Atlantic Economy* (Cambridge: Cambridge University Press, 1954); Charles P. Kindleberger, *Europe's Postwar Growth: The Role of Labor Supply* (Cambridge: Harvard University Press, 1967), chap. 9; Theodore W. Schultz, "Migration: An Economist's View," in William H. McNeill and Ruth S. Adams, eds., *Human Migration: Patterns and Policies* (Bloomington: Indiana University Press, 1987), pp. 377–386. These and other works by economists deal with the benefits and costs as well as the determinants of migration. For a useful bibliography on the economics of migration, see Julian L. Simon, *The Economic Consequences of Immigration* (New York: Basil Blackwell, 1989).

11. Aristide R. Zolberg, Astri Suhrke, and Sergio Aguayo, *Escape from Violence: Conflict and the Refugee Crisis in the Developing World* (New York: Oxford University Press, 1989); and Michael R. Marrus, *The Unwanted: European Refugees in the Twentieth Century* (New York: Oxford University Press, 1985), are among the most comprehensive treatments of the major world regions that have produced refugees in this century.

security. Such a framework should consider political changes within states as a major determinant of international population flows, and migration, including refugee flows, both as cause and as consequence of international conflict.

A security/stability framework can be contrasted with an international political economy framework, which explains international migration primarily by focusing on global inequalities, the economic linkages between sending and receiving states including the movement of capital and technology and the role played by transnational institutions, and structural changes in labor markets linked to changes in the international division of labor. The two frameworks have much in common. Both turn our attention from individual decision-making by migrants to the larger social, political, and economic context within which individuals act; both are interactive frameworks emphasizing the linkage between migration processes and other global processes; and both pay close attention to the behavior of states and to the importance of borders, although the security/stability framework gives somewhat greater importance to state decision-making than does a political economy approach, which often regards the state as a weak actor buffeted by larger global forces.

The two frameworks direct us to study different aspects of international migration, to ask different questions, to offer different explanations for international flows, and to create different conceptual tools for analysis. While they are at times complementary, the frameworks often yield different outcomes. A more narrowly economic perspective, for example, may lead the analyst to regard the movement of people from a poor country to a rich country as mutually advantageous (the one benefiting from remittances, the other from needed additions to its labor force), whereas a security/stability perspective of the same migration flow may lead one to point to the political risks associated with changes in the ethnic composition of the receiving country, and the attending international strains that result if there are clashes between natives and migrants. Alternately, an economic perspective might lead the analyst to conclude that migration results in a brain drain from the sending country while worsening unemployment and creating housing shortages in the receiving country, while a security/stability framework might lead the analyst looking at the same migration flow to argue that internal security and international peace can be enhanced because the migrants are an ethnic minority unwelcomed in their home country but readily accepted by another country. The movement of people may be acceptable to both countries even though each incurs an economic loss. Thus, cost/benefit analyses may yield different assessments and policies, depending upon which framework is chosen.

Much of the contemporary literature on international migration focuses on global economic conditions as the key determinants of population movements.[12] Differentials in wages and employment opportunities—a high demand for labor in one country and a surplus in another—stimulate the movement of labor. According to economic theories of migration, individuals will emigrate if the expected benefits exceed the costs, with the result that the propensity to migrate from one region or country to another is viewed as being determined by average wages, the cost of travel, and labor market conditions. Accordingly, it is argued, changes in the global economy, such as a rise in the world price of oil or shifts in terms of trade and international flows of capital, will increase the demand for labor in some countries and decrease it in others. Moreover, the development strategies pursued by individual countries may lead to high growth rates in some and low growth rates and stagnation in others. Uneven economic development among states and a severe maldistribution of income within states may induce individuals and families to move across international boundaries to take advantage of greater opportunities.

These economic explanations go a long way toward explaining a great deal of international population movements, but they neglect two critical political elements. The first is that international population movements are often impelled, encouraged, or prevented by governments or political forces for reasons that may have little to do with economic conditions. Indeed, much of the international population flows, especially within Africa and South

---

12. On the political economy of international migration see, for a neo-Marxist perspective, Saskia Sassen, *The Mobility of Labor and Capital: A Study in International Investment and Labor Flow* (Cambridge: Cambridge University Press, 1988); Alejandro Portes and John Walton, *Labor, Class, and the International System* (New York: Academic Press, 1981); Stephen Adler, *International Migration and Dependence* (Westmead: Saxon House, 1977); and Stephen Castles and Godula Kosack, *Immigrant Workers and Class Structure in Western Europe* (London: Oxford University Press, 1973). For other political economy interpretations, see Kindleberger, *Europe's Postwar Growth*; Michael Piore, *Birds of Passage: Migrant Labor in Industrial Societies* (Cambridge: Cambridge University Press, 1979); Wolf R. Bohning, *The Migration of Workers in the United Kingdom and the European Community* (London: Oxford University Press, 1972); and Wolf R. Bohning, *Studies in International Labour Migration* (London: Macmillan, 1984). Two recent works by economists on migration to the United States do not deal with the political or security dimensions of international migration. See Simon, *The Economic Consequences of Immigration*; and George J. Borjas, *Friends or Strangers: The Impact of Immigrants on the U.S. Economy* (New York: Basic Books, 1990).

Asia, are determined only marginally, if at all, by changes in the global or regional political economy. And secondly, even when economic conditions create inducements for people to leave one country for another, it is governments that decide whether their citizens should be allowed to leave and governments that decide whether immigrants should be allowed to enter, and their decisions are frequently based on non-economic considerations. Moreover, governments vary in their capacity to control entry. States that are capable of defending themselves against missile, tank, and infantry attacks are often unable to defend themselves against the intrusion of thousands of illegals infiltrating across a border in search of employment or safety. Governments want to control the entry of people and regard their inability to do so as a threat to sovereignty. Any effort, therefore, to develop a framework for the analysis of transnational flows of people must also take into account the political determinants and constraints upon these flows.[13]

A security/stability framework complements rather than replaces an economic analysis by focusing upon the role of states in both creating and responding to international migration. The object of this article is to identify some of the circumstances in which security/stability considerations become paramount in how states deal with issues of international migration. I do so in three ways, first, by identifying types of international movements generated by considerations of state security and stability, as distinct from those flows largely shaped by the regional or international political economy. I provide a brief description of forced and induced emigrations as examples of politically-driven population movements with international repercussions.

---

13. Among the studies that focus on the political determinants of refugee flows, the most comprehensive is Zolberg, Suhrke, and Aguayo, *Escape from Violence*. Few other studies so directly consider the relationship between population flows and the political processes within and between states that create them. For a study of the *effects* of migration, especially on foreign policy, see the particularly useful set of essays edited by Robert W. Tucker, Charles B. Keely, and Linda Wrigley, *Immigration and U.S. Foreign Policy* (Boulder, Colo.: Westview Press, 1990). Also see Michael S. Teitelbaum, "Immigration, Refugees and Foreign Policy," *International Organization*, Vol. 38, No. 3 (Summer 1984), pp. 429–450. For an examination of how refugee flows affect and are affected by international relations, see Gilbert Loescher and Laila Monahan, eds., *Refugees and International Relations* (New York: Oxford University Press, 1989); and Leon Gordenker, *Refugees in International Politics* (London: Croom Helm, 1987). It should be noted that the standard works in international relations and in the political economy of international relations do not discuss international migration and refugee flows. See, for example, Robert O. Keohane and Joseph S. Nye, Jr., *Power and Interdependence* (Boston: Little, Brown, 1977); Robert Gilpin, *The Political Economy of International Relations* (Princeton: Princeton University Press, 1987); Kenneth Waltz, *Theory of International Politics* (Reading, Mass: Addison-Wesley, 1979); Stephen D. Krasner, *Defending the National Interest* (Princeton: Princeton University Press, 1978); Robert O. Keohane, *After Hegemony* (Princeton: Princeton University Press, 1984).

Secondly, I identify those circumstances when international migration is regarded as a threat to a country's security and stability. This leads us to consider how and when refugees and economic migrants come to be regarded as threatening by receiving and sending countries. And thirdly, I consider the various ways states react when faced with population movements they regard as a threat to their international security and internal stability.

Forced and Induced Emigrations: A Global Perspective

It would be inaccurate to use the passive voice to describe much of the world's population flows. They do not merely happen; more often they are made to happen. We can identify three distinct types of forced and induced emigrations in the contemporary world.

First, governments may force emigration as a means of achieving cultural homogeneity or asserting the dominance of one ethnic community over another. Such flows have a long and sordid world-wide history. The rise of nationalism in Europe was accompanied by state actions to eject religious communities that did not subscribe to the established religion, and ethnic minorities that did not belong to the dominant ethnic community. In the fifteenth century the Spanish crown expelled the Jews. In the sixteenth century the French expelled the Huguenots. In the seventeenth and eighteenth centuries the British crown induced Protestant dissenters to settle in the American colonies. And in the early decades of the twentieth century minorities throughout Eastern Europe—Bulgarians, Greeks, Jews, Turks, Hungarians, Serbs, Macedonians—were put to flight.[14]

Contemporary population movements in post-independence Africa, the Middle East, South Asia, and Southeast Asia are similarly linked to the rise of nationalism and the emergence of new states. The boundaries of many of the new post-colonial regimes divided linguistic, religious, and tribal communities, with the result that minorities, fearful of their future and often faced with discrimination and violence, migrated to join their ethnic brethren in a neighboring country. Many Third World countries also expelled their ethnic minorities, especially when the minorities constituted an industrious

---

14. See Eugene M. Kulischer, *Europe on the Move: War and Population Changes, 1917–47* (New York: Columbia University Press, 1948), pp. 248–249.

class of migrant origin in competition with a middle-class ethnic majority.[15] Governments facing unemployment within the majority community and conflicts among ethnic groups over language and educational opportunities often regarded the expulsion of a prosperous, well-placed minority as a politically popular policy. Minorities have often been threatened by the state's antagonistic policies toward their religion, their language and their culture, as the state sought to impose a hegemonic ethnic or religious identity upon its citizens.[16] Economically successful minorities have often been told that others would be given preferences in employment, a policy of discrimination which effectively made it difficult for minorities to compete on the basis of merit.[17] Many governments expelled their minorities or created conditions that induced them to leave, and thereby forced other countries, on humanitarian grounds or out of cultural affinity, to accept them as refugees. The list of expulsions is long: Chinese from Vietnam, Indians and Pakistanis from East Africa, Tamils from Sri Lanka, Bahais from Iran, Kurds from Turkey, Iran and Iraq, Ahmediyas from Pakistan, Chakmas from Bangladesh, and in Africa the Tutsi from Rwanda, Eritreans and others from Ethiopia, and non-Arab peoples from the south in Sudan, to name a few.[18] To this list from the Third World, we must now add the minorities in each of the successor states of Yugoslavia.[19]

Secondly, governments have forced emigration as a means of dealing with political dissidents and class enemies. The ancient Greeks were among the

---

15. In 1969 Kenya announced that eighty thousand noncitizen Asians must leave and in 1972 Uganda expelled its Indian population, most of whom were part of the country's middle class. See Zolberg, Suhrke, and Aguayo, *Escape from Violence,* pp. 65–66.
16. Sri Lanka is an example. See Stanley J. Tambiah, *Ethnic Fratricide and the Dismantling of Democracy* (Chicago: University of Chicago Press, 1987); and Stanley J. Tambiah, *Buddhism Betrayed? Religion, Politics, and Violence in Sri Lanka* (Chicago: University of Chicago Press, 1992).
17. Two examples are Malaysia, where the government adopted a policy of giving preferences in employment and education to Malays over Chinese, and Sri Lanka, where government gave preference to Sinhalese over Tamils. For these and other examples see Donald L. Horowitz, *Ethnic Groups in Conflict* (Berkeley: University of California Press, 1985), pp. 185–228.
18. Ibid., pp. 198–199, 200–201, 208–209.
19. The war for "ethnic cleansing" in Yugoslavia is the latest example of governments seeking to force populations to move in an effort to establish ethnic hegemony over a territory; in this particular instance it is combined with an effort to force a change in the borders themselves by establishing Serbian demographic and military preponderance in areas of Croatia and Bosnia-Herzegovina that could then be incorporated into Serbia. For an account see Misha Glenny, "Yugoslavia: The Revenger's Tragedy," *The New York Review of Books,* Vol. 34, No. 14 (August 13, 1992), pp. 37–43. Glenny notes that majority-minority conflicts in Kosovo and Macedonia, accompanied by similar refugee flights, could lead to military action by Albania, Bulgaria, Greece, or Turkey.

earliest to strip dissidents of citizenship and cast them into exile. Socrates himself was offered the option of going into exile rather than being executed. Contemporary authoritarian governments have expelled dissidents or allowed them to go into exile as an alternative to imprisonment. Exiles from the Third World—from Ethiopia, Iran, Cuba, South Korea, Nicaragua, Vietnam, Chile—have largely replaced exiles from Europe in the United States.[20]

Governments may expel not just a handful of dissidents, but a substantial portion of the population hostile to the regime. Revolutionary regimes often see large-scale emigration of a social class as a way of transforming the country's social structure. The exodus of more than a half million members of the Cuban middle class was regarded by the Castro regime as a way of disposing of a social class hostile to socialism. In 1971 the Pakistani government sought to weaken the insurgency in East Pakistan by forcing large numbers of Bengali Hindus out of the country. The Vietnamese government justified expulsions as a way of eliminating a bourgeois social class opposed to the regime. The Khmer Rouge regime killed or forced into exile citizens tainted with French and other western cultural influences in an effort to reduce Cambodia's cultural and economic ties with the West. And in Afghanistan, the Soviet and Afghan military forced populations hostile to the regime to flee to Pakistan and Iran.[21]

A third type of forced emigration can be described as part of a strategy to achieve a foreign policy objective. Governments may, for example, force emigration as a way of putting pressure on neighboring states, although they may deny any such intent. The refugee-receiving country, however, often understands that a halt to unwanted migration is not likely to take place unless it yields on a demand made by the country from which the refugees come. In 1981, for example, the United States government believed that the government of Haiti was encouraging its citizens to flee by boat to Florida to press the United States to substantially increase its economic aid. (It did.)[22]

---

20. On exile politics see the articles in *Third World Quarterly*, Vol. 9, No. 1 (London: Third World Foundation, January 1987); and Yossi Shain, *The Frontier of Loyalty: Political Exiles in the Age of the Nation-State* (Middletown, Conn.: Wesleyan University Press, 1989).

21. For accounts of forced migration as an instrument of both domestic and foreign policy, see Michael S. Teitelbaum, "Forced Migration: The Tragedy of Mass Expulsions," in Nathan Glazer, ed., *Clamor at the Gates: The New Migration* (San Francisco: ICS Press, 1985); and Peter H. Koehn, *Refugees from Revolution: U.S. Policy and Third-World Migration* (Boulder, Colo.: Westview Press, 1991).

22. As part of its effort to halt Haitian migration to the United States, the Reagan administration promised increased amounts of foreign aid to improve the conditions that purportedly promoted the flow. For an account of how the United States utilized its aid program to persuade the

In the 1980s, Pakistani officials believed that Soviet pressure on Afghans to flee was intended in part to force Pakistan to seek a settlement with the Afghan regime and to withdraw military aid to the insurgents.[23] The Malaysian government feared that the government of Vietnam sought to destabilize it by forcing Malaysia to accept Chinese refugees.[24] The Federal Republic of Germany believed that the German Democratic Republic was permitting Tamil refugees to enter through the Berlin border to force the FRG to establish new rules of entry that would tacitly recognize the East German state or, alternatively, as a bargaining ploy for additional financial credits (which the FRG subsequently granted in return for a halt to the flow).

In the eighteenth and nineteenth centuries, colonization was an instrument of foreign economic policy that served to extend control over a territory. The British settled their colonies in the western hemisphere, in southern and eastern Africa, and in the Pacific; the French settled North Africa; the Portuguese populated Angola and Brazil; the Russians moved into nearby territories in the east, south, and southwest.[25]

The imperial powers also moved populations from one territory to another in pursuit of their own economic interests. Slaves were transported from Africa to the Caribbean and to North and South America. After the abolition of slavery, the British established a system of indentured labor that enabled them to satisfy the labor needs in their colonies (especially on British-owned plantations) by moving Indians to East Africa, Mauritius, the Caribbean, and Fiji.[26] The colonial powers also encouraged the migration of entrepreneurial

---

Haitian government to prosecute those engaged in trafficking in illegal migrants and to pledge not to mistreat return migrants, see Jorge Domínguez, "Immigration as Foreign Policy in U.S.-Latin American Relations," in Robert Tucker, Charles B. Keely, and Linda Wrigley, eds., *Immigration and U.S. Foreign Policy* (Boulder, Colo.: Westview Press, 1990). Also see Gil Loescher and John A. Scanlan, *Calculated Kindness: Refugees and America's Half-Open Door, 1945 to the Present* (New York: Free Press, 1986).

23. U.S. Department of State, *Afghanistan: Eight Years of Soviet Occupation* (Washington, D.C.: U.S. Government Printing Office, December 1987).

24. For an account of Malaysian and Thai government responses to refugees from Vietnam, see Loescher and Scanlan, *Calculated Kindness*, p. 135. Also see Lesleyanne Hawthorne, *Refugee: The Vietnamese Experience* (London: Oxford University Press, 1982).

25. For a political analysis of Russian colonization policy, see Alexandre A. Bennigsen and S. Enders Wimbush, "Migration and Political Control: Soviet Europeans in Soviet Central Asia," in McNeill and Adams, *Human Migration*.

26. For accounts of how the British settled South Asians in British colonies in Burma, Uganda, Kenya, Malawi, Mauritius, Guyana, Malaysia, South Africa, Fiji, and in the Caribbean, see Hugh Tinker, *The Export of Indian Labour Overseas 1830–1920* (London: Oxford University Press, 1974); and Hugh Tinker, *The Banyan Tree: Overseas Emigrants from India, Pakistan, and Bangladesh* (Oxford: Oxford University Press, 1977).

communities, traders, and money lenders whom they regarded as politically pliable, e.g., Indians to the Gulf, Lebanese to West Africa, and Chinese to Southeast Asia.

While the colonization of distant territories rarely led to enduring political or economic control, the colonization of nearby territories has almost always had permanent consequences. Americans moved westward into Mexican and Indian territories. The Chinese colonized non-Han areas. The Russians colonized the Ukraine, Moldavia, the Baltic states, and portions of Muslim-populated Soviet Central Asia. And the Germans moved eastward in central Europe. These flows displaced the local populations and transformed the politics of the areas that were colonized.

With independence from European colonialism, many newly-established regimes sought to "decolonize" themselves by pressing for the exodus of populations they regarded as imposed upon them by the imperial power. With few exceptions, white settlers were pressed to return home. French settlers vacated Algeria; most Portuguese left Angola and Mozambique; many British left Zimbabwe. The new regimes often pressed for the exodus of those who had been brought in by the imperial rulers as indentured servants, although they were now free laborers and many had become prosperous businessmen and members of the middle class. Uganda forced South Asians to leave.[27] Sri Lanka pressed for the departure of Tamil tea estate workers. The Fijian military overthrew an elected government dominated by Indian descendants of estate workers, and native Melanesian Fijians rioted against Indians in an apparent effort to force them to leave the island.[28] A similar process of rejection may soon be at work in the former Soviet republics, where millions of Russian "colons" are regarded as illegitimate settlers imposed by the Soviet regime.[29]

Forced emigration can be an instrument by which one state seeks to destabilize another, force recognition, stop a neighboring state from interfering

---

27. M. Mamdani, *From Citizen to Refugee: Ugandan Asians Come to Britain* (London: Pinter Publishers, 1973).
28. Colonel Sitveni Rabuka, a Melanesian, took over the government and arrested all cabinet members. The coup was endorsed by the Great Council of Chiefs and was quickly followed by race riots and attacks on Indian property. For an account of the 1987 coup, see the *Far Eastern Economic Review*, June 4, 1987, p. 38. It is estimated that in 1987 Fiji's population of 714,000 was 48.6 percent of Indian origin and 46.2 percent of Melanesian origin. For an account of subsequent emigration by many Indians from Fiji see the *Far Eastern Economic Review*, June 28, 1990, p. 15.
29. Rogers Brubaker, "Ethnopolitical Migration from and among Soviet Successor States," in Myron Weiner, ed., *International Migration and Security* (forthcoming).

in its internal affairs, prod a neighboring state to provide aid or credit in return for stopping the flow, or extend its own political and economic interests or those of a dominant ethnic group through colonization or decolonization. An examination of both historical and contemporary population movements thus demonstrates that countries of emigration have more control over international population flows than is usually accounted for by political analysts, and that what often appears to be spontaneous emigration and refugee movements may represent deliberate emigration policies on the part of sending countries. To view refugee flows as simply the unintended consequences of internal upheavals or economic crises is to ignore the eagerness of some governments to reduce or eliminate from within their own borders selected social classes and ethnic groups, and to affect the politics and policies of their neighbors.[30]

When is Migration a Threat to Security and Stability?

Migration can be perceived as threatening by governments of either population-sending or population-receiving communities. The threat can be an attack by armed refugees; migrants can be a threat to either country's political stability; or migrants can be perceived as a threat to the major societal values of the receiving country.

"Security" is a social construct with different meanings in different societies. An ethnically homogeneous society, for example, may place a higher value on preserving its ethnic character than does a heterogeneous society and may, therefore, regard a population influx as a threat to its security. Providing a haven for those who share one's values (political freedom, for example) is important in some countries, but not in others; in some countries, therefore, an influx of "freedom fighters" may not be regarded as a threat to security. Moreover, even in a given country, what is highly valued may not be shared by elites and counter-elites. The influx of migrants regarded as radicals may be feared by a monarch, but welcomed by the opposition. One ethnic group may welcome migrants, while another is vehemently opposed to them. The business community may be more willing than the general public to import migrant workers.

---

30. For a useful bibliographical guide to the vast literature on refugees, see *Displaced Peoples and Refugee Studies: A Resource Guide,* edited by the Refugee Studies Programme, University of Oxford (London: Hans Zell Publishers, 1990).

Similarly, countries differ in whether or not they regard the mistreatment of their citizens abroad as a threat that calls for state action. While some countries are prepared to take armed action in defense of their overseas citizens, others prefer not to antagonize a government that has enabled its citizens to find employment and a country that is a source of much-needed remittances.

Any attempt to classify types of threats from immigration quickly runs into distinctions between "real" and "perceived" threats, or into absurdly paranoid notions of threat or mass anxieties that can best be described as xenophobic and racist. But even these extreme notions are elements in the reaction of governments to immigrants and refugees. It is necessary to find an analytical stance that, on the one hand, does not dismiss fears, and, on the other, does not regard all anxieties over immigration and refugees as a justification for exclusion.

Before turning to an analysis of how, why, and when states may regard immigrants and refugees as potential threats, it is first necessary to note that some obvious explanations for the response of population-receiving countries are of limited utility. One example is economic absorptive capacity. It is plausible, for example, that a country with little unemployment, a high demand for labor, and the financial resources to provide the housing and social services required by immigrants should regard migration as beneficial, while a country low on each of these dimensions should regard migration as economically and socially destabilizing. Nevertheless, using these criteria, one might expect Japan to welcome migrants and Israel to reject them, when in fact the opposite is the case.[31]

A second plausible but unsatisfactory explanation is the volume of immigration. A country faced with a large-scale influx should feel more threatened than a country experiencing a small influx of migrants. From this perspective one might have expected the Federal Republic of Germany to regard a trickle of Sri Lankan Tamils in the mid-1980s with equanimity, but to move swiftly to halt the 1989 influx of 2,000 East Germans daily, or for the countries of Africa to feel more threatened by the onrush of refugees and hence less receptive than the countries of Western Europe confronted with a trickle from the Third World. Again, however, the opposite has been the case.

---

31. In fact, when Soviet Jewish migration reached 200,000 in one year, there were "euphoric expectations of a million-and-a-half newcomers within two or three years," wrote the editor of the Jerusalem *Post*. David Bar-Illan, "Why Likud Lost—And Who Won," *Commentary*, Vol. 94, No. 2 (August 1992), p. 28.

Economics does, of course, matter. Even a country willing to accept immigrants when its economy is booming is more likely to close its doors in a recession. But economics does not explain many of the differences between countries, nor does it explain the criteria countries employ to decide whether a particular group of migrants or refugees is acceptable or is regarded as threatening. Similarly, volume can matter, but again it depends upon who is at the door.

The third and most plausible explanation for the willingness of states to accept or reject migrants is ethnic affinity. A government and its citizens are likely to be receptive to those who share the same language, religion, or race, while it might regard as threatening those with whom such an identity is not shared. But what constitutes "ethnic affinity" is, again, a social construct that can change over time. Australians and Americans, for example, redefined themselves so that Asians are no longer excluded as unassimilable peoples. Many West Europeans now regard East Europeans as fellow-Europeans, more acceptable as migrants than people from North Africa. Who is or is not "one of us" is historically variable. To many nineteenth-century American Protestants, Jews and Catholics were not "one of us," and today, for many Europeans, Muslims are not "one of us." Moreover, what constitutes cultural affinity for one group in a multi-ethnic society may represent a cultural, social, and economic threat to another: note, for example, the hostile response of some African-Americans in Florida to Cuban migrants,[32] Indian Assamese response to Bangladeshis, and Pakistan Sindhi response to Biharis. Cultural affinity—or its absence—clearly plays a critical role in how various communities within countries respond to a population influx; this is a theme to which we shall return.

We can identify five broad categories of situations in which refugees or migrants may be perceived as a threat to the country that produces the emigrants, to the country that receives them, or to relations between sending and receiving countries. The first is when refugees and migrants are regarded as a threat—or at least a thorn—in relations between sending and receiving countries, a situation that arises when refugees and migrants are opposed to the regime of their home country. The second is when migrants or refugees

---

32. The ambivalent attitude of African-Americans toward immigration is described by Lawrence H. Fuchs, "The Reactions of Black Americans to Immigration," in Virginia Yans-McLaughlin, ed., *Immigration Reconsidered: History, Sociology and Politics* (New York: Oxford University Press, 1990).

are perceived as a political threat or security risk to the regime of the host country. The third is when immigrants are seen as a cultural threat or, fourth, as a social and economic problem for the host society. And the fifth—a new element growing out of recent developments in the Gulf—is when the host society uses immigrants as an instrument of threat against the country of origin.

REFUGEES AND IMMIGRANTS AS OPPONENTS OF THE HOME REGIME

Conflicts create refugees, but refugees can also create conflicts. An international conflict arises when a country classifies individuals as refugees with a well-founded fear of persecution,[33] thereby accusing and condemning their country of origin for engaging in persecution. The mere granting of asylum can create an antagonistic relationship. Thus, the January 1990 debate in Congress over whether Chinese students should be permitted to remain in the United States because of the persecutions in China was regarded by the People's Republic of China as "interference" in its internal affairs. President Bush was prepared to permit graduating students and other Chinese in the United States to remain by extending their visas, but not to grant asylum, while many Congressmen wanted to grant formal asylum status in order to condemn China. Moreover, to classify individuals as refugees with a well-founded fear of persecution is also to acknowledge that they have a moral (as distinct from a political) right to oppose their country's regime. The view of the United Nations High Commission for Refugees (UNHCR) is that the granting of refugee status does not necessarily imply criticism of the sending by the receiving country, but such a view contradicts the conception of the

---

33. The language is from the 1951 United Nations Convention Relating to the Status of Refugees, subsequently modified in a 1967 protocol. The Convention states that a refugee is a person who "owing to a well-founded fear of being persecuted for reasons of race, religion, nationality, membership of a particular social group or political opinion, is outside the country of his nationality and is unable, or unwilling to avail himself of the protection of that country." This definition is the centerpiece of most Western law dealing with refugees. Some critics (see Zolberg, Suhrke, and Aguayo, *Escape from Violence*) believe that the definition is too narrow because it excludes those who only flee from violence. For a defense of the United Nations definition, see David A. Martin, "The Refugee Concept: On Definitions, Politics, and the Careful Use of Scarce Resources," in Howard Adelman, ed., *Refugee Policy: Canada and the United States* (Toronto: York Lanes Press, 1991), pp. 30–51. A wider definition of refugee was adopted in 1969 by the Organization of African Unity in its Refugee Convention, according to which the term refugee applies to every person who "owing to external aggression, occupation, foreign domination or events seriously disturbing public order in either part or the whole of his country of origin or nationality, is compelled to leave his place of habitual residence in order to seek refuge in another place outside his country of origin or nationality."

refugee as one with a fear of *persecution*.[34] Moreover, democratic regimes generally allow their refugees to speak out against the regime of their country of origin, allow them access to the media, and permit them to send information and money back home in support of the opposition. The host country's decision to grant refugee status thus often creates an adversary relationship with the country that produces the refugees. The receiving country may have no such intent, but even where its motives are humanitarian the mere granting of asylum can be sufficient to create an antagonistic relationship. In the most famous asylum episode in this century, Iranian revolutionaries took violent exception to the U.S. decision to permit the shah of Iran to enter the U.S. for medical reasons; many Iranians regarded it as a form of asylum and used it as an occasion for taking American hostages.

A refugee-receiving country may actively support the refugees in their quest to change the regime of their country of origin. Refugees are potentially a tool in inter-state conflict. Numerous examples abound: the United States armed Cuban refugees in an effort to overthrow the Castro regime at the Bay of Pigs; the United States armed Contra exiles from Nicaragua; the Indian government armed Bengali "freedom fighters" against the Pakistan military; the Indian government provided military support for Tamil refugees from Sri Lanka to give the Indian government leverage in the Tamil-Sinhalese dispute; Pakistan, Saudi Arabia, China, and the United States armed Afghan refugees in order to force Soviet troops to withdraw from Afghanistan; the Chinese provided arms to Khmer Rouge refugees to help overthrow the Vietnamese-backed regime in Cambodia; and Palestinian refugees received Arab support against Israelis. Refugee-producing countries may thus have good reason for fearing an alliance between their adversaries and the refugees.

Non-refugee immigrants can also be a source of conflict between receiving and sending countries. A diaspora made up primarily of refugees is, of course, likely to be hostile to the regime of the country from which they fled. But even economic migrants may become hostile, especially if they live in democratic countries while the government of their homeland is repressive. Thus, many overseas Chinese lost their sympathy for China's government in 1989 when the regime became repressive at Tiananmen Square. Thereafter, many overseas Chinese supported dissidents within China and pressed their

---

34. For an analysis of the UNHCR's concept of protection, see Leon Gordenker, *Refugees in International Politics* (New York: Columbia University Press, 1987), pp. 27–46.

host governments to withdraw support for China. The Beijing government came to regard many overseas Chinese as a source of support for dissidents.[35] There are numerous examples of diasporas seeking to undermine the regime of their home country: South Koreans and Taiwanese in the United States (who supported democratic movements at home), Iranians in France (Khomeini himself during the reign of the Shah, and opponents of Khomeini's Islamic regime thereafter), Asian Indians in North America and the UK (after Indira Gandhi declared an emergency), Indian Sikhs (supporting secession), and dissident Sri Lankan Tamils and Northern Irish Catholics among others.[36]

The home country may take a dim view of the activities of its citizens abroad, and hold the host country responsible for their activities. But host countries, especially if they are democratic, are loath to restrict migrants engaged in lawful activities, especially since some of the migrants have already become citizens. The home country may even plant intelligence operators abroad to monitor the activities of its migrants,[37] and may take steps to prevent further emigration. The embassy of the home country may also provide encouragement to its supporters within the diaspora. The diaspora itself may become a focal point of controversy between the home and host countries, among contending groups within the diaspora, or between sections of the diaspora and the home government.[38] Thus, struggles that might overwise take place only within a country become internationalized if the country has a significant overseas population.

---

35. They have some cause to do so: in March 1990 the Chinese government sealed Tiananmen Square after receiving word that overseas Chinese, using fax machines, had called upon dissidents to protest peacefully by gathering in large numbers in the Square. For a history of Communist China's relationship with its diaspora, see Stephen FitzGerald, *China and the Overseas Chinese: A Study of Peking's Changing Policy 1949–1970* (Cambridge: Cambridge University Press, 1972).

36. For an analysis of the role played by Asian migrants and their descendants in the United States in supporting movements for democratization or for self-determination in their "home" countries, see Myron Weiner, "Asian Immigrants and U.S. Foreign Policy," in Tucker, Keely, and Wrigley, *Immigration and U.S. Foreign Policy*, pp. 192–213; for an analysis of the political role of other diasporas in the United States, see Yossi Shain, "Democrats and Secessionists: U.S. Diasporas as Regime Destabilizers," in Weiner, *International Migration and Security.*

37. On the role played by the Taiwanese security apparatus in attempts to thwart support for Taiwanese independence sentiments within the Taiwanese community in the United States, see Weiner, "Asian Immigrants and U.S. Foreign Policy," p. 197.

38. Examples include conflicts between Turkish Muslim fundamentalists and their opponents within Germany and, earlier, among Indians in Britain who were divided in their attitude toward Prime Minister Indira Gandhi's government after she declared an emergency in 1975 and arrested members of the opposition.

REFUGEES AND IMMIGRANTS AS A POLITICAL RISK TO THE HOST COUNTRY
Governments are often concerned that refugees to whom they give protection may turn against them if they are unwilling to assist the refugees in their opposition to the government of their country of origin. Paradoxically, the risk may be particularly high if the host country has gone so far as to arm the refugees against their country of origin. Guns can be pointed in both directions, and the receiving country takes the risk that refugees will seek to dictate the host country's policies toward the sending country. For example, the decision by Arab countries to provide political support and arms to Palestinian refugees from Israel created within the Arab states a population capable of influencing their own foreign policies and internal politics. Palestinians, for example, became a political force within Lebanon in ways that subsequently made them a political and security problem for Lebanon, Syria, Jordan, Israel, France, and the United States. The support of Iraqi invaders by Palestinians in Kuwait was an asset to Iraq since some of the 400,000 Palestinians in Kuwait held important positions in the Kuwaiti administration. The decision after the war by the Kuwaiti government to expel Palestinians reflected its view that Palestinians had become a security threat.[39] Throughout the Middle East, governments must consider the capacity of the Palestinians to undermine their regimes should they adopt policies that are unacceptable to the Palestinians. Similarly, the arming of Afghan refugees in Pakistan limited the options available to the government of Pakistan in its dealings with the governments of Afghanistan and the Soviet Union. The Pakistani government armed the Afghans in order to pressure the Soviets to withdraw their forces and to agree to a political settlement, but the Pakistani government was also constrained by the knowledge that it could not sign an agreement with the Soviet or Afghan governments that was unacceptable to the armed Afghans in Pakistan.

Refugees have launched terrorist attacks within their host country, illegally smuggled arms, allied with the domestic opposition against host-government policies, participated in drug traffic, and in other ways eroded governments' willingness to admit refugees. Palestinians, Sikhs, Croats, Kurds, Armenians, Sri Lankan Tamils, and Northern Irish, among others, have been regarded

---

39. For an analysis of the changing attitudes of Kuwaitis toward Palestinian migrants and toward foreign workers in general, see Jill Crystal, *Kuwait: The Transformation of an Oil State* (Boulder, Colo.: Westview Press, 1991), pp. 166–169.

with suspicion by intelligence and police authorities of other countries and their requests for asylum have been scrutinized not only for whether they have a well-founded fear of persecution, but for whether their presence might constitute a threat to the host country.

Such fears, it should be noted, are sometimes exaggerated, and governments have often gone to extreme lengths to protect themselves against low-level threats[40] but these fears are nonetheless not always without foundation, especially in the context of an increase in international terrorism.

MIGRANTS PERCEIVED AS A THREAT TO CULTURAL IDENTITY

How and why some migrant communities are perceived as cultural threats is a complicated issue, involving initially how the host community defines itself. Cultures differ with respect to how they define who belongs to or can be admitted into their community. These norms govern whom one admits, what rights and privileges are given to those who are permitted to enter, and whether the host culture regards a migrant community as potential citizens. A violation of these norms (by unwanted immigrants, for example) is often regarded as a threat to basic values and in that sense is perceived as a threat to national security.

These norms are often embedded in the law of citizenship that determines who, by virtue of birth, is entitled as a matter of right to be a citizen, and who is permitted to become a naturalized citizen. The main distinction is between citizenship laws based on *jus sanguinis*, whereby a person wherever born is a citizen of the state of his parents, and those based on *jus soli*, the rule that a child receives its nationality from the soil or place of birth. The ties of blood descent are broader than merely parentage, for they suggest a broader "volk" or people to whom one belongs in a fictive relationship. The Federal Republic of Germany, for example, has such a legal norm. Under a law passed in 1913—and still valid—German citizenship at birth is based exclusively on descent (*jus sanguinis*); thus the children of migrants born in Germany are not thereby automatically entitled to citizenship (no *jus soli*). The Basic Law (Germany's postwar "Constitution") also accords citizenship

---

40. One of the more extreme responses was the McCarran-Walter Immigration Act passed by the U.S. Congress in 1952, which excluded any aliens who might "engage in activities which would be prejudicial to the public interest, or endanger the welfare, safety or security of the United States." The Immigration and Naturalization Service interpreted the act to go beyond barring known or suspected terrorists to exclude writers and politicians known to be critical of the United States.

to those Germans who no longer live in Germany and who may no longer speak German but came (or are descended from those who came) from Germany, including the territories from which Germans were expelled after the war.[41] Thus, thousands of immigrants who entered the Federal Republic from East Germany or from Poland after the Second World War were regarded as German citizens returning "home." Other countries share a similar concept. Israel, for example, has a Law of Return, under which all Jews, irrespective of where they presently live, are entitled to "return" home to reclaim, as it were, their citizenship. Nepal also has a law which entitles those who are of Nepali "origin," though they may have lived in India, Singapore, Hong Kong or elsewhere for several generations, to reclaim their citizenship by returning home.

Where such notions of consanguinity dominate citizenship law, the political system is capable of distinguishing between an acceptable and unacceptable influx, without regard either to the numbers or to the condition of the economy into which the immigrants move. In general, countries with norms of consanguinity find it difficult to incorporate ethnically alien migrants, including refugees, into citizenship. These countries are also likely to have political groups that advocate sending immigrants home even though expulsion may impose severe economic consequences for the host as well as the home countries.

A norm of indigenousness may also be widely shared by a section of a country's population and even incorporated into its legal system. This norm prescribes different rights for those who are classified as indigenous and those who, irrespective of the length of time they or their ancestors resided in the country, are not so classified. An indigenous people asserts a superior claim to land, employment, education, political power, and the central national symbols that is not accorded to others who live within the country. The indigenous—called *bhoomiputras* in Malaysia, "sons of the soil" in India, and native peoples in some societies—may assert exclusive rights denied to others, often resting on the notion that they as a people exist only within one country, while others have other homes to which they can return. Thus, the Sinhalese in Sri Lanka, the Malays (the *bhoomiputras*) in Malaysia, the Assamese in Assam, and the Melanesians in Fiji, among others, subscribe to

---

41. Kay Hailbronner, "Citizenship and Nationhood in Germany," in William Rogers Brubaker, ed., *Immigration and the Politics of Citizenship in Europe and North America* (Lanham, Md.: University Press of America, 1989).

an ideology of indigenousness which has, in various guises, been enshrined in the legal system and which shapes the response of these societies to immigrants. The *bhoomiputras* in Malaysia regarded the influx of Chinese and others from Vietnam as a fundamental threat, indeed so threatening as to lead the government to sink Vietnamese boats carrying refugees. Similarly, the Assamese rejected the influx of Bengalis, Indian-born Nepalis, and Marwaris from other parts of India (as well as immigrants from Nepal and Bangladesh), fearing that any resulting demographic change would threaten their capacity to maintain the existing legal arrangement under which native Assamese are provided opportunities in education and employment not accorded other residents of the state.[42] Nativism, a variant of the norm of indigenousness, played an important role in shaping the U.S. Immigration Act of 1924, particularly its national origins clause providing for national quotas. This legislation, and the political sentiment that underlay it, resulted in a restrictive policy toward refugees throughout the 1930s and early 1940s. After the war, however, the older American tradition of civic pluralism became politically dominant. It shaped the 1965 Immigration Act, which eliminated national quotas and gave preferences to individuals with skills and to family unification. The numbers and composition of migrants then significantly changed. From the mid-1960s to the later 1980s, between five hundred thousand and one million migrants and refugees entered each year, with nearly half the immigrants coming from Asia.

Citizenship in the United States is acquired by birth or by naturalization. Originally, American law permitted naturalization only to "free white persons," but subsequent acts permitted naturalization without regard to race. Apart from the usual residence requirements, U.S. naturalization law requires applicants to demonstrate their knowledge of the American Constitution and form of government, and to swear allegiance to the principles of the U.S. Constitution. Political knowledge and loyalty, not consanguinity, are thus the norms for membership. It is in part because the United States has political rather than ethnic criteria for naturalization that the United States has been more supportive of immigration and in the main has felt less threatened by immigration than most other countries.

For much of its history a low level of threat perception has also characterized the French response to immigration. While a concern for cultural unity

---

42. For an analysis, with examples, of the notion of indigenousness as providing the basis of group legitimacy, see Donald L. Horowitz, *Ethnic Groups in Conflict* (Berkeley: University of California Press, 1985), pp. 202–216.

is a central element in the French conception of nationhood, the French have also had a political conception of citizenship derived from the revolutionary origins of the notion of citizenship. The French, as Rogers Brubaker has written, are universalist and assimilationist in contrast with the *Volk*-centered Germans.[43] The result is that the French have been more willing to naturalize immigrants than have the Germans and more open to political refugees than most other West European countries. Even so, France has a strong anti-migrant movement, the National Front, led by Jean-Marie Le Pen, a North African–born Frenchman who has won considerable support for his position that guest-workers from North Africa, and their French-born children, should "return" home to North Africa.

Legal definitions of citizenship aside, most societies react with alarm when there is an unregulated large-scale illegal migration of people who do not share their culture and national identity. Examples abound. Illegal migration into the Sabah state of Malaysia from the Philippines and Indonesia—an estimated 400,000 or more of Sabah's 1.4 million population—has created anxieties there. The government of Malaysia is particularly uneasy since the Philippines lays claim to Sabah and some Filipino leaders insist that, so long as the dispute continues, Malaysia has no right to consider Filipinos as illegal aliens. Should the Filipinos acquire citizenship, it has been noted, they might win a third or more of Sabah's parliamentary seats and pursue a merger with the Philippines. The Philippines might thereby acquire through colonization what it is unable to win through diplomatic or military means.[44]

Colonization as a means of international conquest and annexation can in fact be the deliberate intent of a state. The government of Morocco, for example, moved 350,000 civilians into Western Sahara in an effort to claim and occupy disputed territory. The Israeli government has provided housing subsidies to its citizens to settle on the West Bank. Since the annexation of the Turkic regions of central Asia in the nineteenth century, the Czarist and

---

43. William Rogers Brubaker, ed., "Introduction," in Brubaker, *Immigration and the Politics of Citizenship in Europe and North America*, p. 8.

44. Concern over colonization, it should be noted, can also be an internal affair in multi-ethnic societies. Territorially-based ethnic groups may consider an influx of people from other parts of the country as a cultural and political threat. Hence, the Moros in Mindanao revolted at the in-migration of people from other parts of the Philippines, Sri Lanka's Tamils oppose settlement by Sinhalese in "their" region, Nicaragua Miskito Indians object to the migration of non-Miskito peoples into "their" territory on the Atlantic coast, and a variety of India's linguistic communities regard in-migration as a form of colonization. In some cases such settlements can provoke an internal conflict between migrants and indigenes, with international consequences.

Soviet regimes have encouraged Russian settlement, while a similar policy of settling Han people has been pursued by the Chinese government in Sinkiang province and other areas.

Many governments are concerned that migration may lead to xenophobic popular sentiments and to the rise of anti-migrant political parties that could threaten the regime. Under such circumstances governments may pursue anti-migration policies in anticipation of public reactions.

MIGRANTS PERCEIVED AS A SOCIAL OR ECONOMIC BURDEN

Societies may react to immigrants because of the economic costs they impose or because of their purported social behavior such as criminality, welfare dependency, delinquency, etc. Societies may be concerned because the people entering are so numerous or so poor that they create a substantial economic burden by straining housing, education, and transportation facilities. In advanced industrial societies, services provided by the welfare state to migrant workers, permanent migrants, or refugees may generate local resentment. In less developed countries, refugees may illegally occupy private or government lands; their goats, sheep, and cattle may decimate forests and grazing land; they may use firewood, consume water, produce waste, and in other ways come to be regarded as an ecological threat. The willingness to bear these costs is likely to be low if the host government believes that the government of the sending country is engaged in a policy of population "dumping," by exporting its criminals, unwanted ethnic minorities, and "surplus" population at the cost of the receiving country. The United States, for example, distinguished between those Cubans who fled the Communist regime in the 1960s, whom it welcomed, and Cuban convicts removed from prisons and placed on boats for the United States in the 1970s, whom it did not.[45] After the 1947 partition, India accepted Hindus from Pakistan who preferred to live in India, but regarded as destabilizing and threatening the forced exodus of East Pakistanis in the early 1970s, which India saw as a Pakistani effort to turn West Pakistan into the majority province by "dumping" East Pakistanis into India. Governments also distinguish between situ-

---

45. For an account of the history of Cuban migration to the United States from 1959 until the Mariel boatlift in 1980, see Gil Loescher and John A. Scanlan, "U.S. Foreign Policy, 1959–1980: Impact on Refugee Flow from Cuba," *Annals*, Vol. 467 (May 1983), pp. 114–137. Also see Jorge I. Domínguez, "Immigration as Foreign Policy in U.S.-Latin American Relations," in Tucker, Keely, and Wrigley, *Immigration and U.S. Foreign Policy*; and Felix Roberto Masud-Piloto, *With Open Arms: Cuban Migration to the United States* (Totowa, N.J.: Rowman and Littlefield, 1988).

ations in which ethnic minorities are permitted to leave (e.g., Jews from the Soviet Union) and those from which minorities are forced to flee (e.g., Bulgarian Turks or Sri Lankan Tamils), and are therefore more likely to accept the former than the latter.

In the eighteenth and nineteenth centuries, several European governments promoted emigration as a way of easing the social and political burdens that might result from poverty and crime. It has been estimated that between 1788 and 1868 England exiled 160,000 of its criminals to Australia as a convenient way to get rid of prisoners and reduce the costs of maintaining prisons.[46] In the middle of the nineteenth century, the British regarded emigration as a form of famine relief for Ireland. In seven famine years, from 1849 to 1856, one and a half million Irish emigrated, mostly across the Atlantic.[47] In Germany, from which 1,500,000 emigrated between 1871 and 1881, local officials believed that "a large body of indigent subjects constitute a social danger and a serious burden on meager public funds; better let them go."[48] Reacting to these policies, one American scholar wrote in 1890 that "there is something almost revolting in the anxiety of certain countries to get rid of their surplus population and to escape the burden of supporting the poor, the helpless and the depraved."[49] His reaction foreshadowed some of the popular concerns over Third World migration that grew in Western Europe in the latter part of this century.

The fears of western countries notwithstanding, however, population dumping has not been a significant element in the flow of migrants from the Third World to advanced industrial countries. To the extent that population dumping has occurred, it has largely been of ethnic minorities; flights—at least before the Yugoslav crisis—have primarily been to neighboring developing countries rather than to advanced industrial countries.

Forced population movements of ethnic minorities took place in Eastern Europe during the interwar period, placing enormous economic and social strains upon the receiving countries, taking a heavy toll upon the migrants themselves, and worsening relations among states. But because there was

---

46. Robert Hughes, *The Fatal Shore* (New York: Knopf, 1987).

47. H.J.M. Jonston, *British Emigration Policy 1815–1830: Shovelling out Paupers* (Oxford, UK: Clarendon Press, 1972).

48. Mack Walker, *Germany and the Emigration 1860–1885* (Cambridge: Harvard University Press, 1964).

49. Richmond Mayo-Smith, *Emigration and Immigration: A Study in Social Science* (New York: Charles Scribner and Sons, 1890); reprinted 1986, pp. 197–198.

an element of exchange, and minorities moved to states in which their ethnic community was a majority, settlement was possible and violent international conflict was avoided. In 1922–23 Greeks fled Turkey and Turks fled Greece. An estimated 1.5 million people from both nations were involved. In a related population exchange, in 1923 the Greek government, in an effort to Hellenize its Macedonian region, forced the exodus of its Bulgarian population. As the Bulgarian refugees moved into Greek-speaking areas of Bulgaria, the local Greek population fled southward to Greece.[50] The world's largest population exchange was in South Asia, where fourteen million people moved between India and Pakistan between 1947 and 1950. But since both countries respected the wishes of each other's ethnic minorities to settle in the country in which they constituted a majority, the exchange took place without causing a conflict between the two countries.[51] Similarly, the forced exit of Jews from North Africa to Israel in the 1950s was not a source of international conflict, since the refugees were welcomed by Israel. In contrast, however, the flight of Arabs from Israel in 1948 led to an interminable conflict between Israel and its Arab neighbors since the Arab states did not recognize the legitimacy of the new state.[52]

Government officials, otherwise concerned with the plight of refugees, may fear that a decision to grant refugee status to a small number of individuals might open the floodgate beyond what society is prepared to accept. One reason states hesitate to grant refugee and asylum status to those fleeing because of economic and even violent conditions at home—as distinct from having a personal "well-founded fear of persecution"—is the concern that the number of asylum requests would then increase. States prefer restrictive criteria in order to keep the influx small. Since laws of asylum are often imprecise and the policy that states will admit refugees with a well-founded fear of persecution is subject to varied interpretations, individuals who wish to enter a country but cannot do so under existing guestworker and migration laws may resort to claiming political asylum. Western European governments are thus torn between a humanitarian sentiment toward refugees and the

---

50. Michael R. Marrus, *The Unwanted: European Refugees in the Twentieth Century* (New York: Oxford University Press, 1985).
51. The population exchange proved to be violent, as the various communities slaughtered one another. However, it was neither the exchange nor the killings that led to war between India and Pakistan. The Indo-Pakistan war of 1947–48 was over the disputed territory of Kashmir.
52. Benny Morris, *The Birth of the Palestinian Refugee Problem, 1947–1949* (Cambridge: Cambridge University Press, 1987).

recognition that the more generous the law of asylum, the greater the number of applicants. As the number of asylum-seekers grows, governments become more restrictive, insisting on evidence that the individual does indeed have a well-founded fear of persecution, not "merely" a fear of being killed in a violent civil conflict. A major increase in asylum applications to Switzerland in 1986 and 1987, for example, led to passage of a referendum imposing a ceiling on the number of entries under the laws of asylum. In recent years Western Europe has become more restrictive as the requests for asylum have increased. Policy makers argue that to admit even a small number of refugees who enter because of political conditions or violence at home would be to open the door to larger numbers than their society is prepared to admit.

MIGRANTS AS HOSTAGES: RISKS FOR THE SENDING COUNTRY
Recent actions of the governments of Iran, Iraq, and Libya all demonstrate how migrants can be used as an instrument of statecraft in order to impose restraints upon the actions of the home government. Following the invasion of Kuwait on August 2, 1990, the government of Iraq announced a series of measures using migrants as instruments for the achievement of political objectives. The Iraqis declared that Westerners living in Iraq and Kuwait would be forcibly held as a shield against armed attack, in an effort to deter the United States and its allies from launching airstrikes against military facilities where hostages might be located. The Iraqi government then indicated its willingness to treat the migrants of those countries that did not send troops to Saudi Arabia, such as India, more favorably than the migrants of those countries that did, such as Pakistan and Bangladesh. The Iraqi government subsequently declared that food would not be provided for Asian migrants (including Indians) unless their countries sent food supplies and medicines in violation of the United Nations embargo.

While the Iraqi strategy of using their control over migrants for international bargaining is thus far unique, the mere presence of migrants in a country from which they could be expelled has been for some time an element affecting the behavior of the migrants' home country. Since the late 1970s the countries of South Asia have been aware of their dependence upon migration to the Gulf and have recognized that any sudden influx of returning migrants would create a major problem for domestic security as remittances came to an end, balance of payments problems were created, families dependent upon migrant income were threatened with destitution, and large numbers of people were thrown into labor markets where there already existed substantial unemployment. Since the Gulf War, all of these fears have materialized. Sending governments aware of these potential consequences have hesitated to criticize host governments for the treatment of migrant workers.[53] When workers have been expelled for strikes and other agitational activities, the home governments have sought to pacify their migrants—and the host government—in an effort to avoid further expulsions. Governments have often remained silent even when workers' contracts have been violated. Thus, the understandable reaction of some governments with migrants in Kuwait and Iraq was to see first whether it was possible for their migrants to remain, and to assure the security of their citizens, rather than to support international efforts against Iraqi aggression.

More recently there were reports that Libya threatened to expel migrants of any home government that voted for the UN Security Council resolution invoking sanctions against Libya for its failure to extradite two men accused of terrorism in the Pan American flight which fell over Lockerbie, Scotland. The target of Libya's threat was clearly Egypt, which had one million citizens working and living in Libya.

A security threat, as Robert Jervis has reminded us, is often a matter of perception.[54] What are the enemy's capabilities? What are its intentions? Perceptions similarly shape decision-makers' assessments of whether refugees and migrants constitute a security threat. Time and again we have seen how different are the assessments that various governments make of the threat posed by a population influx. With the rise of anti-migrant right wing parties in France, Germany, Italy, Switzerland, and elsewhere in Europe, European governments have virtually halted migration and made entry difficult for refugees from Third World countries; in contrast, the United States, Canada, and Australia, all traditional immigration countries, have strong pro-immigrant constituencies that have sustained pro-immigration policies even in the midst of substantial unemployment.[55] Moreover, perceptions of

---

53. For a description of working conditions of South Asian migrants in the Persian Gulf, and the reluctance of South Asian governments to protest the mistreatment of migrants, see Myron Weiner, "International Migration and Development: Indians in the Persian Gulf," *Population and Development Review*, Vol. 8, No. 1 (March 1988), pp. 1–36. For accounts of the benefits to Asian countries of migration to the Gulf see Godfrey Gunatilleke, ed., *Migration of Asian Workers to the Arab World* (Tokyo: United Nations University, 1986); and Rashid Amjad, ed., *To the Gulf and Back: Studies in the Economic Impact of Asian Labour Migration* (Geneva: International Labor Organization, 1989).

54. Robert Jervis, *Perception and Misperception in International Politics* (Princeton: Princeton University Press, 1976).

55. These countries have their anti-immigrant sentiments as well. Patrick Buchanan, candidate

risk change. Prior to the invasion by Iraq, Kuwait had a larger number of guest workers than native workers, yet did not feel insecure in their presence. But as a result of the invasion and the support to Iraq reportedly given by some migrant communities, the government and citizens of Kuwait now have a different assessment of the political risks of foreign workers and are concerned both with their numbers and national origin. Moreover, a country's concern that a refugee influx is the result of population "dumping" by its neighbor—clearly a matter of perception of intentions—is likely to be greatest when there is a history of enmity between sending and receiving countries, as in the case of Pakistan and India. Countries almost always feel threatened if their neighbor seeks to create a more homogeneous society by expelling its minorities—the phrase now is "ethnic cleansing"[56]—but we have also seen that there can be circumstances when a population "exchange" or an orderly "return" of an ethnic minority can be regarded as non-threatening by the receiving country.

How governments assess one another's intentions with respect both to economic migrants and political refugees is thus critical to how conflictual population movements may become. A government is more likely to accommodate a refugee flow from a neighboring country if it believes that the flight is the unfortunate and unintended consequences of a civil conflict than if it believes that the flight of the refugees is precisely what is intended.[57] Similarly, a government's response to reports that its citizens abroad are maltreated will depend upon whether it believes that the host country is culpable.

But perception is not everything. As we have seen, there are genuine conflicts of interests among countries on matters of migrants and refugees.

---

for president in the 1992 Republican primaries, was opposed to migration, particularly for what he regarded as its impact on employment and on welfare. The Australian debate is more pertinent to this article for its focus on the security dimensions of migration: Australian advocates of migration have argued that Australia's security is improved by opening its doors to migrants from Asia; opponents have been concerned with multiculturalism and population growth. See Katharine Betts, *Ideology and Immigration: Australia 1976 to 1987* (Victoria: Melbourne University Press, 1988); and Robert Birrell, Douglas Hill, and Jon Nevill, eds., *Populate and Perish? The Stresses of Population Growth in Australia* (Sidney: Fontana/Australian Conservation Foundation, 1984).

56. The older expression "unmixing of peoples" was reportedly used by Lord Curzon to describe the situation during the Balkan Wars; Marrus, *The Unwanted*, p. 41.

57. The European community stiffened its views toward Serbia when it became clear that Serbs were seeking to force the exodus of Croatians and Bosnians; many German officials then concluded that their willingness to accommodate refugees was enabling the Serbs to achieve their objective of clearing areas of non-Serbs.

Countries quarrel over each other's entry and exit rules as some countries want those whom another will not let go, while some countries force out those whom others do not want.[58] How states react to international population flows can itself be a source of international conflict.

State Responses to Population Movements

How do states react when they are confronted with an unwanted population influx, either of economic migrants or of refugees? For the foreseeable future the numbers of people who wish to leave or are forced to leave their countries will continue to exceed substantially the numbers that other countries are willing to accept. What strategies are available to states confronted with a rising demand for entrance? One possible response is to increase immigration. For many industrial countries, migration is advantageous, providing more young people to offset low national birthrates, manpower for service sector jobs that local people do not want, skilled manpower for labor-short occupations, and new investments by energetic, entrepreneurial newcomers. "The absorptive capacity of West European countries," wrote *The Economist*, "though not as great as that of America or Australia, is still bigger than timid people think. European politicians who run scared of racist or anti-immigrant feeling will be doing their countries no favours. Their guiding principle as they map out Europe's immigration plans should not be 'How few can we get away with letting in?', but rather, 'How many can we possibly take without creating unbearable social strain?' "[59]

But even countries that are relatively open to economic migrants and to refugees will not be able to admit all who want to enter. Sealing borders is one response, but rarely wholly effective even in the case of islands. Control is difficult for any country with large coastlines or land borders. Regulation of employers (including penalties for employing illegals) and the use of identity cards has made a difference in the countries of Western Europe, but is not a useful option for a country with large numbers of small firms, a poorly developed administrative structure, and officials who are easily cor-

---

58. For an analysis of how the congruence or incongruence of rules of entry and exit influence the patterns of conflict and cooperation among states, see Myron Weiner, "On International Migration and International Relations," *Population and Development Review,* Vol. 11, No. 3 (September 1985), pp. 441–455.

59. *Economist,* "The Would-be Europeans," August 4, 1990, p. 15. The *Economist* adds, "For West Europeans it will be easier to absorb East Europeans than North Africans."

rupted. Moreover, however opposed the government and a majority of the population are to illegal migration, there are often elements within the society who welcome refugees and migrant workers: employers, ethnic kinfolk, political sympathizers, or officials willing to accept bribes. Finally, even if a country is able to fine-tune the number and characteristics of the economic migrants it admits, how can it cope with a massive influx of refugees in flight from a neighboring country?

Faced with unwanted flows whose entrance they cannot control, governments have increasingly turned to strategies for halting emigration.[60] We can identify three such strategies.

The first is to pay to avoid what one does not want. It has been suggested that an infusion of aid and investment, an improvement in trade, the resolution of the debt crisis, and other measures that would improve income and unemployment in low-income countries would reduce the rate of emigration. Meritorious as these proposals are, there is no evidence that they can reduce emigration in the short run. Indeed, high rates of emigration have often been associated with high economic growth rates. It was so for Great Britain in the nineteenth century, and in recent years for South Korea, Taiwan, Turkey, Algeria, and Greece. Only after an extended period of economic growth and a significant rise in wages do we see a substantial reduction in pressures for emigration.[61] Economic aid, however, may not be intended to remedy a country's high unemployment or low economic growth rate, but rather as payment to a government to halt a refugee flow. As noted earlier, United States economic assistance to Haiti halted a growing refugee flow (although

---

60. For a somewhat different view than is presented here, arguing that the challenge of migration can best be dealt with as part of dealing with other global issues, see Jonas Widgren, "International Migration and Regional Stability," *International Affairs*, Vol. 66, No. 4 (October 1990), pp. 749–766: "The long-term solutions to the migration challenge are the same as those outlined for all the other burning global problems that we face: stabilizing world population at a reasonable level, reinstalling human rights, reinforcing democracy, peacefully settling regional conflicts, halting environmental degradation, allowing for continued economic growth, abolishing trade protectionism, alleviating poverty, relieving the debt burden, increasing sound development aid, strengthening UN cooperation—and in general maintaining peace, regionally and globally" (p. 766). To the extent states regard migration and refugee flows as threats to their security, more direct and immediate measures will be taken.

61. For an attempt to deal with the relationship between migration, investment, and trade, see *Authorized Migration: An Economic Development Response* (Washington, D.C.: Report of The Commission for the Study of International Migration and Cooperative Economic Development, 1990). The bipartisan Commission, created by Congress in the Immigration Reform and Control Act of 1986, concluded that "any serious cooperative effort to reduce migratory pressure at their source must be pursued over decades, even in the face of intermediate contrary results" (p. xvi).

it resumed again in early 1992, following a coup); similarly, the flow of Sri Lankan refugees to West Germany from East Germany was reduced when the Federal Republic of Germany agreed to provide credits to the German Democratic Republic. In the Haitian case, government-to-government aid was intended by the donor country to persuade the recipient of the aid to halt the exodus; in the German case, the aid was intended to persuade the recipient of the aid to cease providing transit to unwanted refugees.

Assistance can also be used by governments to persuade other governments to retain refugees. Thus, the United States and France have been willing to provide economic assistance to Thailand if the Thais would hold Vietnamese refugees rather than permit these refugees to seek entrance into the United States and France.[62] The United Nations High Commission for Refugees and other international agencies, largely financed by the West and Japan, provide resources to refugee receiving countries—especially in Africa—not only as an expression of humanitarian concerns, but also as a means of enabling refugees to remain in the country of first asylum rather than attempting to move elsewhere, such as to advanced industrial countries.[63] International financial support has also been important in inducing refugees to return home when a conflict subsides. Funds for transportation, resettlement, and mine clearance are often critical for a successful speedy repatriation process.

Secondly, where generosity does not work or is not financially feasible, receiving countries may employ a variety of threats to halt emigration. Diplomatic pressures, including coercive diplomacy, may be exerted. The Indian government, for example, pressured the government of Bangladesh to halt Bangladeshi land settlement in the Chittagong Hill tracts, which had led local Chakma tribals to flee into India. The Indian government is in a position to damage Bangladeshi trade and to affect the flow of river waters if the Bangladesh government is not accommodating. When Burmese Muslim refugees

---

62. John R. Rogge, "Thailand's Refugee Policy: Some Thoughts on Its Origin and Future Direction," in Howard Adelman and C. Michael Lanphier, ed., *Refuge or Asylum: A Choice for Canada* (Toronto: York Lanes Press, 1990), pp. 150–171. Rogge describes how the Thais came to regard the influx from Vietnam as a security threat (pp. 162–163).

63. In 1991–92 the United States sought to use its financial leverage to induce the government of Israel not to settle Soviet Jews on the West Bank, arguing that the settlement policy was damaging to the peace negotiations between Israel, the Palestinians, and Israel's neighboring Arab states. The Israeli Labor Party's opposition to settlements, and the implication that the suspension of settlements would lead the United States to provide guarantees for $10 billion in bank loans, may have been a factor in the Labor victory. See Bar-Ilan, "Why Likud Lost—And Who Won," p. 28.

moved from the Arakan region of Burma into Bangladesh as a result of a Burmese government policy of settling non-Muslim Burmese in Arakan, the Bangladesh government threatened to arm the Burmese Muslim refugees if settlement was not halted. In both cases the threats worked to reduce or, for a while, halt the flow. In another example, the Arab League representative to the United Nations argued that the influx of Soviet Jews into Israel could constitute a threat to international peace and security under the UN charter.[64] Palestinians threatened international carriers who agreed to carry Soviet Jews to Israel, an instance of intervention by a third party which did not want an unimpeded flow between a sending and receiving country.

Coercive diplomacy to induce a country to halt actions that are forcing people to flee may be more effective when there are collective international sanctions. But thus far it has been exceedingly difficult for counties burdened by refugee flows to persuade the international community that sanctions should be imposed on the country producing the refugees.

Thirdly, there is the extreme sanction of armed intervention to change the political conditions within the sending country. In 1971 an estimated ten million refugees fled from East Pakistan to India following the outbreak of a civil war between the eastern and western provinces of Pakistan. This refugee flow was regarded by India as the result of a deliberate policy by the Pakistan military to resolve Pakistan's own internal political problems by forcing East Pakistan's Hindu population into India. Many Indian officials believed that the Pakistan government was seeking to change the demographic balance in favor of West Pakistan by shifting millions of East Pakistanis to India. The Indian government responded by sending its armed forces into Pakistan; its occupation of East Pakistan forced the partition of the country, and within months India had sent the refugees home.

In two other instances in South Asia, armed support for refugees was an instrument of policy by the receiving country. The Pakistani government armed some of the three million Afghan refugees who entered Pakistan following the April 1978 communist coup in Kabul and the subsequent Soviet invasion of Afghanistan in December 1979. The aim of the Pakistan government was for the armed Afghans to force a Soviet withdrawal, bring down the Soviet-supported Communist regime, and repatriate the refugees. The other instance of intervention was the initial Indian support for the Tamil

---

64. *New York Times*, February 8, 1990.

Tigers, a militant group fighting against the Sri Lankan government. The Indian government supported Tamil Tiger refugees in India and enabled arms to flow into Sri Lanka in an effort to force a political settlement between the Tamils and the Sri Lankan government, but the result was that the ethnic conflict worsened and the refugee exodus continued, prompting direct intervention by the Indian military.

The high level of threat or violence among the countries of South Asia to deal with unwanted refugee flows may foreshadow similar behavior elsewhere. The factors at work in South Asia include the ethnic affinity between the migrants and the people of the region into which they have migrated (a factor affecting the decision of refugees to flee and also increasing the anger of the receiving population), the adversarial relationship among some of the countries in the region, the porosity of borders, and the lack of administrative, military, and political capacity to enforce rules of entry. Faced with large unwanted population movements whose entry they cannot control, governments in the region have looked for ways to influence the exit policies of their neighbors.

The Kurdish revolt in Iraq after the Gulf war provides another example of the use of force to deal with an unwanted refugee flow. As Kurdish refugees entered Turkey, the government of Turkey made clear its unwillingness to add to its own Kurdish population and used its troops to seal the borders. The United States, Great Britain, and other allies in the war used their military power to force Iraq to place the Kurdish region under allied protection; the intervention enabled an estimated 1.5 million Kurds who had fled to Iran and Turkey to return, and the Kurds to form their own government.[65]

With the outbreak of war among the successor states of Yugoslavia, and a large outpouring of Croatian and Bosnian refugees to Germany, Hungary, Austria, and other former Yugoslav states, there were calls for armed intervention by NATO or by the United Nations.[66]

---

65. Allied intervention to protect the Kurds is a rare instance of a UN-sanctioned military intervention to protect a minority within a country. For a useful account of the history of the efforts by the Kurds to create a state of their own, see Gerard Chaliand, ed., *People Without a Country: The Kurds and Kurdistan* (London: Zed Press, 1980). The Kurds have reportedly created their own government in the territory within the allied protected security zone; "Kurds Creating a Country on the Hostile Soil of Iraq," *New York Times*, August 12, 1992, p. 1.
66. For useful brief historical as well as contemporary accounts of refugee movements throughout the Balkans, see Minority Rights Group, *Minorities in the Balkans*, Report No. 82 (London: Minority Rights Group, October 1989).

In each of these instances the high profile and highly conflictual nature of population movements has affected which institutions make exit and entry rules and engage in international negotiations. Decisions on such matters have come to be dealt with, not by ministries of labor, border control officials, or the courts, but at the highest levels of government, in the foreign and defense ministries, the security and intelligence agencies, and by heads of government. The very form and intensity of response to unwanted migrations is itself an indication that such population flows are regarded as threats to security or stability. These responses also suggest that states do not regard refugee flows and emigration as purely an internal matter, despite the assertions of the United Nations and other international agencies that countries do not have the right to interfere in the internal affairs of states that produce refugees, even when there is a perceived threat to the security and stability of countries upon whom the burden of unwanted refugees falls.

While the notion of sovereignty is still rhetorically recognized, a variety of "internal" actions by states are increasingly regarded as threats by other states. Thus, the spewing of nuclear waste and other hazardous materials into the atmosphere and the contamination of waterways which then flow into other countries is no longer regarded as an internal matter. In the same spirit, a country that forces its citizens to leave or creates conditions which induce them to leave has internationalized its internal actions.

A conundrum for Western liberal democratic regimes, however, is that they are reluctant to insist that governments restrain the exit of citizens simply because they or others are unwilling to accept them. Western liberal democracies believe in the right of emigration by individuals, but they simultaneously believe that governments retain the right to determine who and how many shall be permitted to enter. Liberal regimes may encourage or even threaten countries that produce refugees and unwanted immigrants in an effort to change the conditions that induce or force people to leave, but they are often reluctant to press governments to prevent people from leaving, or to force people to return home against their will. They do not want regimes to prevent political dissidents or persecuted minorities from leaving their country; rather, they want governments to stop their repression.

Advanced industrial countries that admit immigrants prefer an immigration policy that creates the fewest domestic or international political problems. One policy option is to admit those who best satisfy the requirements of the receiving country: those who have skills needed in the labor market, or capital to create new businesses, or relatives who would facilitate their integration into the society.[67] But a limited, largely skill-based immigration policy for Western Europe or the United States would still leave large numbers of people banging on the doors, seeking to enter as refugees or, failing that, as illegals.

An alternative policy based upon the needs of immigrants and refugees, though morally more attractive, is more difficult to formulate, more difficult to implement, and legally and politically more contentious. But no policy, short of the obliteration of international boundaries and sovereign states, can deal with the vast numbers of people who want to leave their country for another where opportunities are greater and life is safer. A moral case can be made for giving preference to those in flight, even at the cost of limiting the number of immigrants admitted to meet labor needs or to enable families to reunite. If countries have a ceiling on the number of people they are willing to admit, there is a strong moral argument for providing admissions first to those who are persecuted or whose lives are in danger, and have few places to go. But for reasons indicated above, only a narrow definition of what constitutes a refugee, with a case-by-case review, will enable states to put a cap on what they regard as potentially unlimited flows.

As a matter of political realism, then, a significant increase in the flow of refugees or of unwanted illegal economic migrants is likely to lead the governments of population-receiving countries to consider various forms of intervention to change the domestic factors that force or induce people to leave their homeland. If a people violate the boundaries of a neighboring country, then they and their government should expect others to intervene in their internal affairs.

---

67. See Ben J. Wittenberg and Karl Zinsmeister, "The Case for More Immigration," *Commentary*, Vol. 89, No. 4 (1990), 19–25; and Simon, *The Economic Consequences of Immigration*.

Down and Out in Warsaw and Budapest

| F. Stephen Larrabee

Eastern Europe and East-West Migration

In the last few years the issue of migration flows has emerged as a significant political problem, especially in Europe.[1] In the early postwar period, the free movement of people had generally been considered to be a positive development and a spur to economic growth. But in the 1970s, this attitude began to change as economies in Western Europe began to contract and the need for cheap labor declined. At the same time, during this period Europe changed from a net emigration region to an area of net immigration. This change was largely due to two factors: (1) economic growth in Western Europe made it an attractive area for many in developing countries; and (2) traditional markets for unskilled labor began to contract.[2]

Nevertheless, immigration was largely considered a manageable problem, at least in the medium term, well into the 1980s. The collapse of communism in Eastern Europe and the Soviet Union, however, has given the question of East-West migration an entirely new dimension.[3] In the 1970s and the early 1980s, the outflows of people from Warsaw Pact states numbered only about 100,000 annually. This changed dramatically in 1989 when a total of 1.2

F. Stephen Larrabee is a Senior Analyst in the International Policy Department at RAND in Santa Monica, California.

This article is a revised version of a paper originally presented at a conference on "Prospective Migration from the USSR" in Santa Monica, November 17–19, 1991, sponsored by RAND. It is part of a larger RAND project on "Current and Emergent Migration and Emigration from the Former USSR: Domestic and International Consequences." The views expressed in the article are the author's own and do not necessarily reflect those of RAND or its sponsors.

---

1. See Jonas Widgren, "International Migration and Regional Stability," *International Affairs*, Vol. 66, No. 4 (October 1990), pp. 749–766. Also Hans Arnold, "The Century of the 'Refugee': A European Century?" *Aussenpolitik*, No. 3 (1991), pp. 271–280; and Peter Opitz, "Refugee and Migration Movements," ibid., pp. 261–270. For a useful survey of the literature on the subject, see Kimberly A. Hamilton and Kate Holder, "International Migration and Foreign Policy: A Survey of the Literature," *Washington Quarterly*, Vol. 14, No. 2 (Spring 1991), pp. 195–211. See also the contributions in the special silver anniversary issue, "International Migration: An Assessment for the '90s," *International Migration Review*, Vol. 23, No. 3 (Fall 1989).
2. Widgren, "International Migration and Regional Stability," pp. 753–754. The "push factor" was more powerful.
3. See François Heisbourg, "Population Movements in Post–Cold War Europe," *Survival*, Vol. 33, No. 1 (January–February 1991), pp. 31–43.

International Security, Spring 1992 (Vol. 16, No. 4)
© 1992 by the President and Fellows of Harvard College and the Massachusetts Institute of Technology.

million people left the former Warsaw Pact states.[4] With the passage of the new passport law in the former Soviet Union in May 1991, allowing freedom of travel to all Soviet citizens, this number could increase significantly.

In addition, as economic restructuring and privatization gather momentum in both the former Soviet Union and Eastern Europe, they will create further pressures for out-migration. According to recent estimates, a rapid demilitarization of the Soviet economy could put as many as 35–40 million people out of work.[5] Many might seek employment in Western Europe. Some, however, might go to Eastern Europe, especially Poland.

These migratory pressures will create major dilemmas for both Eastern and Western Europe. Western Europe has long pressed for freedom of travel for East European and Soviet citizens. Now that this has become possible, can Western Europe close its doors to these new immigrants? Having themselves fought hard to win the right to travel freely, can the East European countries now deny that right to the citizens of the former Soviet Union?

The prospective new wave of migration comes, moreover, at a time when Western Europe finds itself facing significant constraints on its ability to absorb a massive influx of new populations. In the last few years Western Europe received 800,000 regular migrants, including a record number of refugees seeking political asylum from non-European, Third World countries. In the period 1983–89 the number of asylum seekers more than tripled. A growing number of these were from Eastern Europe.

The unexpected increase in the number of asylum seekers, together with changes in U.S. and Australian policies that are slowing down admission of refugees, has aggravated the difficulties for traditional transit points, like Austria and Italy, for immigrants to the United States and Australia. These countries now find themselves host to a growing number of migrants from the East who have nowhere else to go.

Perhaps even more importantly, the motivations behind the new emigration from the East are changing. A decade ago most immigrants from the East were political refugees: they sought asylum from persecution based on their political beliefs. Today the majority of refugees and asylum seekers are

4. Widgren, "International Migration and Regional Stability," p. 757.
5. Jean-Claude Chesnais, "Migration from Eastern to Western Europe, Past (1946–1989) and Future (1990–2000)," paper presented at the Conference of Ministers on the Movement of Persons Coming from Central and Eastern European Countries, sponsored by the Council of Europe, Vienna, January 24–25, 1991, p. 23.

"economic refugees"; that is, the primary motivation for emigration is economic betterment, not political persecution. As a result, they are not eligible for asylum under the 1951 Geneva Convention on Refugees. This has left a large pool of refugees essentially stranded, causing major headaches for governments in Eastern and Western Europe.

At the same time, as a result of the greater freedom of travel in the East, irregular migration has increased. Many immigrants from the East arrive on tourist visas and find illegal employment. This has created new economic and social problems in Western Europe. The problem, moreover, is no longer confined to the traditional receiving countries in the north (France, Germany, and Austria); it has also begun to affect countries in southern Europe.

The problem posed by migration, however, is not limited to Western Europe. Some countries in Eastern Europe such as Poland and Hungary are already beginning to face an influx of refugees and asylum seekers from other Eastern European countries, especially Romania. Many of these eventually move on, but some stay, creating new social and economic burdens at a time when these countries face massive economic problems due to the need to restructure their economies along market lines.

These trends highlight the degree to which migration from the East is beginning to become a major security issue. Moreover, large-scale unrest in the former Soviet Union or an outbreak of ethnic tensions elsewhere in Eastern Europe could accentuate these problems. Thus there is a need for both East and West to address the question of East-West population migration more seriously, and to cooperate more closely to manage its consequences.

To date, however, little scholarly work has been devoted to the implications and policy dilemmas posed by the potential migrations from the Soviet Union and Eastern Europe.[6] In part this is due to the difficulty of obtaining data; many of the countries in Eastern Europe have not published or do not have detailed figures on immigration. Moreover, much of the migration is "irregular" or illegal; which makes its dimensions difficult to assess. But the lack of attention is also due to a slowness in appreciating the broader security implications of the issue.

This article seeks to help fill the current void in the scholarly literature. It is divided into five parts. The first section examines the pattern and possible dimensions of migration from the former Soviet Union. The second section

---

6. Two notable exceptions are Heisbourg, "Population Movements in Post–Cold War Europe," and Chesnais, "Migration from Eastern to Western Europe."

discusses the problem posed for Eastern Europe by increased migration from the former Soviet Union and the efforts undertaken by these countries to cope with this increased migration. The third section focuses on the problem of migration within Eastern Europe itself, that is, from one East European country to another. The fourth section examines the impact of migration from the East to the Federal Republic of Germany (which is the main recipient of the emigrants from the East), and the policy dilemmas that this migration poses. A final section focuses on the future policy agenda and the ways in which East and West might cooperate to control and manage the population outflows.

Migration from the Former Soviet Union: How Many? How Soon?

The disintegration of the Soviet Union has focused attention on the issue of emigration and its security implications. Many in Eastern and Western Europe fear that the collapse of the Soviet Union could lead to a massive flight of Soviet citizens to the West. How realistic are these fears? How many people are likely to leave? And what would be the consequences of any mass exodus for Eastern as well as Western Europe? To answer these questions it may be useful to view emigration from the Soviet Union in historical perspective. In the postwar period there have been four major waves or stages of Soviet emigration.[7] (See Table 1.)

The first stage (1949–70) was one of relatively low levels of emigration. The second stage (1971–80) witnessed a dramatic increase in emigration—largely due to the improvement in East-West relations—although levels began to taper off toward the end of the 1970s as détente soured. The third stage (1981–86) was a period of reduced emigration as East-West relations deteriorated.

The fourth stage (1987 through at least the end of 1991) has seen an unprecedented upsurge in the number of emigrants. During 1990 more Soviet citizens (377,200) left the Soviet Union than in any preceding 12-month period. Moreover, the pattern and motivation for emigration also began to change. In the past, emigration was limited primarily to three groups: Jews,

---

7. For a detailed discussion of the dimensions of this emigration and its causes, see Sidney Heitman, *Soviet Emigration since Gorbachev* (Cologne: Bericht des Bundesinstituts für ostwissenschaftliche und internationale Studien [BIOSt], 1989) and by the same author, "Soviet Emigration in 1990," ibid., 1991. Also Klaus Segbers, *Wanderungs-und Flüchtlingsbewegungen aus der bisherigen UdSSR* (Ebenhausen: Stiftung Wissenschaft und Politik, January 1991).

Table 1. Soviet Emigration 1948–1990.

Period	Total
1948–1970	59,600
1971–1980	347,300
1981–1986	44,000
1987–1989	308,200
1990	377,200
	1,136,300

SOURCE: Heitman, *Soviet Emigration in 1990,* p. 5.

Germans, and Armenians. But in 1990 other groups such as Pentacostal Christians and Pontian Greeks began to join the ranks of emigrants from the Soviet Union.[8]

There were three main reasons for the increased emigration. First, an increasing number of Jews and Germans were motivated to emigrate by concerns about rising ethnic conflict. Second, many Jews and Armenians feared that prospective changes in U.S. immigration regulations would foreclose their option to emigrate at a later date. Third, Soviet emigration regulations and practices were relaxed. While many previous restrictions remained on the books, they were more leniently applied and the overall emigration procedure was speeded up.

Despite the increase, however, emigration has until now remained an "ethnic privilege": 95 percent of the emigrants have come from one of four major ethnic groups: Jews, Germans, Armenians, and Greeks. Emigration, moreover, has been almost entirely to four countries: Israel, Germany, the United States, and Greece. (See Table 2.)

The passage of a new Soviet passport law in May 1991, which gave every Soviet citizen (except those dealing with military secrets) the right of free travel,[9] together with the growth of ethnic unrest in the various republics, has increased concern that the West could be faced with a massive exodus of Soviet citizens. The figures on how many people may leave vary. Some

8. Heitman, *Soviet Emigration since 1990,* p. 13.
9. For a detailed discussion of the law and its implications, see Sidney Heitman, *The Right to Leave: The New Soviet Law on Emigration* (Cologne: BIOSt, 1990); also Heitman, *Soviet Emigration since 1990,* pp. 23–31.

Table 2. Destinations of Soviet Emigrants by Country, 1948–90.

Destination	Group	1948–89	1990	Subtotals by group	Totals by destination
United States	Jews	170,800	6,500	177,300	268,500
	Armenians	63,800	6,500	70,300	
	Evan. and Pent.	14,000	4,100	18,100	
	Other	200	2,600	2,800	
Israel	Jews	191,900	181,800		373,700
Germany	Germans	266,400	148,000	414,400	420,400
	Jews	—	6,000	6,000	
France	Armenians	12,000	—		12,000
Greece	Greeks	10,000	14,300	24,300	25,800
	Armenians	1,500	—	1,500	
Other		28,500	7,400	—	35,900

*NOTE: "Others" refers to emigrants who resettled in countries other than those listed in this table. These include 14,000 Jews who went to Poland and later re-emigrated to Israel; 21,300 Jews who resettled in various Western countries; 300 Evangelical and Pentecostal Christians; and 800 Armenians.

SOURCE: Heitman, "Soviet Emigration Since Gorbachev," p. 7.

Soviet officials have claimed that the figures may be as high as seven or eight million,[10] while others such as Vladimir Scherbakov, Chairman of the State Committee on Labor and Social Services and head of the Soviet Delegation to the Conference of Ministers on the Movement of Persons from Central and Eastern European Countries (sponsored by the Council of Europe in Vienna, January 24–25, 1991) have put the figure at 1.5–2 million.[11]

At the moment it is impossible to say with certainty how great the outflow will be. This will depend on internal developments in the former Soviet Union, above all the success of the reform process in the Western republics (Russia, Ukraine, and Belorussia [Belarus]) and the degree of social unrest

10. Judith Dempsey, "Seven Million May Leave Soviet Union," *Financial Times*, January 26, 1991.
11. Celestine Bohlen, "Moscow Predicts 1.5 Million Will Move West," *New York Times*, January 27, 1991.

and ethnic violence that occurs as the former Soviet Union reconstitutes itself. Three factors in particular, however, are likely to restrict the outflow: (1) the capacity of the underdeveloped and dilapidated Soviet transportation system to transport large masses of people; (2) visa and other restrictions by the potential receiving countries; and (3) the personal and practical costs of emigrating.

The second factor is particularly important. Migratory pressures do not automatically result in massive migration. As many international migration theorists emphasize, it is the policies of the receiving countries that determine whether migration takes place, and what kind of migration occurs.[12] Thus if the countries of Western and Eastern Europe impose visa restrictions, this may act as a disincentive for many citizens from the former Soviet Union to emigrate and thus reduce the number of potential immigrants.

In addition, one needs to differentiate between a *desire to emigrate* and an actual *willingness to emigrate*. The two are by no means the same. Many Soviet citizens may contemplate emigration, but be unwilling to undergo the practical hardships—the loss of friends, cultural isolation, uprooting of family, etc.—when confronted with the choice of actually leaving. This too may constrain the outflow.

These factors have led some Western analysts to take a skeptical view about the prospects for a large wave of emigration from the Soviet Union.[13] Some analysts have argued that large-scale migration is likely to be primarily internal. They point out that with the exception of the Jews, Armenians, and Germans, Soviet citizens have little tradition of emigration. This is particularly true in the case of the Central Asians, who seldom leave their own republics in spite of low living standards and high unemployment.[14]

However, the pattern and extent of emigration could change if social and economic conditions in many areas of the former Soviet Union continue to deteriorate. In this connection, it is important to note that the pattern of internal migration has been changing since the mid 1970s. Prior to the mid-1970s the principal internal migration was from Siberia and Central Russia to the southern republics (Moldavia, Ukraine, Trans-Caucasus, and central Asia). Since the mid-1970s, however, the pattern has been in the opposite

---

12. See Aristide R. Zolberg, "The Next Waves: Migration Theory for a Changing World," *International Migration Review*, Vol. 23, No. 3 (Fall 1989), pp. 405–406.
13. Segbers, *Wanderungs-und Flüchtlingsbewegungen aus der bisherigen UdSSR*, p. 19.
14. Chesnais, "Migration from Eastern to Western Europe," p. 22.

direction, from the southern republics and districts to central and eastern Russia.[15]

In particular, there has been a trend toward "re-migration" on the part of the Russian population back to Russia. This re-migration has been caused principally by increased population growth in the southern republics, which has put growing pressures on the labor market. As a result, more and more jobs have been taken by the native population, forcing the Russian population to migrate back to Russia.[16] This trend is likely to intensify with the proclamations of sovereignty and independence in the other republics. Changes in citizenship laws and other regulations may put the Russian population at a disadvantage, causing many to leave these republics. However, if conditions continue to deteriorate in Russia, many of these Russians will be unable to find good jobs and suitable housing in Russia and they may decide to emigrate abroad.

The Impact on Eastern Europe

The prospect of large-scale emigration from the former Soviet Union has important implications not only for the West, but also for Eastern Europe. Even the lower figure of 1.5 million emigrants cited by Scherbakov would pose major problems for the countries of Central and Eastern Europe, which have a limited capacity to absorb refugees or provide gainful employment for new emigrants at a time when their economies are facing radical restructuring. Moreover, some of these countries could become transit points for former Soviet citizens trying to move on to the West.

POLAND

Poland would be particularly affected by a massive outflow of Soviet nationals. The number of Soviet tourists to Poland has grown rapidly in recent years. In 1990 nearly a quarter of all tourists to Poland (4,200,000 out of 18,000,000) came from the Soviet Union. This represents a 67 percent increase over the previous year.[17] In 1991 the number is expected to reach 6,000,000

---

15. Zhanna Zaiyontchkovskaya, "Effects of Internal Migration on Emigration from the USSR," paper presented at the RAND conference on "Prospective Migration from the USSR," Santa Monica, November 17–19, 1991, p. 6.
16. Ibid., p. 21.
17. Christopher Wellisz, "Soviet Coup Renews Fear of Exodus," Radio Free Europe/Radio Liberty (RFE/RL), *Report on Eastern Europe,* September 13, 1991, p. 19.

(out of an expected 21–22 million tourists). How many of these will stay in Poland is not known. However, according to Polish officials, Soviet citizens account for nearly 80 percent of illegal immigrants.[18]

Soviet citizens entering Poland need either a visa or an officially certified invitation letter. However, there is a large black market for false travel documents. The growing number of Soviet citizens entering Poland with false travel documents is becoming a serious problem and source of concern to Polish officials. According to an internal Polish report, around 300 Soviet citizens trying to enter Poland with false travel documents are turned back at the border daily.[19]

Poland has taken a number of measures in order to prepare for a massive wave of emigration from the Soviet Union. In January 1991 the Ministry of Internal Affairs announced a plan to tighten security along Poland's eastern frontier. The plan called for the construction of fourteen new watch towers and the modernization of border control equipment. A contingency plan for the mobilization of troops to stem a large influx of refugees was also prepared.[20]

Poland has also set up a Refugee Office within the Ministry of Internal Affairs. However, according to Colonel Zbigniew Skoczylas, advisor to the Refugee Office, Poland could afford to accept only 50,000 refugees at most, at a cost of 1.5 trillion zloty per year ($130 million). He warned that there will be a complete breakdown of the economy if Poland is forced to accept several million refugees.[21] Even 200,000–300,000 would pose enormous problems, particularly at a time of recession and rising unemployment.

Interestingly, the coup attempt in the Soviet Union in August 1991 did not lead to a massive outflow of Soviet citizens into Poland. During the three days of the coup, only fifty Soviet citizens applied for asylum in Poland. Moreover, the number of Soviet citizens entering and leaving Poland remained more or less equal.[22] This has led some Polish officials to conclude that the emigration problem may not prove as serious as they initially feared.

A more immediate problem is the large influx of Soviet citizens who enter Poland for a short stay (1–3 days). Polish authorities estimate that on any

---

18. Private discussions with Polish officials, October 1991.
19. Thomas Urban, "Polen verstärkt Grenzkontrolle," *Süddeutsche Zeitung*, September 28, 1991.
20. Wellisz, "Soviet Coup Renews Fear of Exodus," p. 19.
21. Mary Battiata, "Poland, Others Forecast Flood of Refugees," *Washington Post*, November 14, 1990.
22. Private discussions with Polish officials, October 1991.

given day, there are about 140,000 Soviet and Baltic citizens on Polish territory, most of whom come for short stays. Many of them engage in smuggling and blackmarketeering in order to earn hard currency. Upon returning, they smuggle vodka into Poland and sell it, converting their zloty into dollars. They then convert their dollars into rubles, making a substantial profit. The illicit vodka smuggling deprives Poland of important tax revenues at a time when Poland badly needs hard currency. According to one estimate, $80 million leaves Poland every month through illicit vodka sales.[23]

Another problem is posed by Soviet citizens who seek to work illegally in Poland. According to official Polish estimates, there are 20,000–30,000 illegal Soviet workers in Poland, most of them engaged in construction and agriculture.[24] These workers work for about half the normal Polish wage. However, this is still 2–3 times what they would earn at home. As unemployment increases—it reached 9.4 percent in July 1991—and more Poles find it hard to get work, the issue of illegal Soviet workers could become a serious problem, exacerbating social and political tensions.

A third and potentially more serious problem could be posed by the large-scale emigration of the Polish minority living in the Soviet Union. According to the 1989 census, there were 1,126,334 Poles residing in the Soviet Union; the actual figure is probably somewhat higher. Eighty percent of the Soviet Union's Polish population resided in the three republics of Belorussia (417,720), Lithuania (257,994), and Ukraine (219,179). In addition there were sizeable Polish populations in the Russian SFSR (94,594), Latvia (60,416), and Kazakhstan (59,956).

In the last several years there has been a growing interest in repatriation on the part of many of the Poles in the Ukraine. Unlike the Poles in the West who have much-needed skills and hard currency, the Poles in the Soviet Union are poor, old, and unskilled. Many of them are retirees. They would pose a burden on the Polish economy if they returned. According to a recent study by the Polish Foreign Ministry, the repatriation of one million Poles over the next five years would cost 20–30 trillion zloty ($1.8–2.7 billion). Thus the report recommends that Poland discourage their repatriation. Instead it suggests that Poland should support a general improvement in the conditions of the minority in order to help them maintain their national identity and to provide an incentive for them not to emigrate.[25]

---

23. *Gazeta Wyborcza*, July 17, 1991.
24. Wellisz, "Soviet Coup Renews Fear of Exodus," p. 20.
25. Ibid.

There are also about 260,000 ethnic Poles in Lithuania. They make up about 7 percent of the population. The treatment of the Polish minority in Lithuania has traditionally been a source of friction between the two countries.[26] During the communist period this friction was largely kept under control. However, as Lithuania moved closer toward independence, tensions with Poland over the treatment of the Polish minority resurfaced. Relations were strained in particular by the decision of the Lithuanian government in September 1991 to disband the self-governing councils in the Salcininkai and Vilnius districts, in which Poles make up 80 and 60 percent of the population, respectively, on the grounds that the councils had allegedly supported the coup attempt in Moscow.[27]

Rising nationalist tensions or a drastic deterioration in economic conditions in the Ukraine, Belorussia, or Lithuania could result in a decision by many members of the Polish minority in these areas to emigrate to Poland. In such a case, Poland would be hard pressed, morally and politically, not to accept these refugees.[28] But a massive influx of these refugees would significantly exacerbate Poland's already serious economic problems, severely undercutting the prospects for successful reform.

Polish officials believe, however, that the likelihood of a massive emigration by the Polish minorities in the Ukraine and Belorussia is small. The minorities in both republics are highly assimilated and relatively well-treated. Moreover, Poland has made respect for minority rights an issue in its effort to improve relations with both republics. In October 1990 it signed a Declaration-of-Friendship Agreement with the Ukraine which contained a provision guaranteeing respect for the rights of minorities.[29] A similar agreement was signed with Belorussia in October of 1991.

The Friendship Declarations are part of a broader effort by Warsaw to improve relations with both republics as they move toward greater sover-

---

26. For a comprehensive discussion, see Stephen Burant, "Polish-Lithuanian Relations: Past, Present and Future," *Problems of Communism*, May–June 1991, pp. 67–84.

27. See Christopher Bobinski, "Lithuania Warned on Polish Minority," *Financial Times*, September 16, 1991; Edward Lucas, "Lithuania Dispute with Poles Worsens," *The Independent*, September 19, 1991; and Jan de Weydenthal, "The Polish-Lithuanian Dispute," RFE/RL, *Report on Eastern Europe*, October 11, 1991, pp. 20–23.

28. According to a recent poll by the Public Opinion Institute CBOS in Poland, 80 percent of those polled felt that members of the Polish minority in the USSR should be allowed to settle in Poland without any restrictions. See Thomas Urban, "Polen verstärkt Grenzkontrollen," *Süddeutsche Zeitung*, September 28, 1991.

29. An agreement containing similar guarantees was signed with Russia as well. For background, see Anna Sabbat-Swidlicka, "Friendship Declarations Signed with Russia and the Ukraine," RFE/RL, *Report on Eastern Europe*, November 2, 1990, pp. 25–27.

eignty or independence. One of the basic aims of Polish policy is to encourage the integration of both republics, particularly the Ukraine, into pan-European institutions and processes like the Conference on Security and Cooperation in Europe (CSCE), the negotiations on reducing Conventional Forces in Europe (CFE), and the Council of Europe. Poland views such integration as an important safeguard against the emergence of a highly nationalistic and chauvinistic regime in Kiev that would curtail the rights of the Polish minority. Polish authorities also believe that the Ukraine's need for Western assistance will act as a moderating constraint on Kiev's treatment of the minority.

The situation with Lithuania is more complicated. Unlike the Ukraine, Lithuania feels more threatened by Poland. Its nationalism also has a stronger anti-Polish edge. However, the two countries, in January 1992, signed a Declaration of Friendship similar to the Declarations signed by Poland with Ukraine and Belorussia. This should help to reduce tensions and provide important guarantees for minority rights. Moreover, the fact that the Poles in Lithuania are less educated (educational level generally has a strong impact on emigration) suggests that the rate of outmigration is likely to be modest.

HUNGARY

Hungary's problems are of a less urgent nature and magnitude. There is a small Hungarian minority (150,000–200,000) in the Trans-carpathian *oblast* of the western Ukraine. However, members of the minority have generally been well-treated and have shown little inclination to emigrate or request repatriation. Like Poland, Hungary has consciously sought to improve relations with Ukraine lately. In June 1991 the Ukraine and Hungary signed a declaration of basic principles as well as a joint statement guaranteeing the rights of national minorities.[30] This statement is regarded by Hungarian officials as an important means of ensuring that the ethnic, cultural, educational, and linguistic rights of the Hungarian minority in the Ukraine will be respected. They believe that the general improvement in the situation of the Hungarian minority in recent years reduces the likelihood of any large-scale emigration of the Hungarian minority in the Ukraine to Hungary.[31] However, if the

---

30. For details see Alfred A. Reisch, "Agreements Signed with Ukraine to Upgrade Bilateral Relations," RFE/RL, *Report on Eastern Europe*, June 21, 1991, pp. 14–17. See also Alfred Reisch, "Hungary and Ukraine Agree to Upgrade Bilateral Relations," ibid., November 2, 1990, pp. 6–12.

31. See the interview with former Foreign Minister Gyula Horn, Chairman of the Hungarian Socialist Party, *Magyar Nemzet*, April 24, 1991. Translated in Foreign Broadcast Information Service (FBIS) EEU-91-084, May 1, 1991, p. 22.

situation of the minority deteriorated and many decided to emigrate, there would be strong moral pressure on Hungary to allow them to be repatriated.

Hungary has set up an Office of Refugee Affairs within the Interior Ministry and has built several refugee camps, including one sponsored by the United Nations at Bieske (outside of Budapest) to house refugees. Hungarian officials, however, do not expect to face a major wave of immigrants from the Soviet Union. They believe they can handle any increase in immigration through measures already in force or which can be introduced quickly, such as visa and currency requirements. In October 1991 Budapest introduced stricter border controls on foreigners, including currency restrictions. While the restrictions were mainly aimed at curbing the influx of Romanians, especially gypsies, they also apply to Soviet citizens.

In addition, Hungary tightened the regulations on hiring foreigners. According to a decree passed in October 1991, foreign citizens wishing to work in Hungary will have to apply for a special "work permit visa" at Hungarian missions in their respective countries. The move is designed to reduce the influx of illegal foreign workers at a time of rising unemployment in Hungary.

CZECHOSLOVAKIA

Czechoslovakia does not seem likely to face a serious immigration problem from the Soviet Union. Unlike Poles or Hungarians, there are few Czechs or Slovaks living in the Soviet Union. About 15,000 Czechs and Slovaks live in the Volyn area of the Ukraine. Few of these, however, have expressed a desire to be repatriated. And even if many of them did seek to emigrate, the number is not so large as to prove unmanageable.

Nevertheless, the Czechoslovak government has made preparations to handle an increased flow of refugees. A Refugee Affairs Office has been set up, staffed by officials from the Defense and Interior Ministries. Czechoslovakia has also doubled the number of guards along the Soviet border. In addition, in December 1990, a law was drafted that would make it legal to use the army to contain any large-scale migration.

In November 1990, Czechoslovakia passed a new Law on Refugees, which went into effect on January 1, 1991. Under the new law, a refugee must declare his or her intention to claim refugee status at the border and is obliged to stay in a special camp until his or her application for refugee status has been accepted or rejected. The Federal Ministry of Internal Affairs is obligated to act on the application within 90 days. After five years, a refugee whose application is accepted can apply for citizenship.

To date the influx of refugees has been limited. As of January 1991, there were some 1,200 refugees in Czechoslovakia.[32] They are housed in four camps and several "emergency stations" in the Czech republic. In addition, Slovakia is setting up five refugee camps for potential Soviet refugees, which will be paid for by the Czechoslovak Red Cross. However, government spokesmen have said that the camps could not accommodate more than 12,000 people annually.[33]

ROMANIA

Romania is a major "exporter" of emigrants, rather than an importer. According to the Romanian media, more than 800,000 Romanians emigrated from Romania in the first eight months of 1990.[34] Many of these were young and highly educated. If accurate, this would represent a major hemorrhage for a country of 23 million people.

In the foreseeable future, Romania is likely to remain a migration exporter rather than an importer. Developments in Moldavia (Moldova), however, could complicate this assessment. There are 3,350,000 "Moldavians" in the area of the former Soviet Union, including 2.8 million in Moldavia and 320,000 in the Ukraine. They are ethnic Romanians. While they feel a strong sense of kinship with their brethren in Romania, they have little inclination to emigrate to Romania, in large part because of the low standard of living in Romania and the chaotic political conditions existing there. However, if Russia were to attempt to reassert control over Moldavia or if there was a serious rise of ethnic tensions between the Russian minority (about 13 percent of the population) in Moldavia and the Romanian majority, many Moldavians might decide to emigrate to Romania. A mass migration of Moldavians to Romania would exacerbate Romania's already serious economic and political problems, adding to the chaotic conditions that exist there and making any effort to establish a stable democratic system all the more difficult, if not impossible.

BULGARIA

Bulgaria is unlikely to be seriously affected by any migration from the Soviet Union. There are some 370,000 Bulgarians in the Soviet Union: 23,000 in the

---

32. Vladimir Kusin, "Refugees in Central and Eastern Europe: Problem or Threat?" RFE/RL, *Report on Eastern Europe*, January 18, 1991, p. 37.
33. Ibid.
34. See Dan Ionescu, "The Exodus," RFE/RL, *Report on Eastern Europe*, October 26, 1990, pp. 25–31, and Ionescu, "Recent Emigration Figures," ibid., pp. 21–24.

Ukraine and 90,000 in Moldavia. They have not shown any strong inclination to be repatriated or to move West, although this might change if there were to be serious unrest in Russia, the Ukraine, or Moldavia.

The main problem for Bulgaria has been the absorption of the ethnic Turkish minority. Under the Zhivkov regime, discriminatory legislation prompted some 310,000 ethnic Turks to emigrate in 1989. Zhivkov's successors reversed much of the discriminatory legislation in December 1989 and since then about 150,000 ethnic Turks have returned. The reversal of the legislation against the Turks, however, sparked large-scale demonstrations in several Bulgarian cities in January 1990. The question of minority rights for the Turks continues to be a controversial issue in Bulgarian politics.[35]

Migration Within Eastern Europe

A second problem is created by the emigration within Eastern Europe itself from one East European country to another. Here the main problem is posed by the emigration of Romanians, many of them gypsies. The goal of most of these gypsies is to reach the West—Austria or Germany—rather than settle in the East European countries through which they pass. However, many of them do not have visas or valid papers and are turned back at the German or Austrian border. They are forced to return to various East European transit countries. For the countries of Central Europe, these gypsies are becoming a growing social problem. Many of them remain in limbo, eking out a meager living and often resorting to begging or petty crime.

Poland in particular has been faced with a large influx of Romanian gypsies. It is estimated that there are today between 50,000 and 70,000 Romanian gypsies in Poland.[36] In order to stem the influx, Poland tightened its regulations for admission to the country in December 1990. Romanians now must produce an officially certified invitation for the visit as well as a return ticket and must show that they have at least 200,000 zloty in cash for each day of their expected stay.

The influx of gypsies has caused growing popular resentment and social tension. In July 1991, hundreds of gypsies fled from Poland to Sweden after

---

35. See Duncan Perry, "Ethnic Turks Face Bulgarian Nationalism," RFE/RL, *Report on Eastern Europe*, March 15, 1991, pp. 5–8.
36. Dan Ionescu, "Recent Emigration Figures," RFE/RL, *Report on Eastern Europe*, February 15, 1991, p. 21.

a mob of Poles in the town of Mlawa attacked a group of gypsies and ransacked their homes.[37] The gypsies are particularly resented because many have become wealthy through illicit deals and smuggling.

The large influx of gypsies has also led to an increase in the number of illegal border crossings.[38] Many of the gypsies enter Poland illegally and then proceed on to Germany, where they seek to cross the border illegally. Those that are caught are turned back, where they remain in legal limbo, often waiting to make another attempt to cross the border illegally. The sharp rise in the number of illegal border crossings has exceeded the capacity of the German border guards to deal with the problem and created strains in Warsaw's relations with Bonn.[39]

The vast majority of the refugees in Czechoslovakia are also from Romania. Many of them have entered illegally. In June 1991, Czechoslovakia deported a total of 226 refugees, most of them Romanians, who had tried to cross Czechoslovakia illegally on their way to Germany. Another 800 were deported in July on special aircraft, after the Hungarian government refused to allow trains carrying them out of Czechoslovakia to cross Hungary on the way back to Romania.[40]

Hungary has faced similar problems. According to the Office of Refugee Affairs, nearly 30,000–35,000 Romanian citizens entered Hungary before 1989. Most of these were ethnic Hungarians and were integrated relatively easily into Hungarian society. However, more recently the refugees have included a growing number of ethnic Romanians, many of them gypsies. In order to reduce the influx, in early October 1991 Hungary introduced stricter border controls on foreigners, including currency restrictions. This move, however, has been criticized by the Hungarian minority in Romania, who claim it complicates their situation.

The conflict in Yugoslavia has seriously exacerbated Hungary's refugee problem.[41] According to the Red Cross, there were more than 35,000 refugees

37. "Poles Vent Their Economic Rage on Gypsies," *New York Times*, July 25, 1991.
38. According to Jaroslaw Zukowicz, press spokesman of the headquarters of the Polish border guards, between January and June 1991, 4,406 persons sought to cross the Polish border illegally. The vast majority of these were Romanians (1,679) followed by Bulgarians (407) and Czechoslovaks (206). RFE/RL, *Daily Report No. 146*, August 2, 1991.
39. Ulrich Reitz, "Zwischenstation Polen," *Die Welt*, July 22, 1991.
40. "The Other Europeans on the Move," *Financial Times*, August 17/18, 1991.
41. See Judith Pataki, "Refugee Wave From Croatia Puts Strain on Relief Efforts," RFE/RL, *Report on Eastern Europe*, September 27, 1991, p. 12.

in Hungary as of October 1991.[42] The majority of these (some 67 percent) are ethnic Croats, who are seeking only temporary refuge and want to return home once the fighting stops. However, about 25–26 percent are ethnic Hungarians.[43]

Hungarian authorities are particularly concerned about the large Hungarian minority in Yugoslavia. There are nearly 430,000 ethnic Hungarians in Yugoslavia, most of them located in the Vojvodina region of Serbia. Along with the Albanians of Kosovo, they have had their political rights progressively restricted by the Serbs since 1989. If their rights continue to be curtailed, many of them might decide to flee or emigrate. Absorbing another major influx of refugees would impose a serious burden on the Hungarian economy, already severely strained by the need to feed and house the large number of other refugees, and could aggravate social tensions.

The growing problems posed by the increased influx of migrants and refugees have prompted the three countries of Central Europe (Hungary, Poland, and Czechoslovakia) to step up cooperation. As a first step the three countries agreed in October to coordinate their policies regarding refugees, and to work out uniform laws and regulations for handling applications for refugee status. This move is part of a general trend toward increased cooperation between the three countries since the Visegrad summit of February 1990, which could have important regional implications.

Germany and East-West Migration

The prospect of increased emigration from the East poses major dilemmas for Western Europe and especially for the Federal Republic of Germany. In the last decade West Germany has been confronted with a massive influx of foreign immigrants. This began well before the fall of the Berlin Wall in November 1989 and has increased steadily since. A growing number of these have come from Eastern Europe. In 1974, for instance, only 7,994 persons emigrated to the Federal Republic from Eastern Europe. This represented only 5.3 percent of the total inflow of foreigners. In 1988, by contrast, 133,742

---

42. Celestine Bohlen, "Refugees from Yugoslavia are Welcomed in Hungary," *New York Times*, October 18, 1991. Also Peter Maass, "Refugees from Croatia Flood into Hungary," *Washington Post*, October 7, 1991; and Carol J. Williams, "Serbian-Croatian Conflict Spills into Hungary," August 25, 1991. It is difficult to obtain accurate figures about the number of refugees because many stay with relatives and return home when the fighting in their neighborhood stops.
43. Figures provided by Office of Refugee Affairs, Budapest, November 1991.

persons from Eastern Europe emigrated to the FRG,[44] 39.7 percent of the total inflow of foreigners in that year. Of these, Poland sent nearly one-third of the immigrants, followed by Turkey (12.1 percent) and Yugoslavia (8.6 percent).[45]

ETHNIC GERMAN EMIGRATION

The influx of foreigners from Eastern Europe to the FRG has consisted mainly of two types: (1) repatriated ethnic Germans (*Aussiedler*); and (2) non-German asylum seekers (*Asylanten*).[46] The *Aussiedler*, however, have certain advantages not available to non-German refugees from Eastern Europe: they are considered Germans and thus have access to the German labor market and are entitled to certain social benefits. They have also tended to be more highly skilled and have greater proficiency in the German language, though in recent years both the language proficiency and occupational qualifications of the *Aussiedler* have declined. As a result the problems of both groups have become more similar.[47]

Since 1988 the influx of *Aussiedler* has grown steadily. (See Figure 1 and Table 3.) In 1990, 397,073 ethnic Germans emigrated to Germany.[48] This was nearly twice as many as in 1988 (202,673). Of the 1990 immigrants, the largest number (147,950) came from the Soviet Union, followed by Poland (133,872) and Romania (111,150).

The statistics reveal some interesting trends: the number of *Aussiedler* from the Soviet Union has steadily increased (See Table 4). In 1990, the number of *Aussiedler* from the Soviet Union (147,950) increased by more than a third over 1989 (98,134) and tripled over 1988 (47,572). Immigration rose in 1991 as well: in the first nine months more than 113,000 Soviet *Aussiedler* emigrated to the Federal Republic. If this trend keeps up, the German population in the Soviet Union could be nearly depleted within five to ten years.

---

44. Elmar Hönekopp, "Migratory Movements from Countries of Central and Eastern Europe: Causes and Characteristics, Present Situation and Possible Future Trends—The Cases of Germany and Austria," paper prepared for the Conference of Ministers on the Movement of Persons Coming from Central and East European Countries, Vienna, January 24–25, 1991, pp. 25–27.
45. Ibid., p. 27.
46. A third group, emigrants from the former German Democratic Republic GDR (*Übersiedler*), is outside the scope of this analysis and not considered here.
47. Hönekopp, "Migratory Movements from Countries of Central and Eastern Europe," p. 8.
48. "1990 mehr Aussiedler nach Deutschland als je zuvor," *Frankfurter Allgemeine Zeitung*, January 4, 1991. The statistics in the article are based on official figures released by the German Ministry of Interior.

Figure 1.   Ethnic German Immigration to FRG (1950–91), Countries of Origin.

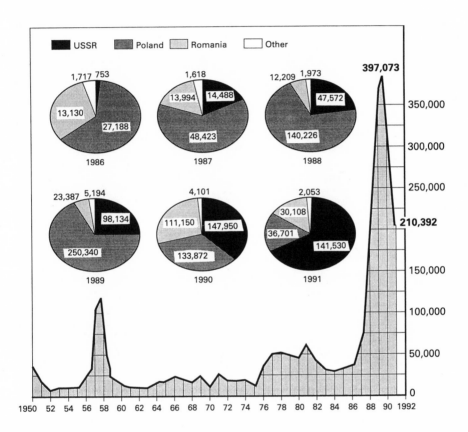

SOURCE: *Die Welt,* January 10, 1992.

In addition, the number of *Aussiedler* from Romania more than quadrupled in 1990 over 1989 (111,150 in 1990 vs. 23,387 in 1989 and 12,902 in 1988.) The 1990 emigrants represented nearly half of all the ethnic Germans in Romania.

Table 3. Ethnic German Emigrants, Country of Origin, 1980–1990.

Year	Poland	USSR	Romania	Total
1980	26,637	6,954	15,767	51,984
1981	50,983	3,773	12,031	69,336
1982	30,355	2,071	12,972	47,992
1983	19,121	1,447	15,501	37,844
1984	17,455	913	16,553	36,386
1985	22,075	757	14,924	38,905
1986	27,188	882	13,130	42,729
1987	48,423	14,488	13,994	78,498
1988	140,226	45,572	12,902	202,645
1989	250,340	98,134	23,387	377,036
1990	133,872	148,000	111,000	397,073
1950–1990	1,372,182	403,308	353,320	2,345,229

NOTE: Only the most important source countries are shown.

SOURCE: Mirjana Morokvasic-Müller, "Beyond the Invasion Scenario: Circular Migrations from and within Eastern and Central Europe," paper presented at the RAND conference on "Prospective Migration from the USSR," Santa Monica, November 17–19, 1991, p. 19.

Table 4. Emigration of Ethnic Germans from the Soviet Union to the FRG.

Period	Total
1948–1970	22,400
1971–1980	64,300
1981–1986	19,500
1987–1989	160,200
1990	147,950
1991	141,530

SOURCE: Heitman, *Soviet Emigration in 1990*, p. 5; 1991 figures from *Die Welt*, January 10, 1992.

If this trend continues, there will be almost no ethnic Germans remaining in Romania within a few years.[49] The main reason for the increase was the

---

49. For a detailed discussion of recent emigration trends and their implications, see Dan Ionescu, "Countdown for the German Minority," RFE/RL, *Report on Eastern Europe*, September 13, 1991, pp. 32–41.

removal of travel restrictions by Ceausescu's successors as well as the increased economic and political unrest in Romania itself.

The number of *Aussiedler* from Poland, on the other hand, declined by nearly half in 1990 (133,872) compared to 1989 (250,340). (See Table 3.)

However, since mid-1990 there has been a decline in the number of ethnic Germans emigrating to the FRG. The decline continued in 1991, when 221,995 *Aussiedler* emigrated to the Federal Republic. Compared to nearly 400,000 in 1990, this represents a drop of nearly half.[50]

The decline in the number of *Aussiedler* is largely due to the change in the German law regarding the emigration of ethnic Germans (*Aussiedleraufnahmegesetz*) in July 1991, which requires prospective *Aussiedler* to make their applications for emigration in their home country before emigrating. Bonn's stepped-up efforts to provide direct material assistance to areas populated by ethnic Germans (*Aussiedlergebiete*) has also played a role. This assistance has been directed particularly at the nearly two million ethnic Germans in the Soviet Union and has been designed to give prospective *Aussiedler* incentives to remain where they are. Bonn has pressed the Soviet—and more recently the Russian—authorities to restore to ethnic Germans the Volga republic from which Stalin deported them in 1941.[51] Gorbachev pledged to restore their homeland in a message to the Congress of Soviet Germans in October 1991. During his visit to Bonn in November 1991, Yeltsin reaffirmed this pledge.[52] However, the pledge prompted protests from many of the inhabitants of the Volga region who fear being displaced by the resettlement, and since then Yeltsin has adopted a more equivocal attitude, calling for a gradual, step-by-step resettlement of the German community.

The prospect of obtaining their own homeland, however, has not succeeded in stemming the flow of *Aussiedler* from the former Soviet Union. Although the number of *Aussiedler* overall declined in 1991, the number of *Aussiedler* emigrating from the former Soviet Union remained about the same as in 1990 (141,350 in 1991, compared to 147,950 in 1990). According to some reports by ethnic German authorities in the former Soviet Union, as many

---

50. "Im vergangen Jahr fast 260,000 Asylbewerber in Deutschland," *Frankfurter Allgemeine Zeitung*, January 4, 1992.
51. See John Tagliabue, "Bonn Wants Russia to Restore Republic for Ethnic Germans," *New York Times*, January 19, 1992.
52. "Yelzin verspricht Wolga-republik," *Die Welt*, November 22, 1991; "Deutsche Wolgarepublik nicht vorrangig—Bundregierung dringt auf konkrete Vereinbarungen," *Suddeutsche Zeitung*, November 23, 1991.

as 90 percent of the ethnic German community are ready to emigrate.[53] How many of these will actually do so depends to a large extent on developments in the various republics, especially Russia. However, unless there is a significant improvement in the situation of the ethnic German community very quickly, a large number are likely to leave, adding to Bonn's already considerable immigration problems.

ASYLUM SEEKERS

In addition to the record number of *Aussiedler* who arrived in Germany in 1990, the number of applicants for asylum in 1990 more than doubled over 1989.[54] In 1990, 193,063 persons applied for asylum in the FRG, an increase of 59 percent over the previous year. This represented close to half of all asylum applications within the EC as a whole. (See Table 5.)

The largest number of applicants (35,345) came from Romania—a nearly ten-fold increase over 1989 (3,121). It was followed by Yugoslavia (22,114 in 1990 vs. 19,423 in 1989) and Turkey (22,082 vs. 20,020 in 1989). The number of applications from Bulgaria also significantly increased (8,341 in 1990 vs. only 429 in 1989). In addition, there was also a sharp increase in applications from a number of Third World countries such as Lebanon and Vietnam.[55]

Table 5. Asylum Seekers in the FRG.

	Country of Origin				
	Romania	**Yugoslavia**	**Turkey**	**Poland**	**Totals**
1989	3,121	19,423	20,020	26,092	121,318
1990	35,345	22,114	22,082	9,155	193,063
1991	40,504	74,854	23,877	3,448	256,112

NOTE: Totals include asylum seekers from other countries also.

SOURCE: *Frankfurter Allgemeine Zeitung,* January 6, 1992.

53. "Reform des Asylrechts: Neuer Vorstoss der Union," *Deutschland Nachrichten,* January 10, 1992.
54. Figures are from "Zahl der Asylbewerber in Deutschland 1990 mehr als verdoppelt," *Frankfurter Allgemeine Zeitung,* May 5, 1991. The article is based on figures released by the German Ministry of the Interior.
55. Most of the Vietnamese had been working in the former GDR prior to unification.

The number of applicants from Poland, by contrast, dramatically declined from 26,092 in 1989 to 9,155 in 1990. This decrease is probably due to the increased freedom of travel. Many Poles travel to the West, especially Germany, seeking temporary (illegal) work and then return to Poland. There is thus less pressure to emigrate. (See Table 5.)

The number of asylum seekers shows no signs of abating. In 1991, 256,112 persons applied for asylum in Germany—32.7 percent more than in 1990.[56] The highest number of these (74,854) came from Yugoslavia, more than three times as many as in 1990. The next largest number came from Romania (40,504), followed by Turkey (23,877) and Bulgaria (12,056). Significantly, the number of asylum seekers from the republics of the former Soviet Union more than doubled (5,690 in 1991, vs. 2,337 in 1990). The number of asylum seekers from Poland, by contrast, continued to decline (3,448 in 1991, vs. 9,155 in 1990 and 26,089 in 1989).

The main reason so many refugees apply for asylum in Germany is the Federal Republic's liberal asylum laws. In contrast to other countries within the EC, Germany cannot turn refugees back at the border. Under the German constitution (Article 16), they have the right to apply for asylum. In addition, the Federal Republic is the only country in the EC in which a rejected applicant has the right to remain in the country.

The political changes in Eastern Europe and the Soviet Union since 1989 have significantly complicated the asylum problem and contributed to the increase in asylum seekers. However, many applicants from Eastern Europe who before 1989 might have qualified for asylum on grounds of political or religious persecution today are rejected. Most applicants for asylum today from Eastern Europe are not political but economic refugees. They thus do not qualify for refugee status. As a result, the number of applicants who are granted asylum has significantly declined. In 1986, for instance, 16 percent of all applicants received asylum. In 1990 the figure dropped to just below 5 percent.[57] Many prolong their stay, however, by dragging out the appeal process.

At the same time there has been a sharp increase in the number of illegal or "irregular" immigrants, who clandestinely cross the German borders from

---

56. "Im vergangen Jahr fast 260,000 Asylbewerber in Deutschland"; "Die meisten Asylbewerber kamen aus dem einstigen Jugoslavien," *Frankfurter Allgemeine Zeitung*, January 6, 1992.

57. "Der Feind des Guten ist das Gutgemeinte—Für eine Europäisierung des Asylrechts und der Einwanderungspolitik plädiert der Vize-Präsident Martin Bangemann," *Frankfurter Rundschau*, September 13, 1991.

Poland and Czechoslovakia. According to figures released by the German Ministry of the Interior, in the first half of 1991 some 42,000 people clandestinely entered Germany. The German authorities seized 5,422 "illegals" on the Czechoslovak-German border and 2,960 illegal entrants on the Polish-German border. Nearly 70 percent of these were Romanians, most of them gypsies.[58]

The sharp increase in asylum applicants has contributed to a visible growth of social tensions in Germany, and a marked increase in violence against foreigners.[59] While this hostility toward foreigners has been most acute in eastern Germany (the former GDR) where unemployment is high, it has increased significantly in the western part of Germany as well. Some polls, in fact, suggest that support for right-wing hostility against foreigners may actually be stronger in West Germany than in the former GDR.[60]

Concern about the influx of refugees has become a major issue in German domestic politics. In the local elections in Bremen at the end of September 1991, the German People's Union (DVU), a right-wing political party that campaigned to increase restrictions on foreigners seeking to take advantage of Germany's liberal asylum law, won 6.2 percent of the vote, gaining seats in the local parliament for the first time. The big loser, the Social Democrats (SPD), opposed any change in the constitution to tighten restrictions on asylum. The DVU drew much of its new-found strength from voters, especially in working-class districts, who had traditionally voted for the SPD.[61]

The asylum issue has become the focal point of an increasingly heated debate between the major parties in Germany over the last year.[62] The Chris-

---

58. See "Schäuble regt internationale Konferenz über illegale Einreise an," *Frankfurter Allgemeine Zeitung*, August 3, 1991.

59. In September there were more than 200 attacks against asylum seekers, immigrants, and foreign workers. See Stephen Kinzer, "German Vote Raises Foreigner's Fears," *New York Times*, October 8, 1991; Stephen Kinzer, "A Wave of Attacks on Foreigners Stirs Shock in Germany," ibid., October 1, 1991; Stephen Kinzer, "German Visits Refugees, Attacks Go On," ibid., October 5, 1991; Quentin Peel, "Racist Attacks Mar German Unity Anniversary," *Financial Times*, October 4, 1991; Marc Fisher, "Anti-Immigrant Violence Grows in Germany," *Washington Post*, September 30, 1991. For German views see, for example, Robert Leicht, "Hoyerswerda in den Kopfen," *Die Zeit*, September 26, 1991; Thorsten Schmidtz, "Die braven Burger von Hoyerswerda," ibid.; and Gunter Hoffmann, "Hilflos vor dem Fremdenhass," ibid., October 3, 1991.

60. According to a poll taken by the public opinion research institute EMNID in Bielefeld in September 1991, 21 percent of East Germans and 38 percent of West Germans expressed "understanding" for right-wing hostility aimed against foreigners. See *Der Spiegel*, No. 40, 1991, p. 30.

61. Klaus-Dieter Frankenberger, "Protest der 'Kleinen Leute'," *Frankfurter Allgemeine Zeitung*, October 11, 1991.

62. See "Tauziehen um die Asylrechtsreform in Bonn," *Neue Zürcher Zeitung*, September 29/30,

tian Democratic Union (CDU), together with its sister party the CSU, has called for changes in the German constitution that would allow border guards to turn back refugees at the border. The Social Democratic Party (SPD) and Free Democratic Party (FDP), however, oppose any changes in the constitution. Given the fact that a change in the constitution would require a two-thirds majority and thus support of the SPD, it is unlikely that the CDU's efforts will succeed. However, in order to defuse the current tensions, the three main parties agreed in October 1991 to speed up the procedures for processing asylum applications, and to increase the number of refugee centers, especially in the new *Länder* in the former GDR.

Some SPD politicians have argued that Germany should abandon special rights for ethnic Germans (*Aussiedler*) and simply set quotas for all immigrants. The Kohl government, however, has rejected any restrictions on the number of ethnic Germans—the *Aussiedler* are an important CDU constituency—while insisting that Germany is not an "immigration country."[63] Instead it has advocated a combination of policy measures to address the migration/refugee problem:

- increased financial and material assistance to the East designed to provide incentives for would-be emigrants to stay home;
- changes in the constitution restricting the right of asylum;
- a harmonization of visa and asylum policies within the EC;
- a more equitable division of refugees within Europe (not just the EC).

Bonn has called for greater cooperation within the EC to address the problem. At the Luxembourg summit in June 1991, Kohl pressed for a common EC policy toward asylum and immigration.[64] Such a policy is essential if the EC is to meet its target of scrapping all borders by the end of 1992. Once these borders are removed, all EC citizens will have unlimited freedom

---

1991; "Political Parties Draw Closer on Emotional Issue of Asylum," *German Tribune*, August 18, 1991; "Weitere starre Fronten in der Asyl-Debatte," *Die Welt*, September 25, 1991; "Asylrecht: Schäuble dämpft Erwartungen," ibid., September 27, 1991; "Bewegungen in der Asyl-Debatte," ibid., September 28/29, 1991; and "Die Bonner Parteien sehen keine Mehrheit für eine Änderung des Asyl-Grundrechts," *Frankfurter Allgemeine Zeitung*, September 28, 1991.

63. See "Schäuble: Aussiedler werden ohne Einschränkungen aufgenommen," *Frankfurter Allgemeine Zeitung*, April 13, 1991.

64. At the EC summit in Luxembourg, in June 1991, Kohl pushed the EC leaders to agree to a harmonization of individual members' policy on asylum. See "L'Allemagne propose de définit une strategie commune européenne en matière d'immigration," *Le Monde*, June 30–July 1, 1991. Also Christopher Parkes, "Germany Calls for EC Asylum Policy," *Financial Times*, September 3, 1991.

of movement within the internal market, but also all persons legally residing within the Community, including applicants for asylum, will be able to move freely. A common EC asylum policy within the EC, however, would probably require a change in the German constitution, since few West European governments are likely to agree to the liberal rights of asylum provided under Article 16 of the German constitution.

Bonn has also intensified cooperation with the individual countries of Eastern Europe, in order to manage and control the problem of illegal entry better. Cooperation with Poland in particular has been strengthened in an effort to reduce the number of immigrants who illegally cross the Polish-German border. In December 1990 Poland introduced visa and currency restrictions on Romanians entering Poland. This has helped to diminish the number of illegal immigrants who transit Poland into Germany.

These measures alone, however, are unlikely to resolve the problem. Sooner or later it seems likely that Germany must admit that it is becoming an immigration country and must establish quotas for immigrants rather than relying on the cumbersome system of granting asylum for political refugees. While there is still considerable resistance to this idea, particularly within the CDU/CSU, over the long run this may prove the most effective way to manage what has become a major social, economic, and political problem. It would allow Germany to channel the influx of immigrants and harmonize their entry with the labor and housing market. It would also reduce the number of illegitimate asylum seekers and illegal migrants.

Toward East-West Cooperation: The Policy Agenda

The problems faced by the Federal Republic, while more acute than elsewhere in Western Europe, are part of a larger problem in Europe as a whole.[65] In the last decade, the number of asylum seekers in Europe has dramatically increased from a few thousand in the early 1970s to nearly 500,000 in 1990. The unexpected arrival of so many refugees has caught Western European countries unprepared and has overtaxed procedural systems for handling these refugees. Administrative difficulties have been further compounded by the fact that many arrive without travel documents or valid visas. Costs of

---

65. For a detailed discussion of Europe's attempts to deal with the growing refugee crisis, see Gil Loescher, "The European Community and Refugees," *International Affairs*, Vol. 65, No. 4 (Autumn 1989), pp. 617–636.

processing have also soared. In 1989 the cost for the care of asylum seekers in ten European countries plus Canada was at least $4.5 billion; by 1992 it is expected to rise to $8 billion.[66]

The process of political liberalization in the former Soviet Union and Eastern Europe since 1989 has added to these problems. Exactly how large the population outflow from the East will be in the coming decade is difficult to estimate since it is highly scenario-dependent. However, given the gulf between the two parts of Europe and the length of time needed for adaptation by the economies of Eastern Europe, it seems likely that the number of people wishing to leave will be higher in the short term than Western Europe will be able to absorb.[67]

By the early twenty-first century, however, the drop in the birth rate in Western Europe in the 1960s and 1970s should lead to a chronic labor shortage and provide new opportunities for workers from the East. Even countries like Italy, Greece, and Spain, which have traditionally been exporters of labor, will face a labor shortfall and could benefit from an influx of labor from the East over the long run.

The problem is the short term—the next decade, especially the coming 2–5 years when the former Soviet Union and Eastern Europe will face massive adjustment problems and rising unemployment. This is likely to increase the number of migrants to Western Europe and parts of Eastern Europe. Even if the worst scare scenarios do not transpire, increased cooperation between East and West will be necessary to manage the large westward flow of populations. The problem of irregular migration in particular is likely to become acute.

To date the response by many countries in Western Europe to the growing migration pressure from the East has been to tighten border controls and visa restrictions. However, such measures alone are unlikely to stem the migration because they do not deal with the root causes of the outflow, which are the "push factors" in the East. Moreover, they contravene the basic spirit and objectives of Basket Three of the Helsinki Final Act, which calls for the free flow of people, information, and ideas.

What is needed is a broad-gauged, multi-faceted long-term strategy that combines some tightening of controls with development measures that address the root causes of the outflow. However, if this strategy is to be

---

66. Robert Rice, "Europe's Need for a Common Front," *Financial Times,* July 23, 1991.
67. Chesnais, "Migration from Eastern and Western Europe," p. 24.

successful, it cannot be a purely national or even Western endeavor. It must involve cooperation with the prospective sending countries in the East.

In particular, Russia, Ukraine, and the Baltic states need to become integrated in West European efforts to control migration. These areas are likely to be the main sources of emigration from the former Soviet Union.[68] Their cooperation is therefore essential in trying to regulate and stabilize East-West migration.

At the same time, more attention must be paid to the security implications of the possible large-scale emigration of the Soviet scientific intelligentsia, especially those who have worked in sensitive areas of the military-industrial complex. As the impact of market reforms and arms control agreements begins to be felt, tens of thousands of highly skilled scientists will be forced out of work. Many may be tempted to emigrate to countries like Libya or Syria by the prospect of immediate employment and high salaries. Were these scientists to put their skills and knowledge at the disposal of such regimes, this could have a damaging impact on Western security. Thus a concerted Western policy must be worked out to ensure that such a development does not occur.

In addition, several other measures should be part of a comprehensive strategy for dealing with the consequences of possible large-scale migration:

- *Harmonization of rules and practices related to granting asylum within the EC.* In particular, the Community members must agree on criteria for refugee status and streamline the process of asylum adjudication.
- *EC cooperation with the countries of Eastern Europe and the Western republics of the former Soviet Union regarding visa policy, measures to prevent illegal immigration, and deportation agreements.* East European visa and immigration policies in many cases are very liberal for Third World nationals. Consequently, South-North immigration flows are diverted to Eastern Europe and subsequently reach Western Europe illegally. Greater cooperation could reduce this flow, as well as that of East European nationals to Western Europe.
- *Harmonization of policy within the EC on immigration from Eastern Europe and the former Soviet Union.* The goal should be a European Migration Conven-

---

68. In 1989 64 percent of all emigrants from the USSR came from Russia, the Ukraine, and Kazakhstan (which has a large Russian population). Segbers, *Wanderungs- und Fluchtlings-bewegungen aus der bisherigen UdSSR*, p. 16.

tion that establishes immigration quotas for East Europeans and former Soviet nationals, and provides for effective and orderly migration.

- *Increased financial and development assistance to the countries of Eastern Europe and the key republics of the former Soviet Union.* This assistance should be designed to help these countries and republics address the consequences of large-scale immigration as well as to create incentives to keep their own populations from migrating. Such aid can have a dual effect: it can counteract the "push factor" by improving the economic conditions in the sending countries; it can also weaken the "pull factor" by helping to narrow the gap between the sending and receiving countries.[69]

In the final analysis, the migration problem is closely linked to the larger question of the success of the reform process in the East as a whole. If the reforms are successful, the pressure on sizable numbers of citizens from the East to move West will be gradually reduced. But if the reforms fail, many in the East will "vote with their feet." This gives the West a strong incentive to support measures to help stabilize the reform processes now underway in Eastern Europe and the former Soviet Union. Without such support, these reforms could falter, increasing the prospects for instability and disorder in both parts of Europe.

---

69. The relationship between development and migration is complex. Push and pull factors are rarely the only factors determining migration flows. Other socioeconomic factors, such as kinship ties between migrants in the receiving countries, and the political relationships between sending and receiving countries also play a role. Thus migratory flows may persist even after the original economic causes have been considerably weakened.

Part IV:
Nationalism and
International Security

Hypotheses on Nationalism and War

Stephen Van Evera

Scholars have written widely on the causes of nationalism[1] but said little about its effects, especially its effects on international politics. Most strikingly, the impact of nationalism on the risk of war has barely been explored. Most authors take the war-causing character of nationalism for granted, assuming it without proof or explanation.[2] Factors that govern the size of the dangers posed by nationalism are neglected. What types of nationalism are most likely to cause war? What background conditions catalyze or dampen this causal process? These ques-

Stephen Van Evera teaches in the political science department at the Massachusetts Institute of Technology.

Thanks to Robert Art, Don Blackmer, David Laitin, John Mearsheimer, Barry Posen, Jack Snyder, and Stephen Walt for sharing their thoughts on nationalism and their comments on this paper. A version of this article will appear in 1994 in a Council on Foreign Relations volume edited by Charles Kupchan.

1. A survey is Anthony D. Smith, *Theories of Nationalism*, 2nd ed. (New York: Harper & Row, 1983). Prominent recent works include: Ernest Gellner, *Nations and Nationalism* (Ithaca: Cornell University Press, 1983); Anthony D. Smith, *The Ethnic Origins of Nations* (Oxford: Basil Blackwell, 1986); E.J. Hobsbawm, *Nations and Nationalism Since 1780* (New York: Cambridge University Press, 1990); Benedict Anderson, *Imagined Communities: Reflections on the Origin and Spread of Nationalism*, rev. ed. (London: Verso, 1991); Liah Greenfeld, *Nationalism: Five Roads to Modernity* (Cambridge: Harvard University Press, 1992); and Barry R. Posen, "Nationalism, the Mass Army, and Military Power," *International Security*, Vol. 18, No. 2 (Fall 1993), pp. 80–124. However, the nationalism literature leaves ample room for more work on nationalism's causes: much of it fails to frame hypotheses clearly and much does not systematically test hypotheses against empirical evidence; hence the literature leaves many questions unresolved.
2. Thus Anthony Smith notes that "the prevailing image of nationalism in the West today is mainly negative," and Boyd Shafer states his "belief that nationalism, especially when carried to extremes, leads to war and destruction." Smith, *Theories of Nationalism*, p. 8; Boyd C. Shafer, *Faces of Nationalism* (New York: Harcourt Brace Jovanovich, 1972), p. xiii. Yet the entry under "Nationalism and War" in Louis Snyder's 435-page *Encyclopedia of Nationalism* fills only two pages, and its bibliography lists no works focused on the topic. Louis L. Snyder, *Encyclopedia of Nationalism* (New York: Paragon, 1990), pp. 248–250. Exceptions exist: a few scholars have held a less purely critical view of nationalism, arguing that it has the potential for both good and evil. See, for example, Carlton J.H. Hayes, *Essays on Nationalism* (New York: Macmillan, 1926), pp. 245–275; Hayes's views are summarized in Snyder, *Encyclopedia of Nationalism*, pp. 132–133. And the impact of nationalism on the risk of war is now receiving more attention: see especially Jack Snyder, "Nationalism and the Crisis of the Post-Soviet State," *Survival*, Vol. 35, No. 1 (Spring 1993), pp. 5–26; and Barry R. Posen, "The Security Dilemma and Ethnic Conflict," *Survival*, Vol. 35, No. 1 (Spring 1993), pp. 27–47. The Snyder and Posen pieces are also published in Michael E. Brown, ed., *Ethnic Conflict and International Security* (Princeton: Princeton University Press, 1993).

International Security, Vol. 18, No. 4 (Spring 1994), pp. 5–39
© 1994 by the President and Fellows of Harvard College and the Massachusetts Institute of Technology.

tion are largely undiscussed, hence the causal nexus between nationalism and war presents an important unsolved riddle.

This article explores that nexus. I define nationalism as a political movement having two characteristics: (1) individual members give their primary loyalty to their own ethnic or national community;[3] this loyalty supersedes their loyalty to other groups, e.g., those based on common kinship or political ideology; and (2) these ethnic or national communities desire their own independent state.[4] I leave the origins of nationalism unexplored, instead focusing on its effects on the risk of war. Seven questions are addressed: Does nationalism cause war? If so, what types of nationalism are most likely to cause war? How and why do they cause war? What causes these war-causing nationalisms? Under what conditions are they most dangerous? How, if at all, can the war-causing attributes of nationalism be suppressed

---

3. My usage of "ethnic community" follows Anthony Smith, who suggests that an ethnic community has six characteristics: a common name, a myth of common ancestry, shared memories, a common culture, a link with a historic territory or homeland (which it may or may not currently occupy), and a measure of common solidarity. See Smith, *Ethnic Origins of Nations*, pp. 22–30. Summarizing Smith nicely is Michael E. Brown, "Causes and Implications of Ethnic Conflict," in Brown, ed., *Ethnic Conflict and International Security*, pp. 3–26 at 4–5.

Smith's second criteria (myth of common ancestry) would exclude immigrant societies of diverse origin that have developed the other five characteristics of ethnic community, such as the immigrant peoples of the United States, Cuba, Argentina, Chile, and Brazil. However, the common usage of "nation" and "nationalism" includes these groups as nations that can have a nationalism, e.g., "American nationalism," "Argentine nationalism," "Chilean nationalism." I define nationalism as a movement of a "national community" as well as an "ethnic community" in order to include these nationalisms. My usage of "national" follows the *Dictionary of the Social Sciences*, which defines "nation" as "the largest society of people united by a common culture and consciousness," and which "occupies a common territory." Julius Gould and William L. Kolb, eds., *A Dictionary of the Social Sciences* (New York: Free Press of Glencoe, 1964), p. 451.

4. The academic literature defines nationalism in an annoyingly wide range of ways. My definition follows no other exactly, but it amalgamates the more prominent definitions: each of these include at least one element of my definition, that prime loyalty is owed to one's ethnic/ culture group, and/or that the group to which prime loyalty is given should have its own state. My usage most closely follows Rupert Emerson and Richard Cottam, who define nationalism (in Cottam's words) as "a belief on the part of a large group of people that they comprise a community, a nation, that is entitled to independent statehood, and a willingness of this group to grant their community a primary and terminal loyalty"; quoted in Shafer, *Faces of Nationalism*, p. 4. Similar is Hans Kohn, whose nationalists give "supreme loyalty" to their own nationality, and who see "the nation-state as the ideal form of political organization." Ibid. Also similar are E.J. Hobsbawm and Ernest Gellner, who define nationalism as "primarily a principle which holds that the political and national unit should be congruent." Hobsbawm, *Nations and Nationalism since 1780*, p. 9, quoting and adopting Gellner's definition. However, their definition, by describing nationalism as an idea holding that states and nationalities should be coterminous, omits the many nationalisms that would claim their own state while also denying the statehood aspirations of other nationalities, and also omits more modest nationalisms that are content to allow a diaspora beyond their state borders.

or neutralized? How large are the risks to peace posed by nationalism in today's Europe, and how can these risks be minimized? In answer I offer unproven hypotheses that I leave untested for now. Our stock of hypotheses on the consequences of nationalism is meager, hence our first order of business should be to expand it. This can set the stage for empirical inquiry by others.[5]

Causes of war or peace can be classified as proximate (causes that directly affect the odds of war) or remote (causes of these proximate causes, or background conditions required for their activation.) I explore proximate causes first, then turn to remote causes. Specifically, the next section of this article identifies varieties of nationalism that are most likely to cause war (including both civil and inter-state war). The section that follows it identifies the causes of these dangerous varieties of nationalism and the conditions that govern the size of the dangers they produce. Twenty-one hypotheses are proposed in all—nine main hypotheses and twelve sub-hypotheses. Some focus on the impact of the environment that surrounds nationalist movements; this environment can incline the movement toward peaceful or toward warlike behavior. Others focus on the impact of the movement's internal character, especially its ideology and vision of history; this, too, can incline the movement toward peace or war. These hypotheses are highlighted because they are deductively sound, survive plausibility probes, and in some cases generate policy prescriptions. They are summarized in Table 1.[6] Viewed together, they suggest that the effects of nationalism are highly varied: some types of nationalism are far more dangerous than other types, all types of nationalism are more dangerous under some conditions than under others, and nationalism can even dampen the risk of war under some conditions.

If accepted, these hypotheses provide a checklist for assessing the dangers posed by a given nationalist movement or by the spread of nationalism in a given region. To illustrate, I use them in the concluding section to assess the risks that nationalism now poses in Europe, because Europe is a region in flux whose future is much debated. This exercise suggests that nationalism

---

5. A similar exercise whose example influenced my design is Robert Jervis, "Hypotheses on Misperception," *World Politics*, Vol. 20, No. 3 (April 1968), pp. 454–479; reprinted in Robert J. Art and Robert Jervis, ed., *International Politics: Anarchy, Force, Political Economy, and Decision Making*, 2nd ed. (Glenview, Ill.: Scott, Foresman, 1985), pp. 510–526.
6. The text of this article identifies factors that govern the size of the risk posed by nationalism, and explains the proposed causal relationship. Table 1 restates these factors and explanations as hypotheses.

Table 1. Hypotheses on Nationalism and War: Summary.

I. IMMEDIATE CAUSES
1. The greater the proportion of state-seeking nationalities that are stateless, the greater the risk of war.
2. The more that nationalities pursue the recovery of national diasporas, and the more they pursue annexationist strategies of recovery, the greater the risk of war.
3. The more hegemonistic the goals that nationalities pursue toward one another, the greater the risk of war.
4. The more severely nationalities oppress minorities living in their states, the greater the risk of war.

II. CAUSES OF THE IMMEDIATE CAUSES AND CONDITIONS REQUIRED FOR THEIR OPERATION

Structural Factors:
1. Stateless nationalisms pose a greater risk of war if they have the strength to plausibly reach for freedom, and the central state has the will to resist their attempt.
2. The more densely nationalities are intermingled, the greater the risk of war.
   a. The risks posed by intermingling are larger the more local (house-by-house) rather than regional (province-by-province) the pattern of intermingling.
   b. The risks posed by intermingling are larger if the rescue of diasporas by homelands is difficult but possible; smaller if rescue is either impossible or easy.
3. The greater the defensibility and legitimacy of borders, and the greater the correspondence between these political borders and communal boundaries, the smaller the risk of war.
   a. The less secure and defensible the borders of emerging nation-states, the greater the risk of war.
   b. The greater the international legitimacy of the borders of emerging nation-states, the smaller the risk of war.
   c. The more closely the boundaries of emerging nation-states follow ethnic boundaries, the smaller the risk of war.

---

poses very little danger of war in Western Europe, but poses large dangers in the East, especially in the former Soviet Union. Current Western European nationalisms are benign, and the conditions required for a return to the malignant nationalisms of 1870–1945 are almost wholly absent. In contrast, many Eastern nationalisms have many (though not all) of the attributes that

---

Table 1, cont.

Political/Environmental Factors:

4. The greater the past crimes committed by nationalities toward one another, the greater the risk of war.
   a. The better these crimes are remembered by the victims, the greater the risk of war.
   b. The more that responsibility for past crimes can be attached to groups still on the scene, the greater the risk of war.
   c. The less contrition and repentance shown by the guilty groups, the greater the risk of war.
   d. The greater the coincidence of power and victimhood, the greater the risk of war.
5. The more severely nationalities oppress minorities now living in their states, the greater the risk of war. (This restates Hypothesis No. I.4; I list it twice because it operates as both a direct and a remote cause of war.)

Perceptual Factors:

6. The more divergent are the beliefs of nationalities about their mutual history and their current conduct and character, the greater the risk of war.
   a. The less legitimate the governments or leaders of nationalist movements, the greater their propensity to purvey mythical nationalist beliefs, hence the greater the risk of war.
   b. The more the state must demand of its citizens, the greater its propensity to purvey mythical nationalist beliefs, hence the greater the risk of war.
   c. If economic conditions deteriorate, publics become more receptive to scapegoat myths, hence such myths are more widely believed, hence war is more likely.
   d. If independent evaluative institutions are weak or incompetent, myths will more often prevail, hence war is more likely.

I argue make nationalism dangerous; hence the risk of large-scale violence stemming from the now-rising tide of Eastern nationalism is substantial.

What prescriptions follow? The character and consequences of nationalism are not written in stone. The Western powers have some capacity to influence the character and consequences of Eastern nationalist movements, and should try to channel it in benign directions. Most importantly, the Western powers should promote full respect for minority rights, democracy, and official respect for historical truth; if Eastern nationalisms adopt these programs, the risks they pose will sharply diminish.

Varieties of Nationalism: Which Cause War?

Four primary attributes of a nationalist movement determine whether it has a large or small potential to produce violence. These are: (1) The movement's political status: is statehood attained or unattained? (2) The movement's stance toward its national diaspora (if it has one): if the movement has a national state, but some members of the nation are dispersed or entrapped beyond the state's borders, does the nation accept continued separation from this diaspora, or does it seek to incorporate the diaspora in the national state? And if it seeks the diaspora's incorporation, will it accomplish this by immigration or by territorial expansion? (3) The movement's stance toward other nations: does it respect or deny other nationalities' right to national independence? (4) The movement's treatment of its own minorities: are these minorities respected or abused?

IS NATIONAL STATEHOOD ATTAINED OR UNATTAINED?
Nationalist movements without states raise greater risks of war because their accommodation requires greater and more disruptive change. Their struggle for national freedom can produce wars of secession, which in turn can widen to become international wars. Their freedom struggle can also injure the interests of other groups, displacing populations whose new grievances sow the seeds of future conflict, as Zionism's displacement of the Palestinian Arabs in 1948 sowed the seeds of later Arab-Israeli wars. Finally, the appearance of new states creates a new, less mature regional international system that lacks "rules of the game" defining the rights and obligations of its members toward one another, and norms of international conduct; these rights, obligations, and norms can take years to define, raising the risk of crises and collisions in the meantime.

The international system tolerates change poorly, but the accommodation of new nationalist movements requires it.[7] Thus the first measure of the risks

---

7. The dichotomy between stateless and state-possessing nationalist movements is analogous to the dichotomy in international relations between "satisfied" and "dissatisfied" powers; the latter disturb the peace in their effort to gain satisfaction, while the former cause less trouble.

to the peace of a region posed by nationalism is found in the proportion of its nationalist movements that remain unfulfilled in statehood, a factor expressed in the nation-to-state ratio. Are the supply of and demand for states in equilibrium or disequilibrium? Peace in a region is more likely the more closely a supply/demand equilibrium is approached.[8] Modern nationalism disrupted peace over the past two centuries partly because so many of the world's current nationalist movements were stateless at the outset, requiring vast change to accommodate their emergence. Nationalism still threatens peace because its full accommodation would require vast additional change: the number of states in the world has more than tripled since World War II (up from the 50 signers of the UN Charter in 1945, to 180-odd states today), but many nationalities remain stateless; the world has some 6000 language groups,[9] many of which have dormant or manifest aspirations for statehood.

In Western Europe the transition of nations to statehood is largely behind us: that region's remaining stateless nationalities are relatively few and weak. In Eastern Europe and the former Soviet Union, the problem is more serious because the transition to statehood, while largely fulfilled, is still incomplete. The bulk of these stateless nationalities are found in the former Soviet Union; 15 of the 104 nationalities in the former USSR have attained states, but the other 89 have not; these stateless nationalities total 25.6 million people, comprising 10 percent of the former USSR's total population.[10] Most of these nationalities are not potential candidates for statehood (e.g., the Jews) but

---

8. Wars can result from having too many states, as well as too few. If states are too many, wars of national unification will result, as they did in Germany and Italy in the nineteenth century, and as they might someday in the Arab world. In Europe, however, the problem everywhere is an excess of demand for states over the supply.

9. Alan Thein Durning, *Guardians of the Land: Indigenous Peoples and the Health of the Earth*, Worldwatch Paper No. 112 (Washington, D.C.: Worldwatch Institute, December 1992), p. 9. Durning reports that measured by spoken languages the world has 6000 cultures. Of these some 4000–5000 are indigenous, and comprise some 10 percent of the world's population. See also Michael Krauss, "The Language Extinction Catastrophe Just Ahead: Should Linguists Care?" paper presented at the 15th International Congress of Linguists, Quebec City, Quebec, Canada, August 10, 1992. For another estimate see Gunnar P. Nielsson, "States and 'Nation-Groups': A Global Taxonomy," in Edward A. Tiryakian and Ronald Rogowski, eds., *New Nationalisms of the Developed West* (Boston: Allen and Unwin, 1985), pp. 27–56. He identifies a global total of 589 ethnic groups, most of which are stateless (p. 33). He also found that only 41 of 161 states surveyed were ethnically homogeneous (in which one ethnic group comprises over 95 percent of the state's population); see ibid., Table 2.1, pp. 30–31.

10. These figures are for 1979, and are calculated from John L. Scherer, ed., *USSR Facts and Figures Annual*, Vol. 5 (Gulf Breeze, Fla.: Academic International Press, 1981), pp. 51–52. Of these stateless groups the ten largest are the Tatar (6.3 million), German (1.9 million), Jewish (1.8 million), Chuvash (1.8 million), Dagestan (1.7 million), Bashkir (1.4 million), Mordvin (1.2 million), Polish (1.2 million), Chechen (.8 million), and Udmurt (.7 million).

some might be (e.g., the Tatars, Chechen, Ingush, and Ossetians), and their reach for statehood could sow future friction.

ATTITUDE TOWARD THE NATIONAL DIASPORA: IS PARTIAL OR TOTAL NATIONAL UNITY PURSUED? ARE IMMIGRATIONIST OR EXPANSIONIST TACTICS USED?
Does the nationalist ideology posit that all or only a part of the national ethnic community must be incorporated in the national state? And if the whole nationality must be incorporated, will this be accomplished by immigration (bringing the diaspora to the state) or by territorial expansion (bringing the state to the diaspora)?

These questions suggest a distinction among three types of nationalism: "diaspora-accepting," "immigrationist," and "diaspora-annexing." Some nationalisms (the diaspora-accepting variety) are content with partial union (e.g., Chinese nationalism);[11] such nationalisms are less troublesome because they make fewer territorial demands on their neighbors. Some nationalisms (the immigrationist type) seek to incorporate their diasporas in the national state, but are content to pursue union by seeking immigration of the diaspora (current German nationalism and Zionist Jewish nationalism.) Such immigrationist nationalisms are also easy to accommodate. Finally, some nationalisms seek to incorporate their diasporas by means of territorial expansion (pre-1914 Pan-Germanism and current Pan-Serbianism are examples.) Such diaspora-annexing nationalisms are the most dangerous of the three, since their goals and tactics produce the greatest territorial conflict with others. Thus one scenario for war in the former Soviet Union lies in the possible appearance of a Pan-Russian nationalism that would seek to reincorporate by force the vast Russian diaspora now living in the non-Russian republics. This diaspora includes some 24 million Russians, or 17 percent of all Russians.[12] The future hinges heavily on whether Russian nationalism accepts separation from this diaspora (or seeks to ingather it by immigration), or instead forcibly seeks to annex it.[13]

---

11. The Chinese state has historically left the overseas Chinese to their own political devices. John E. Wills, "Maritime Asia, 1500–1800: The Interactive Emergence of European Domination," *American Historical Review*, Vol. 98, No. 1 (February 1993), pp. 83–105, at p. 87.
12. Calculated from Scherer, *USSR Facts and Figures Annual*, pp. 49–51.
13. Russia's extensive military meddling in the affairs of the other former Soviet republics during 1992–94 and the political rise of Vladimir Zhirinovsky in 1993 warns that a new Russian expansionism is already emerging. On this military meddling see Thomas Goltz, "Letter From Eurasia: The Hidden Russian Hand," *Foreign Policy*, No. 92 (Fall 1993), pp. 92–116.

ATTITUDE TOWARD OTHER INDEPENDENT NATIONALITIES:
TOLERANT OR HEGEMONISTIC?

Does the ideology of the nationalism incorporate respect for the freedom of other nationalities, or does it assume a right or duty to rule them? In other words, is the national ideology symmetrical (all nationalities deserve states) or asymmetrical (only our nationality deserves statehood; others should be denied it)?

Hegemonistic, or asymmetrical, nationalism is both the rarest and the most dangerous variety of nationalism. Interwar Nazi nationalism in Germany, fascist nationalism in Mussolini's Italy, and militarist nationalism in imperial Japan illustrate such hegemonistic nationalism; the wars they caused illustrate its results.[14] No European nationalism today displays such hegemonism, but the vast trouble that it caused in the past advises alertness to its possible reappearance in Europe or elsewhere.

THE DEGREE OF NATIONAL RESPECT FOR MINORITY RIGHTS: HIGH OR LOW?

Is the nationalism minority-respecting, or minority-oppressing? A minority-respecting nationalism grants equal rights to other nationalities lying within the boundaries of its claimed state; it may even grant their right to secede and establish their own state. A minority-oppressing nationalism denies such rights to these other nationalities, subjugating them instead. Many of the nationalisms of immigrant nations (American, Anglo-Canadian) have been relatively minority-respecting (in the Canadian case this includes a tacit right to secession, which the Quebecois may soon exercise.) Non-immigrant nationalisms often display far less tolerance for their minorities: prominent current examples include Iraq's and Turkey's oppression of their Kurdish minorities, Bulgaria's oppression of its Turks, China's cruelties in Tibet, Croatia's intolerance toward its Serb minority, and Serbian oppression of its

---

14. On twentieth-century German nationalism, see Louis L. Snyder, *German Nationalism: The Tragedy of a People*, 2nd ed. (Port Washington, New York: Kennikat Press, 1969); Louis L. Snyder, *From Bismarck to Hitler: The Background of Modern German Nationalism* (Williamsport: Bayard Press, 1935); and Hans Kohn, *The Mind of Germany: The Education of a Nation* (New York: Harper and Row, 1960). On official ideas and perceptions in fascist Italy see Denis Mack Smith, *Mussolini's Roman Empire* (Harmondsworth, U.K.: Penguin, 1977). On domestic currents in imperial Japan see Saburo Ienaga, *The Pacific War, 1931–1945* (New York: Pantheon, 1978); and Ienaga, "The Glorification of War in Japanese Education," *International Security*, Vol. 18, No. 3 (Winter 1993/94), pp. 113–133. Nationalism is not, of course, the only possible source of claims against neighbors. These can also arise from non-nationalist expansionist political ideologies (communism), from hegemonistic religious ideas (the crusading Christianity of the middle ages), from safety concerns arising from the security dilemma, from economic greed, and so forth.

Slavic Moslem and Albanian minorities. Nazi German nationalism was an extreme case of a minority-oppressing nationalism.

The first three attributes—is statehood attained? attitude toward diaspora? attitude toward other independent nationalities?—define the scope of a nationalist movement's claims against others; conversely, the fourth attribute—policy toward minorities?—helps determine the scope of others' claims against the movement. The larger these others' goals become, the more they will collide with the movement's goals, raising the risk of war. Minority-oppressing nationalism can cause war in two ways: (1) by provoking violent secessions by its captive nations; or (2) by spurring the homelands of these captive nations to move forcefully to free their oppressed co-nationals[15] (as Croatian threats against the Serb minority in Croatia helped spawn the Serb attack on Croatia in 1991).[16] Minority-oppressing nationalism is most dangerous if the oppressed minorities have nearby friends who have the capacity to protect the oppressed nation by force. (The Serbo-Croat war exploded partly because Croatia's Serbs had such a friend in Serbia). The attitude of many nationalisms in Eastern Europe and the former Soviet Union toward their minorities remains undefined, and the future hinges on whether they evolve toward minority respect or oppression.

These four attributes can be used to create a nationalism "danger-scale," expressing the level of danger posed by a given nationalism, or by the spread of nationalism in a given region. If all four attributes are benign, the nationalism poses little danger of war, and may even bolster peace. Specifically, a nationalism is benign if it has achieved statehood; has limited unity goals (i.e., accepts the existence of any unincorporated diaspora) or adopts an immigrationist strategy for ingathering its diaspora; posits no claim to rule other nationalities living beyond its national territory; and respects the rights of minorities found in this territory. Multiplied, such nationalisms may even dampen the risk of war, by making conquest more difficult: where these nationalisms are prevalent, conquest is harder because nation-states are

---

15. Thus the second and fourth attributes are related: if some states oppress their minorities (the fourth attribute) this affects other states' propensity to pursue diaspora recovery (the second attribute).

16. On the war's origins, including the important role of Croatia's pre-war threats against its Serb minority, see Misha Glenny, "The Massacre of Yugoslavia," *New York Review of Books*, January 30, 1992, pp. 30–35, at 30–31; and Misha Glenny, *The Fall of Yugoslavia: The Third Balkan War* (London: Penguin, 1992), pp. 12–14, 123. An account stressing international aspects of the war's origins is Morton H. Halperin and David J. Scheffer with Patricia L. Small, *Self-Determination in the New World Order* (Washington, D.C.: Carnegie Endowment, 1992), pp. 32–38.

among the most difficult type of state to conquer (since nationalism provides an inspirational liberation doctrine that can be used to mobilize strong popular resistance to conquest).[17] As a result strong states will be deterred from reaching for regional or global hegemony, and will also be less fearful that others might achieve it; hence all states will compete less fiercely with one another.[18] In contrast, a nationalism is bound to collide with others if all four attributes are malign: If the nationalism has no state, the risk of civil war arising from its struggle for national independence is increased; this also raises the risk of inter-state war, since civil war can widen to engulf nearby states. If, after achieving statehood, the nationalism seeks to incorporate a diaspora by force, oppresses minorities found in its claimed national territory, and seeks hegemony over nationalities lying beyond that territory, violence between the nationalism and its neighbors is inevitable.

Causes and Conditions for War-Causing Nationalism

What factors determine whether these four variables will have benign or malignant values? What conditions are required for malignant values to have malignant effects? The deciding factors and conditions are grouped below into three broad families: structural (those arising from the geographic and demographic arrangement of a nation's people); political-environmental (those arising from the past or present conduct of a people's neighbors); and perceptual (those arising from the nationalist movement's self-image and its

---

17. On the greater peacefulness of a defense-dominant world, see Robert Jervis, "Cooperation Under the Security Dilemma," *World Politics*, Vol. 30, No. 2 (January 1978), pp. 167–214.
18. Thus the evident power of nationalism helped dampen Soviet-American competition during the Cold War, by persuading some in the West that nationalism imposed a natural limit on Soviet expansion. These observers argued that the Western powers need not actively check Soviet expansionism at every point because local nationalism could defeat it alone, nor move actively to roll back Soviet gains, because these gains would eventually be rolled back by indigenous nationalism, and in the meantime nationalist resistance would bleed Soviet power. For example, George Kennan took a calm approach to containment partly because he believed that resistant local nationalism would check Soviet expansion in the short run, and would rend the Soviet empire in the long run. See John Lewis Gaddis, *Strategies of Containment: A Critical Appraisal of Postwar American National Security Policy* (New York: Oxford University Press, 1982), pp. 42–48. Other arguments for Cold War restraint that rested in part on the power of nationalism included Arthur M. Schlesinger, *The Bitter Heritage: Vietnam and American Democracy 1941–1968*, rev. ed. (Greenwich: Fawcett, 1968), pp. 78–80; Jerome Slater, "Dominos in Central America: Will They Fall? Does It Matter?" *International Security*, Vol. 12, No. 2 (Fall 1987), pp. 105–134, at 113; and Stephen M. Walt, "The Case for Finite Containment," *International Security*, Vol. 14, No. 1 (Summer 1989), pp. 3–49, at 26–27. Had nationalism been weaker, these arguments would have lost force, leaving a stronger case for more aggressive American policies.

images of others, including its images of both sides' past and present conduct and character).

STRUCTURAL FACTORS: THE GEOGRAPHIC, DEMOGRAPHIC, AND MILITARY SETTING

The size of the risks posed by nationalism is influenced by the balance of power and of will between stateless nationalisms and the central states that hold them captive; by the degree and pattern of regional ethnic intermingling; by the defensibility and legitimacy of the borders of new national states; and by the correspondence of these borders with ethnic boundaries.

THE DOMESTIC BALANCE OF POWER AND OF WILL. Unattained nationalisms are more troublesome under two conditions: (1) the movement has the strength to reach plausibly for statehood; and (2) the central state has the will to resist this attempt.

Stateless nationalisms whose statehood is unattainable will lie dormant, their emergence deterred by the power of the central state.[19] Nationalism becomes manifest and can produce war when the power-balance between the central state and the captive nationalism shifts to allow the possibility of successful secession. Thus two safe conditions exist: where national statehood is already attained; and where it is not attained, but clearly cannot be. The danger zone lies between, in cases where statehood has not been attained yet is attainable or appears to be.[20] In this zone we find wars of nationalist secession.[21] Such conflicts can, in turn, grow into international wars: examples include the 1912–14 Balkan secessionist struggles that triggered World War I, and the 1991–92 Serbo-Croatian conflict.

---

19. If nationalism is unattainable it may not even appear: the captive nation will submerge the nationalist thought. This is similar to the realist argument that imperialism is a function of capability: states imperialize simply when and where they can. Likewise, and conversely, nationalism is in part simply a function of capability: it emerges where it can.

20. We can scale up this logic from single states to regions by asking: do nations have states in proportion to their power? That is, does the state-to-nation ratio correspond with the state-to-nation power ratio? Or do nations have fewer states than their power justifies? If the former is the case, peace is more likely. But if nations have fewer states than their power would allow, trouble results in the form of wars of secession.

21. Overall, then, three variables matter: (1) the supply of states; (2) the demand for states; (3) the capacity of submerged nations to acquire states. Peace is stronger if supply and demand are in equilibrium; or if supply and capacity are in equilibrium. In one case, nationalism is satisfied; in the other, it is dissatisfied but impotent. Dangers arise if both supply and demand, and supply and capacity, are not in equilibrium. We then have submerged nationalisms that both desire and can assert the demand for statehood.

The Third World nationalisms of the twentieth century erupted partly because the spread of small arms and literacy shifted the balance of power in favor of these nationalisms, and against their imperial captors. Nationalism emerged because it could. Likewise, nationalism exploded in the former Soviet Union in the late 1980s partly because Soviet central power had waned.

War is inevitable if central states have the will to resist emerging nationalist/ secessionist movements, but these movements can win freedom without violence if that will is missing. Many sub-Saharan African states gained freedom in the 1960s without violence because the European colonial powers lost their imperial will. Likewise, the emergence of non-Russian nationalisms in the former Soviet Union was accompanied by (and encouraged by) the loss of imperial will in Moscow; this loss of will at the center allowed the non-Russians to escape the Soviet empire without waging wars of secession. French decolonization was far more violent, spawning large wars in Vietnam and Algeria, because the French metropole retained its will even after nationalism gained momentum in the French empire.

The will of the central state is largely governed by its domestic politics, but is also determined partly by demographic facts. Specifically, central governments can allow secession more easily if secession would leave a homogeneous rump central state, since permitting secession then sets a less damaging precedent. Thus the Czechs could accept Slovak independence without fear of setting a precedent that would trigger another secession, since there is no potential secessionist group in the rump Czech Republic. Likewise, the United States could grant independence to the Philippines fairly easily in 1946 because the United States had few other colonies, and none of these were large or valuable, hence Philippine independence set no dangerous precedents. Conversely, the Austro-Hungarian empire strongly resisted secessions before 1914 because the empire contained many potential secessionists who might be encouraged if any secession were allowed.

THE DEMOGRAPHIC ARRANGEMENT OF NATIONAL POPULATIONS: ARE THEY INTERMINGLED OR HOMOGENEOUS? Are nationality populations densely intermingled? If they are, does this create large or small national diasporas? Intermingling raises the risk of communal conflict during the struggle for national freedom, as groups that would be trapped as minorities in a new national state oppose its reach for freedom. Dispersion and intermingling will also trap some co-ethnics outside the boundaries of their nation-states; this raises the danger that new nation-states will pursue diaspora-recovering expansionism after they gain statehood, and the possibility that their abuse of minorities will trigger attack from outside.[22]

These dangers are reduced if national populations are compact and homogenous—diasporas and minorities then occur only if political boundaries fail to follow ethnic boundaries. They are intensified if the nationality is dispersed abroad, and intermingled with others at home. The Czechs, for example, can pursue nationalism with little risk to the peace of their neighborhood, because they have no diaspora abroad, and few minorities at home. They need not limit their goals or learn to accommodate minorities. The 1947 partition of India was a far bloodier process than the 1992 Czech-Slovak divorce partly because Hindus and Moslems were far more intermingled than Czechs and Slovaks. The partition of Yugoslavia has been especially violent partly because nationalities in former Yugoslavia are more densely intermingled than any others in Eastern or Western Europe outside the former Soviet Union.[23]

Overall, nationalism poses greater dangers in Eastern than Western Europe because the peoples of Eastern Europe are more densely intermingled. A survey of Eastern Europe reveals roughly a dozen minority group pockets that may seek independence or be claimed by other countries.[24] The ethno-

---

22. The scope and structure of intermingling governs the acuteness of what might be called the "inter-ethnic security dilemma": this dilemma is posed where one group cannot achieve physical security without diminishing the physical security of other groups. It is analogous to the inter-state security dilemma of international relations, except that the clashing units are ethnic or culture groups, not states.

23. Moreover, Yugoslavia's one easy secession—that of Slovenia—was easy because the Slovene population was not intermingled with others. An excellent ethnographic map of the former Yugoslavia that details its intermingling is Central Intelligence Agency, "Peoples of Yugoslavia: Distribution by Opstina, 1981 Census," Map No. 505956 9-83 (543994). A useful though less detailed ethnographic map covering all of Eastern Europe including former Yugoslavia is Central Intelligence Agency, "Ethnic Majorities and Minorities," in Central Intelligence Agency, *Atlas of Eastern Europe* (Washington, D.C.: U.S. Government Printing Office [U.S. GPO], August 1990), p. 6. A good ethnographic map of the former USSR is National Geographic Society, "Peoples of the Soviet Union," supplement to *National Geographic*, Vol. 149, No. 2 (February 1976), p. 144A; back issues of *National Geographic* containing this map are available from the National Geographic Society, Washington, D.C.

24. These include Hungarians in Romania, Slovakia, and Serbia; Poles in Lithuania, Belarus, Ukraine, and the Czech Republic; Germans in Poland and the Czech Republic; Turks in Bulgaria; Greeks in Albania; Albanians in Serbia and Macedonia; Croats in Bosnia-Herzegovina; and Serbs in Croatia and Bosnia-Herzegovina. Summaries include F. Stephen Larrabee, "Long Memories and Short Fuses: Change and Instability in the Balkans," *International Security*, Vol. 15, No. 3 (Winter 1990/91), pp. 58–91; Istvan Deak, "Uncovering Eastern Europe's Dark History," *Orbis*, Vol. 34, No. 1 (Winter 1989), pp. 51–65; Barry James, "Central Europe Tinderboxes: Old Border Disputes," *International Herald Tribune*, January 1, 1990, p. 5; and the CIA map cited above, "Ethnic Majorities and Minorities, 1990."

graphic structure of the former Soviet Union is even more ominous; an ethnographic map of the former USSR reveals massively intermingled nationalities, scattered in scores of isolated pockets, a mosaic far more tangled and complex than any found elsewhere in Europe except the former Yugoslavia.[25]

Two aspects of intermingling determine the size of the dangers it poses: the scope of intermingling, and the pattern of intermingling. All intermingling causes trouble, but some patterns of intermingling cause more trouble than others.

Groups can be intermingled on a regional scale (regions are heterogeneous, small communities are homogeneous) or local scale (even small communities are heterogeneous, as in Sarajevo.) Regional intermingling is more easily managed, because inter-group relations can be negotiated by elites. In contrast, elites can lose control of events when intermingling extends to the local level: conflict can flare against the wishes of elites when unofficial killers seize the agenda by sparking a spiral of private violence. Local intermingling can also produce conflict-dampening personal friendships and inter-ethnic marriages, but the Bosnian conflict shows the limits of this tempering effect. Overall, local intermingling is more dangerous.

The most dangerous pattern of regional intermingling is one that leaves elements of one or both groups insecurely at the mercy of the other, but also allows for the possibility of forcible rescue—either by self-rescue (secession) or external rescue (intervention by an already-free homeland).

If rescue is impossible, then the goal of secession or reunion with a homeland will be abandoned. Israel cannot rescue Soviet Jewry, except by immigration, and Ukraine cannot rescue the Ukrainian diaspora in Russia; hence neither considers forceful rescue. This lowers the risk of war.

If rescue is easy, it may not be attempted, since the threat of rescue is enough to deter abuse of the diaspora. Russia could fairly easily rescue the Russian minority in the Baltics and perhaps elsewhere on the Russian periphery, because much of the Russian diaspora lies clustered near the Russian

---

25. See the maps cited in note 23 above. Overall, 16 percent of the titular peoples of the 15 successor states of the former Soviet Union, totalling 39 million people, live outside their home states ("titular peoples": the peoples after whom republics are named, e.g., Armenians, Kazakhs, Russians, etc.). Calculated from Scherer, *USSR Facts and Figures Annual*, pp. 49–51. And, as noted above, another 10 percent of the former Soviet population (26 million people) are members of the 89 smaller nationalities without titular home republics ("titular home republic": a republic named after the nationality).

border, and Russia holds military superiority over its neighbors. These power realities may deter Russia's neighbors from abusing their Russian minorities, leaving Russia more room to take a relaxed attitude.[26]

It is in-between situations—those where rescue is possible, but only under optimal conditions—that are most dangerous. This situation will tempt potential rescuers to jump through any windows of opportunity that arise. Forceful rescue is then driven by both fear and opportunity—fear that later the abuse of diasporas cannot be deterred by threatening to rescue them (since the difficulty of rescue will rob that threat of credibility), and by the opportunity to rescue the diaspora now by force.[27] Thus Serbia would have probably been unable to rescue the Serb diaspora in normal times: Serbia is too weak, and the Serbian diasporas in Croatia and Bosnia are too distant from Serbia. But rescue was feasible if Serbia made the attempt at a moment of peak Serbian military advantage. Such a moment emerged in 1990, after Serbia consolidated the weaponry of the Yugoslav army under its control, but before the Croatian and Bosnian states could organize strong militaries.[28] In contrast, such a moment may never emerge for Russia, because it can always rescue large parts of its diaspora should the need ever arise, leaving less need to seize an early opportunity.

These in-between situations are most troublesome when the diaspora is separated from the homeland by lands inhabited by others: wars of rescue then cause larger injury. In such cases rescue requires cutting a secure corridor through these lands; this, in turn, requires the forcible expulsion of the resident population, with its attendant horrors and cruelties. In 1991 the Serbian diaspora in Croatia and Bosnia was cut off from the Serb homeland by walls of Moslem-inhabited territory,[29] and the vast Serbian cruelties against the Bosnian Moslems during 1992–93 grew mainly from Serbia's effort to punch corridors through these walls in order to attach these diasporas to Serbia proper. In contrast, more of Russia's diaspora is contiguous to Russia, hence a Russian war of rescue would do relatively less harm to others innocently in the way (though it would still do plenty of harm.)

---

26. Making this argument is Posen, "The Security Dilemma and Ethnic Conflict," pp. 32–35.
27. See Posen, "The Security Dilemma and Ethnic Conflict," pp. 32–38.
28. The intensification of fighting between Armenia and Azerbaijan in 1991–92 had similar origins: Armenia moved to free Nagorno-Karabakh at a moment that Armenia's power relative to Azerbaijan's was at its peak.
29. See Central Intelligence Agency, "Peoples of Yugoslavia."

BORDERS: DEFENSIBILITY, LEGITIMACY, AND BORDER/ETHNIC CORRESPON-
DENCE. The risks to peace posed by a nationalism's emergence are governed
partly by the defensibility and international legitimacy of the nation's borders, and by the degree of correspondence between these political borders
and ethnic boundaries.

The satisfaction of national demands for statehood extends international
anarchy by creating more states: hence nationalism's effects are governed
partly by the character of the extended anarchy that it creates. Some anarchies
are relatively peaceful, others more violent. The acuteness of the security
dilemma is a key factor governing the answer. Anarchy is a precondition for
international war, hence extending anarchy may expand the risk of war, but
this is not always the case: the fragmentation of states can deepen peace if
it leaves the world with states that are more difficult to conquer, hence are
more secure, than the older states from which they were carved. The character of boundaries helps decide the issue: if the new borders are indefen-
sible, the net impact of the creation of new national states will be warlike; if
borders are highly defensible, the net impact may be peaceful.[30]

Defensible boundaries reduce the risk of war because they leave new states
less anxious to expand for security reasons, while also deterring others from
attacking them. The nations of Western Europe can be more peaceful than
those of the East because they are endowed with more defensible borders:
the French, Spanish, British, Italian, and Scandinavian nations have natural
defenses formed by the Alps and the Pyrenees, and by the waters of the
English Channel, the Baltic, and the North Sea. Icelandic nationalism is
especially unproblematic because geography makes Iceland unusually secure,
and almost incapable of attack. In contrast, the nationalities living on the
exposed plains of Eastern Europe and western Asia contend with a harsher
geography: with few natural barriers to invasion, they are more vulnerable
to attack, hence are more tempted to attack others in preemptive defense.[31]
They are therefore more likely to disturb the status quo, or to be victims of
other disturbers.

The international legitimacy of a new nation's borders helps determine the
level of danger raised when it gains independence: if borders lack interna-

---

30. The new states may also be more defensible than their parent states because they can call
upon nationalism as a mobilizing defensive force, as their multi-ethnic parent states could not.
31. Likewise, Germany has produced the most troublesome Western nationalism partly because
German borders are relatively exposed.

tional legitimacy or are unsettled altogether, demands for border changes will arise, providing new occasions for conflict. The successor states of the former Soviet Union find themselves with borders drawn by Stalin or other Bolshevik rulers; these have correspondingly small legitimacy. Israel's post-1948 boundaries at first lacked international legitimacy because they had no historical basis, having arisen simply from truce lines expressing the military outcome of the 1948 war. In contrast, the borders of the recently-freed states of Eastern Europe have greater legitimacy because they have firmer grounding in history, and some were the product of earlier international negotiation and agreement.

Borders may bisect nationalities, or may follow national demographic divides. Nation-bisecting borders are more troublesome, because they have the same effect as demographic intermingling: they entrap parts of nationalities within the boundaries of states dominated by other ethnic groups, giving rise to expansionism by the truncated nation. Thus Hungary's borders bisect (and truncate) the Hungarian nation, giving rise to a (now dormant but still surviving) Hungarian revanchism against Slovakia, Serbia, and Rumania.[32] The Russian/Ukrainian border bisects both nationalities, creating the potential for movements to adjust borders in both countries.

The borders of new states can arise in two main ways: from violent military struggle (e.g., Israel) or as a result of cession of sovereignty to existing administrative units whose boundaries were previously defined by the parent multiethnic state (e.g., former Soviet Union). War-born borders often have the advantage of following ethnic lines, because the cruelties of war often cause ethnic cleansing, and offensives lose strength at ethnic boundaries; inherited administrative borders (e.g., the boundaries of Azerbaijan, which entrap the Armenians of Nagorno-Karabakh) more often plant the charge of future conflict by dividing nations and creating diasporas. The peaceful dissolution of the former Soviet Union was thus a mixed blessing: its successor states emerged without violence, but with borders that captured unhappy diasporas behind them.

---

32. On latent Hungarian revanchism see, for example, Judith Ingram, "Boys Impatient for 'Great Hungary' to Take Wing," *New York Times,* January 15, 1993, p. A4. On its official manifestations see Stephen Engelberg with Judith Ingram, "Now Hungary Adds Its Voice to the Ethnic Tumult," *New York Times,* January 25, 1993, p. A3.

POLITICAL/ENVIRONMENTAL FACTORS: HOW HAVE NEIGHBORS BEHAVED?
HOW DO THEY NOW BEHAVE?
The conduct of nationalities and nation-states mirrors their neighbors' past and present conduct.

PAST CONDUCT: WERE GREAT CRIMES COMMITTED? The degree of harmony or conflict between intermingled nationalities depends partly on the size of the crimes committed by each against the other in the past; the greater these past crimes, the greater the current conflict. Memories of its neighbors' cruelties will magnify an emerging nation's impulse to ingather its diaspora, converting the nation from a diaspora-accepting to a diaspora-annexing attitude. Thus the vast Croatian mass-murders of Serbs during the 1940s were the taproot that fed violent pan-Serbianism after 1990: Serbs vowed "never again," and argued that they must incorporate the Serbian diaspora in Croatia to save it from new pogroms.[33] Past suffering can also spur nations to oppress old tormentors who now live among them as minorities, sparking conflict with these minorities' home countries. Thus the past horrors inflicted on the Baltic peoples by Stalinism fuels their discrimination against their Russian minorities today;[34] this discrimination, in turn, feeds anti-Baltic feeling in Russia. In contrast, non-victim nations are less aggressive toward both neighbors and minorities. Czech nationalism is benign partly because the Czechs have escaped real victimhood; Quebec nationalism is mild for the same reason.

Mass murder, land theft, and population expulsions are the crimes that matter most. Past exterminations foster diaspora-recovering ideologies that are justified by self-protection logic. Past land theft fosters territorial definitions of nationhood (e.g., the Israeli Likud's concept of "the Land of Israel," a place including once-Jewish lands that Likud argues were wrongfully taken by others) and claims to land that excludes the rights of peoples now on that land (the Likud rejects equal rights for the Palestinian inhabitants of these

---

33. See Bette Denich, "Unbury the Victims: Nationalist Revivals of Genocide in Yugoslavia," Paper presented at the American Anthropological Association Annual Meeting, Chicago, Illinois, November 1991.
34. On the Baltic states' policies see Steven Erlanger, "Baltic Identity: Russians Wonder If They Belong: New Citizenship Rules May in Effect Expel the Ex-'Occupiers'," *New York Times*, November 22, 1992, p. 1. This Baltic anti-Russian discrimination reflects the great cruelties inflicted on the Baltic peoples by Stalin's government: during the years 1940–49 some 36 percent of the indigenous population of Latvia, 33 percent of the indigenous population of Estonia, and 32 percent of the indigenous population of Lithuania were killed, deported, or driven into exile. Dag Sebastian Ahlander, "Help Baltics Deal with Russian Minority," *New York Times* (letter to the editor), December 6, 1992, p. E18.

once-Jewish lands; Serbs likewise reject equal rights for Albanian Kosovars who Serbs claim wrongfully took Serb land.) Past expulsions and dispersions feed diaspora-intolerance: if others created the diaspora, it is argued, then others should pay the price for restoring the diaspora to the nation by making territorial concessions.

The scope of the dangers posed by past crimes is a function, in part, of whether these crimes are remembered, and whether victims can attach responsibility for crimes to groups that are still present. Crimes that have faded in the victims' memories have a less corrosive effect on intergroup relations; thus mayhem that occurred before written records poses fewer problems than more recent crimes that are better-recorded.[35]

Crimes committed by groups still on the scene pose more problems than crimes committed by vanished groups. This, in turn, is a matter of interpretation: who committed the crime in question? Can inherited blame be attached to any present group? Thus the Ukrainians can assess responsibility for Stalin's vast murders of Ukrainians in several ways.[36] Were they committed by a crazed Georgian? This interpretation is benign: it points the finger at a single man who is long gone from the scene. Were they committed by that now-vanished tribe, the Bolsheviks? This interpretation is also benign: those responsible have miraculously disappeared, leaving no target for violence. Or, more ominously, were these the crimes of the Russian empire and the Russian people? This interpretation would guarantee bitter Russian-Ukrainian conflict, because the crimes in question were so enormous, and many of the "criminals" live in Ukraine,[37] making ready targets for hatred, and setting the stage for a Russian-Ukrainian conflict-spiral. Such a spiral is more likely because Russians would not accept the blame assigned them: they count themselves among the victims, not the perpetrators, of Bolshe-

---

35. For example, native Americans can coexist, albeit uneasily, with European immigrants partly because the enormous horrors that the Europeans inflicted on the natives have faded into the mists of history. On these horrors see David E. Stannard, *American Holocaust: Columbus and the Conquest of the New World* (New York: Oxford University Press, 1992). Stannard estimates that the native population of the Americas fell by roughly 95 percent—in absolute numbers by about 71–95 million people—after the European arrival in 1492 (p. 268). If so, this was the greatest human-caused human death in world history.

36. On these murders see Robert Conquest, *The Harvest of Sorrow: Soviet Collectivization and the Terror-Famine* (New York: Oxford University Press, 1986). Stalin's other crimes are covered in Robert Conquest, *The Great Terror: A Reassessment* (New York: Oxford University Press, 1990).

37. Ukraine contains 10.5 million Russians, 21 percent of its total population. Calculated from Scherer, *USSR Facts and Figures Annual*, p. 49.

vism's crimes, and they would view others' demands that they accept blame as a malicious outrage.

The danger posed by past crimes also depends on the criminal group's later behavior: has it apologized or otherwise shown contrition? Or has it shown contempt for its victims' suffering? Nazi Germany's crimes were among the greatest in human history, but Germany has re-established civil relations with its former victims by acknowledging its crimes and showing contrition, e.g., by postwar German leaders' public apologies and symbolic acts of repentance. Conversely, Turkey has denied the great crimes it committed against the Armenian people during World War I;[38] this display of contempt has sustained an Armenian hatred that is still expressed in occasional acts of violent anti-Turkish retribution.

A final significant factor lies in the degree of coincidence of power and victimhood. Are the groups with the greatest historic grievances also the groups with the greatest power today? Or is past victimhood confined to today's weaker groups? Things are more dangerous when power and aggrievement coincide, since this combination brings together both the motive and the capacity to make trouble; when power and aggrievement are separated, grievances have less effects. On this count the past crimes of the Russian and Bolshevik states leave a less dangerous legacy than the crimes committed in the former Yugoslavia during World War II, because the strongest group in the former Soviet Union (the Russians) is the least aggrieved; in contrast, in former Yugoslavia the strongest group (the Serbs) is the most aggrieved.

CURRENT CONDUCT: ARE MINORITY RIGHTS RESPECTED? As noted earlier, nations are less diaspora-accepting if others abuse the rights of that diaspora; such abuse magnifies the impulse to incorporate the territory of the diaspora by force. Thus Serbia's 1991 attack on Croatia was spurred partly by Croatian threats against the Serbian minority.[39] Likewise, Russia's attitude toward the

---

38. On Turkish denial of these murders see Roger W. Smith, "The Armenian Genocide: Memory, Politics, and the Future," in Richard G. Hovannisian, ed. *The Armenian Genocide: History, Politics, Ethics* (New York: St. Martin's, 1992), pp. 1–20; Vahakn N. Dadrian, "Ottoman Archives and Denial of the Armenian Genocide," in Hovannisian, *Armenian Genocide*, pp. 280–310; and Roger W. Smith, "Genocide and Denial: The Armenian Case and Its Implications," *Armenian Review*, Vol. 42 (Spring 1989), pp. 1–38. On the general disappearance of the Armenian people from Turkish historical writings, see Clive Foss, "The Turkish View of Armenian History: A Vanishing Nation," in Hovannisian, *Armenian Genocide*, pp. 250–279.

39. Glenny, "The Massacre of Yugoslavia," pp. 30–31; and Glenny, *The Fall of Yugoslavia*, pp. 12–14, 123.

Russian diaspora will be governed partly by the treatment of the Russian diaspora in their new homelands. Oppressive policies will provoke wider Russian aims.[40]

PERCEPTUAL FACTORS: NATIONALIST SELF-IMAGES AND IMAGES OF OTHERS

The effects of nationalism depend heavily on the beliefs of nationalist movements, especially their self-images and their images of their neighbors. Nations can co-exist most easily when these beliefs converge—when they share a common image of their mutual history, and of one another's current conduct and character. This can be achieved either by common convergence of images on something close to the "truth," or by convergence on the same distortion of the truth. Relations are worst if images diverge in self-justifying directions. This occurs if nations embrace self-justifying historical myths, or adopt distorted pictures of their own and others' current conduct and character that exaggerate the legitimacy of their own cause. Such myths and distortions can expand a nation's sense of its right and its need to oppress its minorities or conquer its diaspora. If carried to extreme such myths can also transform nationalism from symmetrical to asymmetrical—from a purely self-liberating enterprise into a hegemonistic enterprise.[41]

---

40. Even moderate Russian officials have voiced deep concern over the rights of Russian minorities in nearby states. See, for example, Sergei Stankevich, "Russia in Search of Itself," *The National Interest*, No. 28 (Summer 1992), pp. 47–51, at 49–51; and "Four Comments" in ibid. pp. 51–55, at 51–53. They have so far proposed solutions within the framework of international law and institutions: for example, Russian Foreign Minister Andrei Kozyrev suggested in 1992 that the UN establish a mechanism to protect the rights of Russians in non-Slavic former Soviet republics. Thomas Friedman, "Russian Appeals to U.N. to Safeguard Minorities," *New York Times*, September 23, 1992, p. A17. If the rights of these minorities remain otherwise unprotected, however, it seems likely that Russia will act on its own to protect them.

41. In the past I referred to such myth-poisoned nationalism as "hypernationalism." See Stephen Van Evera, "Primed for Peace," *International Security*, Vol. 15, No. 3 (Winter 1990/1991), pp. 7–57, at 47–48n ("Hypernationalism is artificially generated or magnified by chauvinist myths. Conflicts arising from hypernationalism thus derive from the beliefs of nations," not from their circumstances.) However, my usage is narrower than others: see, for example, John Mearsheimer, who defines hypernationalism as the belief that other nationalities are "both inferior and threatening," and as an "attitude of contempt and loathing" toward other nations; Mearsheimer suggests these beliefs can arise from false propaganda or from real experience. John Mearsheimer, "Back to the Future: Instability in Europe After the Cold War," *International Security*, Vol. 15, No. 1 (Summer 1990), pp. 5–56, at 21. Others use the term "hypernationalism" still more broadly to refer to any type of nationalism that spawns aggressive conduct and war. I avoid the term in this paper because it has acquired these several meanings. I regret adding to the confusion, and suggest we settle on a single usage—probably Mearsheimer's, since it has seniority.

Chauvinist mythmaking is a hallmark of nationalism, practiced by nearly all nationalist movements to some degree.[42] These myths are purveyed through the schools, especially in history teaching;[43] through literature; or by political elites. They come in three principal varieties: self-glorifying, self-whitewashing, and other-maligning. Self-glorifying myths incorporate claims of special virtue and competence, and false claims of past beneficence toward others.[44] Self-whitewashing myths incorporate false denial of past wrong-doing against others.[45] Both types of myths can lead a nation to claim a right

---

42. Indeed, the intellectual history of Western nationalisms is largely a record of false claims of special self-virtue and of overwrought blaming of others. See examples in Shafer, *Faces of Nationalism*, pp. 313–342. However, myth is not an essential ingredient of nationalism: nationalism can also rest on a group solidarity based on truth, and the effects of nationalism are largely governed by the degree of truthfulness of the beliefs that a given nationalism adopts; as truthfulness diminishes, the risks posed by the nationalism increase.

43. As Ernst Renan has said, "Getting its history wrong is part of being a nation." Quoted in Hobsbawm, *Nations and Nationalism since 1780*, p. 12.

44. World War I–era European nationalists provide abundant examples of such self-glorification. General Friedrich Bernhardi, the German army's main propagandist, proclaimed in 1912 that the Germans are "the greatest civilized people known to history," and have "always been the standard-bearers of free thought" and "free from prejudice." Friedrich von Bernhardi, *Germany and the Next War*, trans. Allen H. Powles (New York: Longmans, Green, 1914, first published in Germany in 1912), pp. 14, 72. In 1915 German economist Werner Sombart declared that the Germans were "the chosen people of this century," and that this chosenness explained others' hostility: "Now we understand why other people hate us. They do not understand us but they fear our tremendous spiritual superiority." Kohn, *Mind of Germany*, p. 300–301. Richard Dehmel, a German writer, proclaimed in 1914: "We Germans *are* more humane than the other nations; we *do have* better blood and breeding, more soul, more heart, and more imagination." Klaus Schröter, "Chauvinism and its Tradition: German Writers and the Outbreak of the First World War," *Germanic Review*, Vol. 43, No. 2 (March 1968), pp. 120–135, at 126, emphasis in original. In Britain Thomas Macaulay wrote that the British were "the greatest and most highly civilized people that ever the world saw" and were "the acknowledged leaders of the human race in the causes of political improvement." Paul M. Kennedy, "The Decline of Nationalistic History in the West, 1900–1970," *Journal of Contemporary History*, Vol. 8, No. 1 (January, 1973), pp. 77–100, at 81. In the United States Senator Albert Beveridge proclaimed in 1899 that "God . . . has made us the master organizers of the world. . . . He has made us adept in government that we may administer government among savage and senile peoples. . . . He has marked the American people as His chosen nation . . ." Albert K. Weinberg, *Manifest Destiny: A Study of Nationalist Expansionism in American History* (Chicago: Quadrangle, 1963), p. 308. The Soviet government continued this tradition after 1918: the standard Soviet school history text of 1948 claimed that Russian scientists invented the telegraph, steam engine, electric lamp, and the airplane. E.H. Dance, *History the Betrayer: A Study in Bias* (Westport: Greenwood, 1960), pp. 67–68.

45. Innocence can be asserted by denying a barbarous action, or by reinterpreting the action to put a benign "spin" on it. Post-1919 German textbooks illustrate whitewash-by-denial: Weimar German textbooks denied German responsibility for World War I, falsely claiming that "there was no wish for war in Berlin" in 1914, and that "today every informed person . . . knows that Germany is absolutely innocent with regard to the outbreak of the war, and that Russia, France, and England wanted the war and unleashed it." Dance, *History the Betrayer*, p. 62. Nazi-era texts likewise claimed that "England willed the war" in 1914 after having "set Japan on Russia" in 1904. Dance, *History the Betrayer*, p. 57. Whitewash-by-spin is also common. When Nazi forces

to rule others ("we are especially virtuous, so our expansion benefits those we conquer"). They also lead a nation to view others' complaints against them as expressions of ungrateful malice: ("we have never harmed them; they slander us by claiming otherwise"). This can produce conflict-spirals,[46] as the nation responds to others' legitimate complaints with hostility, in expectation that the claimant knows its claims are illegitimate and will back down if challenged. The targets of this hostility, in turn, will take it as further evidence of the nation's inherent cruelty and injustice. Self-glorifying myth, if it contains claims of cultural superiority, can also feed false faith in one's capacity to defeat and subdue others, causing expansionist wars of optimistic miscalculation.

Other-maligning myth can incorporate claims of others' cultural inferiority, false blame of others for past crimes and tragedies, and false claims that others now harbor malign intentions against the nation.[47] Such myths sup-

---

overran Norway and Denmark in 1940 the Nazi party newspaper announced the invasion, but its headline proclaimed "GERMANY SAVES SCANDINAVIA!" William L. Shirer, *The Rise and Fall of the Third Reich: A History of Nazi Germany* (New York: Simon and Schuster, 1960), p. 698n. Similarly, after Soviet forces invaded Afghanistan in 1979 Leonid Brezhnev admitted the action but told the Soviet public: "There has been no Soviet 'intervention' or 'aggression' at all." Rather, Soviet forces were sent to Afghanistan "at its government's request," to defend Afghan "national independence, freedom and honor." L.I. Brezhnev, "Interview for Pravda, January 13, 1980," from *SShA: Ekonomika, Politika, Ideologiya*, No. 2 (February 1980), trans. Joint Publication Research Service, in *U.S.S.R. Report*, No. 75485 (April 14, 1980), p. 3. Japanese imperialists of the 1930s and 1940s claimed Japan was saving China from the "death grip" of the Comintern, and liberating Asia from the Western imperialism. Robert J.C. Butow, *Tojo and the Coming of the War* (Stanford: Stanford University Press, 1969), p. 134; Ienaga, *Pacific War*, pp. 153–154. Earlier a French textbook proclaimed the philanthropy of the French North African empire—"France is kind and generous to the peoples she has conquered." Dance, *History the Betrayer*, p. 44.

46. Thus German whitewashing of German responsibility for World War I helped fuel German hostility toward Europe during the interwar years, and laid the basis for popular German support for Nazi foreign policy. On the post-1918 German "innocence" campaign see Holger H. Herwig, "Clio Deceived: Patriotic Self-Censorship in Germany After the Great War," *International Security*, Vol. 12, No. 2 (Fall 1987), pp. 5–44. A good account of Germany's actual pre-1914 conduct is Imanuel Geiss, *German Foreign Policy, 1871–1914* (Boston: Routledge & Kegan Paul, 1976).

47. For example, Wilhelmine and Nazi German nationalists often asserted others' inherent inferiority. Kaiser Wilhelm II declared in 1913: "the Slavs were not born to rule but to serve, this they must be taught." Fritz Fischer, *War of Illusions: German Policies from 1911 to 1914*, trans. Marian Jackson (New York: W.W. Norton, 1975), p. 222. Historian Heinrich von Treitschke thought the English suffered from "cowardice and sensuality," and the French from "besotted-ness," while an earlier German textbook declared France was "a fermenting mass of rottenness." Snyder, *From Bismarck to Hitler*, p. 35; Antoine Guilland, *Modern Germany and Her Historians* (Westport: Greenwood Press, n.d., reprint of 1915 ed.), pp. 304, 154, quoting an 1876 text by A. Hummel. Writer Richard Dehmel described an England with "only practical talents but not 'culture'." Schröter, "Chauvinism and its Tradition," p. 125. Later, Hitler thought Russia was "ripe for dissolution" because it was ruled by the Jews, who were "a ferment of decomposition." Jeremy Noakes and Geoffrey Pridham, eds., *Naziism 1919–1945: A History in Documents and*

port arguments for the rightness and necessity of denying equal rights to minorities living in the national territory, and for subjugating peoples further afield. These minorities and distant peoples will appear to pose a danger if they are left unsuppressed; moreover, their suppression is morally justified by their (imagined) misconduct, past and planned.

Self-whitewashing myths are probably the most common of these three varieties.[48] The dangers they pose are proportional to the gravity of the crimes they whitewash. If small crimes are denied, their denial is disrespect that victims can choose to overlook. The denial may even spring from simple ignorance; if so, it conveys little insult. If great crimes are denied, however, their denial conveys contempt for the victims' very humanity. The denial cannot be ascribed to unintended ignorance; if truly great crimes are forgotten, the forgetting is willful, hence it conveys greater insult. And being willful, the denial implies a dismissal of the crime's wrongness, which in turn suggests an ominous willingness to repeat it. As a result, the denial of great crimes provokes greater hostility from the victims than the denial of minor crimes.[49] Thus Croatian historians and politicians who whitewashed the Croatian Ustashi's vast murders of Serbs during World War II were

---

Eyewitness Accounts, Vol. 2 (New York: Schocken, 1988), pp. 615–616. He likewise viewed the United States, in Gerhard Weinberg's paraphrase, as a "mongrel society, in which the scum naturally floated to the top," that "could not possibly construct a sound economy." Gerhard L. Weinberg, "Hitler's Image of the United States," *American Historical Review*, Vol. 69, No. 4 (July 1964), pp. 1006–1021, at 1010.

Wilhelmine German nationalists also falsely accused others of malign intentions. Pan-German nationalists wove what Hermann Kantorowicz later termed a "fairy tale of encirclement" that posited a British-French-Russian plot to destroy Germany. See Geiss, *German Foreign Policy*, pp. 121–127. Imperial Japanese nationalists likewise saw a mythical anti-Japanese "ABCD encirclement" by America, Britain, China, and the Dutch, with the USSR and Germany sometimes thrown in as co-conspirators. See Butow, *Tojo and the Coming of the War*, chapter 8, pp. 188–227. During the Korean War Chinese writers demonized the United States as a "paradise of gangsters, swindlers, rascals, special agents, fascist germs, speculators, debauchers and all the dregs of mankind." President Truman and General Douglas MacArthur became "mad dogs," "blood-stained bandits," "murderers," "rapists," and "savages." At the same time General MacArthur warned that China "has become aggressively imperialistic, with a lust for expansion." John G. Stoessinger, *Nations in Darkness: China, Russia, and America*, 5th ed. (New York: McGraw-Hill, 1990), pp. 50–51.

For an example of falsely blaming others for past tragedies see notes 45 and 46 on the German post-1918 innocence campaign: in making this claim of innocence Germans also blamed others for starting the war.

48. Conversely, other-denigration is less common than both self-whitewashing and self-glorification, but is often implicit in self-glorification (others suffer in comparison to the virtuous self-image: if one's own group is spotlessly virtuous, others look worse by comparison).

49. Moreover, the victims' charges will anger the criminal nation, since it believes itself innocent, hence it views the victims' charges as malicious slander.

playing with especially powerful dynamite:[50] the crimes they denied were enormous, hence their denial had serious ramifications, feeding Serb hostility that led to the Serbo-Croatian war of 1991–92. Likewise, the question of historical responsibility for Stalin's crimes in the former Soviet Union is especially explosive because the crimes in question are so vast.

Why are myths purveyed? They emanate largely from nationalist political elites, for whom they serve important political functions. Some of these functions also serve the nation as a whole, while others serve only the narrow interests of the elite. Self-glorifying myths encourage citizens to contribute to the national community—to pay taxes, join the army, and fight for the nation's defense. These purposes are hard to fault, although the myths purveyed to achieve them may nevertheless have pernicious side-effects. Myths also bolster the authority and political power of incumbent elites: self-glorifying and self-whitewashing myths allow elites to shine in the reflected luster of their predecessors' imagined achievements and the imagined glory of the national institutions they control; other-maligning myths bolster the authority of elites by supporting claims that the nation faces external threats, thus deflecting popular hostility away from national elites and toward outsiders. Myths that serve only these purposes injure intercommunal relations without providing countervailing benefits to the general community.

Although mythmaking is ubiquitous among nationalisms, the scope and character of mythmaking varies widely across nations. Myths flourish most when elites need them most, when opposition to myths is weakest, and when publics are most myth-receptive. Four principal factors govern the level of infection by nationalist myth:

THE LEGITIMACY OF THE REGIME (or, if the national movement remains stateless, the legitimacy of the movement's leaders). As just noted, nationalist myths can help politically frail elites to bolster their grip on power. The temptation for elites to engage in mythmaking is therefore inversely propor-

---

50. After Germany and Italy conquered Yugoslavia in 1941 they established a puppet state, the Independent State of Croatia, under the leadership of the Croatian Ustashi, a nationalist Croat extremist-terrorist organization headed by Ante Pavelic. Without prompting from the Nazis the Ustashi then launched a mass murder campaign against other ethnic groups, killing by one estimate 500,000–700,000 Serbs, 50,000 Jews, and 20,000 Gypsies. Alex N. Dragnich, *Serbs and Croats: The Struggle for Yugoslavia* (New York: Harcourt Brace, 1992), pp. 96, 101–103. Dragnich reports that even the Germans were reportedly horrified by the nature and extent of the killings, and German officials protested to Pavelic (p. 103). On these murders see also Aleksa Djilas, *The Contested Country* (Cambridge: Harvard University Press, 1991), pp. 120–127; he endorses a smaller estimate by Bogoljub Kočović of 234,000 Serbs murdered (p. 126). Noting Croatian denials of the Ustashi's mass murders is Denich, "Unbury the Victims," pp. 5–6.

tional to their political legitimacy: the less legitimate their rule, the greater their incentive to make myths.

A regime's legitimacy is in turn a function of its representativeness, its competence and efficiency, and the scope of the tasks that face it. Unrepresentative regimes will face challenge from under-represented groups, and will sow myths to build the support needed to defeat this challenge.[51] This motive helped fuel the extreme nationalism that swept Europe in the late nineteenth century: oligarchic regimes used chauvinist myths, often spread through the schools, to deflect demands from below for a wider sharing of political and economic power.[52] Corrupt regimes or regimes that lack competence due to underinstitutionalization will likewise deploy chauvinist myths to divert challenges from publics and elites. This is a common motive for mythmaking in the Third World. Finally, regimes that face overwhelming tasks—e.g., economic or social collapse, perhaps caused by exogenous factors—will be tempted to use myths to divert popular impatience with their inability to improve conditions. Thus the Great Depression fueled nationalist mythmaking in some industrial states during the 1930s.[53]

These factors correlate closely with the ebb and flow of nationalist mythmaking through history. Nationalist mythmaking reached high tide in Europe when Europe's regimes had little legitimacy, during 1848–1914. It then fell dramatically as these regimes democratized and their societies became less stratified, which greatly lessened popular challenge to elites.[54]

THE SCOPE OF THE DEMANDS POSED BY THE STATE ON ITS CITIZENRY. The more the regime asks of its citizens, the harder it must work to persuade its

---

51. Such mythmaking has two targets: the public at large, and state instruments of coercion, which may need special motivation to carry out their tasks.

52. Regime illegitimacy provides the largest motive for elite mythmaking when the state cannot rule by pure force: mythmaking is then the elite's only means to preserve its rule. The proximate cause of mythmaking can therefore sometimes be found in the decline of the state monopoly of force, not the decline of elite legitimacy. This was the case in Europe in the nineteenth century: nationalist mythmaking rose with the rise of mass armies and popular literacy, which diminished the capacity of the state to govern by pure coercion. Elites were therefore forced to resort to persuasion, hence to mythmaking. (Mass literacy in this context proved a double-edged sword for newly-literate publics. Literacy enabled mass political mobilization by spreading social knowledge and ideas; this led to popular empowerment, but literacy also made publics easier to control from above, by enabling elites to purvey elite-justifying myths through the written word; this limited or reduced popular power.)

53. Making a similar argument, although casting it in somewhat different terms, is Snyder, "Nationalism and the Crisis of the Post-Soviet State," pp. 14–16.

54. On the decline of nationalistic history in Europe since the world wars see Kennedy, "Decline of Nationalistic History in the West."

citizens to fulfill these demands; this increases its temptation to deploy nationalist myths for purposes of social mobilization. Regimes at war often use myths to motivate sacrifice by their citizens and to justify their cruelties against others.[55] These myths can live on after the war to poison external relations in later years. Mass revolutionary movements often infuse their movements with mythical propaganda for the same reason; these myths survive after the revolution is won.[56] Regimes that are forced by external threats to sustain large peacetime military efforts are likewise driven to use myths to sustain popular support. This is especially true if they rely on mass armies for their defense.[57] Finally, totalitarian regimes place large demands on their citizens, and use correspondingly large doses of myth to induce their acquiescence.

DOMESTIC ECONOMIC CRISIS. In societies suffering economic collapse, myth-making can take scapegoating form—the collapse is falsely blamed on domestic or international malefactors. Here the mythmaking grows from increased receptivity of the audience: publics are more willing to believe that others are responsible when they are actually suffering pain; when that pain is new and surprising, they search for the hand of malevolent human agents. Germany in the 1930s is the standard example.[58]

THE STRENGTH AND COMPETENCE OF INDEPENDENT EVALUATIVE INSTITU-
TIONS. Societies that lack free-speech traditions, a strong free press, and free universities are more vulnerable to mythmaking because they lack "truth squads" to counter the nationalist mythmakers. Independent historians can provide an antidote to official historical mythmaking; an independent press is an antidote to official mythmaking about current events. Their absence is a permissive condition for nationalist mythmaking.[59] Wilhelmine Germany

---

55. See, for example, Omer Bartov, *Hitler's Army: Soldiers, Nazis, and the War in the Third Reich* (New York: Oxford University Press, 1991), pp. 106–178, describing the myths purveyed by the Nazi regime to motivate its troops on the Eastern Front.
56. Advancing this argument is Stephen M. Walt, "Revolution and War," *World Politics*, Vol. 44, No. 3 (April 1992), pp. 321–368, at 336–340.
57. For this argument see Posen, "Nationalism, the Mass Army, and Military Power."
58. This hypothesis is widely accepted but has not been systematically tested; more empirical research exploring the relationship between economic downturns and scapegoating would be valuable.
59. The existence of a free press and free universities does not guarantee that myths will be scrutinized; these institutions also require a truth-squad ethos—a sense that mythbusting is among their professional missions. This ethos is often missing among university faculties, who frequently pursue research agendas that have little relevance to the worries of the real world. A discussion that remains valuable is Robert S. Lynd, *Knowledge For What? The Place of Social Science in American Culture* (Princeton: Princeton University Press, 1939). A recent discussion is

illustrates: the German academic community failed to counter the official myths of the era, and often helped purvey them.[60]

Several conclusions follow from this discussion. Democratic regimes are less prone to mythmaking, because such regimes are usually more legitimate and are free-speech tolerant; hence they can develop evaluative institutions to weed out nationalist myth. Absolutist dictatorships that possess a massive military superiority over their citizens are also less prone to mythmaking, because they can survive without it. The most dangerous regimes are those that depend on some measure of popular consent, but are narrowly governed by unrepresentative elites. Things are still worse if these governments are poorly institutionalized, are incompetent or corrupt for other reasons, or face overwhelming problems that exceed their governing capacities. Regimes that emerged from a violent struggle, or enjoy only precarious security, are also more likely to retain a struggle-born chauvinist belief-system.

Conclusion: Predictions and Prescriptions

What predictions follow? These hypotheses can be used to generate forecasts; applied to Europe, they predict that nationalism will pose little risk to peace in Western Europe, but large risks in Eastern Europe.

Most of the nationalisms of the West are satisfied, having already gained states. Western diasporas are few and small, reflecting the relative homogeneity of Western national demography, and Western minorities are relatively well-treated. The historic grievances of Western nationalities against one another are also small—many of the West's inter-ethnic horrors have faded from memory, and the perpetrators of the greatest recent horror—the Germans—have accepted responsibility for it and reconciled with their victims. The regimes of the West are highly legitimate, militarily secure, and economically stable; hence chauvinist mythmaking by their elites is correspondingly

---

Russell Jacoby, *The Last Intellectuals: American Culture in the Age of Academe* (New York: Basic Books, 1987), pp. 112–237. On this problem in political science see Hans J. Morgenthau, "The Purpose of Political Science," in James C. Charlesworth, ed., *A Design for Political Science: Scope, Objectives, and Methods* (Philadelphia: American Academy of Political and Social Science, 1966), pp. 63–79, at 69–74. German academics also cooperated with official German myth-making after World War I; see Herwig, "Clio Deceived."

60. A good survey of German historiography of this era is Snyder, *German Nationalism*, chapter 6 (pp. 123–152). An older survey is Guilland, *Modern Germany and Her Historians*. Also relevant are John A. Moses, *The Politics of Illusion: The Fischer Controversy in German Historiography* (London: George Prior, 1975), chapter 1 (pp. 7–26); and Snyder, *From Bismarck to Hitler*, chapter 3 (pp. 25–35).

rare. The West European nationalisms that caused the greatest recent troubles, those of Germany and Italy, are now clearly benign, and the conditions for a return to aggressive nationalism are absent in both countries. Outsiders sometimes fear that outbreaks of anti-immigrant extremism in Germany signal the return of German fascism, but the forces of tolerance and decency are overwhelmingly dominant in Germany, and the robust health of German democracy and of German academic and press institutions ensures they will remain dominant. As a result nationalism should cause very little trouble in Western Europe.

In the East the number of stateless nationalisms is larger, raising greater risk that future conflicts will arise from wars of liberation. The collapse of Soviet power shifted the balance of power toward these nationalisms, by replacing the Soviet state with weaker successor states. This shift has produced secessionist wars in Georgia and Moldova, and such wars could multiply. The tangled pattern of ethnic intermingling across the East creates large diasporas. Eastern societies have little tradition of respect for minority rights, raising the likelihood that these diasporas will face abuse; this in turn may spur their homelands to try to incorporate them by force. The borders of many emerging Eastern nations lack natural defensive barriers, leaving the state exposed to attack; some borders also lack legitimacy, and correspond poorly with ethnic boundaries. Some new Eastern regimes, especially those in the former Soviet Union, lack legitimacy and are under-institutionalized, raising the risk that they will resort to chauvinist mythmaking to maintain their political viability. This risk is heightened by the regional economic crisis caused by the transition from command to market economies. Evaluative institutions (free universities and a free press) remain weak in the East, raising the risk that myths will go unchallenged. The Soviet regime committed vast crimes against its subject peoples; this legacy will embitter relations among these peoples if they cannot agree on who deserves the blame.[61]

---

61. The emerging nations of the former USSR now stand knee-deep in the blood of Stalin's victims, and in the economic ruin that Bolshevism left behind. If every nation blames only others for these disasters, civil relations among them will be impossible: each will hope to someday settle accounts. Civil relations depend, then, on a convergence toward a common history of the Bolshevik disaster. Things would be best if all converged on a version that blamed the Bolsheviks—who, having vanished, can be blamed painlessly. (Bolshevism would then usefully serve as a hate-soaker—its final, and among its few positive, functions in Soviet history.) Absent that, things would be better if the successor nations agree on how to allocate blame among themselves.

The Eastern picture is not all bleak. The main preconditions for democracy—high levels of literacy, some degree of industrial development, and the absence of a landed oligarchy—exist across most of the East. As a result the long-term prospects for democracy are bright. Moreover, the East's economic crisis is temporary: the conditions for prosperous industrial economies (a trained workforce and adequate natural resources) do exist, so the crisis should ease once the market transition is completed. These relatively favorable long-term prospects for democracy and prosperity dampen the risk that chauvinist mythmaking will get out of hand.[62] The fact that the new Eastern states managed to gain freedom without violent struggles also left them with fewer malignant beliefs, by allowing them to forgo infusing their societies with chauvinist war propaganda. The power and ethnographic structures of the East, while dangerous, are less explosive than those of Yugoslavia: historic grievances and military power coincide less tightly—there is no other Eastern equivalent of Serbia, having both military superiority and large historical grievances; and ethnographic patterns create less imperative for a diaspora-rescue operation by the state most likely to attempt such a rescue, Russia.

---

62. However, in the East's heterogeneous interethnic setting democracy is a mixed blessing: if it takes a strict majoritarian form it can produce majority tyranny and the oppression of minorities, as it has in the past in Northern Ireland and the American Deep South. To produce civil peace in a multi-ethnic setting, democracy must adopt non-majoritarian principles of power-sharing, like those of Swiss democracy. On this question see Arend Lijphart, "Consociational Democracy," *World Politics*, Vol. 21, No. 2 (January 1969), pp. 107–125; Arend Lijphart, *Democracy in Plural Societies: A Comparative Exploration* (New Haven: Yale University Press, 1977); Arend Lijphart, *Democracies: Patterns of Majoritarian and Consensus Government in Twenty-One Countries* (New Haven: Yale University Press, 1984); Arend Lijphart, "The Power-Sharing Approach," in Joseph V. Montville, ed., *Conflict and Peacemaking in Multiethnic Societies* (Lexington, Mass.: Lexington Books, 1990), pp. 491–509; Kenneth D. McRae, "Theories of Power-Sharing and Conflict Management," in Montville, *Conflict and Peacemaking*, pp. 93–106; Jurg Steiner, "Power-Sharing: Another Swiss 'Export Product'?" in Montville, *Conflict and Peacemaking*, pp. 107–114; Hans Daalder, "The Consociational Democracy Theme," *World Politics*, Vol. 26, No. 4 (July 1974), pp. 604–621; Kenneth D. McRae, ed., *Consociational Democracy: Political Accommodation in Segmented Societies* (Toronto: McClelland and Stewart, 1974); and Vernon Van Dyke, "Human Rights and the Rights of Groups," *American Journal of Political Science*, Vol. 18, No. 4 (November, 1974), pp. 725–741, at 730–740. See also James Madison, "The Same Subject Continued . . ." (Federalist No. 10), *The Federalist Papers*, intro. by Clinton Rossiter (New York: New American Library, 1961), pp. 77–84, which addresses the danger of majority tyranny and remedies for it; Madison discusses the risks that arise when "a majority is included in a faction" (p. 80) and the dangers of tyranny by "the superior force of an interested and overbearing majority" (p. 77). Also relevant is Robert M. Axelrod, *Conflict of Interest: A Theory of Divergent Goals with Applications to Politics* (Chicago: Markham, 1970), whose theory of winning coalition membership explains why majoritarian rules distribute power unequally in deeply divided societies.

All in all, however, conditions in Eastern Europe are more bad than good; hence nationalism will probably produce a substantial amount of violence in the East over the next several decades.[63]

What policy prescriptions follow? The Western powers should move to dampen the risks that nationalism poses in the East, by moving to channel manipulable aspects of Eastern nationalism in benign directions. Some aspects of Eastern nationalist movements are immutable (e.g., their degree of intermingling, or the history of crimes between them). Others, however, can be decided by the movements themselves (e.g., their attitude toward minorities, their vision of history, and their willingness to reach final border settlements with others); these can be influenced by the West if the movements are susceptible to Western pressure or persuasion. The Western powers should use their substantial economic leverage to bring such pressure to bear.

Specifically, the Western powers should condition their economic relations with the new Eastern states on these states' conformity with a code of peaceful conduct that proscribes policies that make nationalism dangerous. The code should have six elements: (1) renunciation of the threat or use of force; (2) robust guarantees for the rights of national minorities, to include, under some stringent conditions, a legal right to secession;[64] (3) commitment

---

63. Nationalism is also likely to produce substantial violence in the Third World, largely because a high nation-to-state ratio still prevails there; hence many secessionist movements and wars of secession are likely in the decades ahead. A discussion of the policy issues raised by this circumstance is Halperin, Scheffer, and Small, *Self-Determination in the New World Order;* for a global survey of current self-determination movements see ibid., pp. 123–160.

64. Minority rights should be defined broadly, to include fair minority representation in the legislative, executive, and judicial branches of the central government. The definition of minority rights used in most international human rights agreements is more restrictive: it omits the right to share power in the national government, and includes only the right to political autonomy and the preservation of minority language, culture, and religion. See Edward Lawson, *Encyclopedia of Human Rights* (New York: Taylor & Francis, 1991), p. 1070; on the neglect of minority rights by Western political thinkers, see Vernon Van Dyke, "The Individual, the State, and Ethnic Communities in Political Theory," *World Politics,* Vol. 29, No. 3 (April 1977), pp. 343–369.

When should minority rights be defined to include the right to secession and national independence? Universal recognition of this right would require massive redrawing of boundaries in the East, and would raise the question of Western recognition of scores of now-unrecognized independence movements worldwide. One solution is to recognize the right to secede in instances where the central government is unwilling to fully grant other minority rights, but to decline to recognize the right to secede if all other minority rights are fully recognized and robustly protected. In essence, the West would hold its possible recognition of a right to secede in reserve, to encourage governments to recognize other minority rights. A discussion of the right to secession is Vernon Van Dyke, "Collective Entities and Moral Rights: Problems in Liberal-Democratic Thought," *Journal of Politics,* Vol. 44, No. 1 (February 1982), pp. 21–40, at 36–37. Also relevant is Halperin, Scheffer, and Small, *Self-Determination in the New World Order.*

to the honest teaching of history in the schools,[65] and to refrain from the propagation of chauvinist or other hate propaganda; (4) willingness to adopt a democratic form of government, and to accept related institutions—specifically, free speech and a free press;[66] (5) adoption of market economic policies, and disavowal of protectionist or other beggar-thy-neighbor economic policies toward other Eastern states; and (6) acceptance of current national borders, or agreement to settle contested borders promptly though peaceful means. This list rests on the premise that "peaceful conduct" requires that nationalist movements renounce the use of force against others (element 1), and also agree to refrain from policies that the hypotheses presented here warn against (elements 2–6).

Hypothesis I.4 (see Table 1) warns that the risk of war rises when nationalist movements oppress their minorities; hence the code requires respect for minority rights (element 2). Hypothesis II.6 warns that divergent beliefs about mutual history and current conduct and character raise the risk of war; hence the code asks for historical honesty and curbs on official hate propaganda (element 3). Hypothesis II.6.a warns that illegitimate governments have a greater propensity to mythmake, and hypothesis II.6.d warns that chauvinist myths prevail more often if independent evaluative institutions are weak; hence the code asks that movements adopt democracy (to bolster legitimacy) and respect free speech and free press rights (to bolster evaluation) (element 4). Hypothesis II.6.c warns that economic collapse promotes chauvinist mythmaking; hence the code asks movements to adopt market reforms, on grounds that prosperity requires marketization (element 5). Hypothesis II.3.b warns that the risk of war rises if the borders of emerging nation states lack legitimacy; hence the code asks movements to legitimize their borders through formal non-violent settlement (element 6).[67]

---

65. States should not be asked to accept externally-imposed versions of history in their texts, since no society can arbitrarily claim to know the "truth" better than others. But states could be asked to commit to international dialogue on history, on the theory that free debate will cause views to converge. Specifically, they could be asked to accept the obligation to subject their school curricula to foreign criticism, perhaps in the context of textbook exchanges, and to allow domestic publication of foreign criticisms of their curricula. Schemes of this sort have a long history in Western Europe, where they had a substantial impact after 1945. See Dance, *History the Betrayer*, pp. 127–128, 132, 135–150. This West European experience could serve as a template for an Eastern program.

66. These democratic governments should adopt consociational power-sharing rules, not majoritarian rules; otherwise ethnic minorities will be denied equal political power (see footnote 62.)

67. Such a code could be applied more widely, and serve as the basis for an international regime

The Western powers should enforce this code by pursuing a common economic policy toward the states of the East: observance of the code should be the price for full membership in the Western economy, while non-observance should bring exclusion and economic sanctions.[68] This policy should be married to an economic aid package to assist marketization, also conditioned on code observance.

The Bush and Clinton administrations have adopted elements of this policy, but omitted key aspects. In September 1991, then–Secretary of State James Baker outlined five principles that incorporate most of the six elements in the code of conduct outlined above (only element 3—honest treatment of history—was unmentioned), and he indicated that American policy toward the new Eastern states would be conditioned on their acceptance of these principles.[69] During the spring and summer of 1992 the administration also proposed a substantial economic aid package (the Freedom Support Act) and guided it through Congress.

However, Baker's principles later faded from view. Strangely, the Bush administration failed to clearly condition release of its aid package on Eastern compliance with these principles. It also failed to forge a common agreement among the Western powers to condition their economic relations with the Eastern states on these principles. The principles themselves were not elaborated; most importantly, the minority rights that the Eastern states must protect were not detailed, leaving these states free to adopt a watered-down definition. The Bush administration also recognized several new Eastern governments (e.g., Azerbaijan's) that gave Baker's principles only lip service while violating them in practice.[70] The Clinton administration has largely

---

on nationalist comportment; a nationalist movement's entitlement to international support would correspond to its acceptance and observance of the code.

68. The Western powers should also offer to help the Eastern powers devise specific policies to implement these principles, and offer active assistance with peacemaking if conflicts nevertheless emerge. Specifically, Western governments and institutions should offer to share Western ideas and experience on the building of democratic institutions; the development of political and legal institutions that protect and empower minorities; the development of market economic institutions; and the best means to control nationalism in education. (On this last point an account is Dance, *History the Betrayer*, pp. 126–150.) Finally, if serious conflicts nevertheless emerge, the West should offer active mediation, as the United States has between Israelis and Arabs.

69. For Baker's principles see "Baker's Remarks: Policy on Soviets," *New York Times*, September 5, 1991, p. A12. Baker reiterated these principles in December 1991; see "Baker Sees Opportunities and Risks as Soviet Republics Grope for Stability," *New York Times*, December 13, 1991, p. A24. Reporting Baker's conditioning of American recognition of the new Eastern governments on their acceptance of these standards is Michael Wines, "Ex-Soviet Leader Is Lauded By Bush," *New York Times*, December 26, 1991, p. 1.

70. See "Winking at Aggression in Baku" (editorial), *New York Times*, February 14, 1992, p. A28.

followed in Bush's footsteps: it continued Bush's aid program, but omitted clear political conditions.[71]

There is still time for such a policy, but the clock is running out. A policy resting on economic sticks and carrots will be too weak to end major violence once it begins; hence the West should therefore move to avert trouble while it still lies on the horizon.

---

71. In April 1993 the Clinton administration forged agreement among the Group of Seven (G7) states (Britain, France, Germany, Italy, Canada, Japan, and the United States) on a $28 billion aid package for the former Soviet Union, and Congress approved a substantial aid package in September 1993. See Serge Schmemann, "Yeltsin Leaves Talks With Firm Support and More Aid," *New York Times,* April 5, 1993, p. 1; David E. Sanger, "7 Nations Pledge $28 Billion Fund To Assist Russia," *New York Times,* April 16, 1993, p. 1; Steven Greenhouse, "I.M.F. Unveils Plan for Soviet Lands," *New York Times,* April 21, 1993, p. A16; and Steven A. Holmes, "House Approves Bill Including 2.5 Billion in Aid for Russians," *New York Times,* September 24, 1993, p. A6. The aid was conditioned on Eastern moves toward marketization, but political conditions were omitted. President Clinton did declared that "we support respect for ethnic minorities," and "we stand with Russian democracy" as he announced the American aid pledge. Schmemann, "Yeltsin Leaves Talks." However, press accounts do not mention explicit political conditions.

Nationalism, the Mass Army, and Military Power

Barry R. Posen

The collapse of the Soviet Union and the end of the Cold War have precipitated an epidemic of nationalist conflicts. Nationalism was hardly quiescent during the last forty-five years: it played a key role in the decolonization process, fueling both revolutionary and inter-state warfare. But students of strategy concerned themselves with the dynamics of superpower conflict and its effects on regional enmities more than with the dynamics of nationalist rivalries. Thus, we lack sufficient analysis to explain our current predicament; instead, we invoke folk theories about ancient hatreds, or sorcerer leaders who have miraculously called them forth.

We fear nationalism because of its close association with the destructive warfare of the first half of the century. Many believe that nationalism permitted or even compelled leaders to conduct reckless foreign policies that produced wars; prolonged the wars by promoting escalation of war aims; increased the destructiveness of war by providing distilled industrial power in the form of vast quantities of armaments; and sustained the most intense combat imaginable with the energies and the blood of millions of young men.[1] Although these widely held propositions about the dangerous consequences of nationalism are by no means proven, when we express concerns today about the re-emergence of long-suppressed nationalism, this is what we fear.

Given that so much curiosity about nationalism is driven by its apparent association with war, it is noteworthy that few scholars have tried directly to connect the two phenomena. Most scholarship on the origins of nation-

Barry R. Posen is Professor of Political Science at MIT and a member of its Defense and Arms Control Studies Program.

The author would like to thank Omer Bartov, Liah Greenfeld, Jack Snyder, and Stephen Van Evera for comments on earlier drafts. The Committee on International Conflict and Cooperation of the National Research Council arranged for several helpful reviews. The Levitan Prize and the Carnegie Corporation of New York provided financial support.

1. For an example of such views, see Michael Howard, *War in European History* (New York: Oxford University Press, 1976), pp. 109–115; Carlton J.H. Hayes, *Nationalism: A Religion* (New York: Macmillan: 1960), pp. 120–124.

International Security, Vol. 18, No. 2 (Fall 1993), pp. 80–124
© 1993 by the President and Fellows of Harvard College and the Massachusetts Institute of Technology.

alism addresses the political, social, and economic development processes that have affected the formation of national identities. This literature is striking in its richness, but it pays little attention to war. Most scholarship on the origins and conduct of the great wars we associate with nationalism, especially the two world wars, traces only imprecisely their connection with nationalism.

In this article I argue that nationalism increases the intensity of warfare, and specifically the ability of states to mobilize the creative energies and the spirit of self-sacrifice of millions of soldiers. Several of the elements of nationalism long stressed by scholars of the subject are caused or intensified by the task of preparation for warfare, and by the experience of warfare, particularly "mass mobilization" warfare. It is not merely coincidental that nationalism seems to cause intense warfare; I argue that it is purveyed by states for the express purpose of improving their military capabilities.

Security Competition and Military Imitation

I define nationalism as the propensity of individuals to identify their personal interest with that of a group that is too large to meet together; to identify that interest on the basis both of a "culture" that the group shares, and a purported history that the group purportedly shares; and to believe that this group must have a state structure of its own in order to thrive.[2] Nationalism would thus help generate the individual commitment and the organized cooperation that make for combat power on the battlefield. Once nationalism is in place, the kind (although not necessarily the incidence) of warfare that we have seen since the French Revolution follows. Most of the interesting questions arise as to how both the beliefs and the shared culture come to be, and how they come to be in many states more or less simultaneously. Usually the answer to these questions is presumed to lie at the level of individual

---

2. This definition is consistent with that offered by Ernst Haas, "What is nationalism and why should we study it?," *International Organization*, Vol. 40, No. 3 (Summer 1986), p. 709. It also draws on Karl W. Deutsch, *Nationalism and Social Communication: An Inquiry into the Foundations of Nationality*, 2nd ed. (Cambridge, Mass.: MIT Press, 1966), chap. 4, "Peoples, Nations, and Communication," pp. 86–105. I have also borrowed from Ernest Gellner, who posits that a shared "high" or literary culture is the fundamental element of nationalism. Because he views culture as the glue that holds industrial capitalism together, he sees the spread of capitalism as the main cause of modern nationalism. Below I develop a different argument. Gellner, *Nations and Nationalism* (Ithaca: Cornell University Press, 1983); for a useful summary, see pp. 139–143; and for elaboration, pp. 35–38.

societies; if nationalism emerges in many neighboring societies simultaneously, then it is assumed that they are all experiencing similar political,
social, economic, or demographic changes.

By contrast, my argument stresses the causal role of the international
system; structural realism deduces from the anarchical condition of international politics that states that wish to remain autonomous will compete for
security. Military capabilities are a key means to such security, and thus
states will pay close attention to them. States will be concerned about the
size and effectiveness of their military organizations relative to their neighbors. As in any competitive system, successful practices will be imitated.
Those who fail to imitate are unlikely to survive.[3] The development of the
professional officer corps in the 1600s was one such practice, which provided
modern states with a permanent organization dedicated to the improvement
of war-making capacity, and to the observation of such improvements by
prospective adversaries.[4]

The mass army is a successful practice from the point of view of state
survival in international politics. The mass army makes land powers much
more capable of aggression. It is difficult to oppose a mass army without a
mass army. Once the French Revolution, and later Napoleon, proved the
efficacy of this pattern of military organization, others who valued their
sovereignty were strongly encouraged to imitate this example. It is this
imitation, I argue, that helped to spread nationalism across Europe.

THE MASS ARMY

Although historians, military and otherwise, speak of the rise of the "mass
army" in the French Revolution, and its subsequent spread across the world,

---

3. The standard work is Kenneth Waltz, *Theory of International Politics* (Reading, Mass.: Addison-
Wesley, 1979); see esp. pp. 123–128. "Contending states imitate the military innovations con-
trived by the country of greatest capability and ingenuity," p. 127. This is also the theme of
Charles Tilly, ed., *Formation of National States in Western Europe* (Princeton: Princeton University
Press, 1975). The essays in Tilly's collection stress competition and imitation in the development
of the whole administrative apparatus of states, including their military; they address the
development of nations less directly. See also Stanislav Andreski, *Military Organization and Society*
(Berkeley: University of California Press, 1971), pp. 68–71.
4. William H. McNeill, *The Pursuit of Power* (Chicago: University of Chicago Press, 1982), pp.
123–124, views the Thirty Years War as the event marking the institutionalization of a "professional" officer corps in the sense of a Europe-wide, self-conscious group of technical experts in
the "management" of violence, dedicated to the improvement of their craft. After the Thirty
Years War, the institution of the standing army spread throughout Europe, providing regular
employment for these professionals. As noted elsewhere in this article, the notion that one plied
one's trade for a single state throughout one's career had not yet caught on.

clear definitions, as well as explanations of its emergence and spread, are hard to find. The essence of the mass army is only partly its size, although it *is* a great deal larger than most of its predecessors.[5] The essence of the mass army is its ability to maintain its size in the face of the rigors of war: the attrition exacted by the unhealthful conditions of the campaign, the temptation of individuals to desert, and the firepower of the enemy. Its second essential quality is that it can also to a very large extent retain its "combat power." Replacements can be armed, trained, and organized rapidly so that they can be maneuvered over great distances and employed in engagements. Thus the recruits must arrive with a certain willingness to become soldiers, a certain educability, and a certain commitment to the outcome of the battle. This makes political motivation, and ultimately literacy, key elements of the mass army.

The development of the mass army depended physically on a general increase in population and wealth, so that society could provide from its surplus the reserves of manpower, weapons and supplies necessary to its effectiveness. The army needed the spread of literacy, initially down to the level of the non-commissioned officer, to facilitate command, training, and political motivation. The first mass army depended ultimately upon a political revolution whose ideology, redolent of nationalism, stressed the equality and community of all Frenchmen;[6] the first coalition's invasion of France in 1793 forced a beleagured leadership to order mass conscription.

Finally, the politically motivated mass army was a response to a "technological" problem—a constraint. (Developments in military techology reward some behaviors and penalize others, but they seldom directly determine military practice.) By the mid-1700s improvements in firearms made infan-

---

5. Louis XIV put the largest *ancien regime* army into the field; at 450,000 it represented a feat unequalled by his royal successors. Russell F. Weigley, *The Age of Battles* (Bloomington: Indiana University Press, 1991), p. 260. By late 1793, the revolutionary government had 700,000 soldiers. Jean-Paul Bertaud, *The Army of the French Revolution*, trans. R.R. Palmer (Princeton: Princeton University Press, 1988), p. 243. Under Napoleon strength fluctuated, but between 1800 and 1812, 1.3 million conscripts were reportedly absorbed. McNeill, *The Pursuit of Power*, p. 200.
6. The germ of this argument is found in Carl Von Clausewitz, *On War*, ed. and trans. Michael Howard and Peter Paret (Princeton: Princeton University Press, 1976, 1984), pp. 591–593. Of France he notes, "in 1793 a force appeared that beggared all imagination. Suddenly war again became the business of the people . . . all of whom considered themselves to be citizens. . . . The full weight of the nation was thrown into the balance." Of the consequences, he wrote, "Since Bonaparte, then, war, first among the French and subsequently among their enemies, again became the concern of the people as a whole. . . . There seemed no end to the resources mobilized; all limits disappeared in the vigor and enthusiasm shown by governments and their subjects."

trymen potent killers on their own and, combined with improvements in artillery, made it dangerous for more than a few infantrymen to cluster together.[7] Dispersal would improve the odds for survival. Since the 1700s, professional soldiers have understood that the motivation, command, and control of dispersed infantry on the battlefield are extremely difficult.[8] The problem becomes how to keep these dispersed, scared, lonely individuals risking their own lives, and cooperating to take the lives of others. An important related problem is how to replace the high casualties that may arise from armed clashes using these technologies. The deliberate sponsorship of both the cultural and ideological components of nationalism was perceived by many as a critical element, sometimes as *the* critical element, of the solution. Those states who do this better, all other things being equal, will be more competitive than others.[9]

States, therefore, act purposefully to produce nationalism because of its utility in mass mobilization warfare. Two aspects of nationalism—literacy and ideology—are subject to state action through schools, media, and indoc-

---

7. Most historians date the problem to the appearance of muzzle-loading percussion-fired rifles in the mid-1800s, but I find evidence that the problem emerged and was recognized a century earlier.

8. By the end of the Napoleonic wars, fighting in open order, or skirmishing, had become common practice in many European armies. Three different methods had been developed to produce troops who could use these tactics. The first was to train them from birth, as on the border of the Austro-Hungarian empire or the American frontier. This method was unavailable to central Europeans. The second was to drill and train the troops meticulously, as was pioneered by the British. This could not produce large numbers of troops, nor replacements for high attrition. It was uniquely suited to an offshore seapower which could control the size of its land commitment and the pace of battle, as did Wellington in Spain. The final mechanism was to improve the political motivation, solidarity, and learning skills of the average recruit, as pioneered by the French Revolution. This method spread throughout continental Europe, and ultimately the world, in the form of the mass army. For a superb introduction, see David Gates, *The British Light Infantry Arm, 1790–1815* (London: Batsford, 1987), esp. chap. 1.

9. Since the publication in the west of certain Second World War studies of the German Army, and particularly since the Vietnam War, the U.S. security studies community has stressed the impact of "small unit cohesion" on the combat power of infantry units. Much of this work was stimulated by E.A. Shils and Morris Janowitz, "Cohesion and Disintegration in the Wehrmacht in World War II," *Public Opinion Quarterly*, Vol. 12, No. 2 (Summer 1948), pp. 280–315. See also Martin van Creveld, *Fighting Power: German and U.S. Army Performance, 1939–1945* (Westport, Conn.: Greenwood, 1982). The impact of ideology, patriotism, or nationalism on combat power has until recently been derogated. There is, however, new literature that goes some way to restore sensitivity to the impact of these "wholesale" factors on combat power. Cited at length below is John A. Lynn, *The Bayonets of the Republic, Motivation and Tactics in the Army of Revolutionary France, 1791–94* (Urbana: University of Illinois Press, 1984). See also Omer Bartov, *Hitler's Army: Soldiers, Nazis, and War in the Third Reich* (New York: Oxford University Press, 1991); John Dower, *War Without Mercy: Race and Power in the Pacific War* (New York: Pantheon, 1986). All three of these works stress the conscious systematic manipulation of soldiers' attitudes.

trination within the military. States promote compulsory primary education to spread literacy in a standard version of the spoken language to enhance the technical military utility of their soldiers. In doing so, they spread the "culture" and the version of history that are central to the national identity. Culture means mainly a written language, but also a shared set of symbols and memories. Both formal language and these shared symbols and memories facilitate communication, training, and geographical and social mobility.[10] Although Ernest Gellner believes these arise from economic requirements, any argument that one can make for the economic function of literacy and a shared culture is at least as plausible for a military function, particularly in mass warfare.[11] The military fate of armies composed of several distinct communities and faced by relatively homogeneous armies tells the tale; the Austro-Hungarian army was nearly the least successful army of the First World War.[12]

The regimented presence of boys and young men in classrooms and in military units is also exploited to spread crude nationalist ideology among them. Schools, military training, and the newspapers spread the idea that the group has a shared identity and fate that can only be protected by the state. A highly patriotic and militarized version of the group's history is a critical building block of this idea.

States institute compulsory education and engage in propaganda because military and political leaders believe that such ideas enhance the commitment of the troops to the purposes of the war, increase their willingness to sacrifice their lives, and improve their solidarity with one another. Wars provide new incentives for both the winners and the losers to purvey the elements of

---

10. Gellner, *Nations and Nationalism*, p. 57. "It [nationalism] means the generalized diffusion of a school-mediated, academy-supervised idiom, codified for the requirements of reasonably precise bureaucratic and technological communication. It is the establishment of an anonymous, impersonal society, with mutually substitutable atomized individuals, held together above all by a shared culture of this kind."

11. "There seems to be in most countries a direct proportion between the degree of popular literacy and that of unquestioning national loyalty." Carlton J.H. Hayes, *Nationalism: A Religion* (New York: Macmillan, 1960), p. 87. He goes on to note the difference in resilience between the illiterate Russian conscripts of 1914–18 and the literate ones of 1941–45.

12. Max Weber, commenting on the Austro-Hungarian Army during World War I, argues this position: "Consider the fundamental difficulty confronting Austrian officers, which stems from the fact that the officer has only some fifty German words of command in common with his men. How will he get on with his company in the trenches? What will he do when something unforeseen happens, that is not covered by this vocabulary: What in the event of a defeat?" Weber, quoted in David Beetham, *Max Weber and the Theory of Modern Politics* (Cambridge, U.K.: Polity Press, 1985), p. 129.

nationalism, if the wars demonstrate the military advantages that come with literacy and solidarity. War also provides new ammunition, from disastrous military history as well as glorious, for subsequent purveyors of national-ism.[13]

Below, I focus largely on developments in land warfare from 1750 to 1914 and how they affected the development of nationalism in Prussia (and ulti-mately Germany) and in France. The patterns identified in this limited case study suggest that nationalism will be found to be part and parcel of prep-aration for mass mobilization warfare of any kind.

THE CASE

To evaluate the plausibility of the argument outlined above, I examine the competitive relationship between France and Prussia/Germany during the period from the Seven Years War (1756–63) to the eve of the First World War. The purpose here is not to test the theory systematically against any of its competitors; rather it is to establish its plausibility. This case should be relatively easy for the theory to pass: France and Germany share a gentle border and a long history of security competition; their struggles from the late 18th through the 20th century are often associated with an obvious and intense nationalism; the professional militaries of the two countries devel-oped more or less simultaneously; and their literatures were easily accessible to each other. There is a vast secondary literature on this competition. Thus both substantively and bibliographically I am, in the parable of the drunkard's search, looking under the light. But if this case does not lend some plausibility to the theory in this military competition, then it probably is a "critical case": if the theory cannot survive here, it probably would not elsewhere, and so we should spend little additional time on it.

The purpose of my argument is not to deny the influence of other political, social, and economic phenomena on the development of nationalism. It is, rather, to stress a causal chain that I believe has received insufficient attention in studies of nationalism and war, and one that I believe has a great deal of potential to explain the spread of nationalism and variations in its virulence.

---

13. Liah Greenfeld, *Nationalism: Five Roads to Modernity* (Cambridge: Harvard University Press, 1992), pp. 159, 180. Greenfeld notes that France's defeat in the Seven Years War stimulated the growth of nationalist sentiment in the French elite, quoting R.R. Palmer, "The National Idea in France before the Revolution," *Journal of the History of Ideas*, Vol. 1 (1940), p. 100. Simon Schama offers a similar judgment in *Citizens: A Chronicle of the French Revolution* (New York: Knopf, 1989), pp. xv, 32–34, 858.

An effort to weigh the power of these military causes, relative to other types of causes, will have to await further research. Nevertheless, if the argument is persuasive, then it suggests that nationalism can be expected to persist wherever the military security of states depends on mass mobilization, and that we must expect future military organizers with even a mediocre knowledge of military history to imitate this military format.[14]

THE PREDICTIONS

From the theory I have developed follow certain predictions about the case. First, we should expect to find that the explanations offered by important actors, such as statesmen and soldiers, of what they do are made in terms that are consistent with the theory. Since the theory predicts change over time in important practices, and since change is never easy, someone has to argue for it. If they argue for it for the reasons I have specified, then the theory is strengthened.

Second, we should find that changes in a given state's military or educational policies often follow the big wars that demonstrate the effectiveness of alternative policies, especially if they are successfully demonstrated by a potential adversary. For example:

- We should see states adopting mass armies if they have been beaten by mass armies, or they expect to have to confront one.
- We should see states embarking on literacy campaigns for the explicit purpose of producing better soldiers.
- We should find that educational materials used in primary schools have both a high nationalist content and a high military content.

Our purpose is to see whether states consciously imitate the successful practices of others, whether the mass army is deemed to be such a successful practice, whether nationalism correlates with the success of the mass army, whether the intensification of nationalism in one's own country is viewed as an essential component of a mass army, and whether actors connect literacy to military success and sponsor literacy to improve military effectiveness.

---

14. The concept of a "military format" is borrowed from Samuel E. Finer, "State- and Nation-Building in Europe: The Role of the Military," pp. 89–90, in Tilly, ed., *Formation of National States*, pp. 84–163. He includes, in the concept of format, the "service basis" of the military force, its composition in terms of main arms, and its social stratification. Finer's general approach in the essay helped inspire my own treatment below.

Third, if we find that states do these things even when they have other reasons not to, the theory is strengthened. And indeed, there are such reasons: narrow elites, such as the Prussian elite during the period in question, have good reason to avoid the mass army because it legitimates popular claims for political participation. Nationalist ideology does the same. By recruiting from every class, the mass army loses its utility as an instrument of domestic repression, and thus changes the balance of power between rulers and ruled. (It also diffuses some military skill throughout the society, as trained conscripts return to civilian life.) Increases in literacy also change the domestic balance of power by improving the political organizational abilities of the newly literate. Thus narrow elites should be opposed to the mass army, to nationalist ideology, and to compulsory education. If they nevertheless opt for the mass army and its necessary supports for security reasons, it strengthens my claim that systemic forces are a powerful cause of the diffusion of nationalism.

Narrow elites will wish to dispense with the mass army and its educational and ideological supports as soon as the national emergency passes, but according to realist theory, this is extremely difficult to do. The problem is somewhat akin to unilateral disarmament: since states cannot easily predict when and whether their neighbors can return to this successful offensive format, they must preserve a capability to return to it themselves, even if they would rather not do so for other reasons. Clausewitz summarized the lessons of mass mobilization in the Napoleonic wars: "once barriers—which in a sense consist only in man's ignorance of what is possible—are torn down, they are not so easily set up again. At least when major interests are at stake, mutual hostility will express itself in the same manner as it has in our own day."[15]

An alternative theory argues that narrow elites purvey nationalism as a kind of "false democracy" when they are under internal assault.[16] Nationalism is viewed as a confidence game in which elites try to convince the lower

---

15. Clausewitz, *On War*, p. 593. Elsewhere (p. 220) he observes, "All these cases have shown what an enormous contribution the heart and temper of a nation can make to the sum total of its politics, war potential, and fighting strength. Now that governments have become conscious of these resources, we cannot expect them to remain unused in the future, whether the war is fought in self-defense or in order to satisfy intense ambition."

16. This argument is implicit in many historical analyses of Wilhelmine Germany. For example see V.R. Berghahn, *Germany and the Approach of War in 1914* (New York: St. Martin's: 1973) pp. 29–31. Stephen Van Evera develops it briefly in "Primed for Peace: Europe After the Cold War," *International Security*, Vol. 15, No. 3 (Winter 1990–91), pp. 28–29.

orders that they are all members of the same community; inequalities of power and wealth are deliberately obscured. But even if these same elites promote nationalism, however, they should avoid the mass army and compulsory education, since these would shift the internal balance of power.

One could argue that nationalist ideology is a mechanism to counterbalance the democratizing force of conscription and compulsory education when the international system forces these expedients on narrow elites. Still, if this were the case, one would expect to find more democratic states purveying nationalism less intensively than less democratic states: the French state should purvey a less virulent nationalist ideology, and do so less intensively, than the German state. Such a fine-grained measurement is beyond the scope of this article, but the case described below does permit the reader to make a crude comparison; I see no obvious differences.

Theories of nationalism that stress its internal cultural sources seem to suggest the unlikelihood that successful military practices will be borrowed from abroad, although no theory explicitly advances this proposition. If nationalism was largely the organic result of a special internal process, borrowing of even successful enemy military practices would be taboo. Where states might argue their own national uniqueness and the complete "non-importability" of foreign models, but instead imitate the military institutions and practices of those who have defeated them, repackaged with a veneer of indigenousness, credibility is lent to the argument that military competition is an important cause of the spread of nationalism.

The Eve of Revolution

From the close of the Thirty Years' War to the end of the eighteenth century, the monarchs of Europe made war with small long-service armies, the rank and file of which were often at least partly "foreign," commanded by a mix of aristocrats, profiteers, and free-lance professionals. These armies tended to fight as relatively compact formations. Combat performance depended in part on drilling the individual soldiers until they could perform elaborate tactical maneuvers and shoot their weapons more or less automatically. Discipline was fierce. Frederick the Great of Prussia was the acknowledged master of this kind of war, and he is noted to have asserted that his troops had to fear their officers more than the enemy.

Already at roughly mid-century, some professional soldiers had become dissatisfied with customary military practices. This is sometimes attributed to a generalized spillover from the Enlightenment to military thought. Rather than quarrel with this position I would add that a practical problem had emerged: European armies had become too good at making war the old-fashioned way.[17] State financial and administrative apparatuses were strong enough to stay at war for several years at a time. But the combination of pre-war drill, improvements in firepower technology, and battlefield leadership had made actual combat almost too costly to sustain.[18] Casualties of 20 percent or more per battle became common in the Seven Years War, and the war lasted long enough for a number of battles to be fought.[19] Yet the infantry casualties could not be replaced at the pace they were incurred. Recruitment in wartime was difficult, and there was no time for the intensive training required to produce new infantrymen capable of the elaborate tactical combinations that officers preferred. The usual expedient was to add more and more artillery to the forces, but given the sheer weight of the guns, this impaired both large-scale and small-scale maneuver.[20]

Prior to the French Revolution, French and German military thinkers were writing about the need for a better motivated soldier, and particularly for a soldier who had some loyalty to the state. The Count de Guibert's *Essai General de Tactique* of 1772 is cited as the main theoretical work of the period that argues for the great military utility of a committed citizen army.[21] Perhaps of equal influence was the German Count Wilhelm zu Schaumburg-Lippe-Buckeburg, chief of a small German state the energies of which were dedicated totally to the count's avocation, "military organization and training."

17. McNeill, *The Pursuit of Power*, pp. 158–166, views the Seven Years War as an immediate catalyst of a new round of innovative thinking in European armies that had performed poorly, particularly the French, and imitative behavior on the part of many others, particularly of Prussia. He also posits a host of other "causes" of strain for the warfare states of Europe.
18. Even Frederick the Great, whom historians consider noteworthy for his willingness to risk battles, nevertheless viewed them as chancy affairs, often forced upon him by the exigencies of the situation. See Hans Delbrück, *History of the Art of War Within the Framework of Political History*, Vol. IV: *The Modern Era*, trans. Walter J. Renfroe (Westport, Conn.: Greenwood Press, 1985; first published Berlin: 1920), pp. 369–383.
19. Weigley, *The Age of Battles*, pp. 179–195.
20. Dennis Showalter, "Weapons and Ideas of the Prussian Army from Frederick the Great to Moltke the Elder," in John A. Lynn, *Tools of War* (Urbana: University of Illinois Press, 1990), pp. 186–191.
21. R.R. Palmer, "Frederick the Great, Guibert Bülow: From Dynastic to National War," in Peter Paret, ed., *Makers of Modern Strategy: From Machiavelli to the Nuclear Age* (Princeton: Princeton University Press, 1986), pp. 107–108. Guibert was also an exponent of mobility, although this was not inconsistent with Frederick's military practice. Guibert did not expect an imminent political revolution that would provide the kind of soldiers he wanted, and later repudiated his arguments as to their utility.

The count, who had instituted universal military service in his little state, also operated a military academy and enjoyed an "international reputation as a soldier." Gerhard von Scharnhorst, who led the reform of the Prussian Army after its defeat at the hands of Napoleon, was educated in this academy, from whence he derived many of his ideas about the value of an army that was representative of the population.[22]

Reforms were also proposed to improve the treatment of the soldier in the ranks, which were rationalized on the grounds of increased combat power.[23] In Prussia in the 1770s, the regiments of the army began to set up their own schools to educate soldiers and their dependents. The main impetus was to improve their economic lot, not their military utility, but the movement represented a shift in attitude toward the soldier.[24]

Similarly there was considerable debate about the utility of skirmishers— dispersed infantry fighting independently of the long, tightly-controlled lines then typical of European army tactics. The purpose of the line was to generate volume of fire, not accuracy; commanders aimed the whole line by maneuvering it into range of the enemy (50–100 meters) at well-chosen points. Skirmishers, in contrast, were meant to fight as individuals and to pick their own targets. The debate was well underway at mid-century, although historians do not quite agree on its causes. The main inspiration seems to have been the extensive use, in the Hapsburg armies, of irregular troops raised and recruited from the disputed lands bordering the Ottoman empire.[25] There soldiers seem to have been bred rather than trained, and they spent much of their everyday life in a war of small-unit actions and raids. When attached

---

22. Peter Paret, *Clausewitz and the State: The Man, His Theories, and His Times* (Princeton: Princeton University Press, 1985), pp. 60–62. Scharnhorst was born in Hanover, served first in that army of that state, and as was the custom of the time, was recruited by Prussia in 1801 on the basis of his established reputation as a soldier.

23. Peter Paret, *Yorck and the Era of Prussian Reform, 1807–1815* (Princeton: Princeton University Press, 1966), pp. 18–19. By the 1790s there is some evidence that the treatment of the common soldier was beginning to improve; see ibid., p. 107.

24. Paret, *Clausewitz*, pp. 46–51. Clausewitz spent his early years in a regiment known for its interest in education.

25. The flintlock musket with socket bayonet made the lone infantrymen a potent weapon. Arguably this weapon was not truly perfected until the mid-1700s, and most soldiers were trained for rapidity of fire rather than accuracy. If trained in aimed fire, a soldier could hit and kill individuals at ranges up to 80 yards, and clusters of individuals at 160 yards, while with the bayonet he could still defend himself in the clinches. With training he could fire three or four rounds a minute. It was now possible, where terrain permitted, to disperse infantrymen to fight alone, and in the right terrain, unseen. Compressed groups of men, the tactical combinations of the preceding century, were vulnerable to these skirmishers, and to artillery. If they failed to disperse, they too would be vulnerable.

to regular units for war in Central Europe, they proved useful for reconnaissance, flank security, and combat in close terrain. As similar units were organized in the Prussian and French armies, they were trained for aimed fire, and often armed with the rifle, rather than the cheaper, less accurate, but faster-loading smoothbore musket.[26] Such troops were slightly expanded in the Prussian Army prior to the French Revolution; expanded yet again in the last decade of the century; and yet again after the defeats of 1806. Light infantry made up 5 percent of the army in 1786, 14 percent in 1800, and 31 percent by 1812.[27]

While the reforms attempted before the French Revolution were meager, they suggest that an important military problem had emerged even before the revolution facilitated the implementation of solutions.

As the early successes of the French revolutionary armies were studied in Prussia after 1795, their widespread employment of skirmishers—*tirailleurs*—became the central issue. Moreover, the connection between these tactics and the nature of the soldier was clearly understood. Peter Paret deserves quotation in full:

To a remarkable, possibly unique, degree all problems concentrated in this issue. If skirmishing was to be more generally employed, the soldier's education, discipline, and drill—all of which bore directly on his ability to fight in open order—would need to be changed. Nor could the old methods of recruitment, exemption, and reliance on mercenaries be retained; a more representative cross-section of the population in the ranks would turn the army into a more national body; the relationship between officer and man, soldier and citizen, and between soldier and sovereign would be modified.[28]

The French Revolution gave Europe its first modern mass army. This mass army depended on nationalism for its combat power. Those who subsequently imitated the mass army were also forced to imitate its nationalism.

THE BIRTH OF THE MASS ARMY

From 1792 to 1815, France was at war with much of Europe. Historians agree that the French Revolution marked a transformation in the conduct of war. The most important factor was the involvement of the French people. The armies became mainly French; they grew in size; and their ability to replace

---

26. Paret, *Yorck*, pp. 23–25; 28–30; 40–42. The cited pages only provide the outlines of these developments. Light forces and skirmishing are one of the main themes of the book.
27. Ibid., p. 269.
28. Ibid., p. 76.

casualties through levies on the population at large made it possible to engage in frequent battles of great violence. The population took an interest in these wars, providing much direct material support in the early years of the revolution. Their commitment also undoubtedly enhanced the morale of the troops. Lengthy movements at greater speed became possible. The baggage trains could be slimmed substantially, since troops could be permitted to forage without too great a risk of the desertions that plagued the armies of the *ancien regime*. The democratic ideals of the army, and the departure of much of the aristocratic officer corps, reduced a good deal of the "life-style" baggage that had formerly slowed movements in the field.[29]

Tactically, the French armies fought with a mix of line, column, and skirmishers. Conventional military histories of the revolution view deployment of skirmishers as the principal mode of combat in the Revolutionary armies (probably not true), and as a natural adaptation by politically motivated but poorly trained military novices (probably true). The widespread employment of skirmishers in "open order" seems to have spread fairly quickly after the revolution, and persisted to some degree in most European armies.[30] It was hard to fight the French without adopting their methods.

Reforms initiated before but not completed by the revolution were extended. These depended not on political revolution but on the departure of many aristocratic officers, and their replacement with ambitious non-commissioned officers (NCOs) and volunteers would have changed the organizational balance between traditionalists and innovators in favor of the latter. The stress of constant combat no doubt eased the way for reforms by testing and proving their utility. French artillery was vastly improved in terms of mobility and range. The "division," now a relatively standard army formation mixing artillery, infantry, and cavalry to permit effective independent combat operations, became a regular organizational form. It improved the overall mobility of the army by permitting movement along separate parallel routes,

---

29. For brief accounts see McNeill, *Pursuit of Power*, pp. 185–206; and Hew Strachan, *European Armies and the Conduct of War* (London: George Allen and Unwin, 1983), pp. 36–42.
30. The open order persisted, at least in the French Army. See Ardant Du Picq, *Battle Studies, Ancient and Modern Battle*, trans. Colonel John N. Greely and Major Robert C. Cotton (New York: Macmillan, 1921), p. 238. Writing on the eve of the Franco-Prussian War, he observed, "Since these wars, our armies have always fought as skirmishers." He also reports that the Prussians fought largely as skirmishers in 1866. Paret, *Yorck*, p. 37, "The decisive innovation in infantry fighting that was to occur at the end of the eighteenth century consisted in the acceptance of open-order tactics by the line infantry."

with a considerable diminution of the risk of defeat in detail. At the same time, divisions could be quickly recombined into larger forces.

While it is commonplace to attribute the size and energy of the French revolutionary armies to the political revolution itself, a closer look at these armies reveals that there was a sustained political campaign to educate and motivate the armies after they were formed, and to forge powerful emotional bonds between the army and the civilian population.[31] The high-water mark of these efforts, and their success, seems to have occurred by roughly 1794.[32]

The identification of the army with the nation was facilitated first by the greater representativeness achieved in the pattern of recruitment.[33] The combination of the first waves of volunteers and the first conscripts produced an army that was by 1794 representative of the society as a whole. This, coupled with a host of other measures, encouraged those within the army to believe that the whole country was behind them. Similarly, recruitment from many parts of the country put large numbers of previously sedentary people on the roads of France. They learned that there was a France, and those who witnessed their passing understood that a great collective experience was underway.[34] The frequent singing of patriotic songs, many of which were commissioned for the purpose, helped reinforce these feelings on a daily basis.[35]

Political propaganda was disseminated in the army camps in the forms of pamphlets and journals, much of it regularly read aloud. Cowardice was punished and heroism rewarded in public ceremonies. Civic festivals brought together soldiers and civilians to celebrate the ideals of the revolution.[36] In contrast to the old regime, and to the practice in the rest of Europe, soldiers

---

31. On these issues, see the very fine work of Jean-Paul Bertaud, *The Army of the French Revolution: From Citizen Soldiers to Instrument of Power*, trans. R.R. Palmer (Princeton: Princeton University Press, 1988); and John A. Lynn, *The Bayonets of the Republic: Motivation and Tactics in the Army of Revolutionary France, 1791–94* (Urbana: University of Illinois Press, 1984).
32. Peter Paret seems to agree. "Rather than reflecting attitudes already widely held in 1793 or 1814—loyalty to a cause, hatred of the foreigner, patriotism—conscription helped create and diffuse these attitudes." Paret, *Understanding War* (Princeton: Princeton University Press, 1992), p. 73.
33. Bertaud, *The Army of the French Revolution*, p. 132.
34. Ibid., pp. 73, 127.
35. A single sentence cannot do justice to the importance of song. See Bertaud, *The Army of the French Revolution*, pp. 137–141; Lynn, *Bayonets of the Republic*, pp. 141–150. Tens if not hundreds of thousands of song books were distributed to the army in 1793 and 1794. The government subsidized patriotic-song writers. Even the act of singing together helped build a certain collective consciousness. Patriot festivals, marches, and even battles were occasions for singing. No one who has seen films of Nazi rallies from the 1930s can doubt their impact.
36. Bertaud, *The Army of the French Revolution*, pp. 205–210.

were portrayed as honored members of society.[37] Class-based barriers to promotion were largely eliminated. Within the constraints of military discipline, the social distance between officers and enlisted men was reduced.

A minor theme of the period was an increased emphasis on literacy within the army as a criterion for promotion.[38] In early 1794 an ability to read and write was made compulsory for commissioned and non-commissioned officers alike.[39] NCOs were required periodically to read *The Rights of Man* and the military laws aloud to their squads.[40] Starting in September 1792, the National Convention began to publish a daily journal especially for the army. These appear to have been read aloud regularly to squads of the Armée du Nord, one of the largest in the field.[41] Four hundred thousand copies of the draft constitution of June 24, 1793, were distributed to the armies. The armies occasionally distributed printed propaganda in enemy territory as well.

In his remarkable study of the Armée du Nord, John Lynn concludes that these efforts were highly successful. Not only did they contribute to the well-known élan of these French troops, but they encouraged a "rise in self- and group-imposed standards of performance and sacrifice." These standards facilitated the rapid training of these French troops, which he concludes was critical to their developing combat power. "Without strong normative compliance, large-scale reliance on open-order combat would have been out of the question."[42]

PRUSSIAN MILITARY REFORMS

Many foreign military observers understood the connection between French tactical innovations, particularly the widespread employment of skirmishers,

---

37. Lynn, *Bayonets of the Republic*, pp. 177–182.
38. As early as 1787 the army had opened schools to teach non-commissioned officers how to read and write. Armies increasingly employed training manuals, personnel records, and written orders, and were doing so with a frequency that required literate corporals and sergeants. McNeill, *Pursuit of Power*, p. 187. This of course had the effect of making revolutionary propaganda accessible to the army.
39. Bertaud, *The Army of the French Revolution*, pp. 174, 189. At that time nearly 85 percent of the NCOs could read and write; more than half also knew some arithmetic. Given that the Army ascribed to promotion on the grounds of merit, it seems likely that the military literacy programs begun in 1787 survived into the revolution. France had quite a high literacy rate at the time of the Revolution. Simon Schama, *Citizens* (New York: Alfred Knopf, 1989), p. 180–181.
40. Bertaud, *The Army of the French Revolution*, p. 199.
41. Lynn, *Bayonets of the Republic*, pp. 122, 136. It is Lynn's judgment that the primary purpose of this political propaganda was to instill obedience to legitimate political authorities; combat motivation was of secondary importance.
42. Ibid., p. 283.

and the political system that produced them.[43] The later Prussian reformers, especially Scharnhorst, were quick to point out the impact of the French *tirailleurs*, although others challenged their views.[44] Field Marshal von dem Knesebeck, a later opponent of Scharnhorst, nevertheless understood the French quite well: "It is here that the education of the individual is of such great benefit to the Republicans, because situations too often occur during the combat of light forces in which the officer's control ceases completely . . . in which each man acts on his own."[45] The Prussians worried about the large number of men the French could throw into the field, and some began to advocate expanded reliance on a militia to beef up their own forces.[46]

The catastrophic defeats of Prussia at Jena and Auerstedt in 1806, and the humiliating peace terms imposed by Napoleon, gave new impetus to those who advocated military reform in Prussia.[47] Under the pressure of defeat, King Frederick William was open not only to military reform proposals, but to reforms of all kinds.[48] While Scharnhorst, as chair of the Military Reorganization Commission, spearheaded the military reformers, Heinrich von Stein guided the effort to reform the political administration of the country. Both civilians and soldiers were working from ideas developed prior to the defeat, but defeat was a major impetus to their efforts.[49] And for soldiers, such as Scharnhorst's collaborator August von Gneisenau, these political reforms had the purpose of releasing military energy.[50]

---

43. Paret treats this debate extensively in *Yorck*, Chapter III, "The Last Years of the Old Monarchy," pp. 47–110. As early as 1796 Scharnhorst declared that, "we shall be victorious when one learns to appeal, like the Jacobins, to the spirit of the people"; quoted in Gunther E. Rothenberg, *The Art of Warfare in the Age of Napoleon* (London: Batsford, 1977), p. 190.
44. Paret, *Yorck*, p. 77; Paret, *Clausewitz*, pp. 32–33.
45. Paret, *Yorck*, pp. 78–79.
46. Ibid., pp. 89–90.
47. William O. Shanahan, *Prussian Military Reforms 1786–1813* (New York: Columbia University Press, 1945), is still widely cited, but should be read in conjunction with Paret, *Yorck*.
48. Liah Greenfeld argues that German "national consciousness" barely existed prior to 1806, but was a "formidable presence" by 1815; Greenfeld, *Nationalism*, p. 277. Elsewhere (p. 372) she comments that, "France gave Germany the Enemy, against whom all strata of the disunited German society could unite. . . . Hatred of France inspired the uncertain patriotism within the German breasts. . . . Without the decade of collective effervescence and common effort, the vital enthusiasm which was sustained by the persistence of the French menace, German nationalism would not have survived its birth." Her definition of nationalism is more complex than my own, but there is sufficient commonality to make her observation relevant.
49. On the political reforms and the impetus given to them by the defeat see Hans Rosenberg, *Bureaucracy, Aristocracy, and Autocracy: The Prussian Experience, 1660–1815* (Boston: Beacon, 1958), pp. 202–205.
50. Gerhard Ritter, *The Prussian Tradition, 1740–1890*: Vol. I, *The Sword and the Scepter, The Problem of Militarism in Germany*, trans. Heinz Norden (Coral Gables, Florida: University of Miami Press,

Although Frederick the Great had considered the possible improvements in his military power that public education could provide, and had issued a set of General School Regulations in 1763, his fears of the socially destabilizing potential of education diluted his support of his own rules.[51] His successors were similarly immobilized. Little progress was made in developing public education until after the defeat at Jena. Efforts to improve the Prussian school system focused largely on the problem of training teachers in a common pedagogical method, which itself had to be arrived at through debate and experimentation. Officials appointed to improve existing schools seem to have agreed that their primary purpose was "to educate to nationhood 'the entire undifferentiated mass'."[52] The Prussian military reformers showed a keen interest in the debate on public education. They considered adapting the then-popular Pestalozzi pedagogical methods to the training of recruits. A Prussian educational official delivered a lecture to seventy officers on the "Influence of the *Volksschule* [primary school] on Military Preparedness."[53] In 1812 a prominent educational official advised that elementary schools should teach "the history of the Germans, not merely . . . that of the Prussians."[54] In spite of the progress made in the education of teachers and the development of curriculum, the poverty born of war probably caused the number of elementary schools and pupils to diminish.[55] The end of the war with Napoleon freed resources to expand and improve the educational system, but was ultimately to produce very conservative policies regarding the structure and the curriculum.

Prussian military reforms initially focused on how better to organize the small (42,000 men) army permitted under the Convention of Paris. Officers most clearly associated with the defeat were purged. The ranks of the officer corps were formally opened to the middle class, although aristocrats continued to dominate. Corporal punishment was abolished, as was the recruitment of foreigners. A host of administrative reforms centralized and rationalized military administration, purging the last elements of "free enterprise"

1969), pp. 70–74. See also Paret, *Clausewitz*, pp. 137–146. Clausewitz was another member of the reform circle, and in a letter to Fichte in 1809 noted the connection of "political arrangements" and "education" to the "warlike spirit"; ibid., p. 177.
51. Karl A. Schleunes, *Schooling and Society: The Politics of Education in Prussia and Bavaria, 1750–1900* (Oxford, U.K.: Berg, 1989), pp. 14–16, 45–49.
52. Ibid., p. 74, quoted a report from 1809.
53. Ibid., pp. 68–69, 75.
54. Ibid., p. 78, quoted a report from 1812.
55. Ibid., p. 79.

from the army. The system of officer education was improved and extended, and greater scope for promotion by ability rather than seniority was provided. A War Academy for senior officers was established in Berlin in 1810.[56]

The French divisional system was imitated and formalized, albeit in smaller brigade-sized units. A small number of reservists were trained in the regular army and sent back to civilian society to give the army some personnel reserves to replace attrition if and when warfare resumed. A much higher proportion of the infantry was trained to fight as skirmishers.[57]

But the reform of greatest long-term import for the peace of Europe was the introduction of a universal military obligation. Actual conscription was adopted only with great reluctance, and Prussia conscripted only a small percentage of its young men after the defeat of Napoleon. Nevertheless, the reforms after Jena, and the fact that mobilized Prussian citizen-soldiers had participated in the final defeat of France, created both the military infrastructure and the legitimating experience that set the stage for the victories of 1866 and 1870.

As early as 1808 the Military Reorganization Commission had proposed broadening the methods of recruitment to the Army, including combining conscripts and volunteers in the regular army, and the formation of volunteer militia. Even this proposal, which fell well short of genuine universal military obligation, was opposed by the king and a broad spectrum of aristocrats and the middle class. Undeterred, the Reorganization Commission in 1810 recommended universal conscription with no exemptions. Both domestic opposition, and the limitations on army size imposed by Napoleon, rendered the issue moot until the emperor's defeat in Russia created an opening for Prussian revolt.

In 1813, universal conscription was implemented. Volunteer units were organized for the wealthy and educated, who were obliged to provide their own equipment. The *Landwehr*, a local militia organization that enrolled all able-bodied males, was formed, and the *Landsturm*, a regional defense militia for all other males, was also organized. The latter saw little action, but the regulars, the volunteers, and the *Landwehr* all saw action against the French.[58]

---

56. Paret, *Yorck*, pp. 170–171.
57. For short summaries see Rothenberg, *The Art of Warfare in the Age of Napoleon*, pp. 190–194; Delbrück, *History of the Art of War*, Vol. IV: *The Modern Era*, pp. 449–455. For a lengthier treatment see Paret, *Yorck*, pp. 11–153.
58. Paret, *Yorck*, pp. 133–138. Paret reports that during the 1700s the Prussian army had drawn its recruits from foreigners, and from draft districts or military cantons within the country. But

The Army grew from 60,000 in December 1812 to 130,000 three months later, and to 270,000 by the fall.[59] These measures were not met with universal acclaim, and popular support for the rising against the French does not seem to have equalled the level of public support achieved by the French in 1793–94.[60] Nevertheless, there is reason to believe that the combination of technical reforms, broader recruitment, and the fact of political rebellion against external domination provided the Prussian Army of 1813–15 with motivation and combat power that was vastly increased over its predecessor of 1806.[61]

SUMMARY OF THE REFORM PERIOD

The security relationship between France and Prussia from the mid-seventeenth to the early eighteenth century illustrates every aspect of the argument developed at the outset of this essay. Military professionals faced with a host of battlefield constraints, many of them technological in nature, theorize about ways to solve their problems. The development of greater emotional commitment to the state is widely perceived to be essential to a solution. This is particularly clear in the identification of success at open-order tactics with political commitment. Education becomes interesting both in the narrow technical sense of the facilitation of military administration, and in the broader sense of creating political awareness and commitment. Innovations that produce vast increases in the combat power of the French Army, both of a narrow tactical nature and of a more diffuse political nature, are closely studied by Prussian professionals. Imitation is recommended, and to a considerable extent achieved, including political reforms. The extent of imitation is of course limited by internal political resistance in Prussia, and the degree of necessity; nevertheless it happens. This period of war, crisis, and political change is followed by a period of "reaction" after Napoleon's defeat. Many of the military changes discussed above are suppressed to a considerable degree. Much survives, however, and a second cycle of mass mobilization and military innovation begins in the last third of the nineteenth century.

---

there was a strong bias in local recruitment that put the burden largely on the poorest of the rural population. Moreover, the percentage of foreigners varied during the 1700s; Frederick the Great strongly favored reliance on them, proposing a ratio of 2 foreigners to every native. For a lengthier treatment of this hybrid system, see Delbrück, *History of the Art of War*, Vol. IV: *The Modern Era*, pp. 247–252.

59. Paret, *Clausewitz*, pp. 234–237., See also Rothenberg, *Art of Warfare*, pp. 194–196.

60. Paret, *Clausewitz*, p. 236; Paret, *Yorck*, p. 218.

61. I believe this to be a fair summary of Paret's judgment, in spite of his cautionary observations noted above. See for example Paret, *Yorck*, p. 219.

Reaction, 1815–1870

After Napoleon's defeat, the statesmen of Europe tried to restore the status quo both domestically and internationally. Since domestic political revolution in France was closely linked to more than two decades of French expansionism, the restoration of monarchical power in France was seen as a key to peace. Similarly, political reforms that had been made in the societies that opposed the French for the instrumental purpose of beating them were to a great extent reversed. With the lessons of two decades of painful war still fresh, Europe's statesmen strove for moderation in their external relations. The need for highly motivated mass armies was removed; and monarchs were happy to see an ebbing of the domestic political energies that war had released.

Nevertheless, in Prussia and in France several military innovations associated with the Revolutionary and Napoleonic wars were preserved. In both countries, the principle of homogeneous national armies, without foreign units or foreign private soldiers, was retained.[62] Both also retained the form, although not quite the fact, of a general military obligation of the citizenry to the state.

In France the Bourbons abolished conscription in 1814, but found it necessary to implement a highly unfair system of "selective service" in 1818. Each year roughly 20,000–30,000 men were chosen by lottery from the 300,000 eligible for a seven-year term of service.[63] Those drawing "bad" numbers could hire a substitute, or after 1855 simply pay a fee to the state, so military service was actually the obligation of the poor. Troops often re-enlisted in the army after their first lengthy term of service; now unsuited for the civilian world, they sold their services as substitutes to those rich enough to pay. More than half of the officer corps in this period was drawn from the ranks.[64] The 1818 Law continued the revolutionary tradition of conditioning promo-

62. Unlike the early Revolutionary armies, Napoleon did rely in his later campaigns on foreign units to a considerable degree, and recruits from border areas often had a different mother tongue.
63. This discussion relies on Richard Challener, *The French Theory of the Nation in Arms, 1866–1939* (New York: Columbia University Press, 1955), pp. 10–28; and David B. Ralston, *The Army of the Republic: The Place of the Military in the Political Evolution of France, 1871–1914* (Cambridge, Mass.: MIT Press, 1967), pp. 9–25.
64. Richard Holmes, *The Road to Sedan: The French Army 1866–70* (London: Royal Historical Society, 1984), pp. 90–100.

tion to officer rank (non-commissioned and commissioned) on literacy.[65] A study of incoming conscripts in the late 1820s revealed that only about half could read, which helped prompt national reforms in primary education in 1833.[66] Regimental schools were also instituted to teach the necessary skills.[67] To the extent that regimental educational materials communicated any message, it seems to have stressed martial virtues and heroic episodes of French military history, but not explicit nationalism.[68] The army was keenly concerned with fitness, tactical training, and marksmanship.[69] An interest in athletics, especially gymnastics and fencing, developed in the regiments.

In sum, although the French Army was much less representative of society as a whole than it had been during Napoleon's reign—no longer the revolutionary "Nation in Arms"—it was more representative and homogeneous than it had been prior to the Revolution.

French officers developed a strong belief that long service produced *l'esprit militaire*, a powerful sense of discipline and military identity, which were presumed to contribute to superior battlefield performance.[70] The precise source of this belief, which persisted well into the twentieth century, is unclear. I speculate that it was in part a return to pre-revolutionary professional military attitudes. It is likely that many early nineteenth-century officers were veterans who had bitter memories of their experiences with hastily raised, ill-trained troops during the last years of Napoleon's rule.[71] Constant warfare against great coalitions decimated the experienced cadre of the army,

---

65. Ibid., pp. 189–192, notes that the quality of the education received in these schools was questioned even then.
66. Paddy Griffith, *Military Thought in the French Army, 1815–51* (Manchester, U.K.: Manchester University Press, 1989), p. 103.
67. Eugen Weber, *Peasants Into Frenchmen* (Stanford, Calif.: Stanford University Press, 1976), p. 298. The Army also taught French to the many provincial French recruits, such as Bretons, who still spoke their own native language; ibid., p. 299. The state's general interest in literacy was growing. The 1833 law required every commune to organize at least one elementary school, and that the school be certified by the state. Every department was obliged to organize or help organize a "normal" (secondary) school for the training of teachers. Compliance was not always enthusiastic, but in at least one coastal province local political leaders strongly supported the school because local young men tended to serve in the army and the navy where literacy was necessary for advancement. Ibid., pp. 307–308, 327. For a lengthy discussion of regimental education, see Griffith, *Military Thought*, pp. 101–113.
68. Griffith, *Military Thought*, p. 105.
69. Ibid., pp. 114–130.
70. Holmes, *The Road to Sedan*, pp. 90–91.
71. See Griffith, *Military Thought*, pp. 8–9.

and populated the ranks with inexperienced, teen-aged recruits.[72] Combat effectiveness deteriorated.[73]

From 1815–60 the organization of the Prussian Army, including the recruitment, training, and organization of the rank and file, and the recruitment and education of the officer corps, was a central matter of domestic political dispute. The king and the Junker aristocracy mistrusted the *Landwehr* and aimed to destroy its autonomy; they hoped to preserve and expand aristocratic dominance of the officer corps. The purpose was to secure the army as a defense of monarchical power against the growing political power of the middle and working classes. At the same time, however, considerations of security were also accommodated. By 1866 Prussia had achieved a competently commanded, highly motivated mass army, which was at the same time politically reliable.

Concern about the political reliability of the Army during this period had its counterpart in the question of primary school curriculum. From the end of the Napoleonic Wars Prussia developed an increasingly effective system of compulsory education for males.[74] The proportion of children enrolled reportedly increased to nearly 80 percent by 1837. The organization of the schools was calculated to divide people into distinct social classes and to restrict upward mobility. Reading, writing, arithmetic, religion, and singing were the main primary school subjects. The purpose of the latter two was apparently to instill "discipline, order, and obedience to authority."[75] The impetus was primarily to instill loyalty to the monarchy, not national identity.[76] Explicit German nationalism played a minor role, if any, in the curriculum prior to the victories of 1866 and 1870.[77] The fact that statistics were

---

72. David G. Chandler, *The Campaigns of Napoleon* (London: Weidenfeld and Nicolson, 1967), pp. 333–334.
73. Presumed political reliability was also an attraction of long-service troops, both in France and in Prussia.
74. Gordon A. Craig, *Germany 1866–1945* (New York: Oxford University Press, 1978), pp. 186–187.
75. Craig, *Germany*, pp. 188–189. The School Regulations of 1854 placed religion at the center of the curriculum for primary school, where it apparently influenced the teaching of reading, writing, and arithmetic. Very little time was given over to history or science. Schleunes, *Schooling and Society*, p. 153.
76. Craig, *Germany*, pp. 157–158. Religious instruction was apparently increased for the same reason in 1879.
77. Schleunes, *Schooling and Society*, pp. 97–98, 109. Teachers themselves, however, became somewhat politicized and were blamed for the revolution of 1848. One suspects that in spite of the formal curriculum, teachers must have found it difficult to avoid including some political content in their teaching. Ibid., pp. 129–130.

collected on the literacy of recruits suggests that the original reform-era military interest in education was sustained.[78] In 1844 it was suggested that retired Army NCOs be recruited as primary school teachers to remedy a chronic shortage.[79]

There was little change in Prussian military institutions from 1815 to 1860. The standing army was kept small, roughly 200,000, largely for budgetary reasons. Conscripts served three years with the colors and two with the reserve, then joined the *Landwehr*.[80] Those not called up joined the *Landwehr* directly. *Landwehr* officers were chosen from the local elite, and included many members of the middle class.[81]

In two major mobilizations to provide military muscle for international crises in 1831 and 1859, *Landwehr* troops made a poor showing. In combat against the Poles in 1831, and against the Danes in 1848, the Army on the whole did not perform well. In civil disturbances associated with the brief liberal revolution of 1848, both *Landwehr* and regular infantry troops had proven weak supports of the crown.[82] Napoleon III's victory in Italy in 1859, and the incompetence of the concomitant Prussian mobilization, provided the final impetus for further reform.[83]

The purpose of the reforms was to expand the regular army and establish its complete dominance of the *Landwehr*. The Army Bill of 1860 was ultimately to double the size of the standing army, and preserve the three-year term.[84] Conscripts would then serve four years with the reserves, and only after that pass into the *Landwehr*. The regular army was to become the only source of *Landwehr* recruits; the *Landwehr* would fall entirely under its administration. The army could now draw upon seven annual classes of trained men at mobilization. The Prussians were thus able to field 355,000 soldiers against the Austrians, and, with the allies of the North German Confederation, a million in 1870.[85]

---

78. Schleunes, ibid., p. 109, notes that by 1841 only one Prussian recruit in ten had never attended school. 40 percent of the recruits from the annexed Polish province of Posen had never attended school. Ibid., p. 100.
79. Ibid., pp. 112, 122–123.
80. In practice, conscripts apparently served only two years with the colors. Michael Howard, *The Franco-Prussian War* (New York: Macmillan, 1962), p. 20.
81. Ibid., pp. 8–12.
82. Alfred Vagts, *A History of Militarism, Civilian and Military*, rev. ed. (New York: Free Press, 1959), p. 191.
83. Howard, *The Franco-Prussian War*, p. 20.
84. Vagts, *A History of Militarism*, pp. 192–193.
85. Howard, *The Franco-Prussian War*, p. 22; Gordon Craig, *The Battle of Königgratz* (New York:

This commitment to the development of a rapidly mobilizable, well-trained, professionally-officered mass army was seen to depend in some measure on widespread basic literacy among the common soldiers.[86] Much progress had been made in Prussia, more than in any other country; by 1850 the adult literacy rate was reportedly 80 percent.[87] And the Prussian officer corps, even prior to 1806, considered itself to have a special "educational mission."[88] In Gerhard Ritter's words, "If the *Landwehr* of 1814 had meant a partial civilianization of the army, the royal mass army of 1860 already displayed a marked inclination toward militarization of the whole nation."[89]

In one of the formative domestic crises of modern Germany, the Prussian parliament declined to fund the reforms proposed in 1860. But the government implemented them in any case over the next eight years, and ultimately extended them to the North German Confederation.[90]

Officer quality also improved. Warfare was perceived to be increasing in complexity as the products of the industrial revolution, particularly the railroad and telegraph, began to find military employment. Education was expected to have a greater impact on combat performance. Future officers were obliged to study in higher military schools or to have a university education. Candidates for the initial officer entrance examination were required to demonstrate competence in grammar and spelling, apparently a problem area for some of the Junker applicants. On the whole, officer quality did improve.[91] The General Staff under Helmuth von Moltke's leadership skimmed off the intellectual cream of the German War Academy and subjected it to additional exacting training in the problems of wartime command of the very large forces that would now become available.[92]

The victory of the Prussians over the Austrians in 1866 impressed observers all over Europe, particularly Napoleon III, Emperor of the French. The fully

Lippincott, 1964), p. 17. It is likely that this figure, which is close to that used by most historians, refers to the field army; more troops were probably available in garrison, in fortresses, and along lines of communication.

86. Paul Kennedy, *The Rise and Fall of the Great Powers* (New York: Random House, 1987), p. 184.

87. Schleunes, *Schooling and Society*, p. 109.

88. Vagts, *A History of Militarism*, p. 172. "Far from being alienated from the people, this army was to be a great national school in which the officer would be an educator in the grand style, a shaper of the people's mind"; Ritter, *Sword and Scepter*, p. 118.

89. Ritter, *Sword and Scepter*, p. 119.

90. Howard, *The Franco-Prussian War*, pp. 18–22.

91. Vagts, *A History of Militarism*, pp. 194–195.

92. Howard, *The Franco-Prussian War*, pp. 24–25.

mobilized Prussian Army was expected to outnumber the French by 2 to 1 as of 1866, without even counting Prussia's allies.[93] Napoleon III could see the merits of short-service conscription backed by a large reserve organization. The French military attaché in Berlin pointed out that the Prussians had perfected the "nation in arms" that the French had invented, and enhanced its effectiveness with the addition of universal primary education.[94] Indeed, French educators were beginning to articulate a keen sense of inferiority *vis-à-vis* Prussia.[95] But the French officer corps for the most part remained wedded to its preference for long-service troops, and the French legislature, which had gained considerable power by this time, was unwilling to support truly large scale conscription. In January 1868 a compromise bill was passed. Active army service was reduced to five years, but it was to be followed by a four-year reserve obligation. More conscripts were to be called up each year, but a substantial number would serve only five months in the active forces, the remainder of their nine-year obligation in the reserves or in the anemic French counterpart to the old Prussian *Landwehr*, in the *Garde Nationale*.[96] Ultimately, these changes were expected to produce a mobilizable force of 800,000 men or more.

Other reform efforts included Napoleon's futile attempt to induce the Army to imitate the Prussian General Staff; modest progress in the development of an efficient railroad mobilization plan; and the re-equipment of the French Army with the Chassepot breech-loading rifle, then the finest in the world.[97]

Several lessons emerge from this relatively quiet period in European politics. First, reactionary elites clearly understood the relationship between an expanded military and expanded political participation. Opposed to the second, they suppressed the first. Second, the military advantages of a relatively homogeneous national army were not forgotten, and the basic notion of the state's legitimate right to conscript citizens for the military was preserved. As quiet as European international politics were during these years, such a useful security asset was not thrown away, even given domestic incentives to do so. Third, as Prussian ambitions began to grow at mid-century, and again in the face of considerable aristocratic resistance, the state adopted a

---

93. Holmes, *The Road to Sedan*, p. 92.
94. Allan Mitchell, *Victors and Vanquished: The German Influence on Army and Church in France after 1870* (Chapel Hill: University of North Carolina Press, 1984), p. 4.
95. Mitchell, *Victors*, pp. 143–148.
96. Howard, *The Franco-Prussian War*, pp. 29–34.
97. Ibid., pp. 35–38.

professionally controlled mass army. Conservatives began to believe that the army itself might prove a useful tool to socialize young men to their political image of Prussia. Fourth, although they feared its social consequences, the Prussian government expanded and improved compulsory education faster than any other country in Europe. Fifth, the French perceived themselves to be the most affected by Prussian reforms, and moved rather quickly after 1866 to develop a response in kind, albeit somewhat paler.

Finally, an observation on military technology is in order. Improvements in firepower were seen to necessitate even more battlefield dispersion than had evolved in the Napoleonic wars, and even more dependence on the individual commitment of the soldier.[98] The deployment of the muzzle-loading percussion military rifle, the later widespread adoption of the breech-loader after 1866, and analogous improvements in artillery posed new tactical problems for European soldiers. Increased range and rate of fire meant that when fighting occurred, soldiers tended to disperse automatically, regardless of the intentions of their officers. To preserve some semblance of battlefield order, officers in France and Prussia placed a greater weight on training and length of service as a source of combat motivation than on the political commitment of the preceding period.[99] At the same time, however, there is a good deal of scattered evidence that the leaders of the armies were concerned about the education level and political attitudes of the conscripts that came to them, and paid some attention to their "patriotic" education in the military. These somewhat muted concerns become much more explicit after the Franco-Prussian War.

---

98. Showalter, "Weapons and Ideas," pp. 198–199. See also the influential essays by Colonel Ardant Du Picq, *Battle Studies: Ancient and Modern Battle* (New York: Macmillan, 1921), pp. 100–101, 151–169.

99. Du Picq, *Battle Studies*, p. 96. Du Picq is often taken to advocate long service, although to the extent that he offers a figure, he seems to view three or four years as sufficient (p. 131). His main point, however, is that soldiers can be kept fighting under the conditions of modern firepower only with tremendous internalized self-discipline. This he believed came from long "mutual acquaintanceship" of men and officers. In this he anticipated the modern military emphasis on small-unit cohesion. Interestingly, however, he also stressed something else that individuals brought to the small unit: "French sociability creates cohesion in French troops more quickly than could be secured in troops in other nations. Organization and discipline have the same purpose. With a proud people like the French, a rational organization aided by French sociability can often secure desired results without it being necessary to use the coercion of discipline" (p. 225). One suspects that Prussian officers would substitute some perceived positive attribute of their own young soldiers, such as "respect for authority," for French "sociability." I would substitute "shared culture" more generally.

The Franco-Prussian War and Its Aftermath

The immediate cause of the Franco-Prussian War was the Spanish attempt to recruit a minor prince of the Hohenzollern family to assume the Spanish throne. The blow to French prestige and power precipitated their immediate opposition, which actually encouraged the prince to withdraw. But clumsy diplomacy by the French, and clever exploitation of their mistakes by Bismarck, ended in a clash of arms with France widely viewed in Europe as the guilty party.[100] The underlying cause of the war, however, was the growing power of Prussia, the declining position of France, and the inability of the two states to establish their relative diplomatic weight in Europe through any measures other than war.[101]

The magnitude of the initial French defeats would probably have sufficed to cause a new wave of military reform in postwar France. The French legislature ordered mobilization on July 14. By August 19, its best army, 155,000 strong, was bottled up in Metz by about 170,000 Germans. (It was to surrender on October 29.) On September 2, Napoleon III surrendered France's "reserve" army of 100,000 at Sedan. In roughly six weeks, the cream of the French long-service troops and their senior commanders had been eliminated. The French had succumbed to superior numbers, organization, tactics, commanders, and—in the case of artillery—even weaponry.[102] By any criterion the Prussian victory was extraordinary.[103] The Prussian armies now marched on Paris.

In Paris, then a heavily fortified city full of mobilized troops, the remnants of Napoleon's government took steps to form a Government of National Defense, even as moderate and extreme left-wing political forces moved to

---

100. See Howard, *Franco-Prussian War*, pp. 48–57, for a lucid summary of this convoluted matter.
101. Ibid., p. 40; In terms of population and wealth, Prussia and its German allies did not overmatch France. The Prussians won due to greatly superior military organization. Had the French military reforms progressed unhindered for another five years, a war with Prussia in 1875 might not have produced quite so lopsided an outcome. For a material assessment, see Kennedy, *Rise and Fall*, pp. 149, 171, 187.
102. Here I include both tactics, the method of fighting at the level of small and medium-sized units, and "operational art," the method of orchestrating the movement of corps and armies moving independently to try to achieve a single military goal. In the latter, the Prussians vastly outclassed the French; in the former the superiority was less marked, and depended largely on the exploitation of technically superior artillery.
103. I rely for the preceding and subsequent analysis on the classic work by Michael Howard, *The Franco-Prussian War*.

overthrow the old regime altogether. The moderate left took control and proceeded to establish its writ throughout unoccupied France. Since the new government's claim to legitimacy was based on national defense, it met little political resistance. Informal peace overtures foundered on Prussia's demands for Alsaçe and Lorraine.[104]

The new government intended that Paris would be the decisive battle of the war. Two weeks of frenetic activity strengthened its fortifications and armaments, and assembled some 200,000 largely untrained soldiers. The Prussians opted for a siege, however. Then the scene of action shifted to the rest of France, much to the surprise of the Prussians.

The agent of this shift was 32-year-old Leon Gambetta, the Minister of the Interior, who had been smuggled out of Paris in a balloon. He organized resistance in the rest of the country, assisted by Charles de Freycinet, a professional engineer. Together they not only led the organization of new armies, they mobilized the whole apparatus of the state and relevant civilian professions. Theoretically, the Law of 1868 left a million men with some kind of military obligation for Gambetta to exploit (not counting the soldiers in Paris, surrounded in Metz, or surrendered to the Germans). With a superior navy intact, imports of weapons and equipment from abroad helped arm these soldiers. The industrial resources of unoccupied France were pressed into the business of manufacturing weapons. Time and the availability of both officers and NCOs were short, so for the most part the soldiers remained poorly trained and poorly led. But, in Michael Howard's words, the "amplitude" of this national mobilization "far surpassed anything on the German side," and "was not to be seen again until the First World War was far advanced on its course."[105] In a vain hope to relieve Paris, the armies thus organized fought a series of bloody and unsuccessful campaigns against the Prussians; the battles raged across northern France and drew the Prussians deeper and deeper into the country. By the end of January, however, Gambetta's improvised forces had all been defeated and driven from the field. This regular, if incompetent, resistance was accompanied by French partisan activity in the Prussian rear.[106] These actions usually elicited retaliation against the local population, and captured partisans were generally shot.[107]

---

104. Ibid., pp. 224–228.
105. Ibid., p. 245.
106. Ibid., pp. 249–256.
107. Ibid., pp. 378–381. In the words of one German officer, "The war is gradually acquiring a

On January 28, aware that the military situation was hopeless, the Government of National Defense signed an armistice with Prussia; following elections that returned a majority of peace advocates to the French National Assembly, German terms were accepted. This included the cession of Alsaçe and Lorraine and a 5-billion-franc indemnity to be paid over four years. On March 1 the National Assembly ratified the agreement.

The effects of the Franco-Prussian War on subsequent French military planning, indeed on military planning throughout Europe, were profound. Michael Howard wrote that, "any continental power which wished to escape annihilation as swift and overwhelming as that which overtook the Second Empire had to imitate the German pattern and create a Nation in Arms—a nation whose entire man-power was not only trained as soldiers, but could be mobilized, armed, and concentrated on the frontiers within a very few days."[108] France set out to rebuild its own military, and in many respects relied on the Prussian model. While they never matched Germany in terms of mobilizable troops, armament, and organization, they nevertheless achieved a major transformation in their army.[109]

To this important military lesson was added the living symbol of two lost provinces; the experience of a large scale national mobilization; the fact that public support for the mobilization had been erratic, particularly in the interior, and the memory of a German occupation that had been anything but gentle. These were to provide the initial impetus for a wave of French military reforms, and later a set of larger social reforms.

The first pillar of French military regeneration was a commitment to obligatory military service for nearly the entire male population.[110] The 1872 debates on new military legislation brought repeated allusions to the lesson offered by the Prussian reformist response to their defeat at Jena in 1807.[111] Along with a better ability to field a large and well-trained army, many

---

hideous character. Murder and burning is now the order of the day on both sides, and one cannot sufficiently beg Almighty God finally to make an end of it"; p. 379.

108. Ibid., p. 455.

109. Mitchell, *Victors and Vanquished*, argues that the French consciously imitated much German military practice. Yet he judges them harshly for the measured pace and limited extent of their imitation and improvement, especially on the breadth of conscription of the adult male population, and the organization of men who had completed their term of service into reserve units. I am struck by what was done and thus I judge the evidence as supporting my theory.

110. The Army itself instituted a number of reforms, most prominently the institution of a General Staff and the permanent peacetime organization of all large military units, including Army Corps of several tens of thousands of men.

111. Challener, *The French Theory of the Nation in Arms*, pp. 33–36.

conservative delegates thought that conscription would instill discipline and solidarity in the youth of France.[112] The initial law, however, did include exemptions for teachers, priests, and those studying for certain professions, who committed themselves to ten years of service to the state. University students could volunteer for one year in the military, if they paid their own way and passed an exam to prove their military competence. Everyone else was theoretically vulnerable to the five-year term, although a lottery would divide them into two groups, one serving a year with the colors, the other serving five.[113] Military conservatives had been able to preserve this lengthy term of service on the strength of the pre-1870 arguments, seen both in France and in Prussia, that long service imparted a special discipline and cohesion that would produce a high-quality soldier.

In actual practice, the distinction between the one-year and five-year active troops was gradually eroded. French military critics regularly argued for reducing the term of service to three years, and thus increasing the percentage of the annual class of eligible young men who would receive extensive military training. But until 1889, such arguments were rebuffed on the basis of the professional officer corps' preference for the longer term of service. In reality, however, most recruits to the infantry served at most forty months, which was codified in 1880.[114] The nominally long term of service, carried out against overall active-service manpower ceilings, meant that perhaps 200,000 eligible young men did not receive military training in the 1870s.[115] Legislation in 1889 and 1905 further equalized the burdens of military service.

The Army was increasingly considered "a school in which French youth acquired basic principles of citizenship."[116] Those from provinces where French was not the mother tongue learned the language of their countrymen.[117] Until roughly 1890, French troops did not serve close to home, so military service introduced vast numbers of rural and small town young men to the rest of the country as a whole.[118] Many simply did not return to their

---

112. These hopes had their parallels in Prussia, prior to the war. Apparently, the effort to use the army to inculcate these "conservative" values evaporated by 1877–78. Ralston, *The Army of the Republic*, p. 48.
113. Ibid., pp. 40–41.
114. Mitchell, *Victors and Vanquished*, p. 79.
115. Ibid., p. 80.
116. Challener, *The French Theory of the Nation in Arms*, p. 47.
117. Weber, *Peasants into Frenchmen*, p. 299.
118. Ralston says that after about 1890, for reasons of economy, the French Army did regularly station soldiers close to home; Ralston, *The Army of the Republic*, p. 284.

villages after their military service. Eugen Weber concludes, "the army turned out to be an agency for emigration, acculturation, and in the final analysis, civilization, an agency as potent in its way as the schools."[119] Indeed, the Law of 1872 provided additional advantages to conscripts who could read and write, and threatened the illiterate with an additional year of service.[120]

What of the schools? In the words of Peter Paret, there developed "the collaboration of the elementary schools and the conscript army to teach nationalism to the masses."[121] Contemporary analyses of the Prussian success gave considerable credit to the Prussian system of primary education.[122] A series of laws passed between 1880–82 made education compulsory and free for children aged six–thirteen, and defined the content of the curriculum.[123] This content was decidedly patriotic.[124] One academic remarked early in the Third Republic, "If the schoolboy does not become a citizen fully aware of his duties, and a soldier who loves his gun, the teacher will have wasted his time."[125] The late nineteenth century also saw the beginning of French interest in physical education in the schools, an interest first driven by the connection to fitness for military service.[126]

As part of the Freycinet Plan (a huge public works program aimed at jump-starting the French economy), plenty of money went to the construction of schools. More went to the construction of roads and railroads, particularly

---

119. Weber, *Peasants into Frenchmen*, p. 302. See also Ralston, *The Army of the Republic*, p. 48.
120. Weber, *Peasants into Frenchmen*, p. 327.
121. Peter Paret, "Nationalism and the Sense of Military Obligation," *Military Affairs*, Vol. 34, No. 1 (Winter 1970), p. 5. He asserts that the explicit teaching of nationalism in school and in the army was a direct imitation of the Prussians.
122. Holmes, *The Road to Sedan*, p. 192.
123. Carlton Hayes, *France: A Nation to Patriots* (New York: Columbia University Press, 1930), pp. 35–36. The main theme of this book is the manner in which French patriotism was systematically supported by the educational system, the army, and a host of cultural institutions in post-World War I France.
124. In addition to Weber, *Peasants into Frenchman*, see Hayes, *France*, pp. 38–40.
125. The quotation is from Ernest Lavisse, who in the 1880s wrote several widely used civics and history textbooks; see John Schwarzmantel, "Nationalism and the French Working Class Movement 1905–1914," pp. 65–80, in Eric Cahm and Vladimir Fisera, eds., *Socialism and Nationalism in Contemporary Europe 1848–1945* (Nottingham: Spokesman, 1979), p. 68. Schwazmantel's theme is that national feeling remained quite strong in the French working class.
126. James Albisetti, "The debate on secondary school reform in France and Germany," in Detlef K. Muller, Fritz Ringer, and Brian Simon, eds., *The Rise of the Modern Education System: Structural Change and Social Reproduction 1870–1920* (Cambridge: Cambridge University Press, 1987), p. 187; Mitchell, *Victors and Vanquished*, pp. 151–152, writes: "In addition to a popular mystique about the army becoming the school of the nation . . . , the inverse proposition consequently developed that the schools should prepare pupils for military service." He observes that by the late 1870s some progress in physical education had been made in the secondary schools, but little in the primary schools.

into rural areas. This plan was that of the Freycinet who had helped Gambetta organize the mobilization of French society against the Germans, and who had seen the representatives of rural France end the war in 1871 even though Gambetta wanted to continue the fight. Given Freycinet's personal experience, I am inclined to agree with those who have seen the Freycinet Plan as a deliberate effort to integrate the more backward parts of France into the larger society.[127] Freycinet's subsequent political career suggests his lifelong concern for the improvement of French mobilization capability. As Defense Minister for an unprecedented five years, beginning in April 1888, Freycinet led the successful battle for the three-year term-of-service law passed on July 15, 1889.[128]

Eugen Weber declares that the main function of the new French schools was to teach a "new patriotism." Children were taught that their first duty was to defend the country and, returning to themes we saw in Revolutionary propaganda, schools reminded the students that the Army was now composed of people just like them. The teaching of history and geography was a vehicle for instilling patriotism. New teaching materials were made available to facilitate this task, including maps that showed the lost provinces of Alsaçe and Lorraine as part of France. In the words of one student of education, "The French elementary schools after 1870 became notorious breeding grounds of chauvinism."[129] The long-established connection between basic literacy and the effectiveness of subsequent military training also figured prominently.[130]

The precise connections between all of this state-sponsored activity and the behavior of French troops in World War I are difficult to demonstrate. It would be surprising if *poilu* after *poilu* had left us diaries noting that they were sustained each day by some specific thing they had learned in school,

---

127. Weber, *Peasants into Frenchmen*, pp. 209–210, 309–310. Weber doubts that the plan had this purpose, stressing its stimulative economic aspects.
128. Mitchell, *Victors and Vanquished*, p. 106; "The measures passed under Freycinet cannot be understood simply as products of a self-generated reform movement. The accumulated evidence shows that both the motive and the measurement of reform derived from comparison with Germany" (p. 109). Germany's seven-year defense budget of 1888 had lengthened the obligation of its reservists to report for mobilization to age 45.
129. Albisetti, "The debate on secondary school reform," p. 195. Even textbooks produced by liberals "extolled military virtues, praised France's services to the world, and provided very little information about other countries." Queried on the purpose of studying history, 80% of the candidates for the baccalaureate (secondary school completion exam) are reported to have effectively replied "to exalt patriotism."
130. Weber, *Peasants into Frenchmen*, pp. 333–336.

or some bit of pre-war propaganda. Nevertheless, Stephane Audoin-Rouzeau concludes, from his insightful study of soldier-published trench newspapers during the war, that a profound sense of national feeling, "deeply rooted in the republican patriotism of pre-war days," and "moulded by their primary education" was the primary source of emotional sustenance.[131] This national feeling abandoned the extremes of pre-war chauvinism and was not reanimated by wartime propaganda, particularly of the type directed at the home front. But as the war dragged on, the daily act of "defence of their soil" and remembrance of the comrades who died for it created new sources of resolve. He concludes that, "even in the war's worst moments, the impossibility [unthinkability] of causing the defeat of their own nation by collective weakness constituted a psychological barrier than nothing could overcome."

GERMANY

As the victor in the war of 1870, Prussia/Germany lacked the impetus to innovate that was experienced by the French. But with the ascension of Wilhelm II to the throne in 1888 there was a noticeable increase in the nationalist content of the primary and secondary school curriculum. The main explanation for this offered by most historians is a concern for loyalty to the regime, particularly in the domestic political fight with growing liberal and social-democratic forces. The view that concern about military effectiveness was an important motivating factor is less common, although there is evidence to support it. The content of the motivational efforts also suggests that combat motivation was an important concern.

Both the Prussian War Minister and the Education Minister had believed that the Prussian *Volksschule* teacher deserved much of the credit for the victory over the Austrians in 1866, and so informed the first Kaiser Wilhelm. Bismarck similarly credited them for their role in the victory over the French.[132] During the 1870 war, many pupils in the primary school teacher-training seminars volunteered for military service, suggesting that nationalist sentiment was already deeply embedded in this important group.[133] All of this suggests that in spite of its official stress on religion rather than nation-

---

131. Stephane Audoin-Rouzeau, *Men at War, 1914–1918: National Sentiment and Trench Journalism in France during the First World War* (Providence: Berg, 1992); see chap. 6, "National Sentiment," esp. pp. 176–177, 184.
132. Schleunes, *Schooling and Society*, pp. 160, 191.
133. Ibid., pp. 172–173.

alism, the Prussian primary school curriculum of the 1850s and 1860s must have informally included at least some political component.

New efforts to reform Prussia's schools quickly followed the victory. The official administrative role of the church was eliminated in the Inspection Law of 1871. The role of religion in the curriculum was drastically reduced in new regulations in 1872. "History and the German language and its literature were to replace religion as the core of the curriculum," and the curriculum in the teacher training schools followed suit.[134] Textbooks were standardized with a particular emphasis on the enhancement of national consciousness. For example, a new history text from the mid-1870s explained the Franco-Prussian war this way: "The only cause was France's envy and jealousy of Prussia's growing greatness and Napoleon's desire to stabilize his quaking throne by a war of conquest."[135] Some of the educational reforms must be attributed to Prussian domestic political developments, but the timing of the reforms, the sudden emergence of high-level official respect for Prussia's schoolmasters, and the content of the new curriculum all suggest that military preparedness provided much of the impetus.[136]

Wilhelm II's interest in the content of primary and secondary education was driven initially by the desire to instill regime loyalty; social democracy was to be explicitly addressed as the main enemy. This idea seems to have occurred to him in 1888 and was given impetus by a wave of strikes in 1889. But the new kaiser favored the addition of an even more distinctively nationalist content to the conservative religious approach that had maintained some hold on the curriculum in spite of the 1870 reforms.[137] He was particularly interested in fostering the study of Prussian history.[138] The goal of teaching history for the twin purposes of combatting social democracy and instilling patriotism was furthered by a Cabinet Order of May 1, 1889, and by the kaiser's personal participation in the school conference of 1890.[139]

---

134. Ibid., pp. 177–178.
135. Quoted in ibid., p. 190.
136. Schleunes, ibid., suggests that it was at this juncture that the Prussian schools effectively became apostles of *German* nationalism as a means to legitimate the conquests of the preceding wars; pp. 160–161. It is also noteworthy that a debate emerged on the possibility of centralizing all the schools in Germany, but that was deemed too great a political fight.
137. Walter C. Langsam, "Nationalism and History in the Prussia Elementary Schools Under William II," in Edward M. Earle, ed., *Nationalism and Internationalism* (New York: Columbia University Press, 1950), pp. 241–261, is the most widely cited English language essay on this subject.
138. Craig, *Germany*, p. 189.
139. Albisetti, "The debate on secondary school reform," p. 194.

There was apparently wide consensus among educators that the study of history should replace religion as the source of social cohesion.[140] The Army welcomed the kaiser's initiative, although in subsequent years there were complaints by Army officers that the schools were not doing a good job.[141] Close supervision was also exercised over Prussian teachers, who were viewed as state officials; particular efforts were made to exclude socialists.[142] It was more difficult to control the curriculum and the personnel elsewhere in Germany due to the federal character of the Empire.

While many historians have stressed the domestic problems that the nationalist curriculum was meant to solve, a specifically military motivation for and content of the curriculum is evident. In 1890 Prussian district school inspectors were directed that the primary schools must train the children "as active members of German society, as self-denying subjects, and as men who will be glad to pay the supreme sacrifice for king and country."[143] Prussian pedagogues and writers frequently echoed these themes. The two most popular texts on historical method stressed the importance of military struggle and military power in the history of Prussia, and the special role of history teaching as a source of future willingness to risk all on the field of battle.[144] Prussian national history, particularly military history, dominated the curriculum. There was also a strong emphasis on current military affairs, in terms of both technique and strategic issues.[145] Textbook writers and school teachers may, indeed, have overfulfilled the expectations of the government in their emphasis on military matters.

The military itself was another vehicle for the development of national consciousness in post-unification Germany. Although German conscripts tended to serve close to home, service nevertheless produced an acquaintance with people from different parts of Germany, and often with different parts

---

140. Schleunes, *Schooling and Society*, pp. 226–228. "New texts and readers glorifying the Kaiser and the Fatherland had been introduced. The great deeds of the wars of liberation and unification, of Prussia's kings, of Bismarck, and of the Kaiser were being offered as the fundamental elements of a new national consciousness" (p. 228).
141. Martin Kitchen, *The German Officer Corps 1890–1914* (Oxford: Clarendon Press, 1968), pp. 175–176.
142. Paul Kosok, *Modern Germany: A Study of Conflicting Loyalties* (Chicago: University of Chicago Press, 1933), p. 161. He notes that in Prussia there was very little instruction on the workings of government and society.
143. As quoted in Langsam, "Nationalism and History in the Prussian Elementary Schools," p. 243.
144. Ibid., pp. 245–252.
145. Ibid., pp. 252–258.

of the country itself.[146] Discipline was quite rigorous; indeed sometimes it deteriorated into outright abuse, which may have had the effect of alienating many conscripts.[147]

The officer corps that managed the conscript army became somewhat more heterogeneous than it had been. Prior to 1870 it was populated by politically reliable aristocrats. In the expansion after 1870, it became necessary to bring more middle-class officers into the active and especially into the reserve forces. Propaganda addressed to these officers stressed their personal relationship to the crown, warned against the dangers of domestic subversion, and reminded them of the army's role in blocking such subversion. The political behavior of reserve officers was surveyed, and liberals found themselves deprived of their commissions.[148] But self-policing was the most powerful enforcement mechanism. The prestige of the military was so high in Wilhelmine Germany, and so much elite political energy was directed at keeping it high, that middle-class officers and reserve officers were pleased to have their commissions, and willing to take on the political coloration of their social "betters." The Army identified itself as a key player in the campaign against social democracy and directed considerable energy at the problem.[149] Indeed, up to the outbreak of World War I influential senior officers feared, and in some cases hoped, that they might have to suppress social democracy militarily.

Many measures also aimed at the inculcation of patriotism and nationalism. Religious instruction was stressed within the army, and sermons tended to have a high patriotic content. Like the schools, Army officers attempted to instruct soldiers in the glories of Prussian history. The military published and distributed newspapers and books with patriotic themes. Officers were enjoined to attack social democracy directly in teaching sessions with the troops. This apparently proved embarrassing, as officers unaccustomed to talking politics found themselves bested by enlisted men who were. After 1907, the political content shifted to simpler patriotic appeals.

Martin Kitchen doubts the effectiveness of any of this in combating social democracy, and it is certainly true that it did not stop the growth of the Social Democratic party in Germany. But as late as 1911 some 64 percent of

146. Kosok, *Modern Germany*, p. 136.
147. Ibid., p. 135.
148. Craig, *Germany*, pp. 159–160.
149. The account that follows relies largely on Kitchen, *German Officer Corps*, pp. 168–186.

the recruits to the German army came from rural areas, and were unlikely to have had social-democratic sympathies.[150] They were probably quite receptive to army propaganda and it is likely that many returned to their homes well-indoctrinated. The conscripts from urban areas contained the greatest number of social-democratic sympathizers, and these likely remained unconverted. On the other hand, the propaganda may have had some diffuse effect on the patriotic sentiments of the soldiers. Interestingly, Social Democrats who did serve in the army were enjoined by their party to be exemplary soldiers.[151] It is difficult for human beings to pursue seriously the purposes of an organization without coming to identify with it somewhat. "Even many of the older Social Democratic workers, sitting together around their glasses of beer, took pride in relating their military experiences."[152] Social Democrats readily identified backward Russia as the enemy of Germany, and one prominent Social Democratic theorist shared the officer corps' preference for the offensive. And we must remember that in 1914, the socialists marched.[153]

Both regime loyalty and combat effectiveness were motives for the growing nationalist content of German public education, officer education, and in-service indoctrination of conscripts through the outbreak of World War I. Students of the period stress the impact of regime loyalty. The appearance of both motives in Prussia weakens somewhat my argument that military capability was a primary impetus to the spread of nationalism, but the presence of the same nationalist education in France, where regime loyalty was of less immediate concern, preserves the viability of the hypothesis.[154]

The Evolution of Military Technology, 1870–1914

By 1870, major advances in firepower had been achieved over the weapons of the Napoleonic wars. The importance of firepower, particularly in thwarting the old-fashioned bayonet assault, was already quite clear.

---

150. Ibid., pp. 147–148. In 1907, the German socialist leader Bebel observed that about a third of the mobilized German troops would be Social Democratic Party members. Talmon, *The Myth of the Nation and the Vision of Revolution* (Berkeley: University of California Press, 1981), p. 395.
151. Kitchen, *The German Officer Corps*, p. 167.
152. Kosok, *Modern Germany*, p. 136.
153. Talmon, *The Myth of the Nation and the Vision of Revolution*, pp. 109–110.
154. Albisetti, "The debate on secondary school reform," p. 195, notes that the secondary school curricula in the Second Reich and Third Republic were actually quite similar, with both stressing nationalist and anti-socialist themes. During this period, however, a much smaller percentage of both populations attended secondary school.

Developments after 1870 were to be even more profound.[155] Repeating rifles that fired small-calibre bullets impelled by smokeless powder were widely used by 1890. The accuracy, range, rate, and volume of infantry fire increased markedly. But a prone, entrenched, or camouflaged rifleman was now much harder to detect. Second, the true automatic machine gun made its appearance in the late 1880s. Third, "quick-firing" field guns appeared in the late 1890s. Recoil mechanisms made it unnecessary to re-aim the gun after each shot and permitted a firing rate of ten shrapnel shells per minute. A four-gun battery could mow down any cluster of exposed infantry out to five thousand meters.

Many professional military commentators recognized that these developments favored the tactical defender. They also understood more generally that for offensive or defensive action, troops would have to fight in small units, widely dispersed. Command would have to devolve to lower levels. No longer could a single junior platoon lieutenant hope to keep 80 men within sight and sound of his voice, and control their movements in battle. Any platoon so deployed could be annihilated. The Boer War and Russo-Japanese War at the turn of the century confirmed these lessons for many.

But other professional officers, who increasingly came to dominate the European militaries between 1880 and 1914, recoiled from these lessons.[156] While the improvements in firepower were recognized, their tactical implications were denied. Already in the 1880s, French and German military manuals proposed to counter improvements in firepower with a stress on morale and the positive moral effect of the attack. The notion was that the battle was a struggle for moral ascendancy, and that firepower technology could not compensate for the moral advantage that would redound to the side on the attack. Similarly, there was a strong disinclination to accept the utility of dispersal. Officers wanted to keep their men closer together in order to maintain command and order, which were perceived to be necessary to the ultimate establishment of moral ascendancy.

---

155. See Hew Strachan, *European Armies and the Conduct of War* (London: George Allen and Unwin, 1983), pp. 113–119, for these firepower developments.
156. For the following discussion see ibid., pp. 115–117; Bruce I. Gudmundsson, *Stormtroop Tactics: Innovation in the German Army, 1914–1918* (New York: Praeger, 1989), pp. 1–25 on the debate in the German Army; T.H.E. Travers, "Technology, Tactics, and Morale: Jean de Bloch, the Boer War, and British Military Theory, 1900–1914," *Journal of Modern History*, Vol. 51 (June 1979), pp. 264–286, on analogous developments in the British Army; Jack Snyder, *The Ideology of the Offensive: Military Decision Making and the Disasters of 1914* (Ithaca: Cornell University Press, 1984), pp. 63–67, 77–81, on the French Army.

This tactical cult of the offensive reflected the widespread notion among European soldiers that the battlefield was a place of psychological as well as physical struggle, and that the psychological aspects were dominant.[157] But the effort to win the psychological battle did not begin and end with the order to attack; this was merely its most visible and most idiotic manifestation. In France and Prussia (and in Britain as well), the preparation of the individual began earlier. French officers stressed the cohesion believed to arise from a lengthy term of service. French officers unsuccessfully opposed the government's plan to reduce the term of service from three years to two in 1905, and lobbied for restoration of the third year until they achieved success in 1913.[158] Prussia went over to a two-year term in 1893, although some Prussian officers had agreed with their French counterparts. But Prussia's three-year term was traded away for a major expansion in the size of the standing army, necessitated by the budding Franco-Russian alliance.[159]

A direct connection between the increasing lethality of weaponry and state-sponsored nationalism between 1870 and 1914 is difficult to document.[160] Professional officers understood that firepower improvements presented significant new problems that demanded a better-motivated soldier. The long-service solution was gradually lost after 1870, even as firepower improved. The principal professional military proponent of the offensive and its connection to morale, Ferdinand Foch, was prone to characterize future war as "more and more national in its origin and aims, more and more powerful in

---

157. For a general discussion of these problems as they emerged throughout Europe, see Michael Howard, "Men Against Fire, Expectations of War in 1914," in Steven E. Miller, ed. *Military Strategy and the Origins of the First World War: An* International Security *Reader* (Princeton: Princeton University Press, 1985), pp. 41–57.

158. Ralston, *The Army of the Republic*, pp. 301–302, 350–359. The fight to restore the three-year term, however, seems to have been motivated as much, if not more, by a desire to increase the size of the French standing army, as by its moral qualities. Gerd Krumreich argues that more troops were perceived as necessary to protect the forward concentration areas against a German spoiling attack that would wreck the Plan XVII offensive. To protect the plan's secrecy, more ambiguous arguments were made in public, including the long-service cohesion argument. Krumreich, *Armaments and Politics in France on the Eve of the First World War*, trans. Stephen Conn (Warwickshire: Berg, 1984), pp. 44–52, 107–108.

159. Craig, *Germany*, pp. 257–259;

160. This period saw a wholesale emergence of intense nationalism and social-darwinist ideas in public discourse, which scholars trace to diverse causes. See, for example, Bernard Brodie, *War and Politics* (New York: Macmillan, 1973), pp. 262–270; Snyder, *Ideology of the Offensive*; and Stephen Van Evera, "The Cult of the Offensive," in Miller, *Military Strategy*, pp. 58–63. Travers, "Technology, Tactics, and Morale," suggests that British Army officers became exponents of these ideas in part because of their great concern with how they would deal with the new firepower technology without changing the nature of the soldiers recruited.

its means, more and more impassioned."[161] German theorists at the time also argued the connection between combat performance and the morale and commitment of the troops, and stressed the value of patriotism.[162]

Conclusions

Three basic conclusions emerge from this survey of nearly 150 years of military, political, and social developments in Prussia, Germany, and France. First, professional assessments of the potentialities of military technology, compulsory education for an ever-broadening segment of the military manpower pool, the development and promulgation of nationalist ideology, compulsory military service and the mass army, and actual experiences of wartime were closely connected in both countries.

Developments in military technology that favor dispersal on the battlefield prompt a constant concern for the motivation of soldiers. These same developments may make it difficult to rely on lengthy training and lengthy terms of service to create this motivation, since improved weaponry kills these "custom-made" soldiers too fast. Developments in military technology that increase the human costs of war increase the state's propensity to prepare people to pay those costs, and the sponsorship of nationalism is one solution to the problem.

Developments in military technology, organization, or tactics may also increase the military utility of literacy in conscripts; this causes the state to promote mass literacy for reasons of technical military efficiency. The spread of literacy makes it possible for states to train larger armies in peacetime and mobilize them in wartime with greater speed.

---

161. Stefan T. Possony and Etienne Mantoux, "Du Picq and Foch: The French School," in Edward M. Earle, ed. *Makers of Modern Strategy* (Princeton: Princeton University Press, 1971), p. 222, quoting from Ferdinand Foch, *Principles of War*, trans. Hilaire Belloc (New York: 1920), p. 41. See Foch's original, *Des Principes de la Guerre*, 4th ed. (Paris: Berger-Levrault, 1917), pp. 39–40. In a prior passage he connects effective tactical dispersal to nationalist feelings in the troops, and expresses doubts as to whether either long-service professional troops or multi-national armies could successfully practice such tactics; p. 39.
162. Travers, "Technology, Tactics, and Morale," p. 277. See also General Friedrich von Bernhardi, *Germany and the Next War*, trans. Allen Powles (New York: Longmans, 1914), p. 242: "For while the demands which modern war makes have increased in every direction, the term of service has been shortened in order to make enlistment in very great numbers possible. Thus the full consummation of military training cannot be attained unless recruits enter the army well equipped physically and mentally and bringing with them patriotic sentiment worthy of the honourable profession of arms."

Mass literacy also makes soldiers more accessible to propaganda, both as children and as adults, which facilitates the spread of nationalist ideology. The fact of a shared written language and history promulgated in the schools makes nationalist ideology "self-confirming": it becomes true that the members of the group share special traits.

Second, the internal power of these causes is vastly intensified by the pressure of international competition. Neither political elites nor professional officers "embrace" the mass army. To varying degrees, they are driven to it by the exigencies of international competition. The French revolutionaries were forced to innovate by the magnitude of the military challenges they faced. Others were forced to imitate the French success. As each combatant stumbled into ways to improve the mass army "military format," each successive combat demonstrated to others the new tricks to imitate. Literacy of the officers, NCOs, and enlisted personnel was one such trick. Another was motivation through systematic indoctrination into nationalist ideologies, which stressed the uniqueness and inclusiveness of one's own collectivity, relative to the one next door. And yet another was continuing expansion in the sheer size of the mobilized force. These fed on each other, both within boundaries and across them.

Even if one believes that any of these variables is itself dependent *largely* on other causes, they may nonetheless have the consequences I have described. For example, if literacy is promoted for economic reasons, it still has military effects. If the mass army is an historical accident in one country, and if it is effective, it should still promote imitation by others. If nationalism is a consequence of entire social transformations in one society, it nonetheless provides the motive power for the mass army, which others must imitate if they wish to survive. Imitation of the mass army requires literacy and a nationalist ideology, and therefore these elements will travel with the mass army, and thus nationalism will spread with it. More literacy probably increases the ability of armies to absorb new technology, and thus makes them more lethal, causing a greater necessity for tactical dispersal, and the potential for higher casualties, which will need to be replaced. A more literate population also makes the training and organization of very large forces easier, facilitating mass mobilization.

Third, the argument sheds some light on two persistent mysteries about nationalism and conflict. Nationalism is often posited as a cause of great wars. But the closer we look at the great wars they are often said to have caused, the more complicated the relationship appears. This is because nationalism is as often a consequence of conflict as it is a cause. Leaders use nationalism to mobilize public support for military preparation and sacrifices. When war seems imminent, for any reason, the intensity of propaganda increases. The same is true when wars last for any length of time. Thus it will often be difficult to show that nationalism caused any conflict, because it will generally be accompanied and accentuated by other causes of the conflict. (It may also intensify these other causes.)

The speed and intensity with which nationalism can emerge from apparent dormancy is another mystery. My theory suggests that it is a rational response, not only by elites but also by followers, whenever the geostrategic conditions outlined above seem to hold. States or stateless groups, drifting into competition for whatever reason, will quickly turn to the reinforcement of national identity because of its potency as a military resource. And since states cannot wait for trouble to prepare their citizens for war, much of the preparation is "hidden away" in the schools or in the military experience of conscripts. It is hidden away in the home in long repressed multi-ethnic societies such as Yugoslavia. This material is there for leaders to tap with more open and ubiquitous means of communications in times of threat and crisis.

TASKS FOR FURTHER RESEARCH

The preceding discussion suggests that a number of critical issues remain. The first task is a more extensive examination of the plausibility of the theory. The remaining military competitors in Europe during this period should be subjected to a similar analysis.

A structural realist would argue that the propensity of states to engage in these activities should vary with the threats that they face. States protected by high mountains or deep moats should be less inclined to opt for mass armies, and less dependent on nationalism. States without powerful neighbors depend less on mass armies, and hence depend less on nationalism. States defended by nuclear weapons should be less nationalistic.

In contrast, nationalism should be more intense in continental states with topographically gentle borders, which therefore need their ground forces more. States with powerful neighbors depend more on their armies, and should be more inclined towards nationalism. Where enhanced firepower makes for high casualties, the incentives to purvey nationalism also go up.

It may be that the theory as posited thus far is too limited. Perhaps it applies more generally to any security competition that involves "mass mobilization," that is, requires of society a large-scale financial, organizational, and industrial effort to produce a great military force of any kind, on sea or even in the air as well as on land.

Another line of inquiry would take the theory out of Europe to hold cultural influences constant and thus to improve the focus on the causal influence of the instrumental factors that I have highlighted.

But since many of the non-European conflicts that one could study have occurred among nation-states where socio-economic developments roughly parallel those of late nineteenth-century Europe, this still would not permit an assessment of the independent power of security variables relative to socio-economic ones. Thus a careful search must be mounted for those modern nation-states that find themselves in difficult non-nuclear security competitions. Are they driven to "create" nationalism? There are few such cases. Israel suggests itself. A systematic comparison of the military organizations of the non-nuclear European Cold-War neutrals, Finland, Sweden, and Switzerland, might prove useful. Ukraine may prove an illuminating case if it relinquishes its nuclear weapons and a rivalry with Russia emerges.

Although I have advanced a theory of nationalism based largely on international military competition, clearly domestic factors also affect the development of nationalism. An important if perhaps intractable task is to weigh domestic social, political, and economic influences relative to strategic influences. It is clear, for example, that imitation of the mass army lends itself to the reduction of social inequality, perhaps even to democratization.[163] Where elites do not wish to democratize, powerful tensions arise between the dictates of external and internal survival. Generally, I believe elites will have strong incentives to adopt mass armies and purvey literacy and nationalist ideology when external events warrant. How the tensions between external and internal constraints are resolved may influence the specific content of the nationalist ideology that is purveyed by an elite. And sometimes those tensions cannot be resolved; inferior mass armies will take the field and suffer defeat. These defeats can have major social consequences.

Finally, of course, an examination of the question I have largely begged is essential. How might nationalism cause war? My preliminary hypothesis is that nationalism is a cause of intense widespread public concern for national security, and a public predisposition to accept the judgments of civilian or

---

163. Andreski, *Military Organization and Society*, pp. 73–74.

military "threat inflators" of military dangers from abroad. Since the professional military, in particular, is likely to favor solutions to perceived threats that stress the utility of offensive doctrines and plans, a pressure is created for the adoption of national military policies that will cause or exacerbate conflicts with neighbors. The defensive impulses of nationalism may thus help cause international "spirals" of insecurity.[164]

I would go further and speculate that the mobilization of nationalism for offensive war is dependent to some degree on the intensity of the "security dilemma," the frequent condition in international politics where states cannot make themselves secure without making others insecure. Thus aggressive nationalism is to be most often found in nation-states that have difficulty ensuring their national security through largely defensive military means.

It is thus reasonable to examine the course of state-sponsored nationalism in formerly nationalistic nation-states that have left conventional "mass mobilization" military competitions behind them. It is noteworthy that many Western European states have systematically endeavored to purge national stereotypes from their educational systems.[165] The theory I have outlined suggests that the U.S. nuclear umbrella and the devaluation of non-nuclear forces in the East-West struggle in Europe was a critical permissive condition for the decline of nationalist history. If so, and if one also believes that nationalism is an independent cause of conflict, then nuclear disarmament may not be an unalloyed good, and nuclear proliferation may not always be bad, since it is conventional competitions that depend on the greatest reserves of human courage and commitment.

---

164. A brief if florid version of this argument is found in Carleton Hayes, *Essays on Nationalism* (New York: Macmillan, 1928), pp. 187–195.
165. See, e.g., Paul Kennedy, "The Decline of Nationalistic History in the West, 1900–1970," *Journal of Contemporary History*, Vol. 18, No. 1 (January 1973), pp. 77–100.

Ethnic Nationalism and International Conflict

The Case of Serbia

V.P. Gagnon, Jr.

Does ethnicity affect the international system? What are the causes of violent conflict along ethnic lines? Since the collapse of the Soviet Union and the outbreak of war in the Balkans, these questions have seized the attention of international relations scholars and policy makers.[1] In the former Yugoslavia, war conducted in the name of ethnic solidarity has destroyed the Yugoslav state, leveled entire cities, and resulted in hundreds of thousands of casualties and millions of refugees.[2] It has also brought NATO's first out-of-area actions, the largest United Nations peacekeeping operation in history, and the very real possibility of war spreading to other parts of the Balkans.

Is the Yugoslav case a look into the future of international relations? Are ethnically-mixed regions in the post–Cold War era inevitably the sites of violent conflict that will spill over into the international arena? If so, the only apparent solution would be the creation of ethnically pure states; yet the greatest threats to peace in this century have tended to come from those regions in which partitions along ethnic or religious lines have taken place.[3] This paradox is a

V.P. Gagnon, Jr., is an SSRC-MacArthur Foundation post-doctoral fellow in Peace and Security in a Changing World in the Peace Studies Program, Cornell University. In the current academic year, he is a visiting scholar at Zagreb University in Croatia and Belgrade University in Serbia.

An earlier version of this paper was presented at the September 1992 APSA meeting in Chicago. For helpful suggestions and criticisms, thanks to Dominique Caouette, Roger Petersen, Liz Wishnick, and Peter Katzenstein. Funding for revisions of this paper were provided by the Social Science Research Council–MacArthur Foundation Post-doctoral Fellowship in Peace and Security in a Changing World, and the Department of State Title VIII program in Russian and East European Studies, administered by the Hoover Institution, Stanford University.

1. See, for example, John Mearsheimer, "Back to the Future: Instability in Europe After the Cold War," *International Security*, Vol. 15, No. 1 (Summer 1990), pp. 5–56; Stephen Van Evera, "Hypotheses on Nationalism and War," *International Security*, Vol. 18, No. 4 (Spring 1994), pp. 5–39; Jack Snyder, "The New Nationalism," in Richard Rosecrance and Arthur A. Stein, eds., *The Domestic Bases of Grand Strategy* (Ithaca, N.Y.: Cornell University Press, 1993), pp. 179–200; Michael E. Brown, ed., *Ethnic Conflict and International Security* (Princeton, N.J.: Princeton University Press, 1993).
2. The best English-language sources on the Yugoslav wars include Lenard Cohen, *Broken Bonds: The Disintegration of Yugoslavia* (Boulder, Colo.: Westview, 1993); James Gow, *Legitimacy and the Military: The Yugoslav Crisis* (New York: St. Martin's Press, 1992); Rabia Ali and Lawerence Lifshutz, eds., *Why Bosnia? Writings on the Balkan War* (Stony Creek, Conn.: Pamphleteers Press, 1993).
3. Examples include Greece-Turkey (1922), Ireland (1921), the Sudetenland (1938), India-Pakistan (1947), South African apartheid (1948), Palestine (1948), and Cyprus (1974). John Mearsheimer and Robert Pape, "The Answer: A Partition Plan for Bosnia," *The New Republic*, June 14, 1993, pp. 22–28, argue for partition of Bosnia-Hercegovina as the best solution to the current conflict.

International Security, Winter 1994/95 (Vol. 19, No. 3)

major challenge to international peace and stability, especially given the growing number of violent conflicts described and justified in terms of ethnicity, culture, and religion.

Despite the urgency of this issue, theories of international relations have until quite recently not addressed the question of ethnic nationalist conflict. The main challenge is conceptual: how to establish the causal link between ethnic nationalist sentiment and interstate violence.[4] Existing approaches tend to assume either that ethnic sentiment itself is the main cause of violent conflict, or that external security concerns lead national decision-makers to inflame such sentiment.[5] In this paper I argue that such violent conflict is caused not by ethnic sentiments, nor by external security concerns, but rather by the dynamics of within-group conflict.[6] The external conflict, although justified and described in terms of relations with other ethnic groups and taking place within that context, has its main goal within the state, among members of the same ethnicity.[7]

---

4. One of the shortcomings of the literature on ethnic and nationalist conflict is the lack of a precise conceptual definition. The term "nationalism" (or "hypernationalism") is commonly used, either implicitly or explicitly, to mean simultaneously (and confusingly) ethnic national sentiments or beliefs; political rhetoric that appeals to ethnic nationalist sentiment; and violent conflict that is described and justified in terms of ethnicity. To avoid this confusion, and to clarify the dependent variable (violent conflict, rather than ethnic sentiment) "ethnic nationalism" in this article refers to the rhetoric by which political actors describe, justify, and explain policies with reference to the interest of the "nation" defined in ethnic terms. It does not refer to sentiment or belief. This definition also makes clear that the root causes of a conflict that is described as ethnic may have little to do with ethnicity *per se,* and thereby points to the questions that must be answered to understand ethnic nationalist conflict: when do political elites resort to conflictual definitions of ethnic national interest? When and how do such definitions come to dominate the policies of the state? What are the goals of this conflictual behavior?

5. Examples of international relations works which look to ethnic sentiment as the key to understanding the link between nationalism and foreign policy include Alexis Heraclides, *The Self Determination of Minorities in International Politics* (Portland, Ore.: Cass, 1991); William Bloom, *Personal Identity, National Identity and International Relations* (London: Cambridge University Press, 1990). For those that look to external security concerns, see Mearsheimer, "Back to the Future"; and Barry Posen, "Nationalism, the Mass Army, and Military Power," *International Security,* Vol. 18, No. 2 (Fall 1993), pp. 80–124. The literature on ethnic conflict also tends to explain violent conflict as a response to external threats to or opportunities for the ethnic group *vis-à-vis* other groups. The most prominent such work is Donald Horowitz, *Ethnic Groups in Conflict* (Berkeley: University of California Press, 1985).

6. One work that explores the domestic roots of conflictual nationalist policy is Snyder, "The New Nationalism." For a review of earlier works that look at domestic sources of international conflict, see Jack Levy, "The Diversionary Theory of War: A Critique," in Manus I. Midlarsky, ed., *Handbook of War Studies* (Boston: Unwin Hyman, 1989), pp. 259–288.

7. This type of conflict is one example of the more general phenomenon of violent conflict in the international arena which is described and justified by national leaders in terms of ideas such as religion, class, and culture, as well as ethnicity. Given the extent to which international conflicts have been justified not in purely security terms but rather in such ideational terms, identifying the causal link between such ideas and violent conflicts carried out in their names is clearly of importance.

I argue that violent conflict along ethnic cleavages is provoked by elites in order to create a domestic political context where ethnicity is the only politically relevant identity. It thereby constructs the individual interest of the broader population in terms of the threat to the community defined in ethnic terms. Such a strategy is a response by ruling elites to shifts in the structure of domestic political and economic power: by constructing individual interest in terms of the threat to the group, endangered elites can fend off domestic challengers who seek to mobilize the population against the status quo, and can better position themselves to deal with future challenges.

The dominant realist approach in international relations tells us very little about violent conflict along ethnic lines, and cannot explain the Yugoslav case. Focusing on external security concerns, this approach argues that conflictual behavior in the name of ethnic nationalism is a response to external threats to the state (or to the ethnic group).[8] The general literature on ethnic conflict likewise uses the "ethnic group" as actor and looks to factors outside the group to explain intergroup conflict.[9] But in fact, the Serbian leadership from 1987 onward actively created rather than responded to threats to Serbs by purposefully provoking and fostering the outbreak of conflict along ethnic lines, especially in regions of Yugoslavia with histories of good inter-ethnic relations.[10]

Although the Serbian leadership itself has justified its policies in terms of an external security threat to Serbia and Serbs, over the past thirty years a significant part of the Serbian elite has advocated a very different strategy based on democratic pluralism, peaceful negotiation of political conflict, and modernization of the Serbian economy.[11] This strategy would probably have been

---

8. Mearsheimer, "Back to the Future"; Posen, "Nationalism, the Mass Army, and Military Power." For a realist approach that takes ethnic groups rather than states as actors, see Barry Posen, "The Security Dilemma and Ethnic Conflict," *Survival,* Vol. 35, No. 1 (Spring 1993), pp. 27–47.

9. Horowitz, *Ethnic Groups in Conflict*; and "Democracy in Divided Societies," *Journal of Democracy,* Vol. 4, No. 4 (October 1993), pp. 18–38.

10. In both Croatia and Bosnia, forces allied with Belgrade went to great lengths to destroy the long-standing harmony between Serbs and non-Serbs. Although the Croatian regime had resorted to nationalist rhetoric and actions worrisome to local Serbs, both sides were willing to negotiate over key issues until Belgrade began terrorizing moderate Serbs. This strategy was repeated in Bosnia. In Serbian-controlled regions of Croatia and Bosnia, the extremists in power have silenced and even killed dissenting Serbs. See *NIN,* November 8, 1991, p. 15; *Vreme,* November 4, 1991, pp. 12–15; Milorad Pupovac, head of the Zagreb-based moderate Serbian Democratic Forum, in *Vreme,* October 21, 1991, pp. 12–14; Peter Maass, "In Bosnia, 'Disloyal Serbs' Share Plight of Opposition," *Washington Post,* August 24, 1992, p. 1.

11. For example, Latinka Perović and Marko Nikezić, heads of the Serbian party in the late 1960s and early 1970s [see Perović's *Zatvaranje kruga: Ishod političkog rascepa u SKJ 1971/1972* (Sarajevo: Svjetlost, 1991); and Slavoljub Dukić, *Slom Srpskih Liberala* (Belgrade: Filip Višnjić, 1990)]. On the war in Croatia, nationalist opposition party leader Vuk Drašković from the summer of 1991

much more successful and much less costly than conflict in ensuring the interests of Serbs and Serbia, even if the goal had been an independent, enlarged Serbia.[12] It is difficult to argue that an objective security threat exists when even nationalistically-oriented elites in Serbia denounce the war and claim there was no need for it.

Another common explanation for violent conflicts along ethnic lines, particularly for the Yugoslav case, is that ancient ethnic hatreds have burst to the surface.[13] But this too is unsupported by the evidence: in fact, Yugoslavia never saw the kind of religious wars seen in Western and Central Europe, and Serbs and Croats never fought before this century;[14] intermarriage rates were quite

---

denounced the war in Croatia (*Vreme*, November 4, 1992, pp. 9–11; *Danas*, February 18, 1992). Drašković has also denounced the Bosnian war as harmful to Serbs (see his speech to "Congress of Serbian Intellectuals," May 1994); Milan Panić, first prime minister of the new Serbian-dominated Yugoslavia, also criticized the war ("Four Immediate Tasks," *Review of International Affairs*, no. 1005–6 (June 1-July 1, 1992), pp. 4–6.

12. Indeed, the policies of the Serbian leadership and its allies have alienated the 33 percent of the Serbian republic's population that is non-Serb, thus decreasing its internal security. The Croatian and Bosnian territories that have been gained in the process are among the poorest regions of the former Yugoslavia, with very low rates of education and income, and are for the most part strategically very difficult to defend, since they are connected with Serbian-contiguous lands only by a very thin corridor. The atrocities against and expulsions of most of the very large number of non-Serbs—who before the war made up about 55 percent of the population of the Croatian and Bosnian territories held by Serbian forces in mid-1994—have produced enormous antagonisms and created a situation in which a long-term strategy of low-level guerilla warfare is quite likely. Figures derived from the 1991 Population Census of Bosnia-Hercegovina, cited in Stjepko Golubić, Susan Campbell and Thomas Golubić, "How not to divide the indivisible," in *Why Bosnia*, pp. 230–231; and the 1991 census in Croatia, *Popis Stanovništva 1991* (Zagreb: Republički zavod za statistiku, 1992).

13. See, for example, Robert Kaplan, "Ground Zero," *New Republic*, August 2, 1993, pp. 15–16, "A Reader's Guide to the Balkans," *New York Times Book Review*, April 18, 1994; "History's Cauldron," *Atlantic Monthly*, June 1991, pp. 92–104; and Robert Kaplan, *Balkan Ghosts: A Journey Through History* (New York: St. Martin's Press, 1993). See also Elizabeth Drew, "Letter from Washington," *New Yorker*, July 6, 1992, p. 70.

14. On the history of relations between Serbs and Croats in Croatia before this century, see, for example, Wolfgang Kessler, *Politik, Kultur und Gesellschaft in Kroatien und Slawonien in der ersten Hälfte des 19. Jahrhunderts* (Munich: R. Oldenbourg, 1981); Sergei A. Romanenko, "National Autonomy in Russia and Austro-Hungary," in *Nationalism and Empire* (New York: St. Martin's Press, 1992); Ivo Banac, *The National Question in Yugoslavia: Origins, History, Politics* (Ithaca, N.Y.: Cornell University Press, 1984), p. 410. On cooperation in the first Yugoslavia between Serb and Croat parties in Croatia against Belgrade, see Ljubo Boban, *Svetozar Pribićević u opoziciji (1928–1936)* (Zagreb: Institut za hrvatsku povijest, 1973); Drago Roksandić, *Srbi u Hrvatskoj od 15. stoljeća do naših dana* (Zagreb: Vjesnik, 1991). During World War II, the ruling Ustaša forces in the puppet Independent State of Croatia perpetrated massive atrocities against Serbs and others; they were a marginal party imposed by the Germans and Italians after the highly popular Croatian Peasant Party refused to collaborate. The Ustaša policy of genocide against Serbs, and its use of Muslims to carry out this policy in Bosnia, combined with its authoritarian repression of Croat and Muslim dissent, rapidly alienated most of the state's population. Fikreta Jelić-Butić, *Ustaše i Nezavisna Država Hrvatska* (Zagreb: Sveučilišna Naklada Liber, 1978). And while the Serbian nationalist Četnik

high in those ethnically-mixed regions that saw the worst violence;[15] and sociological polling as late as 1989–90 showed high levels of tolerance, especially in these mixed regions.[16] Although some tensions existed between nationalities and republics, and the forcible repression of overt national sentiment added to the perception on all sides that the existing economic and political system was unjust, the evidence indicates that, notwithstanding claims to the contrary by nationalist politicians and historians in Serbia and Croatia, "ethnic hatreds" are not the essential, primary cause of the Yugoslav conflict.

In the following sections I lay out an alternative theoretical framework and hypotheses about ethnic nationalist conflict that look to internal dynamics to explain external conflict. I then apply this to the specific case of Yugoslavia, concentrating on five episodes in which elites within the Serbian republic resorted to conflictual strategies described and justified in terms of the interest of the Serbian people.[17] In the conclusion I look at how this framework can illuminate other cases, and what it says about strategies for conflict resolution.

Domestic Power and International Conflict: A Theoretical Framework

This section lays out a framework and proposes some hypotheses about the link between ethnicity (and other ideas such as religion, culture, class) and international conflict. It is based on the following four premises: first, the domestic arena is of central concern for state decision-makers and ruling elites because it is the location of the bases of their power. Ruling elites will thus

---

forces perpetrated atrocities against Muslims in Bosnia, most Serbs in Croatia and Bosnia joined the multi-ethnic communist partisan forces rather than the purely nationalistic Četniks. Thus the image of "ethnic groups" in conflict even during World War II must be seen as part of an ideological construct in which "ethnic groups" are portrayed as actors by nationalist politicians and historians.

15. For example, throughout the 1980s, 29 percent of Serbs living in Croatia married Croat spouses. *Demografska statistika* (Belgrade: Savezni zavod za statistiku), 1979–1989 (annual), Table 5–3.

16. Randy Hodson, Garth Massey and Dusko Sekulic, "National Tolerance in the Former Yugoslavia," *Global Forum Series Occasional Papers*, No. 93-01.5 (Durham, N.C.: Center for International Studies, Duke University, December 1993).

17. This article represents part of a broader work that looks at the dynamics of ethnic nationalist conflicts in other Yugoslav republics as well. The Serbian case, however, merits the most attention because the actions of its leadership from the mid-1980s onward have driven the current conflict and created nationalist backlashes in other Yugoslav republics, and because the *de facto* alliance between the Serbian leadership and the Yugoslav Army has given Serbia a massive military and thus political advantage. The Croatian leadership since 1990 has carried out similarly conflictual policies in the name of Croatian ethnic nationalism; but these policies can only be understood within the context of the Serbian strategy.

focus on preserving these domestic bases of power. Second, persuasion is the most effective and least costly means of influence in domestic politics. One particularly effective means of persuasion is to appeal to the interest of politically relevant actors as members of a group. Third, within the domestic arena, appeals for support must be directed to material and nonmaterial values of the relevant target audiences—those actors whose support is necessary to gain and maintain power. Ideas such as ethnicity, religion, culture, and class therefore play a key role as instruments of power and influence, in particular because of their centrality to legitimacy and authority.

Finally, conflict over ideas and how they are framed is an essential characteristic of domestic politics, since the result determines the way political arguments can be made, how interests are defined, and the values by which political action must be justified. The challenge for elites is therefore to define the interest of the collective in a way that coincides with their own power interests. In other words, they must express their interests in the "language" of the collective interest.

These premises lead to the following hypotheses about the conditions under which national leaders will resort to conflictual policies described and justified in terms of threats to the ethnic nation.

First, if ruling elites face challenger elites who seek to mobilize the majority of the politically relevant population in a way that threatens the rulers' power or the political or economic structure on which their power is based, the ruling elites will be willing to respond by undertaking policies that are costly to society as a whole, even if the costs are imposed from outside. Behavior *vis-à-vis* the outside may thus have its main goal in the domestic arena. If the most effective way to achieve domestic goals involves provoking conflict with the outside, then, as long as the net benefit to the threatened elites is positive, they will be willing to undertake such a strategy.

Second, threatened elites will respond to domestic threats in a way that minimizes the danger to the bases of their domestic power. They must gain the support, or neutralize the opposition, of the majority. But if domestic legitimacy precludes the massive use of force against political opponents and depends on respecting certain political forms and "rules of the game," elites are circumscribed in how they can respond to domestic threats. One effective strategy in this context is to shift the focus of political debate away from issues where ruling elites are most threatened—for example, proposed changes in the structure of domestic economic or political power—toward other issues, defined in cultural or ethnic terms, that appeal to the interest of the majority in non-economic terms.[18] But ethnicity or culture in and of itself does not determine policies; the interest of the collective defined in ethnic terms can be defined in any number of ways.

Competing elites will thus focus on defining the collective interest by drawing selectively on traditions and mythologies and in effect constructing particular versions of that interest. The elite faction that succeeds in identifying itself with the interest of the collective, and in defining the collective interest in a way that maximizes its own ability to achieve its goals, wins an important victory. It has framed the terms of political discourse and debate, and thus the limits of legitimate policy, in a way that may delegitimize or make politically irrelevant the interests of challenger elites and prevent them from mobilizing the population on specific issues or along certain lines.

Third, in this competition over defining the group interest, images of and alleged threats from the outside world can play a key role in this domestic political strategy. A strategy relying on such threatening images can range from citing an alleged threat to provoking conflict in order to create the image of threat; conflict can range from political to military. Since political mobilization occurs most readily around grievances, in order to shift the political agenda, elites must find issues of grievance unrelated to those issues on which they are most threatened, and construct a political context in which those issues become the center of political debate. It is at this point that focus on the interest of the group *vis-à-vis* the outside world proves to be useful. If the grievance or threat is to the collective rather than to individuals, it creates an image of potentially very high costs imposed on the group regardless of the direct impact on individuals. It therefore defines the individual's interest in terms of a particular threat to the group. Moreover, if the threat or grievance is outside the direct experience of the majority of politically relevant actors, there is no way to verify whether the grievance is real, or indeed whether it is being addressed or not. Such a strategy also becomes in effect a self-fulfilling prophecy, as the reactions provoked by the conflictual policies are pointed to as proof of the original contention. Thus is created a grievance that, if violence is involved, is sure to continue for years.

The effect of creating an image of threat to the group is to place the interest of the group above the interest of individuals. This political strategy is crucial

---

18. On agenda setting as a power strategy, see P. Bachrach and M.S. Baratz, "The Two Faces of Power," *American Political Science Review*, Vol. 56, No. 4 (1962), pp. 947–952.

because, in the case of aggressive nationalism and images of threats to the ethnic nation, it creates a context where ethnicity is all that counts, and where other interests are no longer relevant. In addition, such an image of overwhelming threat to the group delegitimizes the dissent of those challengers who attempt to appeal to members of the relevant group as individuals or who appeal to identities other than the "legitimate" identity in a "legitimate" way, especially if dissenters can be portrayed as selfish and uninterested in the well-being of the group, and can therefore be branded as traitors.[19]

Thus, by using a strategy of agenda-setting to shift the focus of political attention toward the very pressing issue of threats to the group from the outside, and by actively provoking and creating such threats, threatened elites can maximize the domestic benefits while minimizing the costs imposed on their own supporters, and thus the danger to their own power bases.

Fourth, in this domestic political context, information and control over information play a vital role. Control or ownership of mass media, especially television, therefore bestows an enormous political advantage where the wider population is involved in politics, and is a key element in the success of such a strategy.

Fifth, elites will tend to define the relevant collective in ethnic terms when past political participation has been so defined; when such a definition is encouraged by international circumstances; and when these elites are seen as credible defenders of ethnic interests and concerns. Clearly, for grievances or threats to the group to be politically relevant, a majority of actors must be able to be identified as members of that group. That does not mean, however, that their main or primary identity must be to the group; in fact, people have multiple identities and such identities are highly contextual. The key is to make a particular identity, and a specific definition of that identity, the only relevant or legitimate one in political contexts. This identity will be closely related to the ideas of culture, ethnicity, and religion that the majority of the population values. Ideas such as ethnicity have an impact on the international arena precisely because they are so central to domestic power.

Since conflictual policies tend to take place along these previously politicized lines of identity, they also tend to create the impression of continuity between

---

19. This strategy is thus especially effective in discrediting those who appeal to liberal democratic ideology, which defines the collective interest of the citizenry as best ensured by ensuring the rights and well-being of the individual.

past conflicts and current ones, and indeed are specifically portrayed in this way. But there is nothing natural about ethnic interest that requires it to be defined in a conflictual way.

Sixth, the larger and more immediate the threat to the ruling elite, the more willing it is to take measures which, while preserving its position in the short term, may bring high costs in the longer term; in effect it discounts future costs. The intensity and thus costliness of a conflictual strategy depends on the degree of the threat to the old elites. These factors include, first, the time frame of the threat to power. While the conflictual policies may over the long run result in an untenable position and ultimately undermine their bases of political influence, elites' political behavior in a situation of immediate threat is motivated by that threat and by the concern for keeping the power in the short run, which at least leaves open the possibility of their survival in the long run. This also gives them time to fashion alternative strategies for dealing with change, including shifting the bases of their power.

Also, the strength of the challenger elites also affects the immediacy of the threat. If the challenger elites are successfully mobilizing the majority of the politically relevant population against the status quo, ruling elites will feel quite threatened and be willing to incur high costs to preserve their position. Threatened elites will also attempt to recruit other elites, at the local and regional as well as national levels, to prevent such a mobilization.

A further factor is the costs to the threatened elites of losing power; that is, the resources and fallback positions they have if change does take place. If they have everything to lose and nothing to gain, they will be much more likely to undertake conflictual policies costly to society as a whole than if they have resources that would allow them to remain involved in power to some degree.

For the conflictual strategy to include the use of military force, especially against other states, the status-quo coalition must include a dominant faction within the military.

Seventh, threatened elites may use marginal neo-fascist parties as part of their conflictual strategy in conditions where the wider population is included in the political system. Every country has small extremist groups whose mainstay is ethnic hatred and violence; their motivations may be political, personal, or psychological. But the very existence of this option is clearly not enough for it to come to dominate state policy. An advantage of giving neo-fascists media coverage and weapons is that by bringing extremists into the political realm, the right becomes the "center"; a statement that ten years earlier may have been unacceptably racist may be perceived after this kind of strategy as relatively moderate.[20] By making issues of ethnic nationalism the center of political discourse, this strategy also turns those who are archconservatives on economic issues into moderate centrists.

Eighth, internal costs of a conflictual strategy are closely monitored, since they must be outweighed by benefits. Of particular importance is the need to prevent popular mobilization against costs of the conflictual external strategy. While conflict remains in the realm of political rhetoric, it may have great support among the population, since it is basically costless. But if military conflict is involved, the costs to the general population rapidly start to mount.[21] Conflict will be undertaken with an eye toward minimizing the costs for those parts of the populations which are key for support, and will therefore tend to be provoked outside the borders of the elite's power base, with great efforts taken to prevent war from spilling over to the domestic territory. Thus, in the Soviet case anti-reform conservatives provoked violent ethnic conflict outside of Russia, in Moldova, Georgia, and the Baltics; in the Yugoslav case armed conflict has not taken place within Serbia itself, and the Croatian conservatives' conflictual strategy affected mainly central Bosnia, rather than Croatia.

Of course, if material conditions deteriorate enough and if the discrepancy between the interest of the collective group and the interest of the status quo power elite becomes great enough, challenger elites may successfully lead the wider population to revolt against the power structure. In this case members of the old elite may jump on the bandwagon of the new elites who lead such revolutionary revolts.

Finally, external costs are also key. Such a strategy is most likely when the potential international costs, in terms of how they would affect the status-quo elites' domestic power position, are minimal. But if the cost of external reaction were to threaten elements of the status-quo coalition, they might defect, since losses at the hands of domestic elites could be less than at the hands of external foes, especially if challenger elites were willing to offer a deal to the defectors. This strategy will thus be very sensitive to the kinds of costs it provokes from the outside.

---

20. See Anna Marie Smith, *New Right Discourse in Race and Sexuality: Britain 1968–1990* (New York: Cambridge University Press, 1994).

21. Despite the assumption that ethnic political mobilization inevitably pushes politics towards extremism (referred to as "ethnic outbidding" by Horowitz, *Ethnic Groups in Conflict*, p. 348), there is in fact little evidence of a natural inevitable progression from ethnic mobilization to violent ethnic conflict. See V.P. Gagnon, Jr., "Ethnic Conflict as a Political Demobilizer," forthcoming.

This type of conflictual policy thus comes to dominate some states or regions and not others, depending on the degree of threat to the existing power structure and the size of the coalition (at both national and regional levels) of those within the power elite threatened by change. If a challenge to the existing power structure takes place in such a way that most of the old elite perceives a way out, either by cooptation into the new system or by being permitted to retain some privileges and benefits, a coalition will probably not be strong enough to impose a costly conflictual strategy as state policy. It may nevertheless incite conflict and violence in the hopes of gaining wider support. Such conflict takes the form of violence along ethnic lines when the wider population is involved in political decision making, and when political participation in the past has been defined in ethnic terms.

The Case of Serbia

The violent conflict along ethnic lines in the former Yugoslavia was a purposeful and rational strategy planned by those most threatened by changes to the structure of economic and political power, changes being advocated in particular by reformists within the ruling Serbian communist party. A wide coalition—conservatives in the Serbian party leadership, local and regional party elites who would be most threatened by such changes, orthodox Marxist intellectuals, nationalist writers, and parts of the Yugoslav army—joined together to provoke conflict along ethnic lines. This conflict created a political context where individual interest was defined not in terms of economic well-being, but as the survival of the Serbian people. The conservatives' original goal was to recentralize Yugoslavia in order to crush reformist trends throughout the country, but especially in Serbia itself. By 1990, in a changed international context and with backlashes against their centralization strategy in other republics, the conservative coalition moved to destroy the Yugoslav state and create a new, Serbian-majority state. By provoking conflict along ethnic lines, this coalition deflected demands for radical change and allowed the ruling elite to reposition itself and survive in a way that would have been unthinkable in the old Yugoslavia, where only 39 percent of the population was Serb.

Serbian conservatives relied on the particular idea of ethnicity in their conflictual strategy because political participation and legitimation in this region historically was constructed in such terms. From the nineteenth century, the great powers used the standard of national (usually ethnically-defined) self-determination to decide whether a territory merited recognition as a sovereign state—a practice that continues today. Those elites who could make the best case for representing the interests of an ethnic group could increase their power *vis-à-vis* the domestic arena by being internationally recognized as the representative of their ethnic or national group.[22] In Eastern and Central Europe this factor reinforced the Ottoman, Romanov, and Habsburg empires' definitions of political participation in terms of religion in the first two cases and language in the latter, and the subsequent construction of politicized identities in the nineteenth century.[23] The Serbian national myth, molded in the struggle against the Ottoman Turks and in the expansion of the Serbian state in the nineteenth and early twentieth centuries, played a central role in Yugoslav politics between 1918 and 1941, and remained important for the communist partisans, who relied on popular support during World War II.[24] The ethnic national bases of the Yugoslav republics was the result of this wartime need for popular political support, and was maintained as more than a façade after the 1948 break with the Soviet Union again forced the communists to rely on some level of popular support. This emphasis on ethnicity was reinforced by a system of ethnic "keys" within each republic which determined the distribution of certain positions by ethnic identity according to the proportion of each group in the republic's population.[25] This political reification of ethnicity, along with the suppression of expressions of ethnic sentiment, combined to reinforce the historical construction of political identity in terms of ethnic identity, and made ethnic issues politically relevant when the political system opened up to include the wider population.

---

22. For example, arguments about carving up the Ottoman Empire's European territories were made in terms of "ethnic territories" despite the very ethnically intermixed nature of those territories.

23. On the Romanov Empire's construction of national identity, see John Slocum, "The Boundaries of National Identity: Religion, Language, and Nationality Politics in Late Imperial Russia," Ph.D. dissertation, University of Chicago, 1993; on the Ottomans, Kemal Karpat, "Millets and Nationality: The Roots of the Incongruity of Nation and State in the Post-Ottoman Era," in Benjamin Braude and Bernard Lewis, eds., *Christians and Jews in the Ottoman Empire: The Functioning of a Plural Society*, Vol. 1 (New York: Holmes & Meier, 1982), pp. 141–169; on Hungary, Benedict Anderson, *Imagined Communities* (London: Verso, 1991), pp. 101–109.

24. The relation to religious identity is a complex issue, and is related to the fact that in traditional Serbian national mythology, born in the fight against the Ottomans, the Muslim Turks are seen as the ultimate enemy. Although religion *per se* was minimally relevant to interpersonal relations in Yugoslavia before the most recent wars, as part of the Serbian national mythology it was drawn upon in a selective way to the political ends of demonizing Albanians and Slavic Muslims.

25. On the ways in which socialist regimes reinforced the relevance of ethnic identity, see Katherine Verdery, "Nationalism and National Sentiment in Post-socialist Romania," *Slavic Review*, Vol. 52, No. 2 (Summer 1993), pp. 179–203. A similar process was seen in India, where colonial powers, drawing on real or sometimes mythic differences, politicized cultural difference and played groups off against each other. Paul Brass, *Ethnicity and Nationalism: Theory and Comparison* (Sage: New Delhi, 1991).

In addition, the rhetoric of threats to the ethnic nation was available to Serbian conservatives in a way that it was not in other republics, in part because the Serbian party was one of the few that was ethnically homogeneous enough that such a strategy would not automatically alienate a significant portion of the party membership. The Serbian republic (even without its provinces) also had regional differences in economic development that were more extreme and significant than in any other republic. Thus because liberals were stronger, conservatives entrenched in some underdeveloped regions were also more threatened; however, they had a grassroots base upon which to rely for support. Serbia's conservatives were also well-placed to oppose change, given Serbia's importance in the Yugoslav federation and the frequent congruence of interests between Serbian conservatives and conservative elements in the Yugoslav army.

Five episodes are described below in which conservative forces, especially those in Serbia, were threatened with the radical restructuring of political and economic power. In order to test the hypotheses laid out above, each section looks at the threat to the conservatives and the status quo; their responses; and the effect of those responses.

1960S: THREATS TO THE STATUS QUO

In the early 1960s, in response to an increasingly dysfunctional economic system, reformists in the Yugoslav party leadership, with Tito's support, began a radical restructuring of the Yugoslav political and economic system. At the local level the 1965 reform was a direct attack on party bureaucrats in enterprises as well as those in local administrative positions,[26] and also involved a loosening of party control of society, including tolerance of more open expressions of national sentiment.[27]

---

26. Economic decisions were no longer to be made according to political criteria, and Tito himself openly dismissed "propaganda work," the mainstay of many party workers, stressing instead the need for technical knowledge and "detailed understanding" of economics and management. Tito, speech at fifth plenum of League of Communists of Yugoslavia Central Committee, *Borba*, October 6, 1966, p. 2. Economic reform was accompanied by political reform in the form of a radical restructuring of party relations at the local level, with the goal of undermining the position of conservative party bureaucrats by bringing rank-and-file party members into decision-making, and dismantling the institutional bases of bureaucratic power at the local level (including the local party cells and regional party organizations). Gagnon, "Ideology and Soviet-Yugoslav Relations, 1964–1969: "Irrational foreign policy as a rational choice," Ph.D. dissertation, Columbia University, 1992. April Carter, *Democratic Reform in Yugoslavia: The Changing Role of the Party* (London: Frances Pinter, 1982).

27. See Savka Dabcević-Kucar, series of interviews in *Nedeljna Dalmacija*, January 14, 21, and 28, 1990.

At the macro-political level the reform radically decentralized the federation, and almost all decision-making was given to the republics. This allowed the top leadership to bypass the conservatives who dominated the central bureaucracy and to rely instead on the republic-level leaders and central committees, which were dominated by young technocratically-oriented reformists. Indeed, this decentralization was enthusiastically supported by all the party leaderships, including Serbia's. By the summer of 1971 there was also discussion of decentralizing the party itself, a topic which was to be addressed at a party meeting in November 1971.[28] If undertaken, the effect would have been to institutionalize reformism in each republic, remove all power from the conservatives who dominated the center, and remove even the possibility of a conservative comeback.

The conservatives were clearly threatened by the popularity of the young republic-level reformist leaderships within the central committees, as well as among the wider population. Indeed, the goal of the reforms had been in part to broaden the legitimacy of the communist party by building a base in that wider population; this meant, however, that conservatives were faced with leaders who could mobilize the population in support of irreversible radical changes in the structure of power.

RESPONSE TO THE THREATS. The conservatives at first tried to sabotage implementation of the reform. The result, however, was that in 1966 Tito purged conservatives from the leadership of the party, and the reform became even more radically threatening to conservatives. Some conservatives in the Serbian party then began publicly to argue that the reforms were harmful to the Serbian nation, and linked the reforms to the "historical enemies" of Serbia. These conservatives were expelled from the party in 1968; however, by 1971, as the party faced the possibility of radical decentralization, other conservatives in the Serbian party and army pointed in particular to the open expression of nationalist sentiment in Croatia, which included some extremist views. Conservatives blamed the Croatian leadership for revival of Croatian nationalism.[29]

---

28. Dušan Bilandžić, *Historija SFRJ* (Zagreb: Školska Knjiga, 1979), p. 427.

29. Although this period did see some extreme demands, including calls for a Croatian army, a seat for Croatia in the UN, and a division of Bosnia-Hercegovina, as well as some expression of chauvinistic Croatian nationalism, such demands were never made by the Croatian party leadership, which appealed instead in a positive sense to material well-being, freedom of expression, and cultural creativity. Pedro Ramet, *Nationalism and Federalism in Yugoslavia: 1963–1983* (Bloomington: Indiana University Press, 1984), pp. 104–143; Ante Ćuvalo, *The Croatian National Movement, 1966–1972* (New York: East European Monographs, 1990). Indeed, despite the official explanation, the Croatian party leaders never felt either party rule or socialism to be in danger. The then-leader of the Serbian party also subsequently admitted that the purges of the Croatian leadership had been a mistake. See Dabčević-Kučar, interviews in *Nedeljna Dalmacija*, January, 1990; Miko Tripalo, *Hrvatsko proljeće* (Zagreb: Globus, 1990); Perović, *Zatvaranje kruga*.

These conservatives allied with some conservatives in the Croatian and Bosnian parties, party workers and war veterans who had been forced into early retirement, members of the central bureaucracy, elements in the Yugoslav army, and Serbian nationalist intellectuals to invoke the massacre of hundreds of thousands of Serbs by the Croatian Ustaša leadership during World War II and to blame the reforms for undermining socialism and endangering Croatia's Serbs. Conservatives in the security forces and in the army, in particular, convinced Tito to act against the Croatian reformists.[30] The Croatian reformists were purged and tanks were sent to the outskirts of Zagreb. The following year the Serbian reformists were also purged, despite very strong resistance from the republic's central committee; similar purges in the other republics and provinces followed. As a result, the local-level reforms were effectively reversed, and a renewed ideologization took place.[31]

EFFECT OF THE RESPONSE.   By casting the threat posed by reform in terms of ethnic nationalism, the conservatives shifted the focus of political debate away from the cross-republic reformist project, and toward the alleged threats from Croatian nationalism; this allowed them to argue that radical reform had in fact brought the emergence of nationalism and thus of counterrevolution.[32] By using the threat of external and internal enemies of socialism defined in ethnic national terms, they managed to divide the country's popular reformists. This enabled the conservatives to prevent the decentralization of the party and to reverse the essence of the reforms (although decentralization of the federation itself remained and was enshrined in the 1974 constitution).[33] In addition, the Yugoslav army now became a key political player, with the official role of

---

30. On the army's role in mobilizing war veterans against reformists in Croatia and in other republics, see A. Ross Johnson, *The Role of the Military in Communist Yugoslavia: An Historical Sketch,* No. P-6070 (Santa Monica, Calif.: Rand Corporation, January 1978), pp. 31–33; on the army's role in convincing Tito of the dangers of Croatian nationalism, see Robin Remington, "Armed Forces and Society in Yugoslavia," in Catherine McArdle Kelleher, ed., *Political-Military Systems: Comparative Perspectives* (Beverly Hills: Sage, 1974), p. 188; and Gow, *Legitimacy and the Military,* p. 58. On the role of the security forces in supplying Tito with detailed information, see Zdravko Vuković, *Od deformacija SDP do Maspoka i Liberalizma* (Belgrade: Narodna Knjiga, 1989), p. 586.
31. Stephen Burg, *Conflict and Cohesion in Socialist Yugoslavia* (Princeton, N.J.: Princeton University Press, 1983), pp. 181–183, 229. While confederalization remained in place, the economic mechanisms which were meant to integrate the country were removed, resulting in eight statist and autarkic units.
32. The fact that they argued against the reforms, which were reversed, while the confederalization of the country remained even after the purge of liberals, indicates that the main threat was the reforms.
33. Conservatives in Serbia also set the groundwork for a longer-term strategy, for example by allowing Dobrica Ćosić, who had been purged for denouncing reform as anti-Serbian in 1968, to continue to publish his nationalistically-oriented works. Thus throughout the 1970s he constructed a very specific version of Serbian nationalism, whose theme was that Serbs were the greatest

ensuring the domestic order against external and internal enemies; this made the army the natural ally of conservatives in the party. By 1974, 12 percent of the federal central committee were army officers, up from 2 percent in 1969.[34]

1980–87: THREATS TO CONSERVATIVES

When Tito died in May 1980, the debate over reform, which had been muffled, broke out into the open. The economic crisis triggered by the global recession of the late 1970s, the oil shock, and Yugoslavia's huge foreign debt burden ($20 billion by the early 1980s), as well as the negative results brought by ending reform in the early 1970s, all compelled radical systemic change. The reformists' proposals were indeed much more radical than in the early 1960s and their audience—managerial elites, democratically-oriented intellectuals, and party rank-and-file—were much more receptive. The proposals were therefore even more threatening to the conservatives than they had been in the 1960s, especially without Tito to moderate conflicts; the political conflict had become winner-take-all.

Serbian reformists were in the forefront of this struggle, and in the early 1980s the Serbian party was among the most liberal in the country. Members of the Serbian party leadership called for totally removing party influence at the local levels of the economy; for greater reliance on private enterprise and individual initiative; multiple candidates in state and party elections; free, secret elections in the party; and recognition and adoption of "all the positive achievements of bourgeois civilization," i.e., liberal democracy.[35] From within

victims of Yugoslavia, portraying them as a "tragic people." See for example his popular four-part series of historical fiction, *Vreme Smrti,* published in Belgrade between 1972 and 1979, which chronicles the tragedies of Serbia during World War I (during which it lost 25 percent of its population and 40 percent of its army), and which portrays Serbia as the innocent victim of its neighbors, its supposed allies and other Yugoslav ethnic nations. In English, published as Dobrica Ćosić, *Into the Battle* (part 1) (San Diego: Harcourt Brace, 1983); *Time of Death* (part 2) (New York: Harcourt Brace Jovanovich, 1977); *Reach to Eternity* (part 3) and *South to Destiny* (part 4) (San Diego: Harcourt Brace, 1983). See also the series of interviews in Slavoljub Dukić, *Čovek u svom vremenu: Razgovori sa Dobricom Ćosićem* (Belgrade: Filip Višnjić, 1989).

34. Robert Dean, "Civil-Military Relations in Yugoslavia, 1971–1975, *Armed Forces and Society,* Vol. 3, No. 1 (November 1976), p. 46.

35. These liberal positions especially linked the need for radical economic reform and a market system with an equally radical reform of the political system. See article by Serbian party leadership member Najdan Pašić, in *Danas,* October 12, 1982. Another Serbian leader, Mijalko Todorović, argued that the only solution to the economic crisis was "democratization of all political institutions." Similar views were expressed also by Pašić and Drača Marković, head of the Serbian party, indicating that this was the official position of the party. (Cited in *RFE Situation Report* No. 256, November 7, 1983). See also Pašić letter to the central committee on the political situation, November 1982, cited in *RFE Situation Report* No. 125, June 1, 1983; and his calls to purge the party of conservatives who blocked reform, *Politika,* September 10, 1984.

the party were also heard calls for private enterprise to become the "pillar of the economy," and even calls for a multi-party system. Reformists were also very critical of the Army's privileged political and budgetary position, and called very early on for cutting that influence.[36] Once again reformists were seeking to mobilize broader popular sentiment against conservative positions among party rank-and-file as well as the wider population, at a time when the economic crisis had discredited the conservatives' ideological stance.[37]

Due to the consensus nature of federal decision-making, the conservatives were at first able to hinder an outright reformist victory, but the terms of the debate nevertheless shifted in the favor of the reformists. By the mid-1980s secret multi-candidate elections were being held for party officers, and even some state posts were chosen in multi-candidate popular votes.[38]

RESPONSE TO THE THREATS. Conservatives in Serbia responded with a three-pronged strategy. The first was to re-emphasize orthodox Marxist themes, in an attempt to delegitimate liberal trends at the lower levels of the party. Although the conservatives were not very successful in the political debates over reform at the leadership level, at the local level in Serbia they imposed an orthodox ideological line, while at the same time raising the issue of Serbian nationalism. Most notable was the Belgrade party organization which, beginning in 1984, was headed by Slobodan Milošević. Soon after coming to power, Milošević began a campaign stressing ideological orthodoxy,[39] and sent out warnings to all Belgrade party units urging vigilance against "the dangerous

---

36. For example, in December 1982 the army budget was openly criticized in the Federal Assembly for having been increased by over 24 percent without the Assembly's approval. *Politika*, December 15, 1982. In 1984 the Young Slovene Communist Party organization even called for the abolition of the Yugoslav army (A. Tijanić, *Intervju*, March 30, 1984). Army officers enjoyed pay levels much higher than average Yugoslavs as well as housing privileges in a country where housing was in acute shortage. The budget was also quite high (around 4 percent of gross domestic product in the early 1980s at a time of sharp economic decline).

37. The degree of threat that the reforms posed varied, in part by region of the country. In the early 1980s, those party officials and managers from more economically developed regions—Slovenia and Vojvodina—tended to be reformist, while those from underdeveloped Montenegro, Macedonia, Kosovo, and Bosnia tended to oppose them. The Serbian economy was split between the underdeveloped regions in the south and the more developed regions in the north, around Belgrade, and around the other major cities in central Serbia. The Serbian party leadership was very liberal, although there was a constituency of conservatives who were threatened by reform. Croatia, although more developed, was dominated by conservatives mainly because of the 1971 purges. For characterizations of the republic leaderships, see Pedro Ramet, "The Limits to Political Change in a Communist Country: The Yugoslav Debate, 1980–1986," *Crossroads*, No. 23, pp. 67–79.

38. For example, Croatia and Slovenia had multi-candidate party elections by 1986; Bosnia-Hercegovina held multi-candidate popular elections for state presidency representative.

39. Slavoljub Dukić, "Trka za recenzentom," *Borba*, August 12, 1991, p. 11.

increase in anti-Yugoslav propaganda" from internal and external enemies, a warning that also dominated Yugoslav army leadership pronouncements.[40]

The second part of the conservatives' strategy was to shift attention toward ethnic issues. Thus, Milošević's tenure as party chief in Belgrade also saw the start of a nationalist campaign among Belgrade party members and "leftist" intellectuals, including Milošević's sociologist wife Mirjana Marković, which sought to defend "the national dignity of Serbia" and to protect its interest in Yugoslavia.[41] Belgrade also saw growing numbers of protests by Serbs from the province of Kosovo, claiming to be the victims of ethnic Albanian "genocide."[42] The fact that the demonstrations took place without police interference was a sign that they were at least tolerated by the Belgrade party.

In January 1986, despite very strong opposition from within the party leadership, Milošević was elected head of the Serbian party's central committee.[43] This period saw increased attention to the issue of Kosovo by a Belgrade-centered coalition of conservative party members, orthodox Marxist intellectuals, and nationalist-oriented intellectuals who repeated the charges of "genocide" against Serbs in Kosovo.[44] Journalists who were allied with Milošević, especially at the daily newspaper *Politika*, undertook a media campaign to

---

40. Dukić, "Strogo pov. optuznica," *Borba*, August 13, 1991, p. 11. See also the speech of General Jovičić, head of the army's communist party organization, in *Politika*, December 15, 1984.

41. Mira Marković, *Odgovor* (Belgrade, 1994), and *Duga*, December 1993, cited in *Vreme*, February 7, 1994.

42. Kosovo had been the heart of the medieval Serbian kingdom. But by 1981 it was 75 percent ethnic Albanian, and had received a high degree of autonomy in 1974. In the late 1970s Serbian conservatives had used the issue of Kosovo's autonomy as a way of attacking reformist positions. In this they were supported by conservative Serbs from Kosovo, who were being replaced by ethnic Albanians in party and government posts. In 1981, massive demonstrations by ethnic Albanians erupted throughout the province, which the Serbian conservatives cited as evidence of pervasive "Albanian nationalism." For background on Kosovo, see Branka Magaš, *The Destruction of Yugoslavia* (London: Verso, 1993); Banac, *National Question in Yugoslavia;* Elez Biberaj, "The Conflict in Kosovo," *Survey*, Vol. 28, No. 3 (Autumn 1984); Ramet, *Nationalism and Federalism,* pp. 156–171; essays in Arshi Pipa and Sami Repishti, eds., *Studies on Kosovo* (Boulder, Colo.: East European Monographs, 1984); for a Kosovan Albanian view, see *The Truth of Kosovo* (Tirana: Encyclopedia Publishing House, 1993); for a Serbian view, see Miloš Mišović, *Ko je tražio republiku, Kosovo 1945–1985* (Belgrade: Narodna Knjiga, 1987).

43. For how Milošević and his allies overcame strong opposition, see Slavoljub Dukić, "Kroz iglene uši," *Borba*, August 15, 1991, p. 11; "Pod okriljem Stambolića," *Borba*, August 16, 1991, p. 11.

44. Their main charge was that Serbs were the victims of genocide by the majority Albanian population, which they accused of attempting to create an ethnically pure state though rapes of women, children and nuns, destruction of Serbian cultural monuments, and other types of harassment which had resulted, they claimed, in a massive exodus of Serbs and Montenegrins from the province. For details of the charges as well as a rebuttal of them by an independent commission, see Srdja Popović, Dejan Janća, and Tanja Petovar, *Kosovski čvor: drešiti ili seći?* (Belgrade: Chronos, 1990). See also Magaš, *Destruction of Yugoslavia*, pp. 61–73.

demonize ethnic Albanians and to "confirm" the allegations of genocide.[45] Indeed, the issue of Kosovo now became the conservatives' main weapon against reformist forces within Serbia and in the wider federation, as Serbian conservatives insisted that the issue be the priority not only of the local Serbian party but also at the federal level as well.[46]

However, it soon became clear that this coalition's goals were not limited to Kosovo and Serbia. The third part of the conservatives' strategy was to portray Serbia as the victim of Yugoslavia, setting the stage for attacks on the other republics' autonomy. An ideological manifesto written by some members of the Serbian Academy of Sciences and Arts in 1985, although claiming to call for democracy, actually advocated the restoration of the repressive, centralized socialist system that existed before the 1965 reforms. It sharply attacked the 1965 reforms as the root of all evil in Yugoslavia and as being aimed against Serbs; declared Serbs in Kosovo and Croatia to be endangered; and denounced the "anti-Serbian coalition" within Yugoslavia.[47] Indeed, given the nature of decision-making in Yugoslavia, to prevent radical reform in Serbia the conservatives would have to ensure that it did not take hold in the other republics and at the federal level.

EFFECT OF THE RESPONSE. The result of the Serbian strategy was that questions of radical reform were shunted aside in order to deal with the pressing issue of "genocide" in Kosovo. Through a combination of press manipulation, mass rallies, and political manipulation, and a stress on Stalinist notions of "democratic centralism," by September 1987 Milošević managed to consolidate conservative control over the Serbian republic's party organization.[48] Those parts of the Serbian media that had been relatively independent were taken over by conservative editors allied with Milošević.

---

45. For example, see Magaš, *Destruction of Yugoslavia,* p. 109.

46. For example, in January 1986, 200 Serbian intellectuals, including some who had previously been identified as socialist humanists, signed a petition accusing the (reformist) Serbian and federal party leaderships of complicity in what they described as "the destructive genocide" against Serbs in Kosovo. See text in Magaš, *Destruction of Yugoslavia,* pp. 48–52.

47. For text, see "Memorandum SANU," *Naše Teme,* Vol. 33, No. 1–2 (1989), pp. 128–163. On Milošević's quiet support for the Memorandum, see Slavoljub Dukić, "Čudno Miloševićevo ponašanje," *Borba,* August 21, 1991, p. 13.

48. Reformists were purged from being "soft" on Albanians (because they wanted to negotiate a solution with the Albanians rather than impose one); for being openly critical of the media's inflaming of the Kosovo issue; for warning against the demonization of all ethnic Albanians; and for criticizing the chauvinistic version of Serbian nationalism being used by conservatives. Dragiša Pavlović, "Potcenjuje se srpski nacionalizam," *Borba,* September 25, 1987, p. 3; *Borba,* September 11, 1987. See also Slavoljub Dukić, *Borba,* August 26, 1991, p. 11; *Borba,* August 27, p. 11; *Borba,* August 28, p. 13; *Borba,* August 29, p. 11.

1988–90: THREATS TO THE STATUS QUO

The conservative coalition, although it had consolidated control over the Serbian party organization, still faced threats from reformist forces in other Yugoslav republic and provincial organizations (Serbia was only one of eight), as well as in the federal government, especially as the economic situation continued to deteriorate. Slovenia, with strong liberal and democratic currents, was in the vanguard of increasingly vocal calls for an end to the one-party system and for Yugoslavia to move closer to the west, as well as very sharp criticisms of the Yugoslav army.[49] Also threatening were the successes of Federal Prime Minister Ante Marković, a strong reformer who, despite Serbian opposition, managed to get Federal Assembly approval for radical transformation of the Yugoslav economy.[50]

RESPONSES TO THE THREATS. Over the course of 1988 and 1989, Milošević and his allies attempted to subvert the party leadership in other Yugoslav republics and to weaken the federal government through a strategy of appealing to an aggressive version of Serbian nationalism. This strategy was viable despite the Serbs' minority status in Yugoslavia, because Serbs were overrepresented among politically relevant actors including communist party officials and members in other republics, and within the federal bureaucracies.[51] As long as this remained the case, Serbian conservatives could "legiti-

---

49. Tomaž Mastnak, "Civil Society in Slovenia," in Jim Seroka and Vukašin Pavlović, eds., *The Tragedy of Yugoslavia: The Failure of Democratic Transformation* (Armonk: M.E. Sharpe, 1992), pp. 49–66; Gow, *Legitimacy and the Military*, pp. 78–88.

50. Marković, who became federal prime minister in March 1989, pushed the Federal Assembly to pass constitutional amendments setting the foundation for a market economy and for private enterprise to play a large role in the economy. He circumvented unanimity requirements (and thus the Serbian veto) by declaring further reforms as "urgent measures," which required only two-thirds support in the Assembly, and called for an end to subsidies for unprofitable enterprises. By the end of 1989, Marković had the strong support of the federal communist party apparatus, much of the Federal Assembly, the Croatian party and government, and foreign governments and financial institutions. Cohen, *Broken Bonds*, pp. 66–71.

51. This condition was clearly present within the "inner" Serbia (85 percent Serb), Vojvodina (56 percent Serb), and Montenegro (70 percent Montenegrin and Serb). By the early 1980s Serbs made up 60–70 percent of the army's officer corps and 47 percent of all communist party members in the country; they dominated key parts of the federal bureaucracy, and made up disproportionately large parts of the party membership in Croatia (around 35 percent) and Bosnia-Hercegovina (47 percent). Although at the upper levels of the federal bureaucracy an official policy of quotas existed, these were determined not by nationality but by republic. Thus Serbs from Croatia and Bosnia held positions based on their republic status rather than on their nationality. Within the bureaucracy itself Serbs also tended to dominate; for example, 50 percent of the foreign ministry and diplomatic service came from "inner" Serbia alone (without Kosovo or Vojvodina), which held only 25 percent of the country's population. *Vreme* (Belgrade), September 30, 1991, p. 33. See also Ramet, *Nationalism and Federalism*.

mately" gain power in all of Yugoslavia (and thereby legally recentralize the country) if they could dominate the federal party and state collective leaderships by controlling at least five of the eight votes.

To this end Serbian conservatives continued to focus on the image of threatened Serbs in Kosovo. They staged mass rallies of tens of thousands in every major town in Serbia as well as in other republics and in front of party headquarters and during party meetings; these rallies, decrying the "atrocities" in Kosovo, called for party leaders to step down.[52] The result was that the party leaderships in Vojvodina and Montenegro were ousted in October 1988 and January 1989.[53] The Kosovo party leadership, which had been hand-picked by the conservatives in Belgrade, was also pressured to acquiesce in the abolition of Kosovo's autonomy and the recentralization of Serbia. Although these moves provoked massive demonstrations and strikes among the province's Albanian population to protest the threat to its autonomy, in March 1989 the Kosovo assembly, subjected to fraud and manipulation by Belgrade, voted to end the province's autonomy.[54]

Similar pressure was also put on the Croatian government. Massive rallies organized from Belgrade were held in the rural Serb-majority region around Knin, with the intention of eventually moving on to Zagreb to overthrow the Croatian party leadership.[55] Likewise the ruling party in Bosnia-Hercegovina

---

52. These rallies drew on social dissatisfaction caused by the increasingly poor economic situation as well as images of persecution of Kosovo Serbs. They denounced the existing party leaderships at the federal level and in other republics of betraying the interest of Serbs. They were portrayed by the Serbian regime as an "anti-bureaucratic revolution," although, as one commentator points out, they never criticized the Serbian bureaucracy. Magaš, *Destruction of Yugoslavia*, pp. 206–207. One notable feature of these massive rallies was the presence of many posters and slogans praising Milošević personally (*RFE Situation Report* 8/8, September 23, 1988). See also the interview with former Serbian party leader, Dragoslav Marković, "Naš mir je, ipak, bio bolje," *Borba*, August 17–18, 1991, pp. 10–11. The direct link between this anti-reformist movement and extremist Serbian nationalists is seen in the fact that Mirko Jović, an organizer of the 1988 rallies, is also the founder of the Serbian guerrilla group "Beli orlovi," accused by Helsinki Watch of numerous atrocities against civilians in Croatia and Bosnia. Helsinki Watch has requested that Jović himself be investigated for war crimes. Helsinki Watch, *War Crimes in Bosnia Hercegovina* (New York: Human Rights Watch, 1992), p. 6; *Globus* (Zagreb), August 28, 1992, pp. 11–12, citing *Duga* (Belgrade).
53. For details, see Magaš, *Destruction of Yugoslavia*, pp. 170–172, 208; and *RFE Situation Reports*, Yugoslavia, Nos. 8 and 9, September 23 and October 11, 1988. One Montenegrin party official in October 1988 noted that "the protests about the terrorizing of the Serbian and Montenegrin minorities in Kosovo by the Albanian majority" was the work of Serbian "extremists." Reuters, October 13, 1988.
54. *Yugoslavia: Crisis in Kosovo* (New York: Helsinki Watch, 1990); Michael W. Galligan, et al., "The Kosovo Crisis and Human Rights in Yugoslavia," *Record of the Association of the Bar of the City of New York*, Vol. 46, No. 3 (April 1991), pp. 227–231; Magaš, *Destruction of Yugoslavia*, pp. 179–190.
55. Cohen, *Broken Bonds*, p. 130; the Serb-majority region's population was 65 percent Serb, and it included about 25 percent of Croatia's Serbian population; the rest lived in ethnically-mixed regions where they were not a majority.

discovered that Serbia's secret police were active in the republic.[56] In Slovenia the plan was cruder—hundreds of intellectuals and dissidents were to be arrested and the army was to be used to put down protests.[57]

The conservatives' strategy of consolidating control over the other republics through the use of aggressive Serbian nationalism was accompanied by increasingly vehement media demonization not only of Albanians, but also of Croats,[58] as well as an active campaign to portray Tito's Yugoslavia as specifically anti-Serbian.[59] It claimed that an authoritarian, Serb-dominated and centralized Yugoslavia was the only way to ensure the security and interests of all Serbs: such a Yugoslavia also, not coincidentally, would ensure the power interests of the conservative Serbian elites. In the face of the deteriorating economy, Milošević blamed Marković's reforms, and put forward his own program that rejected even the most modest of the reformists' proposals for economic and political change.[60]

Meanwhile the army, under Defense Minister Branko Mamula, openly sided with conservative positions and harshly attacked the political opposition. In the military itself, conservative Markist-Leninist indoctrination was stepped up within the military itself.[61] The army also endorsed Milošević's neo-socialist economic and political program, stressing in particular continued monopoly of the communist party and recentralization of the state.[62] In cooperation with

56. Milan Andrejevich, "Serbia Accused of Interfering in Bosnian Affairs," *RFE*, October 23, 1989, cited in Gow, *Legitimacy and the Military*, p. 128.

57. *Mladina* (Ljubljana), May 20, 1988.

58. Images were stressed which evoked the specter of the wartime Croatian fascists, including prime-time television broadcasts of previously unshown graphic films from the Ustaša concentration camps. The implication—and at times explicit conclusions—of these and other such images was that Croats as a people were "genocidal." On the television images, see Biljana Bakić, "The Role of the Media in the Yugoslav Wars," draft master's thesis, University of Pittsburgh, Spring 1992; see also Ivo Banac, "The Fearful Asymmetry of War: The Causes and Consequences of Yugoslavia's Demise," *Daedalus*, Spring 1992, pp. 141–174.

59. For example, see Robert M. Hayden, "Recounting the Dead: The Discovery and Redefinition of Wartime Massacres in Late- and Post-Yugoslavia," in Rubie S. Watson, ed., *Memory and Opposition under State Socialism* (Santa Fe, N.M.: School of American Research Press, 1993), citing Ljubomir Tadić, "Kominterna i Nacionalno Pitanje Jugoslavije," *Književne novine*, September 15, 1988.

60. Milošević called for more efficient use of existing resources rather than any structural changes, emphasized "social ownership" rather than private property, stressed the priority of reforming (that is, strengthening) the federal organs, and rejected even the possibility of nonsocialist political parties, Cohen, *Broken Bonds*, pp. 55–58. On the multiparty system, see Milošević, in *NIN*, July 3, 1988, p. 14–15; Slobodan Vučetić, "Pravna država slobodnih ljudi," in *NIN*, July 30, 1989, pp. 10–15, cited in Cohen, *Broken Bonds*, p. 58.

61. Anton Bebler, "Political Pluralism and the Yugoslav Professional Military," in Seroka, *Tragedy*, pp. 126–127, 129.

62. Indeed, this platform, laid out in July 1989 by Defense Secretary Kadijević at the Conference of the Yugoslav Army's party organization, was "the most conservative of all the explicitly articulated platforms in Yugoslavia and the most dogmatic as far as political pluralism was concerned." Bebler, "Political Pluralism," pp. 129–131.

Serbian conservatives, the military openly attacked reformists' calls to democratize the country, to reduce the military's political role, and to reform the military-industrial complex. Moreover, statements by top army officers "made it clear that they viewed the Army's internal mission in orthodox ideological terms."[63]

EFFECT OF THE RESPONSE. Although this strategy gained Serbia control over four of the eight federal republics and provinces, and placed the purported threats to Serbdom at the center of political discourse, it also provoked backlashes in the other republics. In Slovenia, publication of the army's plans to crush dissent radicalized the party and wider population in Slovenia, where by mid-1988 an unofficial referendum on independence was held and the party began advocating introduction of a multi-party system. In Croatia, a bastion of conservatism since 1971, the Serbian moves provoked the reformist minority, so that by October 1988 the Croatian party proposed dismantling the communist party's leading role and encouraging private property.[64] Even conservative Serbs within the Croatian leadership criticized Milošević's strategy.[65] Likewise in Bosnia, which had previously been supportive of Milošević, the aggressive nationalist strategy and the threat to the Bosnian party leadership led it to distance itself from Serbia's positions.[66]

By the end of 1989, reformist forces had taken over the Croatian party, and both the Slovene and Croatian parties had scheduled multi-party elections for the spring of 1990 (despite attempts by conservative Serb allies of Milošević to prevent this in Croatia).[67] An attempt by Milošević to recentralize the federal party at an extraordinary League of Communists of Yugoslavia (LCY) Congress in January 1990 failed as the Slovene party walked out when its proposal for *de jure* party independence was rejected, and the Croatian, Bosnian and Macedonian parties refused to continue the meeting.

1990: THREATS TO THE STATUS QUO

In 1990, the greatest threat yet to the conservative Serbian coalition and its allies arose—the emergence of a political system in which the general population

---

63. Ibid., pp. 130–131.
64. Stipe Šuvar (one of the most orthodox of the Croatian leadership), October 17–19, 1988, in RFE Situation Report, Yugoslavia, No. 10/88, November 11, 1988.
65. For example, Dušan Dragosavac, a Serb and conservative leader in the Croatian party, denounced Milošević for creating national hatreds. *Danas,* December 13, 1988, cited in Magaš, *Destruction of Yugoslavia,* p. 216.
66. Gow, *Legitimacy and the Military,* p. 128.
67. See Josip Jović, "Centar bez srpskog krila," *Nedeljna Dalmacija,* February 11, 1990, pp. 10–11.

would choose political leaderships. The strategy of recentralizing Yugoslavia by use of mob rallies and aggressive Serbian nationalism to pressure communist party leaderships was clearly no longer feasible; likewise, there was little chance of winning an election in a country where only 39 percent of the population was Serb, especially since Milošević's strategy had alienated most non-Serbs.

The specific threats were now coming from three directions. The first was the fact that in the spring 1990 elections in Slovenia and Croatia, openly anti-socialist parties committed to a loosening rather than tightening of political ties had taken power, due in large part to a backlash against Milošević.[68] Federal decision-making bodies thus now included representatives from these two republics, marking the introduction of an irreconcilable ideological difference in terms of economic and political viewpoints. Indeed, the Slovenian and Croatian governments soon put forward formal proposals for confederalizing the country, utterly rejecting Serbia's calls for recentralization. Given the pressure for multi-party elections in the other Yugoslav republics, and the fall of communist parties throughout the rest of Eastern Europe, it seemed likely that other republics would join these calls.[69]

The second set of threats came from the policies of federal Prime Minister Marković. By early 1990 these policies were quite successful in lowering inflation and improving the country's economic situation, and he was very popular, especially within Serbia.[70] Taking advantage of these successes, and looking ahead to multi-party elections, he pushed bills through the Federal Assembly legalizing a multi-party system in the entire country, and in July 1990 formed a political party to support his reforms.

The biggest challenge, however, came from within Serbia itself. Encouraged by the fall of communist regimes in the rest of Eastern Europe and the victory of noncommunists in Croatia and Slovenia, opposition forces in Serbia began

---

68. On the Slovenian election, see Cohen, *Broken Bonds*, pp. 89–94; Milan Andrejevich, "On the Eve of the Slovenian Election," *Report on Eastern Europe*, Vol. 1, No. 16 (April 20, 1990), pp. 32–38; on Croatia, see Milan Andrejevich, "Croatia Goes to the Polls," *Report on Eastern Europe*, Vol. 1, No. 18 (May 4, 1990), pp. 33–37; and Cohen, *Broken Bonds*, pp. 94–102. On Milošević's role in the victory of the nationalist CDU in Croatia, see interview with former Croatian party head Stipe Šuvar, in "Jugoslavija nije razbijena i neće biti," *Nedeljna Borba*, May 5–6, 1990, p. 12.

69. Even the Bosnian communist party, formerly quite conservative, denounced Serbian presidency member Jović's statement that democratization was endangering the constitutional order of Yugoslavia. Enver Demirović, "I vanredni kongres obnove," *Borba*, May 18, 1990, p. 3.

70. In May 1990 Marković's popularity in Serbia surpassed that of Milošević; while the Serbian leader received a 50 percent approval rating, the federal prime minister's positive rating in Serbia was 61 percent. *Borba*, May 21, 1990.

organizing and pressuring the regime for multi-party elections, holding massive protest rallies in May. Although Milošević argued that elections could not be held until the Kosovo issue was resolved, by June the Serbian regime recognized that elections were unavoidable.[71]

RESPONSE TO THE THREATS.   Within Serbia, the regime again resorted to the issue of Kosovo, working assiduously to provoke violent resistance from the Albanian population.[72] Despite these actions and the fact that the new Serbian constitution, adopted in September, effectively stripped Kosovo of its autonomy, Albanian response was peaceful resistance.

While turning up the heat on Kosovo, the Serbian party also had to deal with opposition parties at home, including nationalist ones from the right (most notably the Serbian Renewal Movement, SRM, headed by writer Vuk Drašković), as well as from civically-oriented democratic parties. In the face of anti-communist nationalist party opposition, and in order to win the necessary two-thirds of the Serbian vote (since the party had alienated the non-Serbian 33 percent of the republic's population), the Serbian conservatives first undertook a strategy of averting a split of the communist party into a large pro-reform social democratic party that would more credibly appeal to the population's economic interest, and a small hard-line party (as happened in the rest of Eastern Europe). The Serbian party was renamed the Socialist Party of Serbia (SPS). The regime continued its control over the mass media, and greatly limited access of opposition parties to television. Economic problems were blamed on the "anti-Serbian" policies of Yugoslav federal Prime Minister Marković. The government also printed $2 billion (U.S.) in dinars for overdue worker salaries just before the December elections, with funds taken illegally from the federal treasury.

On issues of nationalism, the party had already very much distanced itself from the policies of Tito, especially those which forbade public expression of national sentiment. This fact, plus the fact that Yugoslav agriculture had remained in private hands, ensured the SPS most of the vote of peasants and those one generation off the land (a majority of the voters), and thus dampened anticommunist sentiment against it.[73] The SPS, linking the nationalist SRM to

---

71. Dušan Radulović and Nebojša Spaić, *U Potrazi za Demokratijom* (Belgrade: Dosije, 1991).
72. In July, Serbia dissolved the Kosovo Assembly and took over all institutions of the province; all Albanian language media were closed down; all Albanians were fired from positions of responsibility and replaced with Serbs, many fanatically anti-Albanian; Albanian workers were fired without cause; and there was a general harassment of the Albanian population. Galligan, "The Kosovo Crisis," pp. 231–234 and 239–258; Magaš, *Destruction of Yugoslavia*, pp. 262–263.
73. "Sto dana višestranačke Srbije," *NIN*, March 29, 1991, pp. 77–79.

Serbian extremists during World War II, portrayed the SRM as wanting to drag Serbia into war, and painted itself as a moderating and progressive force.[74] The SPS managed to win an overwhelming majority of parliamentary seats with the support of 47 percent of the electorate (72 percent of Serbia's Serbs).[75]

But the challenge to the conservatives continued from outside of Serbia, in the context of the Yugoslav federation. The Serbian conservatives' response was to continue to demonize other ethnic nationalities, and also to begin provoking confrontations and violent conflicts along ethnic lines and to discredit the very idea of a federal Yugoslavia, calling it the creation of a Vatican-Comintern conspiracy.[76]

Even before the 1990 elections the Belgrade media had stepped up its campaign against Croatia, and after the elections it accused the new Croatian ruling party, the Croatian Democratic Union (CDU) of planning to massacre Croatia's Serbian residents.[77] Nevertheless, in the May 1990 elections only a small minority of Croatia's Serbs had supported the Serbian nationalist party, the Serbian Democratic Party (SDP).[78] Following the elections, throughout the summer of 1990 the Serbian media also ran stories detailing the anti-Serb massacres of the World War II Croatian Ustaša regime, furthering the implicit link with the CDU,[79] and Belgrade and its allies began to provoke violent conflict in the Serbian-populated areas of Croatia. Between July 1990 and March 1991, Belgrade's allies took over the SDP, replacing moderate leaders with hard-liners. It portrayed the CDU as genocidal Ustaša; rejected all compromises with Zagreb; held mass rallies and erected barricades; threatened moderate Serbs and non-SDP members who refused to go along with the confrontational strategy; provoked armed incidents with the Croatian police, and stormed villages adjacent to the regions already controlled by Serbian forces and an-

---

74. Forty-nine percent of SPS voters stressed the importance of good inter-ethnic relations. *Vreme,* January 6, 1992.
75. For a detailed description of how the SPS managed to subvert the elections and cripple the opposition, see Radulović and Spaić, *U Potrazi za Demokratijom.*
76. Magaš, *Destruction of Yugoslavia,* pp. 263–264.
77. Ibid., p. 262.
78. In the 1990 elections, most of Croatia's Serbs, especially those who lived in ethnically-mixed and more economically-developed parts of the republic, had rejected the overt nationalism of the Serbian Democratic Party (SDP), and had voted instead for multi-ethnic parties. While 23 percent of Croatia's Serbs preferred the SDP, 46 percent preferred the reform communists and 16 percent the Coalition of National Reconciliation, both of which advocated harmonious inter-ethnic relations and improved material well-being, and rejected Milošević's strategy of recentralizing the country. Ivan Šiber, "The Impact of Nationalism, Values, and Ideological Orientations on Multi-Party Elections in Croatia," in Seroka, *Tragedy of Yugoslavia,* p. 143.
79. Hayden, "Recounting the Dead," p. 13.

nexed them to their territory.[80] Throughout this period, conciliatory moves by the Croatian regime were rejected, and moderate Serbs who disagreed with Belgrade's conflictual strategy were branded as traitors.[81] Although the campaign rhetoric and the actions of hard-liners in the CDU did give Croatia's Serbs cause for concern, rather than fostering negotiation and compromise with Zagreb, Belgrade exacerbated the Croatian Serbs' concerns.

Following Milošević's December 1990 victory in the Serbian elections, the situation in Croatia became even more confrontational as a hard-line group within SDP, working closely with Belgrade and armed by the Yugoslav Army, began to provoke armed conflicts with Croatian police in areas where Serbs were not in the majority.[82] Croatian Serbs were increasingly pressured to toe the SDP line, and Croats in the Serb-held "Krajina" region were besieged by Serbian armed forces and pressured to leave.[83] These purposely provoked conflicts were publicly characterized by Belgrade as "ethnic conflicts," the result of ancient hatreds, and the Yugoslav army was called in to separate the groups. At the end of February, Krajina proclaimed its autonomy from Croatia.

---

80. Cohen, *Broken Bonds,* pp. 131 and 134; Miloš Vasić, "Labudova pesma dr Milana Babića," *Vreme,* February 10, 1992, pp. 13–15.
81. For example, in June 1990 the CDU offered SDP leader Jovan Rašković a position as vice-president of the parliament; Belgrade's pressure on Rašković and other SDP members led him to reject the offer and walk out of the assembly, and to end negotiations with Zagreb on the Serbs' status in Croatia; Cohen, *Broken Bonds,* p. 86. During the referendum on sovereignty in August, though Zagreb condemned the voting, it made no move to stop it, or to remove the barricades that Serbian forces had thrown up around the territory. Ibid., p. 134. Indeed, outside observers note that despite Serbian accusations of a genocidal regime, Zagreb continued to moderate its rhetoric and act with "restraint." Helsinki Watch, "Human Rights in a Dissolving Yugoslavia," January 9, 1991, p. 7. In October, moderate SDP representatives from areas outside of Krajina (Slavonia, Baranja, Kordun, Istria), in negotiations with Zagreb, received official recognition of the SDP as the legitimate representative of Croatia's Serbian population and the promise (later confirmed) that the draft Croatian constitution would not include the description of the republic as the "national state of the Croatian people," one of the Serbs' main grievances. The CDU delegation also promised to resolve all other disputed questions quickly. SDP hard liners from Knin, however, denounced the moderate Serbs as traitors. Vasić, "Labudova pesma."
82. Jovan Rašković, one of the founders of the SDP, notes that at a February 26 meeting of the SDP leadership, 38 out of 42 members supported his call for moderation against extremist Milan Babić, who advocated a hard-line confrontational and military approach and who was in direct contact with Belgrade. The next day Babić proceeded to found his own party, the SDS Krajina; Rašković stated that at this time "for the first time I warned that this radical group which wanted to take over the SDP is a danger for us and that war will definitely result if they exacerbate things." See interview with Rašković, *Globus,* February 14, 1992, pp. 14–15. Shortly after this, armed clashes with Croatian police broke out in Pakrac, in western Slavonia, and at the Plitvice Lakes national park on the edge of Krajina.
83. The Croat-majority village of Kijevu outside Knin was besieged for eight months. Srdan Španović, "Čudo u Kirjevu," *Danas,* March 12, 1991, pp. 18–20.

These Serbian moves provoked Croat hard-liners to take repressive actions against Serbs in areas where the ruling party controlled the local government: these actions were pointed to by Belgrade's allies as proof of the threat to Serbs.[84] Despite calls by Croatian hard-liners to use military force, Zagreb lacked significant stocks of weapons (although it was seeking sources), and Croatian president Franjo Tudjman clearly feared providing the Yugoslav army with an excuse to crush the Croatian government. He was thus forced to accept the army's gradually expanding occupation of the areas where the SDP's authoritarian rule prevailed. This period saw the groundwork for a similar strategy being laid in Bosnia by Belgrade's ally there, Radovan Karadžić, head of that republic's SDS.[85]

As conflict heated up in Croatia, in negotiations over the future of Yugoslavia, Milošević and his allies refused to budge from his call for a more tightly centralized federation. He declared that if his demand was rejected, then the borders of Serbia would be redrawn so that all Serbs would live in one state.[86]

EFFECT OF THE RESPONSE.   The result of this strategy of conflict was to further the destruction of Yugoslavia. The provocations and repression of even moderate Serbs in Croatia increased the territory under the Yugoslav army's control, and provoked reactions on the part of extremist Croats.

1991: THREATS TO THE STATUS QUO

This apparently successful strategy was suddenly interrupted when Serbia's political opposition held massive protest rallies in Belgrade on March 9 and 10.[87] Appealing to the wider population, the opposition, led by SRM chief Vuk Drašković, threatened to oust the regime by force of street rallies. Initially called to denounce the regime's tight control and manipulation of the media, the rallies also condemned Milošević's disastrous economic policies and his policy

---

84. For example, in western Slavonia, some hard-line CDU members from Hercegovina, "formerly petty criminals," were put into the police force and began harassing Serbs, and even local Croats were frightened. The result was that the SDP, which had little support in the region before, began to attract many Serbs. Zoran Daskalović, "Skupljenje povjerenja," *Danas*, March 12, 1991, pp. 13–14; Milan Bečejić, "Forsiranje straha," *Danas*, March 12, 1991, pp. 16–17.
85. Karadžić openly declared the goal of drawing ethnic borders, citing the Krajina experience, but ignoring the Muslims as a factor. Yet Bosnia's population was so ethnically intermixed that there really were no ethnic borders. See Golubović, Campbell and Golubović, "How not to Divide," in *Why Bosnia*. Karadžić also declared that "we have given Milošević a mandate to represent Serbs in Bosnia-Hercegovina if Yugoslavia disintegrates." *Borba*, February 26, 1991, p.7.
86. *Vreme*, March 4, 1991.
87. See Helsinki Watch, "Yugoslavia: The March 1991 Demonstrations in Belgrade," May 1, 1991; Zoran Miljatović, "9. mart, zvanična verzija," *NIN*, March 29, 1991, pp. 11–13.

of provoking conflict with other republics.[88] They called for the SPS to step down from power as other East European communists had done. Although Milošević's immediate reaction was to call the army to put down the demonstrations (since the republic's police forces were all in Kosovo), the military refused to use massive force.[89] This marked the start of the democratic opposition's rapid rise in popularity, and the beginning of an open split within the ruling SPS by democratic, pro-reform forces. Shortly thereafter massive strikes (including one of 700,000 workers) aimed specifically against Milošević's regime shook Serbia.

RESPONSE TO THE THREATS. Given the refusal of the army to use force, Milošević was forced to negotiate with his opponents. He accepted limited economic reform, printed more money to pay workers, and discussed the formation of a multi-party Serbian national council. At the end of March he secretly met with Croatian President Tudjman to agree on a division of Bosnia-Hercegovina, thus removing the possibility of Tudjman taking advantage of Milošević's then weak position. In April Milošević finally accepted the principle of confederation, and in early June, during talks over the future of Yugoslavia, he agreed to the principles on which such a confederation would be based.[90] Belgrade also pressured its Serbian allies in Croatia to negotiate with Zagreb, although the Serbs refused to reach an agreement.[91]

Yet at the same time, the strategy of provoking conflict along ethnic lines was also stepped up. Milošević himself labeled the protesters "enemies of Serbia" who were working with Albanians, Croats, and Slovenes to try to destroy Serbia, and ominously stressed the "great foreign pressures and threats" being exerted on Serbia and which gave "support to the forces of disintegration of Yugoslavia."[92] The media stepped up its portrayals of Croatia as a fascist Ustaša state, and in April graphically reported on the opening of caves in Bosnia-Hercegovina filled with the bones of thousands of Serb victims of the Ustaša; in August it broadcast the mass interment of the remains.[93]

---

88. For a list of initial demands, see Milan Bečejić, "Rafali u demokraciju," *Danas,* March 12, 1991, pp. 29–31; see also "Objava mira umesto rata," *Politika,* May 8, 1991, p. 8.
89. On use of force, see Helsinki Watch, "Yugoslavia," May 1991.
90. See "Kompromis i ustupci korak ka rešenju," *Borba,* June 7, 1991, pp. 1 and 3; and interview with Bosnian president Izetbegović, co-author (along with Macedonian president Gligorov) of the compromise plan, "Država na ljudskim pravima," *Vreme,* June 17, 1991, pp. 12–14.
91. Tanjug, April 15 and 16, 1991. This occasion was used, however, to further purge the SDP of moderates with the accusation of being "traitors" for having talked with Tudjman. This period saw further marginalization of other moderates, including Rašković, who was sent to Belgrade. Vasić, "Labudova Pesma," p. 14.
92. Milošević speech to Serbian parliament, *Politika,* May 31, 1991, pp. 1–2.
93. The funeral, presided over by the Serbian Orthodox patriarch, included a procession of coffins that stretched for one and one-half kilometers. Hayden, "Recounting the Dead," p. 13.

This period was also one of close cooperation between the Yugoslav army, the Belgrade regime, and the Bosnian SDP, as the three sides implemented "Project RAM," a plan to use military force to expand Serbia's borders westward and create a new Serbian Yugoslavia.[94] Thus in Bosnia in the spring of 1991, the SDP set up "Serbian Autonomous Regions" which were declared no longer under the authority of the republic government, a repetition of the Krajina strategy.[95]

The SPS at this time also began an open alliance with the neo-fascist Serbian Radical Party led by Vojislav Šešelj, ensuring Šešelj's election to the Serbian parliament in a by-election.[96] Šešelj's guerrilla groups were active in the ensuing escalation of conflict in Croatia. In this period, Belgrade also exerted growing pressure on moderate Serb leaders in Croatia's ethnically-mixed Slavonia region (where Serbs were not in the majority) to accept its confrontational strategy; in May, Krajina held a referendum to join with Serbia, and Belgrade-supported guerrillas, including Šešelj's "Chetniks," flowed into Croatia, terrorizing both Serb and non-Serb populations in the more developed regions of Eastern and Western Slavonia (neither of which had Serb majorities).[97] These forces attacked Croatian police, in at least one case massacring and mutilating them, and began a policy of forcible ethnic expulsions in areas coming under their control. Moderate SDP leaders denounced Belgrade for provoking and orchestrating this confrontational strategy.[98]

---

94. On SDP cooperation with the Yugoslav army, see "Skica pakla," *Vreme*, March 9, 1992, p. 25. On project RAM, see *Vreme*, September 30, 1991; and the stenographic notes of the federal cabinet meeting at which this plan was discussed, in *Vreme*, September 23, 1991, pp. 5–12. Related to RAM, just after the street protests, Yugoslav Defense Minister Kadijević held secret talks in Moscow with Soviet Defense Minister Yazov (who would several months later lead the coup attempt against Gorbachev), and without the knowledge of civilian officials arranged for a large quantity of weapons, including planes, rocket systems, and helicopters, to be delivered to the Yugoslav army (ibid., p. 7).

95. Momčilo Petrović, "Odlučivaće sila?" *NIN*, April 19, 1991, p. 11.

96. Miloš Vasić, "Falsifikat originala," *Vreme*, June 17, 1991, pp. 8–9. Šešelj appealed to a virulent Serbian nationalism that demonized other nationalities, especially Albanians and Croats, called for building a Greater Serbia including all of Croatia "except what can be seen from the top of Zagreb's cathedral," and advocated expulsion of non-Serbs from Serbia. See the program of his "Chetnik movement" in *Velika Srbija*, July 1990, pp. 2–3.

97. Other Belgrade-supported paramilitary groups include those of Arkan ("Tigers"), and of Mirko Jović ("White Eagles"). On Belgrade's support of these groups and the local Serbian forces, see "Helsinki Watch Letter to Slobodan Milošević and General Blagoje Adžić," January 21, 1992, in *War Crimes in Bosnia-Hercegovina* (New York: Human Rights Watch, August 1992), p. 275. On the referendum, see *Politika*, May 13, 1991, pp. 1 and 5.

98. Vojislav Vukčević, head of the SDP organization in the Baranja region of Croatia, bordering on Serbia, in *NIN*, April 19, 1991, p. 14. Former SDP leader Rašković also denounced the hard-liners who had taken over the party, as well as Belgrade's strategy of conflict. *NIN*, May 3, 1991, p. 15.

In the face of this pressure, and in preparation for the new confederal agreement, in late June the Croatian government declared the start of a process of disassociation from Yugoslavia, specifically stating that it was not an act of unilateral secession and that Zagreb continued to recognize the authority of federal organs, including the army.[99] When the Serb-controlled army attacked Slovenia following its own declaration of sovereignty, Croatia refrained from helping the Slovenes, in order to avoid giving the army an excuse to attack Croatia.[100]

Nevertheless, the Yugoslav army, despite its public promises not to attack Croatia,[101] escalated the conflict in Croatia, and Serbian forces continued their strategy of provoking conflicts in Slavonia and on the borders of Krajina, terrorizing civilian populations, destroying Croatian villages and Croat parts of towns, bombing cities to drive out the population, and forcing Serbs on threat of death to join them and point out Croat-owned houses.[102] Serbs who openly disagreed with these policies were terrorized and silenced.[103] The human rights group Helsinki Watch noted that in the period through August 1991 (when the Croats finally went on the offensive and Croat extremists themselves undertook atrocities against civilians), by far the most egregious human rights abuses were committed by the Serbian guerrillas and the Yugoslav army, including indiscriminate use of violence to achieve their goals of terrorizing the Serb population into submission and driving out the non-Serb population.[104] This policy, by provoking extremists in Croatia into action, in effect

---

99. See the report by Chuck Sudetic, "2 Yugoslav States Vote Independence to Press Demands," *New York Times*, June 26, 1991, pp. A1 and A6.
100. These Yugoslav army attacks seemed in part to be in response to U.S. Secretary of State Baker's declaration in Belgrade that the most important U.S. priority continued to be a united Yugoslavia, which was apparently crucial in assuring the army that the international costs of military action would not be unbearable. For Baker's statement, see Thomas Friedman, "Baker Urges End to Yugoslav Rift," *New York Times*, June 22, 1991, pp. 1 and 4. Indeed, the usually reliable independent Belgrade weekly *Vreme* reported that just before Baker's visit the United States had sent special emissaries to offer the Yugoslavs the help of the 82nd Airborne Division if necessary; and a few days before the visit, Assistant Secretary of State Lawrence Eagleburger mentioned the possibility of NATO or CSCE aid to Yugoslavia. Roksanda Ninčić, "Kraj druge Jugoslavije," *Vreme*, July 1, 1991, p. 6.
101. Cited in *Danas*, July 23, 1991, p. 7.
102. See "Helsinki Watch Report on Human Rights Abuses in the Croatian Conflict," September 1991, in *War Crimes*, pp. 230–272; and "Helsinki Watch Letter to Milošević and Adžić," pp. 276–302.
103. See *NIN*, November 8, 1991, p. 15; *Vreme*, November 4, 1991, pp. 12–15l; and interview with moderate Zagreb-based Serbian Democratic Forum leader Milorad Pupovac in *Vreme*, October 21, 1991, pp. 12–14.
104. Helsinki Watch noted that "the majority" of human rights abuses by Croats "involved discrimination against Serbs," where individual managers demanded that Serb workers sign loyalty oaths to Croatia or be fired, as well as some police beatings; whereas abuses by the Serbian forces involved "physical maltreatment" and "egregious abuses against civilians and medical

became a self-fulfilling prophecy as the Serbian regime pointed to those atrocities as proof of its original charges.[105]

This war policy also destroyed the chances for Marković's reforms to succeed. Slovenia and Croatia, along with Serbia, had already been trying to block implementation of many aspects of his reform, but the Yugoslav army and Serbian guerrilla attacks killed any support in Slovenia and Croatia for a continued Yugoslavia, even among those who had advocated it; meanwhile, Milošević's moves to take over the federal presidency and marginalize the federal government by September 1991 led Marković to the conclusion that he had no choice but to resign. By summer, the army was also draining the federal hard currency reserves and taking up a vast proportion of the federal budget, which had been carefully managed by Marković.

The war also helped Milošević in his domestic crisis. In April 1991 the democratic opposition had been at a high point, predicting the imminent fall of the SPS. But the SPS used charges of genocide and the subsequent war in Croatia to suppress internal party dissent and to marginalize the democratic opposition by drowning out concerns about economic and political reform, and by accusing those who questioned the war of treason. The regime also used the war to try to destroy the opposition physically: it first sent to the front reservists from counties that had voted for opposition parties. Opposition leaders and outspoken anti-war activists were also sent to the front. Any criticism was met with physical threats and violence from neo-fascist gangs.[106] The regime also targeted the Hungarian minority in Vojvodina (an absolute majority in seven counties); although they were only three percent of Serbia's population, they represented seven to eight percent of reservists at the front and twenty percent of casualties.[107]

---

personnel," including the use of civilians as "human shields" in battle. It also accused the Yugoslav army of committing "serious human rights violations by attacking civilian targets with Serbian forces," including the mortar bombing of such cities as Vukovar and Osijek. Helsinki Watch ("Yugoslavia: Human Rights Abuses in the Croatian Conflict," September 1991). See also Blaine Harden, "Observers Accuse Yugoslav Army," on EC observers' similar charges, *Washington Post*, January 17, 1992, p. A23. The head of the main democratic nationalist party in Serbia, Vuk Drašković, has publicly stated that "there was no particular need for war in Slavonia." *Danas*, February 18, 1992. See also his denunciation of the war in *Vreme*, November 4, 1991, pp. 9–11.

105. For details of atrocities and abuses by Croatian forces, see Helsinki Watch, "Yugoslavia: Human Rights Abuses in the Croatian Conflict, September 1991"; and "Helsinki Watch Letter to Franjo Tudjman," February 13, 1992, in *War Crimes*, pp. 310–359.

106. Milan Milošević, "Srbi protiv Srba," *Vreme*, October 21, 1991, pp. 8–11; Helsinki Watch, Letter to Milošević and Adžić, *War Crimes*, pp. 302 and 304; Milan Milošević, "Panonska pobuna," *Vreme*, November 18, 1991, pp. 12–15.

107. In addition, 25,000 Hungarians fled Serbia. The leader of Serbia's Hungarian community described this policy as "violent changing of the ethnic structure" of Vojvodina. "Bekstvo od rata," *Vreme*, January 20, 1992, p. 31.

By September 1991 the army was attacking Dubrovnik, and thousands of Serbian and Montenegrin reservists were ranging around Bosnia-Hercegovina, terrorizing the Slavic Muslim population.[108] But at the same time there was growing discontent in Serbia about the war.[109] Thousands of young men hid or left the country to avoid being drafted, and whole units of reservists deserted from the front.[110] It was also clear that the SPS's hard-line allies in Moscow had failed in their attempts to seize power.[111] By November 1991, when the European Community threatened economic sanctions against Serbia, and Croat forces began taking back territory, Serbia accepted the principle of UN peacekeeping forces in the areas it controlled in Croatia.

By this time, the opposition in Serbia was again gaining momentum, drawing on the anti-war sentiment and discontent over continued economic decline. Condemning the SPS's economic policy, its war in Croatia, and even its conflictual policy in Kosovo, the opposition by February 1992 was gathering hundreds of thousands of signatures calling for Milošević's resignation and the convening of a constitutional assembly.[112] Once again, the regime pulled back, and it finally allowed UN troops to move into Krajina, put pressure on hardliners in Krajina, allowed moderate Serbs to negotiate with Zagreb,[113] set up meetings with the remaining four Yugoslav republics to negotiate a future Yugoslavia, and called for talks with Croatia.[114]

But at the same time, Serbia also stepped up the pressure on Bosnia, instituting an economic blockade of the areas not controlled by its SDP allies.[115] It now portrayed as the ethnic enemy the allegedly fundamentalist-Muslim

---

108. On reservists, see Mladen Klemenčić, "Srpska kama u trbuhu Bosne," *Globus*, September 27, 1991, p. 9.
109. For polling data, see Milan Milošević, *Vreme*, September 23, 1991, pp. 29–33.
110. See Dragan Todorović, "To nije njihova kolubarska bitka," *Vreme*, October 7, 1991, pp. 24–26; Milan Milošević, "Marš preko Drine," *Vreme*, October 7, 1991, pp. 20–22; Torov, *Danas*, October 1, 1991, p. 32.
111. In fact, the SPS was the only ruling party in Europe to have openly supported the attempted coup, declaring the beneficial effects of its success for the Serbian regime. See Strojan Cerović, "Staljinizam bez Kremlja," *Vreme*, August 26, 1991, pp. 16–17. For specific comments by SPS officials supporting the coup, see Hari Štajner, "Jeltsin preuzeo Gorbačova," *Vreme*, August 26, 1991, pp. 4–6; in *Vreme*, September 2, 1991; and in "Točak istorije ne može nazad," *Borba*, August 21, 1991, p. 4.
112. Milan Milošević, "Dogadjanje potpisa," *Vreme*, February 17, 1992, pp. 9–14; Mirjana Prošić-Dvornić, "Enough! Student Protest '92: The Youth of Belgrade in Quest of 'Another Serbia'," *The Anthropology of East Europe Review*, Vol. 11, Nos. 1–2 (Spring-Fall 1993), pp. 127–137.
113. See interview with chairman of CDU executive council Stipe Mesić, in *Globus*, February 7, 1992, pp. 6–7.
114. "Cetiri republike za zajedničku državu," *Politika*, January 22, 1992, p. 1.
115. Helsinki Watch, *War Crimes*, p. 26.

population of Bosnia, who were said to be seeking to impose an Islamic state and to perpetrate genocide against the Bosnian Serbs.[116] Indeed, the same scenario was beginning in Bosnia. In December the SDP declared that it would form a republic, and in January 1992 the independent "Serbian Republic" was declared in the 66 percent of Bosnian territory that the SDP controlled, the "Serbian Autonomous Regions" that had been formed in 1991. SDP leader Radovan Karadžić declared at this time that Bosnia would never again be undivided.[117] Objecting to a referendum to be held in those parts of the republic not under SDP control, Serbian guerrilla forces began armed attacks on Croat and Muslim civilians in early March.[118] Despite this, the referendum, seeking approval for Bosnia-Hercegovina's independence, was approved by 63 percent of the republic's population (99 percent of those voting), including a large proportion of those Serbs who lived outside of SDP-controlled territory.[119] (Indeed, the Bosnian presidency continues to include Serbian members, as does the Bosnian army, whose deputy commander is a Serb; all have been branded traitors by the SDP.)

Within the next two months Serbian guerrilla groups had committed widespread atrocities, expelling and murdering non-Serbs, mostly in areas already controlled by the SDP.[120] By September 1992, Belgrade's Bosnian Serb allies had increased their territorial holdings by less than ten percent, to about seventy

---

116. One example of this propaganda came in March 1992, at the end of the Muslim holiday of Ramadan, when the SDP's press agency cited a made-up Koran verse in which, they claimed, Muslims were called on to kill Christians at the end of Ramadan. Ejub Štitkovac, "Kur'an po 'SRNI'," *Vreme*, April 27, 1992, p. 33. The Slavic Muslims of Bosnia are generally very secular. See Ivo Banac, "Bosnian Muslims: From Religious Community to Socialist Nationhood and Postcommunist Statehood, 1918–1992," in Mark Pinson, ed., *The Muslims of Bosnia-Hercegovina* (Cambridge: Harvard University Press, 1994), pp. 129–153.
117. The "Republic of the Serbian People of Bosnia-Hercegovina" was declared to include areas where Serbs were in a majority as well as in "those areas where the Serbian people is in a minority because of the genocide against it during the Second World War." Zehrudin Isaković, "Spor oko 'ako'," *Vreme*, January 13, 1992, pp. 17–18.
118. See Helsinki Watch, *War Crimes*, pp. 27–29; "Drugi Sarajevski atentat," *Globus*, March 6, 1992, pp. 3–6.
119. The SDP prevented the referendum from being carried out in the areas under its control, which included large numbers of non-Serbs. Although the SDP called for a total boycott by Serbs, 2 million people (63.4 percent of eligible voters) participated in the referendum. See *Referendum on Independence in Bosnia-Herzegovina: February 29–March 1, 1992*, cited in *War Crimes*.
120. For details of the atrocities and war, see *War Crimes*; *War Crimes in Bosnia-Hercegovina*, Vol. 2 (New York: Helsinki Watch, April 1993); Roy Gutman, *A Witness to Genocide: The 1993 Pulitzer-Prize Winning Dispatches on the "Ethnic Cleansing" of Bosnia* (New York: Macmillan, 1993). Alexandra Stiglmayer, ed., *Mass Rape: The War Against Women in Bosnia-Herzegovina* (Lincoln: University of Nebraska Press, 1994); Zehrudin Isaković, "Pocrveneli ljiljani," *Vreme*, April 6, 1992, pp. 6–7.

percent. As in Krajina, almost the entire non-Serbian population were killed or driven out, and Serbian dissenters were silenced and repressed.[121]

EFFECT OF THE RESPONSE. The Serbian conservatives' strategy had a short-term goal of insuring their survival in power and preserving the structure of economic and political power in Serbia. In the long term, their strategy initially had the goal of creating a centralized, authoritarian Yugoslavia where the conservatives would crush all attempts at radical change and enforce their own orthodoxy. But when in 1990 the bases of political power shifted to the wider population, the conservatives were forced to change this strategy. Having discredited themselves in the eyes of the 61 percent of Yugoslavia's population that was non-Serb, the conservative coalition resorted to destroying the old multi-ethnic Yugoslavia, and creating on its ruins a new enlarged Serbian state with a large majority of Serbs in which they could use appeals to Serbian nationalism as a means of defining political interests, and thereby preserve the existing power structure. The violence itself and the retaliatory violence against innocent Serb civilians in Bosnia and Croatia have created a situation in which grievances defined in ethnic terms are sure to continue to play an important role in Serbian politics. Meanwhile, the regime has restructured and taken firmer control of the economy, and has blamed the accompanying economic hardships on the international sanctions.

Conclusion: Ethnic Conflict as a Political Strategy

Violent conflict described and justified in terms of ethnic solidarity is not an automatic outgrowth of ethnic identity, or even of ethnic mobilization. Violence on a scale large enough to affect international security is the result of purposeful and strategic policies rather than irrational acts of the masses. Indeed, in the case of the former Yugoslavia there is much evidence that the "masses," especially in ethnically-mixed regions, did not want war and that violence was imposed by forces from outside. The current major conflicts taking place along ethnic lines throughout the world have as their main causes not ancient hatreds, but rather the purposeful actions of political actors who actively create violent conflict, selectively drawing on history in order to portray it as historically inevitable.[122]

---

121. See, for example, Blaine Harden, "In Bosnia 'Disloyal Serbs' Share Plight of Opposition," *Washington Post*, August 24, 1992, pp. 1 and 14.
122. On Azerbaijan, see Dmitrii Furman, "Vozvrashchenie v tretii mir," *Svobodnaia mysl'*, No. 11 (1993), pp. 16–28; on various cases in the Caucasus and Central Asia, Georgii Derluguian, "'Ethnic' violence in the post-communist periphery," *Studies in Political Economy*, No. 41 (Summer 1993),

If such conflict is driven by domestic concerns, outside actors can try to prevent or moderate it by making the external costs of such conflict so high that the conflict itself would endanger the domestic power structure. The most obvious way is the use of military force. But to prevent such conflicts, the threat of force must be made early, and it must be credible. In the Yugoslav case the international community has not fulfilled either condition.

Such conflict might also be prevented or moderated by international attempts to influence the situation from within, striking at the root cause of conflictual behavior. While assuring minorities of their rights may be important, that alone does not address the roots of the conflict in cases such as this one. Rather, the target must be the real causes of conflictual policy: the provocation of violence by threatened elites, and the reasons for their conflictual behavior. Such a preventative policy must come early, but it is much less costly than a military solution. The international community can undertake policies such as ensuring multiple sources of mass information and active and early support for democratic forces. But in cases where domestic structural changes are being fostered by international actors, those actors must also be very attentive to the domestic political context into which they are intervening, and in particular should take into account the concerns of those who are most negatively affected by domestic changes. An example is to ensure those elites most affected by change of fall-back positions.

If violence along ethnic lines is caused by internal conflict, then negotiations over interests outside the domestic arena will be without effect, since the goal of the conflict is not in the international environment, *vis-à-vis* another state, but rather at home. To be truly effective, these internal factors must also be brought into negotiations.

What are the implications of this approach for understanding the link between nationalism and violent conflict in other parts of the world? If domestic conflict drives external conflict, and if the potential costs in the outside world are a key part of the domestic calculus, then we would expect such types of external conflict to be less likely in a truly threatening international environment. If the risk is too high, threatened elites will have more motivation to seek

pp. 45–81; on Africa, Binaifer Nowrojee, *Divide and Rule: State Sponsored Ethnic Violence in Kenya* (New York: Africa Watch, 1993); *Somalia: A Government at War with its Own People* (New York: Africa Watch, 1990); Amnesty International, *Rwanda: Mass Murder by Government Supporters and Troops* (New York: Amnesty International, 1994); Catherine Watson, et al., *Transition in Burundi* (Washington, D.C.: American Council for Nationalities, 1993); on India, Susanne Hoeber Rudolph and Lloyd I. Rudolph, "Modern Hate," *The New Republic*, March 22, 1993, pp. 24–29; on Lebanon, Barry Preisler, "Lebanon: The Rationality of National Suicide," Ph.D. dissertation, University of California, Berkeley, 1988.

a compromise solution with challengers at home. On the other hand, in conditions where the external threat to security is minimal, threatened elites may be more tempted to use conflict in the external arena as one part of their domestic political strategy. The end of the Cold War may therefore have its primary effects on the international arena not directly, through its influence on the structure of the international system, but rather indirectly, in domestic spheres around the world.

What explains absence of ethnic conflict under conditions of change? In the Russian case, Gorbachev's evolutionary style of incremental reform, where he brought conservatives step-by-step toward radical change, was one factor preventing a feeling of sudden threat among conservatives. Since then economic change has taken place gradually in Russia, and often the new owners of privatized enterprises are the former managers and party bureaucrats. Although this gives them a stake in the new system, if these firms are unprofitable or poorly run, a rash of bankruptcies may have a drastic effect. In addition, in the Soviet Union and then in Russia, because reformists are in control of the central government, they also control the media, making it very difficult for hard-liners to create images via television.

Extreme Russian nationalist Vladimir Zhirinovsky, who made a surprisingly strong showing in Russia's 1994 elections and whose expansionist rhetoric alarms many in Russia's "near abroad," is an example of a threatened elite resorting to conflictual policies. Zhirinovsky's rhetoric serves the domestic political aims of threatened elites in the security forces, forcibly pensioned party workers, and others. It is thus no coincidence that, like Milošević, Zhirinovsky and other extreme nationalist Russians speak in terms of threats to Russians outside of Russia; any conflict will thus most likely be outside of Russian Federation's borders.

Methodologically, the case of Serbia shows the importance of recognizing that political rhetoric is itself political behavior, and that conflict described in ethnic terms and taking place along ethnic lines, while it may be about ethnic issues, may be caused by issues not related to ethnicity. The ability of violence to create specific political contexts means that those provoking violent conflict may have as their goal something quite outside the direct objects of conflict. It is thus important to realize that the rhetoric of ethnic nationalist purists is exactly that: rhetoric. Within every group the definition of group interest is contested, and in fact that definition is the key to power.

Suggestions for Further Reading

Rethinking Security

Booth, Ken, ed. *New Thinking About Strategy and International Security* (New York: Harper Collins, 1991).

Buzan, Barry. *People, States and Fear: An Agenda for International Security Studies in the Post-Cold War Era*, 2nd edition (Boulder, Colo.: Lynne Rienner, 1991).

Crawford, Neta C. "The Once and Future Security Studies," *Security Studies*, Vol. 1, No. 2 (Winter 1991), pp. 283–316.

Kennedy, Paul. *Preparing for the 21st Century* (New York: Random House, 1993).

Kolodziej, Edward. "Renaissance in Security Studies? Caveat Lector!" *International Studies Quarterly*, Vol. 36, No. 4 (December 1992), pp. 421–439.

Mathews, Jessica Tuchman. "Redefining Security," *Foreign Affairs*, Vol. 68, No. 2 (Spring 1989), pp. 162–177.

Romm, Joseph. *Defining National Security: The Nonmilitary Aspects* (New York: Council on Foreign Relations Press, 1993).

Walt, Stephen M. "The Renaissance of Security Studies," *International Studies Quarterly*, Vol. 36, No. 2 (June 1991), pp. 211–239.

Environmental Issues and International Security

Benedick, Richard Elliott. *Greenhouse Warming: Negotiating a Global Regime* (Washington, D.C.: World Resources Institute, 1991).

Brown, Janet Welsh, ed. *In the U.S. Interest: Resources, Growth, and Security in the Developing World* (Boulder, Colo.: Westview, 1990).

Brown, Neville. "Climate, Ecology and International Security," *Survival*, Vol. 31, No. 6 (November/December 1989), pp. 519–532.

Deudney, Daniel. "The Case Against Linking Environmental Degradation and National Security," *Millenium*, Vol. 19, No. 3 (Winter 1990), pp. 461–478.

Homer-Dixon, Thomas F., Jeffrey H. Boutwell, and George W. Rathjens. "Environmental Change and Violent Conflict: Growing Scarcities of Renewable Resources Can Contribute to Social Instability and Civil Strife," *Scientific American*, Vol. 268, No. 2 (February 1993), pp. 38–46.

Lipschutz, Ronnie D. *When Nations Clash: Raw Materials, Ideology and Foreign Policy* (Cambridge, Mass.: Ballinger, 1989).

Myers, Norman. "Environment and Security," *Foreign Policy*, No. 74 (Spring 1989), pp. 23–41.

Prins, Gwyn, and Robbie Stamp. *Top Guns and Toxic Whales: The Environment and Global Security* (London: Earthscan, 1991).

Renner, Michael. *National Security: The Economic and Environmental Dimensions*, Worldwatch Paper No. 89 (Washington, D.C.: Worldwatch Institute, 1989).

Westing, Arthur. *Cultural Norms, War and the Environment* (New York: Oxford University Press, 1988).

Westing, Arthur. *Global Resources and International Conflict: Environmental Failures in Strategic Policy and Action* (New York: Oxford University Press, 1986).

Migration and International Security

Eberstadt, Nicholas. "Population Change and National Security," *Foreign Affairs*, Vol. 70, No. 3 (Summer 1991), pp. 115–131.

Gordenker, Leon. *Refugees in International Politics* (New York: Columbia University Press, 1987).

Loescher, Gilbert, and Lailan Monahan, eds. *Refugees and International Relations* (New York: Oxford University Press, 1989).

Sarkesian, Sam C. "The Demographic Component of Strategy," *Survival*, Vol. 31, No. 6 (November/December 1989), pp. 549–564.

Tucker, Robert W., Charles B. Keely, and Linda Wrigley. *Immigration and U.S. Foreign Policy* (Boulder, Colo.: Westview, 1990).

Weiner, Myron, ed. *International Migration and Security* (Boulder, Colo.: Westview, 1993).

Widgren, Jonas. "International Migration and Regional Stability," *International Affairs*, Vol. 66, No. 4 (October 1990), pp. 749–766.

Zolberg, Aristide R., Astri Suhrke, and Sergio Aguayo. *Escape from Violence: Conflict and the Refugee Crisis in the Developing World* (New York: Oxford University Press, 1989).

Nationalism and International Security

Anderson, Benedict. *Imagined Communities: Reflections on the Origin and Spread of Nationalism*, rev. ed. (London: Verso, 1991).

Breuilly, John. *Nationalism and the State* (Manchester, England: Manchester University Press, 1982).

Brown, Michael, ed. *Ethnic Conflict and International Security* (Princeton, N.J.: Princeton University Press, 1993).

Brzezinski, Zbigniew. "Post-Communist Nationalism," *Foreign Affairs*, Vol. 68, No. 5 (Winter 1989/90), pp. 1–25.

Connor, Walker. *Ethnonationalism: A Quest for Understanding* (Princeton, N.J.: Princeton University Press, 1994).

Etzioni, Amitai. "The Evils of Self-Determination," *Foreign Policy*, No. 89 (Winter 1992–93), pp. 21–35.

Gellner, Ernest. *Nations and Nationalism* (Ithaca, N.Y.: Cornell University Press, 1983).

Greenfeld, Liah. *Nationalism: Five Roads to Modernity* (Cambridge, Mass.: Harvard University Press, 1992).

Hall, John A. "Nationalisms: Classified and Explained," *Daedalus*, Vol. 122, No. 3 (Summer 1993), pp. 1–28.

Halperin, Morton H., and David J. Scheffer. *Self-Determination in the New World Order* (Washington, D.C.: Carnegie Endowment for International Peace, 1992).

Hannam, Hurst. *Autonomy, Sovereignty, and Self-Determination: The Accomodation of Conflicting Rights* (Philadelphia, Penn.: University of Pennsylvania Press, 1990).

Helman, Gerald, and Steven Ratner. "Saving Failed States," *Foreign Policy,* No. 89 (Winter 1992–93), pp. 3–20.

Hobsbawm, Eric J. *Nations and Nationalism Since 1780* (Cambridge: Cambridge University Press, 1990).

Horowitz, Donald L. *Ethnic Groups in Conflict* (Berkeley: University of California Press, 1985).

Kedourie, Elie. *Nationalism* (London: Hutchinson, 1985 edition).

Mayall, James. *Nationalism and International Society* (Cambridge: Cambridge University Press, 1990).

Maynes, Charles William. "Containing Ethnic Conflict," *Foreign Policy,* No. 90 (Spring 1993), pp. 3–21.

Montville, Joseph V., ed. *Conflict and Peacekeeping in Multiethnic Societies* (Lexington, Mass.: Lexington Books, 1990).

Motyl, Alexander, ed. *Thinking Theoretically about Soviet Nationalities* (New York: Columbia University Press, 1992).

Pfaff, William. *The Wrath of Nations: Civilizations and the Furies of Nationalism* (New York: Simon & Schuster, 1993).

Premas, Ralph R., S.W.R. de A. Samarasinghe, and Alan B. Anderson, eds. *Secessionist Movements in Comparative Perspective* (London: Pinter, 1990).

Seton-Watson, Hugh. *Nationalism, Old and New* (Sydney, Australia: Sydney University Press, 1965).

———. *Nations and States* (London: Methuen, 1977).

Smith, Anthony D. *The Ethnic Revival in the Modern World* (New York: Cambridge University Press, 1981).

———. *State and Nation in the Third World* (New York: St. Martin's Press, 1983).

———. *Theories of Nationalism,* second ed. (New York: Harper and Row, 1983).

———. *The Ethnic Origins of Nations* (New York: Basil Blackwell Ltd., 1986).

———. *National Identity* (London: Penguin Books, 1991).

———. "National Identity and the Idea of European Unity," *International Affairs,* Vol. 68, No. 1 (January 1992), pp. 55–76.

Snyder, Jack. "The New Nationalism: Realist Interpretations and Beyond," in Richard Rosecrance and Arthur A. Stein, eds., *Domestic Bases of Grand Strategy.* (Ithaca, N.Y.: Cornell University Press, 1993), pp. 179–200.

Tilly, Charles, ed. *The Formation of National States in Western Europe* (Princeton, N.J.: Princeton University Press, 1975).

International Security

Center for Science and International Affairs
John F. Kennedy School of Government
Harvard University

The articles in this reader were previously published in **International Security**, a quarterly journal sponsored and edited by the Center for Science and International Affairs at the John F. Kennedy School of Government at Harvard University, and published by MIT Press Journals. To receive subscription information about the journal or find out more about other readers in our series, please contact MIT Press Journals at 55 Hayward Street, Cambridge, MA, 02142.